THE FATHERS
OF THE CHURCH

A NEW TRANSLATION

VOLUME 51

THE FATHERS
OF THE CHURCH

A NEW TRANSLATION

EDITORIAL BOARD

Hermigild Dressler, O.F.M.
Quincy College
Editorial Director

Robert P. Russell, O.S.A.
Villanova University

Thomas P. Halton
The Catholic University of America

Robert Sider
Dickinson College

Sister M. Josephine Brennan, I.H.M.
Marywood College

Richard Talaska
Editorial Assistant

FORMER EDITORIAL DIRECTORS

Ludwig Schopp, Roy J. Deferrari, Bernard M. Peebles

SAINT CYPRIAN

LETTERS
(1-81)

Translated by
SISTER ROSE BERNARD DONNA, C.S.J.

The College of Saint Rose
Albany, New York

THE CATHOLIC UNIVERSITY OF AMERICA PRESS
Washington, D.C.

NIHIL OBSTAT:

REVEREND HARRY A. ECHLE
Censor Librorum

IMPRIMATUR:

✠PATRICK A. O'BOYLE, D.D.
Archbishop of Washington

September 11, 1964

The *nihil obstat* and *imprimatur* are official declarations that a book or pamphlet is free of doctrinal or moral error. No implication is contained therein that those who have granted the *nihil obstat* and the *imprimatur* agree with the content, opinions, or statements expressed.

Library of Congress Catalog Card No.: 65-12906

Copyright © 1964 by
THE CATHOLIC UNIVERSITY OF AMERICA PRESS, INC.
All rights reserved
Second Printing 1981
ISBN 978-0-8132-2191-5 (pbk.)

CONTENTS

INTRODUCTION ix
LETTER

1 Cyprian to the Priests and People of Furni... 3
2 Cyprian to Eucratius...................... 5
3 Cyprian to Rogatian...................... 6
4 Cyprian, Cecil, Victor, Sedatus, *et al.*, to
  Pomponius 10
5 Cyprian to the Priests and Deacons.......... 14
6 Cyprian to Sergius, Rogatian, and Other
  Confessors 16
7 Cyprian to the Priests and Deacons.......... 19
8 No heading in Hartel: Clergy of Rome to
  Clergy of Carthage..................... 20
9 Cyprian to the Priests and Deacons of Rome.. 23
10 Cyprian to the Martyrs and Confessors...... 24
11 Cyprian to the Priests and Deacons.......... 28
12 Cyprian to the Priests and Deacons.......... 34
13 Cyprian to Rogatian and Other Confessors... 36
14 Cyprian to the Priests and Deacons.......... 40
15 Cyprian to the Martyrs and Confessors....... 43
16 Cyprian to the Priests and Deacons.......... 46
17 Cyprian to the Brethren.................... 49
18 Cyprian to the Priests and Deacons.......... 51
19 Cyprian to the Priests and Deacons.......... 52
20 Cyprian to the Priests and Deacons of Rome.. 53
21 Celerinus to Lucian....................... 56
22 Lucian to Celerinus....................... 59
23 All the Confessors to Cyprian.............. 62

24	Caldonius to Cyprian and the Carthaginian Priests	63
25	Cyprian to Caldonius	64
26	Cyprian to the Priests and Deacons	65
27	Cyprian to the Priests and Deacons of Rome	66
28	Cyprian to Moses, Maximus, and Other Confessors	69
29	Cyprian to the Priests and Deacons	71
30	Priests and Deacons of Rome to Cyprian	72
31	Moses, Maximus, Nicostratus, Rufinus, *et al.*, to Cyprian	79
32	Cyprian to the Priests and Deacons	85
33	No heading in Hartel: To the Lapsed	85
34	Cyprian to the Priests and Deacons	87
35	Cyprian to the Priests and Deacons of Rome	89
36	Priests and Deacons of Rome to Cyprian	90
37	Cyprian to Moses, Maximus, and Other Confessors	94
38	Cyprian to the Priests and People	97
39	Cyprian to the Priests and People	99
40	Cyprian to the Priests and People	102
41	Cyprian to Caldonius, Herculanus, Rogatian, and Numidicus	103
42	Caldonius, Herculanus, Victor, Rogatian, and Numidicus to Cyprian	106
43	Cyprian to the People	106
44	Cyprian to Cornelius	112
45	Cyprian to Cornelius	114
46	Cyprian to Maximus, Nicostratus, and Other Confessors	118
47	Cyprian to Cornelius	119
48	Cyprian to Cornelius	119

49	Cornelius to Cyprian	121
50	Cornelius to Cyprian	124
51	Cyprian to Cornelius	125
52	Cyprian to Cornelius	127
53	Maximus, Urban, Sidonius, and Macarius to Cyprian	131
54	Cyprian to Maximus, Urban, Sidonius, and Macarius	131
55	Cyprian to Antonian	134
56	Cyprian to Fortunatus, Ahymnus, Optatus, Privatian, et al.	154
57	Cyprian and the Bishops at the Council of Carthage to Cornelius	156
58	Cyprian to the People of Thibaris	162
59	Cyprian to Cornelius	171
60	Cyprian to Cornelius	193
61	Cyprian and His Colleagues to Lucius	196
62	Cyprian to Januarius, Maximus, Proculus, Victor, Modianus, et al.	199
63	Cyprian to Cecil	202
64	Cyprian and the Bishops at the Council of Carthage to Fidus	216
65	Cyprian to Epictetus and the People of Assurae	219
66	Cyprian to Florentius Puppian	223
67	Cyprian and the Bishops at the Council of Carthage to Felix, Aelius, and Their People	230
68	Cyprian to Stephen	239
69	Cyprian to Magnus	244
70	Cyprian and Thirty Bishops to Januarius, Saturninus, et al.	258
71	Cyprian to Quintus	262

72	Cyprian and Other Bishops at the Council of Carthage to Stephen...................	265
73	Cyprian to Jubaian......................	268
74	Cyprian to Pompey.......................	285
75	Firmilian to Cyprian.....................	295
76	Cyprian to Nemesianus and Other Bishops and Martyrs in the Mines...............	313
77	Nemesianus, Dativus, Felix, and Victor to Cyprian	319
78	Lucius and Others to Cyprian.............	321
79	Felix, Jader, Polianus, and Others in the Mines to Cyprian......................	322
80	Cyprian to Successus.....................	323
81	Cyprian to the Priests and People...........	324
INDICES	....	329

INTRODUCTION

THE EIGHTY-ONE LETTERS of this collection, Thasci Caecili Cypriani *Epistulae*, written from c. 249 until Cyprian's death in 258 A.D., give a penetrating insight into the affairs of the Church in Africa in the middle of the third century. They reveal problems of doctrine and of discipline which had to be decided in a period of crisis and persecution when the Church, still in its infancy, had not yet emerged from the catacombs. Most important of all, they make Cyprian vividly alive as an understanding bishop who could be both gentle and firm, enthusiastic and moderate.[1] He was prudent enough to go into exile to direct his flock from afar when his presence was a potential source of danger to the people; he was courageous enough to face the martyrdom that he knew would ultimately be his.

Of these letters, fifty-nine were written by Cyprian himself and six more, emanating from Carthaginian Councils or Synods, were largely his work also. Sixteen letters were written by others; apparently eleven are lost.

The period itself saw persecutions which brought grave difficulties to the Christians and weighty responsibilities to those prelates who had to make decisions regarding the sinfulness of apostasy and the reconciliation of the sinners. Schism, a source of trouble in Rome and in Carthage alike, brought with it a scandalous dissension among Christians. Provincial councils, held every year in Carthage when there was a lull in persecution, permitted the Bishop of Carthage and the other

---

[1] For a brief account of Cyprian's life, cf. Saint Cyprian, *Treatises*, ed. Roy J. Deferrari (Washington: The Catholic University of America Press, 1958), pp. v-xii and select works listed in the bibliography.

African bishops, with their confreres of Numidia and Mauretania, to discuss and try to solve their most urgent problems.

Much that was accomplished is revealed in the letters. They answer questions regarding discipline (1-4). They treat of the Decian persecution, the reconciliation of apostates, and the struggle with schismatics (5-68); some are concerned with the baptism of heretics (69-75) and others with the persecution of Valerian (76-81). After Cyprian sent letters to the martyrs, to the clergy and people of his own Carthage, to the clergy and people of Rome, including Popes Cornelius, Lucius, and Stephen, he sometimes sent copies to his correspondents.

With evident concern for the welfare of his people, he stresses the importance of being in communion with the Church because of the life-giving sacraments it confers: baptism, penance with confession, Holy Eucharist with the Sacrifice of the Mass and the Real Presence, Confirmation (even those who recognize the baptism of heretics do not grant them the right to confer the Holy Spirit), and Holy Orders. Cyprian mentions duties of all of the ranks of the clergy except those of porters; he himself ordains men who are ready for the various steps toward the priesthood. His remarks on virginity include comparisons with marriage which show clearly what Christian marriage means. The bishop is the ordinary minister of penance for Cyprian, but priests may administer the sacrament and, in case of necessity, even a deacon may restore the lapsed. Since his concern is with the attitude of the penitent, Cyprian does not mention that confession to a deacon is not a sacrament.[2]

Outstanding in ability and beloved by pagans and Christians alike, Cyprian was definitely qualified to occupy the most important see in the African Church. More than one hundred and fifty bishops of Africa, Numidia, and Mauretania, then three political divisions, but one religious stronghold, listen with respectful deference to the Bishop of Carthage, who ad-

---

[2] In the third century, there was not yet a beginning of canon law which would later regulate such matters.

vocates both independence of judgment for the bishops (after consultation with the clergy and laity) and union with Rome. Since the See of Peter is the center of unity, Cyprian considers schism as particularly evil. Since he considers bishops directly responsible to God for their actions, he looks upon decisions of the various councils as guides to unity rather than laws binding bishops against their consciences.

In a letter to the people of Furni, early in his episcopate, Cyprian is concerned lest a layman's appointment of a priest as tutor or guardian interfere with priestly obligations. To Eucratius' question as to whether to allow an ex-actor, now a Christian, to teach his forbidden art to others, Cyprian returns a negative answer. If Eucratius cannot support the man from the funds of the Church until he can support himself, Cyprian offers assistance. In a reply to Rogatian, who complains against an insolent deacon, Cyprian upholds the bishop by developing from Scriptural references the dignity of the priesthood and the penalty brought upon those who scorn it. The fourth letter, concerned with religious life for women as it was then lived in Carthage, emphasizes the need for virgins not only to be chaste but to give rise to no suspicion that the opposite may be true.

The next letters, written during the Decian persecution, 249-252 A.D., present the bishop in exile providing for his flock. They show clearly the difficulties of Christians who try to remain faithful. Cyprian advises his priests and deacons to use all circumspection in aiding the confessors in prison and all of the poor so that their work may proceed in peace; he urges the confessors themselves to continue in the way they have chosen, strengthened by the joyful thought of the reward which is to come.

The eighth letter, written with no salutation, apparently by the clergy of Rome, during the vacancy of the Holy See, to the clergy of Carthage, presents another side of the picture because these bishops, who have not heard the full story of Cyprian's retirement, question his action and consider him a hireling. Cyprian, who receives this letter, answers it tactfully as if he doubts its authenticity. He also praises the courage and holiness of the martyred Pope Fabian. Some letters praise the martyrs and confessors for their steadfast courage and exhort them to persevere in their suffering; others urge priests and deacons to continue in their zeal for souls in the midst of the persecution and, above all, to pray for the souls of the brethren who face temptation and to take note of the days on which they suffer so that the faithful may be mindful of their martyrs.

In a letter which praises Rogatian and other confessors for their suffering, but warns against those who are trying to corrupt the confessors, Cyprian depicts the inconsistency of the man who resists torture bravely and then sometimes returns from prison or exile to lead a life unworthy of a Christian. Expressing his longing to see his priests and deacons again, although he knows that this is not prudent at the moment, Cyprian asks his ministers to be diligent for him since their presence is not yet dangerous and it is possible for them to carry out the apostolate without serious difficulty. Good example and good discipline preclude overhasty reconciliation of the lapsed. The clergy are responsible for the attitude of the laity and the latter cannot be blamed for desiring immediate reconciliation with the Church; weakness rather than lack of faith has caused the lapse of many. A worthy reception of the Holy Eucharist is impossible for those who rashly refuse to do penance for their lapse. Cyprian frequently insists that, except in cases involving danger of death, the making of major decisions regarding the lapsed should await his return from exile and consultation with the prelates of the area in the presence of the people. Despite his plea for patience, when summer brings the danger of death to many, Cyprian realistically allows the lapsed who have received petitions from the martyrs to be reconciled if there is danger of death.

Writing to the clergy in Rome, Cyprian, who has already sent thirteen letters to them, explains his past actions in trying to check the indiscriminate flow of petitions from the martyrs in prison because it interferes with the discipline of the Church. In his policy of firmness tempered with mercy, he wishes the truly repentant to make satisfactory atonement before they attempt to resume their place in the Christian community. His desire for uniform policy in Rome and in Carthage is noteworthy.

The twenty-first letter is written by Celerinus, a confessor tortured under Decius at Rome; it is addressed to Lucian, a confessor in danger of death, and requests petitions for two women who had weakened in the persecution. Celerinus shows that the women are penitent and trusts that Lucian may help restore them to communion. In his answer, Lucian quotes the martyr Paul's request that peace be given in his own name to any who desire it. Lucian also lists the names of other martyrs who have died with Paul and whose companion Lucian himself expects to be, in a few days, a victim of starvation. Lucian's vague petition wishes peace for all who ask for it. He ends with the greetings of some of his colleagues, but he is too weary to list them all. Lucian and the other confessors then send a brief note to Cyprian to explain what they have done and to request Cyprian to make this known to the other bishops. This act of Lucian and other well-meaning, heroic, but uninformed laymen, a definite interference in the discipline of the Church, causes concern to other bishops besides Cyprian and is a major obstacle in the way of making the lapsed realize the absolute need for penance. Many of them consider the request of the martyrs sufficient.

When Bishop Caldonius asks advice concerning the repentant lapsed of one persecution who have the courage to remain constant in a later trial, Cyprian agrees with Caldonius that the later fidelity under torture should erase the earlier fall. Requesting Caldonius to transmit their mutual agreement to other bishops, Cyprian informs his own clergy and writes also to the clergy in Rome to explain developments: Lucian's imprudence in handing out petitions indiscriminately and the resulting confusion in the cities as the lapsed try to force compliance with the wishes of the martyrs, Caldonius' request for a decision, and Cyprian's answer. Other letters to the confessors and to the clergy follow as Cyprian continues to keep them informed and to stimulate their minds and hearts to courage in the work of the apostolate, working or suffering.

When the Roman clergy write to Cyprian, they pay tribute to him for encouraging the confessors and animating them to face martyrdom. Not yet able to elect a pope to replace Fabian, they have a plan for the lapsed which is in agreement with that of Cyprian about the necessity for a moderate course which would not deny mercy to those in immediate danger, but would require others to await the decision of the bishops in council after the persecution.

Confessors, too, write to Cyprian to express their gratitude for his inspiration. They agree with him also regarding a firm policy for the lapsed because, otherwise, the lapsed will have without suffering what the faithful have endured so much to keep. Cyprian sends copies of the letters to his clergy. He encourages the lapsed who are truly repentant and wish to abide by the decisions of legitimate authority in being restored to the Church, but he reproves those who rashly usurp membership and attempt to send letters in the name of the Church. He upholds the decision of his priests and deacons to withhold Communion from Gaius and his deacon. In the same letter, he postpones any action concerning Philumenus, Fortunatus, and Favorinus until the bishops are able to deliberate.

In view of the fact that many outside the Church claim to find in Cyprian support for the erroneous theory that the primacy of the Roman See is one of honor rather than of jurisdiction, his practice of informing both the Pope and the Roman clergy about his activities is of special interest. The fact that the position of Rome and of Carthage concerning the lapsed and the heretics is essentially the same gives assurance to Cyprian that his policy is right even though later he does not yield on the question of baptism.

Cyprian's exhortation to Moses and Maximus and other confessors draws parallels between his state and theirs and shows how they are united in spite of separation and differences. Their perseverance is a great comfort to Cyprian himself, who never fails to praise and exhort them to continue in suffering as the way to be united with Christ.

Although his usual practice is to consult his priests and people first, Cyprian explains to them why he has ordained Aurelius and Celerinus readers. Their glorious suffering for Christ and their firmness in faith are for their bishop sufficient reason for waiving ordinary requirements. It is interesting to note in this connection the importance which Cyprian attaches to each step of the way to the priesthood. He pays tribute also to Numidicus, whom he adds to the Carthaginian clergy after the man has survived horrible torture himself and has seen his wife burned with other confessors.

Joy in the newly ordained gives way to grave concern as Cyprian writes Caldonius and others concerning the evil deeds of Felicissimus, who is causing trouble and stirring up dissension among the people. When Cyprian excommunicates Felicissimus, he warns Augendus, another agitator, and others involved that they, too, will be excommunicated if they do not separate from the evildoer. Caldonius and the others write to Cyprian that they have also excommunicated Felicissimus and Augendus and four others engaged with them. Cyprian then sends word to his people, who are expecting his return from exile, that he will not be able to come before Easter because of the activities of Felicissimus, who is trying to stir up and to deceive the lapsed. The timely warning is an exhortation to the flock to avoid all false teachers and to remain steadfast in the faith for which they have suffered in the persecution.

Although, because of the schism of Novatian, the first antipope, Cyprian wisely awaits word from his own trusted colleagues before acknowledging Cornelius' election, the Bishop of Carthage is quick to render the deference due to the See of Rome as soon as Cornelius' position is made clear. When

Cyprian writes to the Pope to explain his actions and his policy, he tells the Pope of the reasons for his prudent delay and of his directives to his own flock supporting Cornelius. After he reproves Maximus and Nicostratus and other confessors for supporting schism, Cyprian reports to Cornelius what he has said to the deceived confessors. In answer to a letter from Cornelius, who is apparently displeased that some letters have been sent to priests and deacons instead of to him, and who evidently has not yet received Cyprian's letters, the Bishop of Carthage explains in detail what he has already indicated in two earlier letters: the caution necessitated by the schism in Rome, the Carthaginian joy in the confirmation of the valid election, and the support of Carthage for Cornelius. The Pope, apparently satisfied, writes back to Cyprian about their mutual problem with schismatics and the return of Maximus and other confessors to the Church.

Several letters exchanged between Cyprian and Cornelius are evidence of mutual cooperation and respect. Each warns the other against treacherous evildoers who shift back and forth between Africa and Italy; each explains present activities of the schismatics and heretics who are trying to lead astray even the confessors. Both rejoice greatly in the return of some of the deceived and lament the fall of others.

When Cyprian receives a letter from Maximus, Urban, and other confessors, reporting their return to the Church, his reply shows his happiness at their good fortune. His obvious grief over their lapse and his personal joy over their return encourage them to persevere.

Cyprian is happy to hear from Antonian that the latter adheres to Cornelius; he regrets receiving a second letter which indicates wavering because of the influence of Novatian. Defending the validity of the election of Cornelius, Cyprian vindicates the Pope's character, explains the errors of Novatian and the problems facing the Church at the time. He deals not only with the whole problem of the lapsed but shows carefully why Trofimus is readmitted to the Church as a layman.

When brother bishops question him regarding confessors who have endured torture bravely for a long time before finally yielding, Cyprian agrees that their three long years of severe penance indicate sorrow and that the mercy of God is not to be closed to the penitents. He considers that these may have another chance to redeem themselves if persecution comes again. Cyprian promises to treat the matter fully with the many bishops who will assemble for the council after Easter.

Letter 57, written by Cyprian and the other bishops at the Council of Carthage to Pope Cornelius, constitutes a report of the proceedings of the synod. It recommends pardon to the sincerely repentant in danger of death, preparation of the people to resist another impending persecution, and, as part of this preparation, the giving of pardon to the lapsed who have not withdrawn from the Church. Present conditions make it imperative that peace now be given to the healthy to enable them to face the persecution strengthened by the reception of Holy Eucharist. The bishops draw a distinction between the lapsed who have apostatized or have become heretics and those who have been doing penance since their lapse to which only weakness drove them. Peace is to be given only as a preparation for battle; reconciliation is imperative to prepare these people to be truly soldiers of Christ. If some are not sincere, the responsibility is theirs and God is Judge. The bishops close their epistle to the Pope with an acknowledgment of their own responsibility as shepherds. Of many of the bishops listed in this letter and in the others written from councils, little is known except what is in the letters. Had it not been for the reports of the synods, many of their names would be in oblivion. E. W. Benson, who writes the brief biographies in a *Dictionary of Christian Biography*, draws almost exclusively upon the letters for his information.

After the Council, in writing to the people of Thibaris, Cyprian advises them to receive Holy Eucharist daily for the grace to remain faithful to Christ in the impending persecution. Since some people take scandal from the defection of others, the Bishop of Carthage warns his correspondents that

Christ predicted persecution to keep His followers from being surprised by it. Scriptural references provide abundant inspiration for Cyprian's exhortation to the people.

In a later letter to Cornelius, Cyprian urges the Pope to disregard the threats of impious men and to be firm against the temptations which always beset bishops. Citing his own difficulties with those who refuse to accept the chosen bishop, Cyprian also gives a rather full report on the most recent activities of some of the chief schismatics and heretics. In spite of their obstinacy and evil, Cyprian shows great Christian charity in his willingness to reconcile them. He will not, however, be moved by threats to yield to anything wrong.

Cyprian, in his last letter to Cornelius, praises the Pontiff for his glorious confession and considers that all bishops share in the reflected glory of the Bishop of Rome and that even men previously lapsed are incited to a glorious confession. As if anticipating martyrdom for them both, Cyprian suggests to Cornelius that whoever dies first should persevere in prayer for all of the brethren before the mercy of God.[3]

When Lucius, the successor of Cornelius, finally returns from banishment, Cyprian and his colleagues express the faithful allegiance of Carthage to the new Pope and the wish that he, too, may accomplish much in being able to confess before his people rather than in exile.

In the same year of 253, expressing his concern for the captives of the barbarian raid in Numidia, Cyprian sends to eight Numidian bishops the names of the contributors and the proceeds of a collection taken up to relieve the wants of the persecuted. His letter to Bishop Cecil concerning Holy Eucharist, a treatise on the Blessed Sacrament, develops the doctrine from prefigurings in the Old Testament to the establishment of the Sacrament in the New. Urging the great necessity of doing what Christ did in this Sacrament, Cyprian attacks those who have fallen into the practice of using water alone for the

---

[3] The Pope dies in exile in 253 A.D., five years before the Bishop of Carthage, who is linked with him in the Proper of the Saints.

Sacrifice. Water is matter for baptism and, whenever water alone is mentioned in Scripture, baptism is signified. If water alone is offered in the Chalice, the Blood of Christ is not offered. Cyprian is disturbed that there are those who do not follow the instructions of Christ in this regard.

In a letter to Fidus, Cyprian and many colleagues present at the Council answer the former's appeal against the too hasty reinstatement of Victor by Therapius. Although the Council is disturbed at the rash action, it decides only to reprimand Therapius, but not to take away from Victor peace once granted by a bishop. Although Fidus does not wish to have infants baptized within the third day after birth, the bishops decree that it is not right to deprive anyone of the grace of God. In explaining the Jewish practice of waiting until the eighth day for circumcision, they say also that, with the coming of Christ, the image ceased and that not even a newborn babe should be deprived of the Sacrament. This decision was of great importance to Saint Augustine in his later efforts to promote infant baptism.

When Cyprian writes to Epictetus, appointed bishop of Assurae to replace the lapsed Fortunatian, expressing his sorrow to both bishop and people, that the deceived former bishop is trying to regain his lost episcopate, the Bishop of Carthage cites Fortunatian as an example of the hold which the devil has over the lapsed. Cyprian urges prayer that the deceived may again petition the Lord for mercy after they prove their sorrow for their lapse.

Florentius Puppian's arrogant letter brings a gentle response from Cyprian, who is willing to let the Lord be the Judge of his actions. In his sorrow that such a valiant confessor should descend so low after his confession, the Bishop of Carthage does, however, refute some of the accusations of Puppian. This letter also has a bit of sarcasm for the actions of Puppian and the assurance that God alone is the final Arbiter of both.

Letter 67, another epistle emanating from a council, is addressed by Cyprian and many other bishops to people in Spain who have had difficulty with the lapsed bishops, Basilides and Martial. These are also anxious to regain their bishoprics although worthier men have been elected to replace them. The Council of Carthage of 254 supports the opinion of the people that the evildoers should not be allowed to resume their places among the clergy because the voice of God, heard through Scripture, forbids such an action. Basilides and Martial have deceived Pope Stephen. The sin of Basilides in going to Rome for this purpose is pointed out by the African bishops, who excuse Pope Stephen from any wrongdoing in the matter. Such actions make it appear all the more to the Africans that the end of the world is approaching and that Antichrist is at hand. If the Spaniards retain their firm allegiance to the Lord, all will be well with them.

In a letter to Stephen to tell the Pope that Marcian is now with Novatian, out of the Church, Cyprian desires the Pontiff to write to the people of Gaul about the status of Marcian in the company of the excommunicated Novatian and to excommunicate and to replace Marcian also. It is interesting to note, as part of Cyprian's encouragement of Stephen, his call to the Pope to emulate his illustrious predecessors, Cornelius and Lucius.

The later letters of Cyprian reveal more and more concern with various questions relating to baptism. In a letter to Magnus, Cyprian gives in detail his view that those baptized by Novatian must be rebaptized when they come into the Church and that those who have received clinical baptism through sprinkling in infirmity and illness, when necessity compels, receive the pardon and grace of God.

In the controversy over baptism, many African bishops found themselves at variance with the Roman practice which recognizes as valid any baptism performed according to the correct formula with the correct intention. This means that Rome recognizes the baptism of many of the heretics and merely imposes hands upon those who return to the fold. Cyprian's great respect for the Sacrament leads him into the error of associating the efficacy of the Sacrament with the

INTRODUCTION   xxi

worthiness of the minister. It is responsible for his theory that, since heretics have no power to baptize, baptism of those returning from heresy is not a second baptism but a first. From this point of view, Cyprian does not believe in rebaptism as such because he does not consider that there is any baptism outside the Church. It is in the light of this opinion that he persists in opposing the direct statement of Pope Stephen, who maintains the doctrine later defined by the Church. In this issue, Africa and Asia Minor, which traditionally rebaptized, were at variance with Rome and Alexandria. A letter, sent in 255 A.D. by Cyprian and the other African bishops at the council to fellow Numidian bishops, repeats the decision of the African Church to baptize those coming from heresy. The bishops of Numidia later confirm the decision of the bishops of Africa, but those in Mauretania hesitate. In a separate letter to Quintus, Cyprian encloses the letter of the council and adds to it his own further ideas about the subject. It is here that he does allow those baptized in the Catholic Church before going over to heresy to be received back without another baptism because their baptism was valid. He does not grant this privilege to those baptized without because the practice is contrary to the earlier decision of bishops of Africa and Numidia under Agrippinus. The Council of Carthage of 256 reaffirms the decision to follow African practice.

Cyprian and the others forward to Stephen the result of their deliberations regarding the baptism of heretics. They also urge that penitent clergy be allowed to return to the Church in a lay capacity only. It is interesting to note that this letter, which is expressing views opposed to those held by Stephen and the Roman Church, ends with the note that bishops should not be forced in their decisions, since each is free in his government of his see and is to render an account of his stewardship to the Lord. It is unfortunate that Pope Stephen's letters are missing, but apparently he threatened excommunication for failure to follow the Roman practice. The Pope also refused to receive legates from Africa.

An inquiry of Jubaian occasions a letter with the various

decisions on baptism. Cyprian does not consider that Novatian's rebaptizing has any bearing on rebaptizing in the Church because Novatian, in his attempt to claim the one baptism for himself, is merely imitating what the Church is doing. Since Novatian's own baptism is in the Church, Cyprian thinks that, if the heretic is at all consistent, he will have himself rebaptized also. If the heretics can give one sacrament, they have the Holy Spirit, and, if they have the Holy Spirit, they are the Church. This he is unwilling to concede. The letters on baptism are filled with what Cyprian considers proof for his arguments, proof which seems very convincing both to him and his African confreres.

In a letter to Pompey, Cyprian expresses his dissatisfaction with the views of Stephen on the baptismal question; the Carthaginian Bishop, very blunt about what he considers stupidity on the part of the Pope, is sarcastic about the position of the latter. Repeating every argument he can think of to justify his opposition to Stephen's opinion, Cyprian ends the letter with the statement that all coming from the heretics must be baptized.

The last letter concerning the controversy about baptism is written to Cyprian by Firmilian, Bishop of Caesarea in Cappadocia, another great man of the third century. In this letter, after Firmilian praises the unity and harmony which have existed among the bishops, he attacks Stephen, who, he declares, is betraying this harmony by his stand on the baptismal question. Firmilian also lauds Cyprian for his fidelity to his views and his conscience in spite of the Pope. Linking Stephen with the various heretics who have plagued the Church, the Bishop of Caesarea chides the Pope for his failure to live up to the high ideals set for him by the Apostles. That the successor of Peter should recognize the baptism of heretics seems to Firmilian a complete abdication of the claims of the Roman See and a desertion of unity. Firmilian, too, is sarcastic in discussing the actions of Stephen and upset to know that the Pope considers Cyprian wrong. This letter actually contains the only intimation of Stephen's threat of excommunication.

The last letters encourage the victims of the persecution of Valerian, which temporarily puts an end to the baptismal controversy.[4] Since he cannot come to them in person,[5] Cyprian sends encouraging messages to bishops and other brethren in the mines to exhort them to continue suffering and sacrificing for the love of God. His pride in all of them and his love for them are incentives to their noble living. The confessors answer in three letters, thanking Cyprian for his encouragemen and praising him for his own good example. They give him the credit for stirring up the souls of the brethren and stimulating them to martyrdom and also for assisting the material wants of those in prison.

Of the last two letters, written shortly before the time of Cyprian's own martyrdom, one is to Successus, a bishop also facing martyrdom, to tell him the provisions of the rescript of Valerian concerning the punishments to be meted out to the various groups of Christians and to give Successus the news of the execution of Pope Sixtus on August 6, 258. The other is Cyprian's farewell to all his people written shortly before his martyrdom. He explains his withdrawal in the face of the official attempt to take him to Utica because he wants to die before his own people. At the moment of writing, he is waiting the return of the proconsul, knowing that this means his own death. He exhorts his flock to maintain discipline; he does not wish them to stir up tumult or to offer themselves voluntarily to the persecutors. He himself will decide his own action at the fitting moment according as the Lord inspires him. On September 13, 258 A.D., Cyprian was taken into custody and executed the next day.

---

4 Africa continued rebaptizing until the Council of Arles in 314 under Constantine. The error was retracted by the Synod of 345-348.
5 Cyprian was exiled to Curubis in August 257 A.D., and remained there one year before he was martyred. He came back to Carthage shortly before his death, but, rather than go to Utica to suffer away from his people, he again went into hiding until Galerius Maximus returned to Carthage.

The letters give us an insight into the activities of the short but fruitful episcopate of a man who was a Christian for only ten years. That Cyprian should have so completely absorbed and transmitted the spirit of Christianity in a brief period is characteristic of the man. His many citations from Scripture show his deep appreciation of the Bible. As far as possible, I have used the Confraternity edition, supplementing it with the Douay version for verses not yet translated by the Confraternity editors.

Particularly important is Cyprian's conception of the Church and his ardent desire for unity centered in Rome as the chief See. His one misconception, his refusal to acknowledge the validity of baptism administered out of the Church, is easily explained by the turbulent condition of those early years when the Church had not yet emerged from the catacombs and when doctrine, present in its entirety from the days of Christ, had not yet been clearly formulated.

The style of the *Letters* is as varied as the writers. The rather awkward constructions of several of Cyprian's correspondents, with far less literary skill than he, sometimes present a difficulty in translation. Cyprian's own style is more straightforward when he is discussing less complicated problems and more eloquent when he is defending a controversial opinion or exhorting confessors to martyrdom. Many of his lengthy sentences are rather involved. Textual difficulties which confront the translator indicate the great need for a definitive Latin text.

The salutations of the letters, which follow the usual epistolary style, simply give the greeting of the sender to his beloved brother or brethren. The formula of the complimentary close frequently is the basic: I trust that you, dearly beloved Brother, are always well. *(Opto te, frater carissime, semper bene valere.)* Interesting variations on it are: I trust that you, dearly beloved and ardently desired Brethren, are always well in the Lord and mindful of us. Farewell. *(. . . in Domino semper bene valere et nostri meminisse. Valete.)* We pray that you, dearly beloved Brother, will be well for many years. *(Oramus te . . . multis annis bene valere.)* I trust that you, dearly beloved and blessed Brethren, are always well in the Lord and that you are attaining the glory of the heavenly crown. *(Opto . . . ad coronae caelestis gloriam pervenire.)* I trust that you, dearly beloved Brethren, are always well and persist in imploring the mercy of the Lord in constant prayers with us. *(. . . circa Domini misericordiam exorandum continuis nobiscum precibus insistere.)*

The fact that many of Cyprian's correspondents are facing martyrdom in the near future makes clear that his use of *valere* refers to spiritual rather than bodily health and that his prayer is for the salvation—the true health—of souls.

The text used is that of Hartel in the *CSEL* with occasional references to Bayard's edition for the Association Guillaume Budé.

My grateful thanks are extended to Dr. Roy J. Deferrari, a stimulating teacher whose enthusiasm for Cyprian has served as a constant incentive to me, for his interest in this translation, and his patient understanding and encouragement when the work was in progress.

SELECT BIBLIOGRAPHY

Text:

Cyprian, Thascius Cecil. *Epistulae. Corpus Scriptorum Ecclesiasticorum Latinorum.* 3.2 Edited by W. Von Hartel. Vienna, 1871.

Translations:

Cyprian. *The Epistles of Cyprian.* Translated by Ernest Wallis. *Ante-Nicene Fathers.* 5. Buffalo: The Christian Literature Company, 1886.

Cyprien, Saint. *Correspondance.* Edited and translated by L. Bayard. 2 vols. Société d'Édition "Les Belles Lettres," 1925.

Secondary Works:

Benson, E. W. *Cyprian: His Life, His Times, His Work.* London: Macmillan and Co., Limited, 1897.

Chapman, John. "Cyprian of Carthage," *Catholic Encyclopedia.* 4.

A Dictionary of Christian Biography. 4 vols. Boston: Little, Brown, and Company, 1877-1887.

Fichter, J. H. *Saint Cecil Cyprian: Early Defender of the Faith.* St. Louis: B. Herder Book Company, 1942.

Godet, P. "Cyprien (Saint)," *Dictionnaire de Théologie Catholique.* Edited by A. Vacant and E. Mangenot. III (1908), 2459-2470.

The Holy Bible. Confraternity edition. New York: Benziger Brothers, Inc., 1961.

SAINT CYPRIAN
LETTERS
(1-81)

1. Cyprian[1] *to the priests, deacons, and people abiding in Furni,*[2] *greeting.*

(1) My colleagues who were present here and our fellow priests who were with us and I were greatly disturbed, dearly beloved Brethren, when we had learned that our brother, Geminius Victor,[3] on his death bed, had appointed Geminius Faustinus,[4] the priest, as tutor in his will although long ago it was decreed in a Council of Bishops that no one should appoint in his will a tutor or a guardian from the clerics and ministers of God because everyone honored by the divine priesthood and consecrated for the clerical ministry ought only to serve the altar and the Sacrifices and to have time for prayers and petitions. For it is written: 'No one serving as God's soldier entangles himself in worldly affairs, that he may please him whose approval he has secured.'[5]

Although this statement has been said about all, how much more ought they not be entangled by vexations and worldly snares who, devoted to divine and spiritual matters, cannot withdraw from the Church and have time for worldly and secular occupations. Levites first held the form of this ordination and religion in the law so that, when the eleven tribes divided the land and distributed the possessions, the tribe of

---
1 c. 249 A.D.
2 Furni, a city of Tunisia in the precincts of Carthage and an episcopal seat then vacant. Cyprian was concerned at the failure of a citizen to observe the decree of the council prohibiting the employment of a cleric in secular business.
3 Geminius Victor, a resident of Furni, named Geminius Faustinus, a priest, as tutor contrary to a Carthaginian canon earlier than Cyprian's episcopate. By law Faustinus would have to serve. Cyprian wanted to set an example so that the canon would be observed in the future.
4 Geminius Faustinus, a priest of Furni, 249 A.D., is probably the same man who was a bishop with Cyprian at the Fourth Council, 254 A.D., and likewise Bishop of Furni at the council in 256.
5 2 Tim. 2.4.

Levi, which had time for the temple and the altar and the divine ministries, received nothing from that apportionment of the division but, while others cultivated the land, that tribe honored God only and received from the eleven tribes for its food and nourishment tithes of the crops which were growing. This whole matter was carried out by divine authority and arrangement so that those who devoted themselves to divine services should, in no way, be distracted nor be forced to consider or to transact secular business.

This plan and form are now kept among the clergy so that those who are advanced into sacerdotal ordination in the Church of the Lord may, in no way, be distracted from their divine ministry, that they may not be hindered by worldly troubles and occupations, but, receiving in honor the gifts of the brethren as if tithes of the crops, they may not withdraw from the altar and the Sacrifices and both day and night may serve heavenly and spiritual interests.

(2) The bishops, our predecessors, conscientiously considering this and wisely providing, decreed that no dying brother should name a cleric for guardianship or for trusteeship and, if anyone had done this, prayers should not be offered for him and the Sacrifice should not be celebrated for the repose of his soul. For he who has wished bishops and priests to be distracted from the altar does not deserve to be named at the altar of God in the prayer of the bishops.

And, therefore, since Victor, contrary to the decree recently promulgated by the bishops in council, has dared to appoint Geminius Faustinus, a priest, as tutor, the Holy Sacrifice is not to be offered among you for his repose, nor is any prayer to be repeated in his name in the Church, so that the decree of the bishops may be conscientiously and exactly observed by us and that, at the same time, an example may be given to the rest of the brethren lest anyone call away to secular pursuits bishops and ministers of God devoted to His altar and Church. For care will be taken for the rest that this does not happen any more regarding the person of clerics if what has now been done is punished. I trust that you, dearly beloved Brethren, are always well.

2. *Cyprian*[1] *to Eucratius,*[2] *his brother, greeting.*

(1) In accordance with your love and our mutual reverence, dearly beloved Brother, you thought to consult me as to what seems best to me for a certain actor who, situated among you, is still persisting in the infamy of the same art and, as master and teacher, not for the instruction but for the downfall of youth, is also teaching others what he has unfortunately learned; [you wanted to know] whether such a one ought to communicate with us. I think that it is fitting neither to the Divine Majesty nor to evangelical discipline that the respect and honor of the Church should be defiled by such base and infamous contamination. For since in the law men are forbidden to wear women's clothing and are judged accursed if they do so,[3] how much greater is the offense not only to wear the garments of women, but also by gesture to imitate the unseemly, the unmanly, and the effeminate, in the office of an instructor of a shameless art.

(2) Let no one excuse himself that he himself has withdrawn from the theater when he is still teaching this to others. For he cannot be considered to have withdrawn who has substituted others and who supplies many proxies for himself alone, instructing them contrary to the plan of God and teaching how a man may be weakened into a woman, and sex may be changed by art, and the divine image may be pleasing to the devil, who stains it through the sin of the corrupt and effeminate body. But if such a one pleads as an excuse want and the necessity of poverty, his necessity can also be helped among the rest who are sustained by the support of

---
1 c. 249 A.D.
2 Eucratius, Bishop of Thena, a seaport in the Byzacene province.
3 Cf. Deut. 22.5.

the Church if only he be content with very frugal and simple food and not think that he must be bought off with a pension to cease from sin since this is an advantage, not for us, but for himself. Let him seek thence what else he wishes. For what is the gain which snatches men from the banquet of Abraham and Isaac and Jacob and leads those feasted wickedly and perniciously in the world to the torments of eternal hunger and thirst?

And, therefore, as far as you can, recall him from this depravity and shame to the way of innocence and to the hope of his life that he may be content with the support of the Church, smaller, indeed, but beneficial. But if the Church there has not enough to furnish food to the afflicted, he may transfer himself to us and receive here whatever may be necessary for himself for food and for clothing, and not teach serious sins to others outside the Church, but himself learn salutary lessons in the Church. I trust that you, dearly beloved Son, are always well.

3. *Cyprian*[1] *to Rogatian,*[2] *his brother, greeting.*

(1) Colleagues who were present and I were deeply and painfully disturbed, dearly beloved Brother, on reading your letter in which you complained about your deacon because, unmindful of your episcopal office and forgetful of his own obligation and of his ministry, he has provoked you with his insults and injuries. And you, indeed, have acted honorably and in accordance with your usual humility toward us in that you preferred to complain to us concerning him although you had power, by virtue of the strength of the episcopate and the authority of the see, by which you could immediately punish him, certain that all of your colleagues would be

---
1 c. 249 A.D.
2 Rogatian, Numidian bishop, who appealed to Cyprian against his contumacious deacon.

pleased with whatever you had done according to your episcopal power regarding your insolent deacon, having in mind the divine precepts concerning men of this type, since the Lord God says in Deuteronomy: 'And any man who has the insolence to refuse to listen to the priest or judge, whoever he may be in those days, that man shall die. . . . And all the people, on hearing of it, shall fear, and never again be so insolent.'³

And that we may know that this voice of God came forth with His true and greatest majesty to honor and avenge His priests, when three of the ministers, Core, Dathan, and Abiron, dared to be proud and to lift up their heads haughtily against Aaron, the priest, and to make themselves equal to the priest set over them, they, devoured and swallowed up by an aperture in the earth, paid the penalty immediately for their sacrilegious insolence. Nor were they alone, but two hundred and fifty others who were their companions in insolence were consumed by fire sent forth by the Lord, that it might be proved that the priests of God are avenged by Him who makes priests. In the Book of Kings also when Samuel, the priest, was despised, as you now, by the people of the Jews on account of his old age, the angry Lord cried out and said: 'They have not rejected thee, but they have rejected me.'⁴ And to avenge this, He raised over them King Saul, who afflicted them with grave injuries and trod under foot and pressed the proud people with all insults and punishments that the priest scorned might be avenged on the proud people by divine vengeance.

(2) Moreover, Solomon, established in the Holy Spirit, testifies and teaches what priestly authority and power are, saying: 'With all your soul fear God and revere his priests.'⁵ And again: 'Honor God with all your soul, and respect his priests.'⁶ Mindful of these precepts, the blessed Apostle, according to what we read in the Acts of the Apostles, when it was

---
3 Cf. Deut. 17.12, 13.
4 Cf. 1 Kings 8.7.
5 Sir. (Ecclus.) 7.29.
6 Cf. Sir. (Ecclus.) 7.31.

said to him: 'Dost thou insult God's high priest?' answered and said: 'I did not know, brethren, that he was the high priest; for it is written, "Thou shalt not speak evil of a ruler of thy people." '[7]

Even our Lord Jesus Christ Himself, our King and Judge and God, even up to the day of the Passion showed honor to the high priests and to the priests although the latter had shown neither fear of God, nor recognition of Christ. For when He had cleansed the leper, He said to him: 'Go and show thyself to the priest, and offer the gift.'[8] With that humility which taught us also to be humble, He still called him whom He knew to be sacrilegious a priest. Under the blow of the Passion, likewise, when He had received a slap and it was said to Him: 'Is that the way thou dost answer the high priest?' He spoke nothing abusively against the person of the high priest, but rather maintained His innocence, saying: 'If I have spoken ill, bear witness to the evil; but if well, why dost thou strike me?'[9] All of these things, therefore, were done by Him humbly and patiently that we might have an example of humility and patience. He taught that true priests are to be lawfully and fully honored while He was conducting Himself in such a way in respect to false priests.

(3) But deacons ought to remember that the Lord chose the Apostles, that is, the bishops and leaders, but, after the Ascension of the Lord into heaven, the apostles appointed deacons for themselves as ministers of their episcopate and of the Church. But if we can dare anything against God, who makes bishops, the deacons can also dare against us by whom they are made. And, therefore, it is fitting for the deacon of whom you write to do penance for his insolence that he may acknowledge the honor of the priest and make amends with full humility to the bishop, his leader. For these are the beginnings of heretics and the origin and the attempt of evil-

---

[7] Acts 23.4, 5.
[8] Cf. Matt. 8.4.
[9] John 18.23.

thinking schismatics to please themselves, to despise their leader with insolent pride. Thus there is separation from the Church; thus a profane altar is erected outside; thus there is rebellion against the peace of Christ and the ordinance and unity of God.

But if he further annoys and provokes you by his insults, you will use against him the power of your office either to depose him or to excommunicate him. For if the Apostle Paul, writing to Timothy, said: 'Let no man despise thy youth,'[10] how much more should your colleagues say to you: 'Let no one despise thy age.'

And since you have written that a certain person has joined himself to that same deacon of yours and is a sharer in his pride and insolence, you may either restrain or excommunicate him also and any others that may appear like him and act against a bishop of God. But we also exhort and remind them that they should perceive rather that they have sinned and make satisfaction and allow us to keep our own purpose. For we greatly wish and desire to overcome the insults and injuries of individuals by merciful patience rather than to punish by our priestly power. I trust that you, dearly beloved Brother, are always well.

---

10 1 Tim. 4.12.

*4. Cyprian,*¹ *Cecil,*² *Victor,*³ *Sedatus,*⁴ *Tertullus,*⁵ *with the priests who were present there, to Pomponius,*⁶ *their brother, greeting.*

(1) We have read your letter, dearly beloved Brother, which you sent by Paconius,⁷ our brother, asking and desiring us to write back what seems best to us about those virgins who, although they once determined to keep their state continuously and firmly, have afterwards been found to have remained together in the same bed with men, one of whom you say is a deacon; the same women, who have confessed plainly that they have slept with men, insist that they are chaste.

Since you have desired our judgment about this matter, know that we do not depart from the evangelical and apostolic traditions that we should look out earnestly and firmly for our brethren and sisters and that ecclesiastical discipline should be preserved by all ways of utility and salvation since the Lord speaks and says: 'And I will appoint over you shepherds after my own heart, who will shepherd you with instruction.'⁸ And again it is written: 'He who despises instruction is doomed.'⁹ And in the Psalms also the Holy Spirit instructs, saying: 'Pay homage lest the Lord perchance be angry

---

1 c. 249 A.D.
2 Cecil, Bishop of Biltha in a proconsular province of Africa, present at several synods, a member of the Committee *de Virginibus subintroductis*, is probably the Cecil of Letters 57, 63, 67, and 70.
3 Victor, another African bishop who served with Cecil at most of the above-mentioned synods, is mentioned in Letters 67 and 70.
4 Sedatus, another African bishop, probably of Tuburbo, served on the Committee *de Virginibus subintroductis* with Cecil, Victor, and Tertullus and is mentioned likewise in Letters 67 and 70.
5 Tertullus, another member of the Committee mentioned above, probably an African bishop, worked with Cyprian and the others in judging the discipline to be used towards virgins suspected of incontinence. A principal adviser of Cyprian's first retirement in the Decian persecution, he is also mentioned in Letters 12, 14, 57, and 70.
6 Pomponius, Bishop of Dionysiana in the province of Byzacena, served in several synods and is mentioned also in Letters 67 and 70.
7 Otherwise unknown.
8 Cf. Jer. 3.15.
9 Wisd. 3.11.

and you perish from the just way, when his anger blazes suddenly against you.'[10]

(2) In the first place, therefore, dearly beloved Brother, both leaders and people must endeavor only that we who fear God should keep the divine precepts with every observance of discipline and that we should not allow our brethren to go astray and to live according to their free will and relish, but to consult faithfully for the life of each one, and not to allow virgins to live with men. I do not say to sleep together, but not even to live together, since both their weak sex and still dangerous age ought to be restrained in all things and ruled by us lest opportunity to injure be given to the devil, who lays snares and desires to vent his rage since the Apostle also says: 'Do not give place to the devil.'[11]

The ship must vigilantly be delivered from dangerous places lest it be broken among the cliffs and rocks. The bundle must be drawn out quickly from the fire before it is burned up by the oncoming flames. No one close to danger is safe for a long time. Nor will the servant of God who has entangled himself in the snares of the devil be able to escape the devil. We must intervene quickly for such as these that they may be separated while as yet they can be separated guiltless since they cannot be parted afterwards by our protest after, with a very guilty conscience, they have been united.

Finally, we see how grievous are the downfalls of many men from this cause and we perceive, with the greatest sorrow of our mind, that very many virgins are corrupted by unlawful and dangerous intimacies of this kind. But if they have consecrated themselves in good faith to Christ, let them remain virtuous and chaste without any rumor to the contrary; let them thus, courageous and unwavering, await the reward of virginity. But if they are unwilling or unable to persevere, let them marry rather than fall into hell for their transgressions. Certainly, let them give no scandal to the brethren or

---
10 Cf. Ps. 2.12.
11 Eph. 4.27.

sisters since it is written: 'If food scandalizes my brother, I will eat flesh no more forever, lest I scandalize my brother.'[12]

(3) Let no one think that she can be defended by this excuse that she can be examined and proved whether she is a virgin since both the hands and the eyes of the midwives are often deceived so that, even though she may have been found an incorrupt virgin in that part in which a woman can be, she may yet have sinned in some other part of the body which can be corrupted and yet cannot be examined. How great a confession of infamy and of reproach, assuredly, are the very act of sleeping together in the same bed, the very embracing, the very conversing, and the kissing, and the scandalous and disgraceful sleeping of two lying together! If a husband, coming upon his wife, should see her lying with another man, is he not indignant and does he not storm about and, through the grief of jealousy, does he not perhaps take a sword in his hand? What does Christ, our Lord and Judge, do when He sees His virgin, dedicated to Him and destined for His holiness, reclining with another man? How indignant and angry He is and what punishments does He not threaten against such unchaste intimacies!

We ought to provide and to strive with all counsel that each one of the brethren may be able to escape His spiritual sword and the coming day of judgment. And although we all ought to keep discipline entirely, it is much more proper for leaders and deacons, who should furnish the example and lesson to the others concerning their conversation and conduct, to be careful of this. For how can they be set over integrity and continence if from themselves begin to come forth corruptions and the teachings of vices?

(4) And, therefore, you have acted wisely and vigorously, dearly beloved Brother, in excommunicating the deacon who has often remained with a virgin and also the others who had been accustomed to sleep with virgins. But if they have done penance for this unlawful lying together of theirs and, in

---
12 1 Cor. 8.13.

turn, separate from each other, let the virgins, meanwhile, be diligently examined by midwives, and, if they have been found to be virgins, let them, after having received Holy Communion, be admitted to the Church, yet with this admonition that, if they should afterward return to the same men, or if they should dwell together with the same men in one house and under the same roof, they should be cast out with graver censure; and such should not afterward easily be received back into the Church. But if anyone of them should be found corrupted, let her do full penance because she who has been guilty of this crime is an adulteress, not against a husband but against Christ, and, therefore, after a time considered just, when she has made a confession of sins, let her return to the Church. But if they persevere obstinately and do not separate from each other, let them know that with this, their shameful obstinacy, they can never be admitted by us to the Church lest, because of their sins, they should begin to give an example to others for their destruction. Let them not think that the way of life or salvation exists for them if they have refused to obey the bishops and priests since the Lord God says in Deuteronomy: 'And any man who has the insolence to refuse to listen to the priest or judge, whoever he may be in those days, that man shall die. . . . And all the people, on hearing of it, shall fear, and never again be so insolent.'[13] God ordered men who did not obey His priests to be killed; He appointed the time of His judgment for the disobedient.

And then, indeed, they were killed by the sword when as yet carnal circumcision also remained; but now since circumcision for the faithful servants of God has begun to be spiritual, the proud and insolent are slain with the sword of the Spirit while they are cast out from the Church. For they cannot live without since the House of God is one and there can be no salvation for anyone except in the Church. But that the undisciplined perish while they neither hear nor heed the life-giving precepts, Sacred Scripture testifies, which says: 'The

---
13 Cf. Deut. 17.12, 13.

senseless man loves not to be reproved. But those who hate reproof will die basely.'[14]

(5) Therefore, dearly beloved Brother, take heed that the undisciplined be not consumed and perish, that you rule the brotherhood as far as possible with salutary counsels, and that you counsel each one for his salvation. Steep and narrow is the way through which we enter into life, but most exalted and great is the reward when we come to glory. Let those who have once made themselves virgins for the kingdom of heaven please God in all things and not offend the priests of God or present themselves also as a scandal in the Church to the brethren. And, if, for the present, they seem saddened by us, we should, nevertheless, admonish them with salutary persuasion, knowing that the Apostle also said: 'Have I then become your enemy because I tell you the truth?'[15] But if they obey, it is most pleasing to us. We have strengthened by the dignity of our speech men standing firm in the way of salvation. But if some of the perverse have refused to obey, according to the same Apostle, who says: 'If I were trying to please men, I should not be a servant of Christ,'[16] if we cannot persuade some to make them pleasing to Christ, we assuredly should, according to our duty, please Christ, our Lord and God, keeping His precepts. I trust that you, dearly beloved and ardently desired Brother, are always well in the Lord.

5. *Cyprian to the priests and deacons, his dearly beloved brethren, greeting.*[1]

(1) Unharmed through the grace of God, I greet you, dearly beloved Brethren, rejoicing because I have learned that all things pertaining to your safety are also unimpaired. And

---
14 Cf. Prov. 15.12, 10.
15 Cf. Gal. 4.16.
16 Cf. Gal. 1.10.

---
1 c. 250 A.D.; written from Cyprian's place of exile during the persecution.

since circumstances do not now permit me to be present, I ask you, in your faith and devotion, to perform there both your duty and mine that nothing be wanting either in discipline or in diligence. As for the expenses to be supplied, whether for those who, having confessed the Lord with a glorious voice, have been put in prison, or for those who labor poor and indigent and yet persevere in the Lord, I ask that nothing be wanting since the whole of the small sum which was collected there has been distributed among the clergy for cases of this very nature that many might have the means to be able to work for the necessities and afflictions of each one.

(2) I ask also that your skill and care to bring back peace may not fail. For, although the brethren in their love are desirous of coming together and visiting the good confessors whom divine honor has already made famous with glorious beginnings, yet I think that this ought to be done cautiously and not in crowds and not through a multitude united together at a single time, lest from that very fact hatred be stirred up and permission for entering be refused and while, insatiable, we wish much, we lose all. Take heed, therefore, and provide that this may be done more safely with moderation so that the priests also who offer Sacrifice there among the confessors may alternate one by one, by turns, with one deacon for each, since a change of persons and an alternation of those assembling lessens ill will. For in all things, gentle and humble, as befits servants of God, we ought to have regard for the times and to look forward to peace and to provide for the people. I trust that you, dearly beloved and ardently desired Brethren, are always well and mindful of us. Greet all the brotherhood. My deacon greets you and those who are with me greet you. Farewell.

6. Cyprian[1] to Sergius[2] and Rogatian,[3] and the other confessors, everlasting greeting in the Lord.

(1) I greet you, dearly beloved Brethren, hoping also myself to enjoy your society if circumstances permit me to come to you. For what more agreeable or more joyful thing could happen to me than now to be close to you that you might embrace me with those hands which, pure and innocent and keeping faith in the Lord, have scorned sacrilegious worship? What would be more delightful and sublime than now to kiss your lips which have confessed the Lord with a glorious voice, than to be seen present by your eyes which, having despised the world, have appeared worthy in the sight of God? But since opportunity to be present for this joy is not given, I send, as substitute for me to your ears and eyes, this letter, in which, at the same time, I congratulate and exhort you to persevere strong and steadfast in the confession of heavenly glory and, having entered the way of honor of the Lord, to continue in the strength of the Spirit to receive the crown, having as Protector and Leader the Lord, who said: 'And behold, I am with you all days, even unto the consummation of the world.'[4] Oh, blessed prison which your presence has illuminated! Oh, blessed prison which sends men of God to heaven! Oh, darkness brighter than the sun itself and clearer than this light of the world, where now temples of God have been erected and your members have been sanctified by divinely inspired confessions!

(2) Now let not anything be considered in your hearts and minds but the divine precepts and the heavenly commandments by which the Holy Spirit has always animated us for

---
[1] c. 250 A.D.
[2] Sergius, a Christian confessor in prison for the faith with Rogatian and others.
[3] Rogatian, an aged priest and confessor, was addressed with other confessors by Cyprian, who wished to commend them for their glorious stand for the faith under torture. Later active for Cyprian during his retirement, Rogatian is mentioned also in Letters 7, 13, 41, 42, and 43.
[4] Matt. 28.20.

the endurance of suffering. Let no one think of death, but of immortality, nor of punishment in time, but of glory everlasting, since it is written: 'Precious in the eyes of God is the death of his faithful ones.'[5] And again: 'My sacrifice to God is a contrite spirit: a heart contrite and humbled God does not despise.'[6] And again, where divinely inspired Scripture speaks of the torments which consecrate and sanctify martyrs of God by the very trial of suffering: 'For if before men, indeed, they be punished, yet is their hope full of immortality; and, chastised a little, they shall be greatly blessed, because God tried them and found them worthy of himself. As gold in the furnace, he proved them, and as sacrificial offerings he took them to himself. In the time of their visitation they shall shine; . . . they shall judge nations and rule over peoples, and the Lord shall be their King forever.'[7]

When, therefore, you reflect that you will judge and reign with Christ the Lord, you must exult and tread under foot present sufferings in the joy of what is to come, knowing that it has been so ordained from the beginning of the world that this same justice should struggle in the worldly conflict since, immediately in the very beginning, Abel the just was killed and thenceforth all the just men and the prophets and the apostles who were sent forth. For all of these, the Lord also set an example in Himself, teaching that only those come to His kingdom who have followed Him in His way, saying: 'He who loves his life in this world will lose it; and he who hates his life in this world will keep it unto life everlasting.'[8] And again: 'Do not be afraid of those who kill the body but cannot kill the soul. But rather be afraid of him who is able to destroy both soul and body in hell.'[9]

Paul also exhorts us that we who wish to attain to the promises of the Lord ought to imitate the Lord in all things. 'We

---
5 Cf. Ps. 115.6.
6 Ps. 50.19.
7 Wisd. 3.4-6, 8.
8 Cf. John 12.25.
9 Matt. 10.28.

are,' he says, 'sons of God. But if we are sons, we are heirs of God also, indeed joint heirs with Christ, provided, however, we suffer with him that we may also be glorified with him.'[10] He added also a comparison of the present time and of the future glory, saying: 'The sufferings of the present time are not worthy to be compared with the glory to come that will be revealed in us.'[11] It is fitting for us, meditating upon the glory of this splendor, to endure all afflictions and persecutions because, although the afflictions of the just are many, yet they who trust in God are delivered from all.

(3) Blessed women also who are placed with you in the same glory of confession, who keep faith in the Lord, and stronger than their sex are, not only themselves very near to the crown, but they have offered to other women also an example by their constancy! And lest anything be wanting to the glory of your number, that each sex and age be with you in honor, divine condescension has united even youths to you in a glorious confession, manifesting to us the very thing which Ananias, Azarias, Misael, illustrious youths, once did. When they had been confined in the furnace, the fires ceased and flames gave way to coolness, the Lord being present with them and approving, because the heat of hell could effect nothing against His confessors and martyrs but, on the contrary, they who believed in God should always persevere unharmed and safe in everything. I ask you to consider more diligently in your regard for sacred things what in those youths must have been the faith which could deserve God so fully. For, prepared for all things, as we all ought to be, they said to the king: 'King Nabuchodonosor, there is no need for us to defend ourselves before you in this matter. For our God, whom we serve, can save us from the white-hot furnace and he will deliver us from your hands, O king! But if not, know that we will not serve your gods and worship the golden statue which you set

---
10 Cf. Rom. 8.16, 17.
11 Cf. Rom. 8.18.

up.'[12] Although they both believed and knew in their faith that they could be delivered even from the present suffering, yet they would not boast of this and claim it for themselves, saying, 'But if not,' lest, without the testimony of suffering, the virtue of confession be weakened. They added that God could do all things, but yet they did not trust in this so as to wish to be delivered in the present but to think of that glory of eternal liberty and salvation.

(4) Let us also, retaining this faith and meditating day and night with our whole heart prepared for God, with contempt for the present, think only of the future, the reward of the eternal kingdom, the embrace and kiss of the Lord, the sight of God, that you may follow in all things the priest, Rogatian, a glorious old man, showing you the way to the glory of our time by devout courage and divinely inspired dignity, who with Felicissimus,[13] our always calm and temperate brother, sustaining the first attack of an unruly people, prepared a lodging for you in prison and, as one who somehow marks out the way for you, now also goes before you. That this may be accomplished in you, we beseech the Lord with ceaseless prayers to bring it about that, from beginnings going forward to the heights, He may cause those whom He has inspired to confess to be crowned also. I trust that you, dearly beloved and blessed Brethren, are always well in the Lord and that you are attaining the glory of the heavenly crown.

7. *Cyprian[1] to the priests and deacons, his dearly beloved brethren, greeting.[2]*

(1) I greet you, dearly beloved Brethren, unharmed through

---

12 Cf. Dan. 3.16-18.
13 Felicissimus, a layman, one of the earliest confessors at Carthage in the Decian persecution.

1 c. 250 A.D.
2 Written from exile to encourage his priests to use all diligence to provide for the poor.

the grace of God, wishing to come to you soon to satisfy my own desire as much as yours and that of all the brethren. We must yet look out for the common peace and, sometimes, although with weariness of our mind, be absent from you lest our presence provoke the hatred and violence of the pagans and we, who ought rather look out for the calm of all, be the instruments of breaking the peace. When, therefore, after matters have been settled, you write that I ought to come or, if before that time the Lord has condescended to show me, then I shall come to you. For where could it be better or more joyful for me to be than there where the Lord wished me both to believe and to grow in belief?

I request you to care diligently for the widows and the infirm and all the poor. Moreover, you may furnish to travelers, if any should be indigent, expenses from my own portion which I have left with Rogatian, our fellow priest.[3] Lest perchance all this amount already may have been distributed, I have sent another portion to the same man by Naricus,[4] the acolyte, that provision for the needy may be made more abundantly and more readily. I trust that you, dearly beloved Brethren, are always well and mindful of us. Greet your brotherhood in my name and urge them to remember us.

Letter 8[1]

(1) We have learned from Crementius, the subdeacon,[2] who came to us from you, that the blessed Pope[3] Cyprian for a certain reason has gone into retirement, something which,

---
3 Cf. Letter 6, n. 3.
4 Naricus, an acolyte of Cyprian, sent by him from his retirement with a second relief for sufferers in the Decian persecution.
1 c. 250 A.D. Addressed by the clergy of Rome during the vacancy of the Holy See to the clergy of Carthage.
2 Crementius (Clementius?), mentioned also in Letters 9 and 20, was the subdeacon who took to Rome the announcement of Cyprian's retirement and who brought back to Carthage the news of the martyrdom of Fabian and the opinion of the Roman clergy as to Cyprian's exile.
3 *Papatem.* The title of Pope was then applied to other bishops also.

indeed, he might do rightly, especially since he is a distinguished person. And, with the struggle at hand which, for the sake of fighting the adversary together with his servants, God has permitted in the world, wishing also to make known this struggle to angels and men that he who conquers may be crowned,[4] indeed, the conquered may bring back upon himself the judgment which has been made known to us. And since it is incumbent upon us who seem to be in charge and in the place of shepherds to guard the flock, if we should be found negligent, there will be said to us what was said to our predecessors who were such negligent leaders that 'we did not seek the lost and we did not bring back the strayed and we did not bind up the injured and we have fed off their milk and worn their wool.'[5]

And finally, the Lord Himself, fulfilling what had been written in the Law and the Prophets, teaches, saying: 'I am the good shepherd who lay down my life for my sheep. But the hireling whose own the sheep are not, when he sees the wolf coming, leaves and flees, and the wolf scatters them.'[6] But to Simon also He says thus: ' "Dost thou love me?" He answered "I love thee." He said to him: "Feed my sheep." '[7] We know that this word was fulfilled from the very act in which he died and the other disciples did likewise.

(2) We wish, therefore, dearly beloved Brethren, to be found not hirelings, but good shepherds, since you know, in this instance, that no trifling danger is involved if you have not encouraged brethren to remain steadfast in faith lest the brotherhood, going headlong into idolatry, be completely destroyed. For not only in words do we encourage you in this, but you will be able to learn from many coming from us to you that, with God assisting, we both have done and do all these things with all solicitude and with danger from the world, having before our eyes rather the fear of God and of eternal

---
4 Cf. 2 Tim. 2.5.
5 Cf. Ezech. 34.3, 4.
6 Cf. John 10.11, 12.
7 Cf. John 21.16.

punishments than the fear of men and a brief injury, not deserting the brotherhood but exhorting them to stand fast in the faith[8] and to be prepared for the necessity of going with the Lord. But when they ascended to that to which they were compelled,[9] moreover, we recalled them. The Church stands firmly in faith although some, compelled by the very terror itself, whether because they were distinguished persons or seized with the fear of men, have fallen. These, indeed, we have not abandoned after their separation from us. But we have exhorted them and we do exhort them to do penance if, in any way, they may receive pardon from Him who is able to grant it, lest, if they should be abandoned by us, they should become worse.

(3) You see, therefore, Brethren, that you also ought to do this so that even those who have fallen, correcting their minds by your exhortation, may confess, if they should be taken again, in order that they may be able to correct their former error. And there are other things which are incumbent upon you and which we have likewise submitted that, if any of those who have yielded to this temptation should begin to be seized by illness and should do penance for their deed and desire Communion, assuredly they ought to be assisted. Whether widows or the confined who cannot support themselves or those who are in prison or excluded from their own dwellings, they ought, indeed, to have some to minister to them. Moreover, catechumens afflicted with infirmity ought not to be deceived in their hope that help may be given to them.

And, what is most important, if the bodies of martyrs or of others be not buried, a great danger threatens those upon whom this work is incumbent. We are certain that everyone of you, therefore, who has done this work on whatever occasion is considered a good servant, 'as he who has been faithful in a very little may have authority over ten towns.'[10] May

---
8 Cf. 1 Cor. 16.13.
9 A reference to ascending the steps to sacrifice.
10 Cf. Luke 19.17.

God, who performs all things for them that hope in Him, bring it to pass that we may all be found in these good works!

The brethren who are in chains and the priests and the whole Church, which itself also watches out with the greatest solicitude for all who invoke the name of the Lord, greet you. But we also ask in return that you remember us.

But know that Bassianus[11] has come to us. And we ask you who have a zeal for God to send a copy of this letter to whomsoever you are able on suitable occasions, either that you make your own or send a message that they may stand strong and steadfast in the faith. We trust that you, dearly beloved Brethren, are always well.

9. Cyprian to the priests and deacons, his brethren, abiding in Rome, greeting.[1]

(1) When the rumor of the death of the good man, my colleague,[2] was uncertain among us, dearly beloved Brethren, and conjecture wavered doubtful, I received from you a letter sent to me by Crementius, the subdeacon,[3] in which I was very fully informed concerning his glorious death and I rejoiced exceedingly that his end also showed itself as honorable as the integrity of his administration. In this I congratulate you exceedingly because you honor his memory with such solemn and illustrious testimony that, through you, it might be known to us both what would be glorious for you regarding the memory of your leader and what also would furnish an example of faith and of virtue for us. For as the ruin of a leader is a dangerous incentive to the lapse of his followers, so, on the other hand, is it useful and salutary when a bishop shows himself to the brethren as one to be imitated in the strength of faith.

---
11 Bassianus, probably a member of the Roman clergy.
1 250 A.D.
2 Pope Fabian.
3 Cf. Letter 8, n. 2.

(2) I have also read a letter[4] in which neither those who wrote nor those to whom it is addressed is plainly indicated. And since in that same letter both the writing and the meaning and the papyrus itself have disturbed me lest anything of the truth has been taken away or changed, I have sent back the same original letter to you that you may examine whether it is the same one which you gave to Crementius, the subdeacon, to deliver. For truly, it is an extremely serious matter if the truth of a clerical letter has been corrupted by any lie and fraud. Therefore, that we may know this, examine whether both the writing and the signature are yours and write back to us what the matter is in truth. I trust that you, dearly beloved Brethren, are always well.

10. *Cyprian to the martyrs and confessors of Jesus Christ our Lord in God the Father, everlasting greeting.*[1]

(1) Joyfully I exult and I congratulate you, very courageous and blessed Brethren, having learned your faith and courage in which Mother Church glories and gloried also recently, indeed, when, after a persevering confession, the punishment which made the confessors of Christ exiles was undergone. Yet the present confession is so much the more brilliant and greater in honor as it is braver in suffering. The combat has increased; the glory of the combatants has also increased. You were not kept back from the conflict by fear of tortures but, by the very tortures themselves, you were more stirred up for the conflict. Brave and firm, you have gone forth with manifest loyalty to the battle of the greatest struggle.

I have found that some of you are crowned; some, assuredly, very near to the crown of victory. But all whom the prison has shut up in a glorious multitude, animated with equal and similar warmth of courage to carry on the struggle as soldiers of

---
4 Cf. Letter 8.

1 250 A.D.

Christ, ought to be in the divine camp so that flatteries may not deceive the incorrupt firmness of faith, nor threats terrify, nor crucifixions and torments conquer because, 'greater is he who is in us than he who is in this world.'[2] Earthly punishment is not more able to cast down than divine protection is to raise. The fact is proved by the glorious struggle of the brethren who, after becoming leaders for others in overcoming torments, have offered an example of valor and faith, fighting in the line of battle until the conquered line of battle yielded.

(2) With what praises then should I commend you, most valiant Brethren? With what laudation of the voice should I extol the strength of your heart and the perseverance of your faith? You have endured, even to the consummation of glory, the hardest questioning; you have not yielded to torments, but rather the torments have yielded to you. An end of sorrows which torments did not give, crowns have given. The butcher's stall has persisted for a time for this, not to cast down your abiding faith, but to send men of God more quickly to the Lord. The multitude of those present, admiring the celestial and spiritual combat of God, the battle of Christ, saw that His servants stood with a free voice, an incorruptible mind, a divinely inspired valor, stripped, indeed, of worldly weapons, but, believing, armed with the arms of faith. The tortured stood braver than the torturers; and battered and wounded limbs conquered hammering and tearing nails. Long repeated cruel flogging was not able to overcome an unconquerable faith although, with the structure of their internal organs ruptured, no longer members, but wounds, of the servants of God were tortured. Blood which might extinguish the conflagration of persecution, which might quiet the flames and fires of hell with glorious gore, was flowing.

Oh, what was that spectacle of the Lord, how sublime, how exalted, how acceptable to the eyes of God in the solemn pledge and devotion of His army, as it is written in the

---
2 Cf. John 4.4.

Psalms when the Holy Spirit speaks to us likewise and warns: 'Precious in the sight of God is the death of his faithful ones'![3] This death which has bought immortality at the price of its blood, which has received the crown from the consummation of its valor, is precious.

(3) How joyful was Christ therein! How willingly in such servants of His has He both fought and conquered as Protector of the faith, giving to the believers as much as he who receives believes he can take! He was present at His own struggle; He lifted up, strengthened, animated the defenders and protectors of His Name. And He who once conquered death for us always conquers it in us. 'But when they deliver you up,' He says, 'do not be anxious what you are to speak; for what you are to speak will be given you in that hour. For it is not you who are speaking, but the Spirit of your Father who speaks through you.'[4]

(4) The present conflict has furnished proof of the matter. A voice filled with the Holy Spirit broke forth from the lips of the martyr when the most blessed Mappalicus[5] said to the proconsul in the midst of his torments: 'Tomorrow you will see the combat.' And what he spoke with the testimony of virtue and faith the Lord fulfilled. A celestial struggle took place and the servant of God was crowned in the contest of the promised combat. This is the struggle which the Prophet Isaia foretold of old saying: 'It is not a weak contest for you with men, since God assures the combat.'[6] And that he might show what this struggle would be, he added, saying: 'Behold a virgin shall conceive in the womb, and bear a son, and you shall name him Emmanuel.'[7] This is the struggle of our faith in which we contend, in which we conquer, in which we are crowned.

---

3 Cf. Ps. 115.5.
4 Cf. Matt. 10.19, 20.
5 Mappalicus, a Carthaginian martyr in the Decian persecution, died under reiterated torture before the proconsul. Mentioned also in Letters 22 and 27, he is commemorated in the African Church.
6 Cf. Isa. 7.13.
7 Cf. *ibid.*, 14.

This is the struggle which even the Blessed Apostle Paul has shown us in which we ought to run and to attain to the glory of a crown. 'Do you not know,' he says, 'that those who run in a race, all indeed run, but one receives the prize? So run as to obtain it; . . . and they indeed to receive a perishable crown, but we an imperishable.'[8] Likewise disclosing his own contest and promising that he would soon be a sacrifice to the Lord, he says: 'I am already being poured out in sacrifice, and the time of my deliverance is at hand. I have fought the good fight, I have finished the course, I have kept the faith. Now there is laid up for me a crown of justice, which the Lord, the just Judge, will give to me in that day; yet not to me only, but also to those who loved his coming.'[9] This combat, therefore, foretold formerly by the prophets, engaged in by the Lord, carried on by the apostles, Mappalicus promised again to the proconsul in his own name and in that of his colleagues. Nor did the faithful voice deceive in its promise. He carried out the combat which he promised and he received the reward which he deserved.

I pray likewise and I exhort the rest of you also to follow that most blessed martyr now and the other sharers in the same conflict, friends also strong in faith, patient in sorrow, victorious under inquisition, that the perfecting of virtue and the heavenly crown may also join together those whom the bond of confession and the lodging of the prison joined together, that by your joy you may dry the tears of Mother Church, who bewails the misfortunes and the destruction of very many, and that, by the encouragement of your example, you may also strengthen the endurance of the others who stand. If the line of battle has called you, if the day of your struggle has come, fight bravely; struggle constantly, knowing that you are fighting under the eyes of God who is present, that you are coming to His glory by the confession of His Name who is not such that He only looks upon His servants,

---
8 1 Cor. 9.24, 25.
9 Cf. 2 Tim. 4.6-8.

but He Himself struggles in us; He Himself joins battle; He Himself in the contest of our struggle both crowns and is likewise crowned.

(5) But if, through the mercy of God, peace intervenes before the day of your contest, yet a blameless will and a glorious conscience remain to you. Let not anyone of you be saddened as if he were inferior to those who, having endured torments before you, after having conquered and trampled upon the world, entered on a glorious journey to the Lord. The Lord is the Searcher of the interior and of the heart;[10] He perceives secret matters and gazes upon what is hidden. To merit the crown from Him, His testimony alone who will judge is sufficient.

Either course, therefore, dearly beloved Brethren, is equally sublime and illustrious; the former, more secure, to hasten to the Lord in the consummation of victory; the latter, more joyful, after a leave of absence has been received, to flourish after glory in the praise of the Church. Oh, blessed Church of ours which the honor of divine condescension so illumines, which the glorious blood of martyrs adorns in our times! It was formerly white in the works of the brethren; now it has become purple in the blood of the martyrs. Neither lilies nor roses are lacking to its flowers. Now let each one contend for the most noble dignity of both honors. Let them receive crowns, either white for their work or purple for their suffering. In the heavenly camp, both peace and warfare have their flowers with which the soldier of Christ is crowned for glory. I trust that you, most valiant and blessed Brethren, are always well in the Lord and mindful of us. Farewell.

11. Cyprian to the priests and deacons, his brethren, greeting.[1]

(1) Although I know, dearly beloved Brethren, from the

---
10 Cf. Apoc. 2.23.
1 250 A.D.

fear which each of us owes to God, that you there also rely earnestly on continual prayers and zealous entreaties, yet I myself also admonish your pious solicitude to lament, not by voice alone, but also by fastings and tears and by every kind of intercession for placating and propitiating God. For we must perceive and confess that the very frightful devastation of that affliction which has destroyed, and is even now destroying, our flock in great part has come about because of our sins since we do not keep the way of the Lord, nor do we observe the heavenly commands given to us for salvation. Our Lord did the will of the Father and we, eager for our patrimony and advantage, following after pride, giving way to envy and to dissension, neglecting simplicity and faith, renouncing the world in words only and not in deeds, each one pleasing himself and displeasing all,[2] do not do the will of God.

We are beaten, therefore, as we deserve since it is written: 'But that servant who knows his master's will and did not obey his will, will be beaten with many stripes.'[3] But what blows, what stripes do we not deserve, when not even confessors, who ought to have been an example in good morals to the rest, keep discipline? While, therefore, a haughty and shameless boasting about their confession excites some immoderately, tortures have come, tortures also without an end of the tormentor, without a way out of condemnation, without the solace of death, tortures which do not easily send forth to the crown, but as long as they wrench them on the rack, so long do they cut down, unless someone, taken away by the divine goodness, should go forth in the midst of the torments themselves, gaining glory, not by an end of torture, but by the quickness of death.

(2) We suffer these things because of our fault and of our deserving, as the Divine Judgment has forewarned us, saying: 'If they have forsaken my law, and have walked not in my judgments, if they have profaned my ordinances and have kept

---
2 Cf. 2 Peter 2.13-15.
3 Cf. Luke 12.47.

not my commands, I will visit their crime with a rod and their guilt with stripes.'[4] We, therefore, who neither please God with our good deeds nor satisfy Him for our sins, feel the rods and the lashes. Let us ask from the depth of our heart and with our whole mind the mercy of God because He Himself adds this, saying: 'Yet my kindness I will not take from them.'[5] Let us ask and we receive; and, if there is delay and tardiness in our receiving because we have offended gravely, let us knock because to him who also knocks it is opened,[6] provided only our prayers and groans and tears knock at the door, in which we ought to persist and to employ much time, provided our prayer is also of one mind.

(3) For you ought to know that what has persuaded and driven me more completely to write this letter to you, as the Lord has condescended to show and to reveal, has been said in a vision: 'Ask, and you receive.'[7] Then afterwards, the people present were instructed to pray for certain persons pointed out to them; but in the petition there were dissonant voices and conflicting wills and this greatly displeased Him who had said: 'Ask, and you receive,' because the disunity of the people was out of harmony and there was not one agreement and simple and mutual concord of the brethren although it is written: 'God makes men of one mind to dwell in a house,'[8] and since in the Acts of the Apostles we read: 'Now the multitude of those who believed acted with one soul and with one mind.'[9] And the Lord has commanded with His voice, saying: 'This is my commandment, that you love one another,'[10] and again: 'I say to you further, that if two of you shall agree on earth about anything at all for which you ask, it shall be done for you by my Father who is in heaven.'[11] But if two of one

---
4 Cf. Ps. 88.31-33.
5 Cf. Ps. 88.34.
6 Cf. Matt. 7.7, 8; Luke 11.10.
7 Cf. Matt. 7.7.
8 Cf. Ps. 67.7.
9 Cf. Acts 4.32.
10 John 15.12.
11 Cf. Matt. 18.19.

mind can accomplish so much, what might it be if there were unanimity among all?

But if, according to the peace which the Lord gave to us, there were agreement among all brethren, we should have gained long ago what we seek from the divine mercy and we should not be wavering nor should we be fluctuating so long in this danger of our salvation and of our faith; nay rather these evils would not have come upon the brethren if the brotherhood had been of one mind.

(4) For it was shown, moreover, that a father of the household sat with a young man sitting at his right hand; this youth, anxious and sorrowful with a certain displeasure, sat with a sad countenance holding his jaw in his hand. But another, sitting on the left side, carried a net, which he threatened to throw out to catch the people standing around. And when he who saw wondered what this might be, it was told to him that the young man who was thus sitting at the right was saddened and grieved because his commands were not observed, but that the one on the left rejoiced because an opportunity was being given to him by the father of the household to assume the power of raging violent. This was made manifest long before the storm of this devastation arose. And we saw fulfilled what had then been shown, that while we despised the precepts of the Lord, while we did not keep the salutary commands of the Law which had been given, the enemy was receiving the power of harming; he was overwhelming with a cast of the net those less armed and less cautious to resist.

(5) Let us pray earnestly and let us lament with constant prayers. For know, dearly beloved Brethren, that we were reproached not long ago in a vision because we are falling asleep in prayer and are not watchfully praying. And God, assuredly, who loves him whom He reproves,[12] when He reproves, He reproves for this, that He may amend; He amends for this, that He may save. Let us shake off, therefore, and break off the chains of sleep and let us pray assiduously and

---
12 Cf. Heb. 12.6.

vigilantly, as the Apostle Paul teaches, saying: 'Be assiduous in prayer, being wakeful therein.'[13] For the apostles also did not cease to pray days and nights, and the Lord also, Himself the Master of discipline and the Way of our example, frequently and vigilantly prayed, as we read in the Gospel: 'He went out to the mountain to pray, and continued all night in prayer to God.'[14] And assuredly, what he prayed, He prayed for us since He Himself was not a sinner, but bore our sins. But He Himself interceded so much for us that we read in another place: 'But the Lord said to Peter: "Behold, Satan has desired . . . that he may sift you as wheat. But I have prayed for thee, that thy faith may not fail." '[15] But if He also labors and watches and prays for us and for our sins, how much more ought we to be instant in prayers and to pray and, first, to ask the Lord Himself, then, finally, through Him to make satisfaction to God the Father!

We have an Advocate and Intercessor for our sins, Jesus Christ, our Lord and God, provided only we repent that we have sinned in the past, and, confessing and acknowledging our sins by which we now offend the Lord, we promise for the rest certainly to walk in His ways and to fear His precepts. The Father both corrects and protects us, who yet stand in faith, both in tribulations and in distresses, clinging, nevertheless, firmly to His Christ, as it is written: 'Who shall separate us from the love of Christ? Shall tribulation, or distress, or persecution, or hunger, or nakedness, or danger, or the sword?'[16] None of these can separate believers; nothing can snatch away those clinging to His Body and Blood. This persecution is the examination and evaluation of our heart. God wished us to be tried and proved, as He has always tried His own, and yet in His trials never, at any time, has His help failed believers.

(6) Finally, even to His least servant laden also with the

---
13 Col. 4.2.
14 Luke 6.12.
15 Cf. Luke 22.31.
16 Rom. 8.35.

greatest offenses and unworthy of His attention, He has yet deigned in His goodness toward us to send word: 'Tell him,' He said, 'that he should be secure because peace will come but that, meanwhile, there is a little delay so that some who still remain may be tested.' But we are admonished by the divine condescensions concerning frugal food and temperate drink, namely, lest worldly allurement deprive the uplifted heart of heavenly vigor, or lest the mind, weighed down by too abundant feastings, be not awake for petitions of prayer.

(7) I ought not to have concealed and to have hidden alone in my own conscience these several matters by which each one of us may both be instructed and ruled. Do not you, finally, yourselves keep this letter hidden away among you, but suggest it be read to the brethren. For to hinder those whom the Lord deems worthy for us to admonish and instruct is the part of one who does not wish his brother to be instructed and admonished. Let them know that we are proved by our Lord; let them not, because of the conflict of the present tribulation, fail the faith by which we have once believed in Him. Let each, recognizing his own sins, immediately also put off the conversation of the old man.[17] 'For no one looking back and putting his hand to the plow is fit for the kingdom of God.'[18] Finally, the wife of Lot, who, when freed, looked back in spite of the prohibition, lost what she had gained.[19] Let us not give heed to the things which are behind, to which the devil calls us back, but to the things which are ahead, to which Christ calls. Let us raise our eyes to heaven lest the earth deceive us with its allurements and charms.

Let each one of us pray to God, not for himself only, but for all of the brethren as the Lord has taught us to pray when He commands not private prayer for each one, but He orders those who pray to pray for all in common prayer and peaceful supplication.[20] If the Lord has observed us peaceful and hum-

---
17 Cf. Eph. 4.22.
18 Cf. Luke 9.62.
19 Cf. Gen. 19.26.
20 Cf. Matt. 6.9.

ble, if united to each other mutually, if fearful of His anger, if corrected and amended by the present tribulation, He will preserve us safe from the machinations of the enemy. Discipline has come forth and pardon will follow.

(8) Let us pray to the Lord alone without ceasing to ask and, with faith in receiving, straightforward and of one mind, entreating with both groaning and weeping, as those who are placed between the ruins of the moaning and the remains of the fearful, between the manifold destruction of the fallen and the paltry strength of the standing, ought to pray. Let us ask for peace to be restored sooner, to be succored quickly in our hiding places and dangers, for what the Lord deigns to manifest to His servants to be fulfilled: the restoration of His Church, the security of our salvation, serenity after the rains, light after darkness, peaceful calm after storms and dangers, blessed aids of His fatherly love, the accustomed grandeurs of His Divine Majesty, by which the blasphemy of the persecutors may be beaten back, and the penance of the lapsed may be accomplished, and the strong and stable faith of the persevering may glory. I trust that you, dearly beloved Brethren, are always well and mindful of us. Greet the brotherhood in my name and urge them to be mindful of us. Farewell.

12. Cyprian to the priests and deacons, his brethren, greeting.[1]

(1) Although I know, dearly beloved Brethren, that you have been frequently advised in my letters that every attention is to be given to those who have confessed the Lord with a glorious voice and have been put in prison, yet again and again I press it upon you that nothing be wanting for the care of those to whom nothing is wanting in glory. And I wish that circumstances of the place and my position would permit me now myself to be able to be present; prompt and willing, I should perform with consecrated ministry all of the duties

---
1 250 A.D.

of love toward our most courageous brethren. But let your diligence carry out my duty and do all that which should be done for those whom the divine condescension has adorned with so many merits of their faith and courage. Let very willing vigilance and care be bestowed, moreover, upon the bodies of all who, although they have not been tortured, yet depart from the prison by the glorious exit of death. Neither their valor nor their honor is less that they themselves should not be included among the blessed martyrs. They have endured, as far as it is in their power, whatever they were prepared and ready to endure. In the eyes of God, the one who offered himself to torments and to death suffered whatever he was willing to suffer. For he himself did not fail the torments, but the torments failed him. 'He who has acknowledged me before men, I also will acknowledge him before my Father,'[2] says the Lord. They have acknowledged Him. 'He who has persevered even to the end, he will be saved,'[3] says the Lord. They have persevered and, even to the end, they have kept the merits of their virtues incorrupt and immaculate. And again it is written: 'Be thou faithful unto death, and I will give thee the crown of life.'[4] They endured even unto death, faithful and steadfast and invincible. When to our wish and to our confession in prison and in chains is added also the end of dying, the glory of martyrdom is consummated.

(2) And of these finally, take note of the days on which they die that we may be able to celebrate their commemorations among the memorials of the martyrs although Tertullus,[5] our very faithful and very devoted brother, who does not fail in that matter regarding the care of bodies, among other things which, in his solicitude and care, he bestows upon the brethren in every duty of service, has written and is writing and indicating to me the days on which our blessed brethren in prison pass through the exit door of a glorious death to

---

2 Cf. Matt. 10.32.
3 Cf. Matt. 10.22.
4 Apoc. 2.10.
5 Cf. Letter 4, n. 5.

immortality. And, for their commemorations, let there be celebrated here by us Oblations and Sacrifices which, with protection of the Lord, we shall celebrate soon with you.

As I have already often written, let not your care and diligence, moreover, fail the poor, those particularly who, standing in faith and fighting valiantly with us, have not left the camp of Christ. We must now show greater love and care, indeed, to them because, neither dejected by poverty nor prostrated by the storm of persecution while they are serving the Lord faithfully, they have also offered an example of faith to the other poor. I trust that you, dearly beloved and ardently desired Brethren, are always well and mindful of us. Greet all of the brotherhood in my name. Farewell.

13. Cyprian[1] to Rogatian,[2] the priest, and to the other confessors, his brethren, greeting.

(1) A long time ago now, dearly beloved and very valiant Brethren, I sent you a letter in which in jubilant words I congratulated your faith and courage and now, not otherwise, among the first our voice is uplifted to foretell frequently and always with a joyful mind the glory of your name. For what can either be greater in my prayers or better than when I see the flock of Christ made illustrious by the honor of your confession? For as all of the brethren ought to rejoice in this, so is the greater portion in the common joy the bishop's, for the glory of the Church is the glory of the head. In proportion as we grieve over those whom the attack of the enemy has prostrated, so much the more do we rejoice in you whom the devil could not overcome.

(2) Yet we exhort you, through our common faith, through the true and simple charity of our heart towards you who have conquered the adversary in this first attack to retain your

---
1 250 A.D.
2 Cf. Letter 6, n. 3.

glory with brave and persevering valor. We are still in the world, still drawn up in line of battle; we fight daily for our lives. Care must be taken that, after such beginnings as these to their fulfillment, there may come also and be accomplished in you what you, with such happy beginnings, have already commenced. It is a slight matter to have been able to gain possession of something; it is of greater value to be able to keep what you have obtained as both faith itself and the salutary birth vivify, not by being received, but by being kept. But final perseverance, not accomplishment, preserves a man immediately for God.

The Lord taught this in His instruction, saying: 'Behold, thou art cured. Sin no more, lest something worse befall thee.'³ Consider that He says this also to His confessor: 'Behold, thou hast been made a confessor. Sin no more, lest something worse befall thee.' Solomon, finally, and Saul, and many others, for as long as they did not walk in the ways of the Lord, could not keep the grace given to them. When the discipline of the Lord withdrew from them, His grace also withdrew.

(3) We must persevere in the straight and narrow way of praise and glory and, since calm and humility and tranquillity of good living are becoming to all Christians, according to the voice of God who looks favorably upon no other than the humble man and the calm man and the man respecting His words,⁴ then so much the more ought confessors to observe and to fulfill this, you who have been made an example to the rest of the brethren for whose living your life and actions ought to be a stimulation. For as the Jews have been alienated from God because, on their account, the name of God is blasphemed among the Gentiles,⁵ so, on the contrary, are they dear to God through whose discipline the name of the Lord is adorned with praiseworthy testimony, as it is written with the Lord forewarning and saying: 'Let your light shine before

---
3 John 5.14.
4 Cf. Isa. 66.2.
5 Cf. Rom. 2.24.

men, in order that they may see your good works and give glory to your Father, who is in heaven.'⁶

And the Apostle Paul says: 'Shine like stars in the world.'⁷ And Peter likewise exhorts: 'As strangers,' he says, 'and pilgrims, abstain from carnal desires which war against the soul, behaving yourselves honorably among the pagans; that, whereas they slander you as evildoers, they may, observing your good works, magnify the Lord.'⁸ To my great joy, a very large part of you, indeed, do this and, made better by the honor of confession itself, guard and preserve their glory with calm and good living.

(4) But I hear that some are corrupting your number and destroying the praise of your great name by their cowardly behaving; these, indeed, you yourselves, as lovers and guardians of your good reputation, ought rather to reprove and to restrain and to correct. For with what shame for your reputation is a fault committed when someone remains alive intoxicated and lascivious, when another returns into the same country from which he was banished to perish when seized, no longer as a Christian, but as a criminal!

I hear that some are puffed up and inflated although it is written: 'Be not high-minded, but fear. For if the Lord has not spared the natural branches, perhaps he may not spare thee either.'⁹ Our Lord was led as a sheep for sacrifice and as a lamb without voice before his shearer; thus he did not open his mouth.¹⁰ 'I am not,' he said, 'obstinate and I do not resist. I gave my back to scourges and my jaws to blows. I have not, moreover, turned away my face from the foulness of the spittle.'¹¹ And does anyone now living through Him and in Him dare to exalt himself and to be proud, unmindful both of the deeds which He did and of the commandments which

---
6 Cf. Matt. 5.16.
7 Phil. 2.15.
8 Cf. 1 Peter 2.11, 12.
9 Cf. Rom. 11.20, 21.
10 Cf. Isa. 53.7.
11 Cf. Isa. 50.5, 6.

He handed down to us either by Himself or by His apostles? But if 'no servant is greater than his master,'[12] let those who follow the Lord keep close to His footsteps, humble and calm and silent, when whoever may have been lower may become more exalted, since the Lord says: 'For he who has been the least among you, he will be great.'[13]

(5) What, then, is that which it seems ought to be cursed by you, which we have learned with the greatest groaning and sorrow of our mind, that there are not wanting those who stain the temples of God, their members, both sanctified and made more glorious after confession, with disgraceful and infamous intercourse, joining promiscuous beds with women since, even though defilement of conscience is wanting to them, that itself is a great crime because the examples of these bring forth the ruins of others with scandal.

There ought also to be no contentions and emulations among you since the Lord left His peace to us and it has been written: 'Thou shalt love thy neighbor as thyself. But if you bite and complain of another, take heed lest you be consumed by another.'[14] Abstain, I beg of you, from wranglings also and from curses, for scurrilous talkers will not obtain the kingdom of God and the tongue which has confessed Christ must be kept free and pure with its honor. For he who speaks words peaceful and good and just, according to the command of Christ, daily confesses Christ. We had renounced the world when we were baptized, but now truly we renounce the world when, tried and approved by God, leaving all our possessions, we have followed the Lord and stand and live in His faith and fear.

(6) Let us strengthen each other by mutual exhortations and more and more let us grow perfect in the Lord, that, when He has made peace according to His mercy, as He promises that He will do, renewed and changed, I may say, we may

---
12 John 15.20.
13 Cf. Luke 9.48.
14 Cf. Gal. 5.14, 15.

return to the Church. And either our brethren or the Gentiles may receive us corrected in all things and reformed for the better; and those who had formerly admired glory in virtues may now admire discipline in living.[15] I trust that you, dearly beloved Brother, are always well.

14. Cyprian to the priests and deacons, his brethren, greeting.[1]

(1) I had hoped, indeed, dearly beloved Brethren, to greet in my letter all of our clergy whole and safe. But, because the evil time which has laid low our people in very great part has added also to our sorrows this overwhelming one that it has touched closely even a portion of the clergy with its devastating force, we pray the Lord that, through the Divine Mercy, we may greet you safe also in the future who, we have learned, stand in faith and in courage.

And although reason urged that I myself ought to hasten and to come to you, first, because of my wish and desire for you, which is the greatest object of my prayers, then afterwards, that we might be able to treat those matters which the common advantage demands regarding the government of the Church and, at the same time, to investigate matters examined by the advice of very many, yet it has seemed more advisable up to this point, meanwhile, to preserve concealment and quiet out of consideration for other advantages which pertain to the peace and safety of all of us, the reason for

---

15 Other texts add the following: And although I have written very fully to our clergy, both recently when you were still stationed in prison and now again also, to supply anything if it were necessary either for your clothing or for food, yet, I myself also have sent to you from my own property which I had with me two hundred and fifty sesterces and I had lately sent another two hundred and fifty. Victor [a companion of Cyprian's exile], from reader also made deacon, who is with me, sent you one hundred and seventy-five. But I rejoice when I learn that very many of the brethren, out of their love, are eagerly coming together also to aid your necessities by their collections.

1 250 A.D.

which will be given to you by Tertullus,² our dearly beloved brother. He, with his other care which he bestows earnestly upon divine works, was even the author of this plan that I should remain cautious and restrained and that I should not rashly commit myself to the public view, most especially in that place where I had been so many times sought and demanded.

(2) Relying, therefore, upon both your love and your devotion which I know fully, in this letter I both exhort and command you, whose presence is least obnoxious there and not yet dangerous, to act in my place regarding those matters to be carried out which the religious administration demands. In the meantime, let the care of the poor be carried on as much as possible and in as many ways as possible, if any yet who stand with unshaken faith have not abandoned the flock of Christ, that, by your diligence, the expense for relieving their penury may be supplied, lest, what the storm did not do in regard to those keeping faith, necessity may do in regard to those laboring. Let more willing care be bestowed also upon the glorious confessors. And although I know that very many of these have been received with the vow and love of the brethren, yet if there remain any who lack either clothing or expense money, as I formerly also had written to you when they were still in prison, let whatever things are necessary be supplied to them, provided that they know from you and are instructed and learn what ecclesiastical discipline demands according to the teaching authority of the Scriptures: that they should be humble and modest and peaceful, so as to preserve the honor of their reputation, that they who have been glorious in voice may also make themselves worthy in life so that, meriting the Lord in all things, they may attain the celestial crown with the consummation of His praise. For more remains than seems to be done since it is written: 'Praise not any man before death.'³ And again: 'Be thou faithful unto death, and

---
2 Cf. Letter 4, n. 5.
3 Cf. Sir. (Ecclus.) 11.28.

I will give thee the crown of life.'⁴ And the Lord also says: 'He who has persevered even to the end, he will be saved.'⁵

Let them imitate the Lord, who, at the very time of His Passion, was not prouder but humbler. For then He washed the feet of His disciples, saying: 'If I, the Master and Lord have washed your feet, you also ought to wash the feet of one another. For I have given you an example, that as I have done, you also should do to one another.'⁶ Let them follow also the teaching of Paul the Apostle, who, after often repeated imprisonment, after scourgings, after exposure to the beasts, persevered through all, meek and humble, and even after the third heaven and Paradise he did not take insolently any credit to himself, saying: 'Neither did we eat any man's bread at his cost, but we worked night and day in labor and toil, so that we might not burden any of you.'⁷

(3) Each one of these matters, I beg you, make known to our brethren. And since he will be exalted who has humbled himself,⁸ it is now that they ought to fear more the insidious enemy who attacks each braver man more and, made bolder by that very fact that he has been conquered, attempts to overcome the conqueror. The Lord will bring it about that I may be able both to see them and to fortify their minds with salutary exhortation to preserve their glory. For I grieve when I hear that some wickedly and insolently run about, give way to trifles or to discords, stain with unlawful concubinage the members of Christ, which have already confessed Christ, and that they cannot be restrained either by deacons or priests, but that they so act that, through the depraved and evil living of the few, the shining glory of the many and good confessors is defiled; these they ought to reverence lest, condemned by their own testimony and judgment, they may be deprived of

---

4 Apoc. 2.10.
5 Cf. Matt. 10.22.
6 Cf. John 13.14, 15.
7 2 Thess. 3.8.
8 Cf. Luke 14.11.

their society. For he, finally, is an honorable and true confessor concerning whom the Church does not later blush but glories.

(4) But as for that which our fellow priests, Donatus,[9] and Fortunatus,[10] and Novatus,[11] and Gordius,[12] wrote to me, I have been able to reply nothing in writing alone because, from the beginning of my episcopate, I decided to do nothing of my own opinion privately without your advice and the consent of the people. When I come to you through the grace of God, then we shall discuss in common either what has been done or what must be done concerning these matters, as our mutual honor demands. I trust that you, dearly beloved and ardently desired Brethren, are always well and mindful of me. Greet particularly the brotherhood in my behalf if there are any with you and urge them to be mindful of us. Farewell.

15. Cyprian to the martyrs and confessors, his dearly beloved brethren, greeting.[1]

(1) The anxiety of our position and the fear of God compel us, most valiant and blessed martyrs, to admonish you in our letter that those same men who so devoutly and bravely keep the faith of the Lord should also observe the law and discipline of the Lord. For, although soldiers of Christ ought to keep the commandments of their Leader, then so much more is it fitting for you, who have been made an example of valor and of fear of God to others, to follow His precepts! And I

---
9 Donatus, priest of Carthage, urged Cyprian to relax the discipline of the lapsed.
10 Fortunatus, priest of Carthage, also one of the five opposed to the election of Cyprian, later false bishop of the lax party with Felicissimus on the question of the lapsed, was consecrated by the excommunicated Bishop Privatus.
11 Novatus, priest of Carthage, an original opponent of Cyprian's election, wrote to Cyprian regarding peace for the lapsed. Cyprian warns Pope Cornelius of the bad character of the man.
12 Gordius of Carthage, an associate of the men mentioned above, was one with them in requesting an easy reconciliation for those who had fallen.

---
1 250 A.D.

had, indeed, believed that the priests and deacons who are present there would warn and instruct you most fully regarding the law of the Gospel, as, in the past, it has always been done under our predecessors, that deacons going back and forth to prison controlled the desires of the martyrs by their advice and by the precepts of the Scriptures.

But now I learn with the greatest sorrow of mind that, not only are the divine precepts not suggested there, but rather are hindered, to this extent, that those matters which are done by you yourselves prudently concerning God and honorably concerning the bishop of God are made void by certain priests who consider neither the fear of God nor the honor of the bishop. Although you sent me a letter in which you ask to have your desires examined and peace given to certain lapsed persons when, after persecution is over, we begin to assemble together and to be gathered with the clergy, there against the law of the Gospel, against your honorable petition also, before penance has been done, before the confession of a very serious and low crime has been made, before hands have been imposed by bishop and priest in penance, they dare to offer the Holy Sacrifice for them and to give them the Eucharist, that is, to profane the Holy Body of the Lord although it is written: 'Who eats the bread or drinks the cup of the Lord unworthily, will be guilty of the body and the blood of the Lord.'[2]

(2) And, indeed, concession can be granted to the lapsed in this. Who, dead, would not hurry to be raised to life? Who would not hasten to come to his own salvation? But it is the duty of those in charge to observe the commandment and to instruct both the rash and the ignorant so that those who ought to be shepherds of the flocks may not become butchers. For to grant these things which lead to perdition is to deceive. The lapsed person is not thereby restored, but is driven rather to ruin through the offense to God. Let them learn, therefore,

---

[2] Cf. 1 Cor. 11.27.

even from you what they ought to have taught. Let them reserve your petitions and desires for the bishop; let them wait for a ripe and peaceful time to give peace to you who ask for it. It is of first importance that the mother receive peace from the Lord, then, according to your desires, that arrangements be made for the peace of the children.

(3) And since I hear, most valiant and dearly beloved Brethren, that you are hard pressed by the shamelessness of some and that your sense of modesty is suffering violence, I beg you with what prayers I can that you, mindful of the Gospel and considering what things and what sorts of things your predecessors, the martyrs, conceded in the past, how solicitous they were in all things, should also carefully and cautiously weigh the desires of your petitioners since as friends of the Lord also, afterward to judge with Him, you should examine both the act and the deeds and merits of each one. You should also consider the kinds and qualities of their defects, lest, if anything be hastily and unworthily promised by you or done by us, our Church should begin to blush even before the Gentiles themselves.

For we are both visited and frequently chastised and admonished that the Commandments of the Lord should remain incorrupt and inviolate. I know, indeed, that there among you is no cessation in that the divine censure prepares very many of you also for the discipline of the Church. But all this can be done if you manage the things asked of you with prayerful contemplation, knowing and restraining those who are doing favors for persons receiving from your benefits or who are receiving the trade of illicit business.

(4) Concerning this matter, I have sent letters both to the clergy and to the people, both of which I have committed to you to be read. But you ought to regulate and correct this matter according to your diligence, so as to designate by name those to whom you desire peace to be given. For I hear that

petitions³ are so given to some that it is said: 'Let such a one be received into communion with his own people.' This was never done at all by the martyrs, so that a vague and indiscriminate petition should heap up hatred against us later. For it opens the door wide when it says 'such a one with his own people.' And twenty and thirty and more who assert that they are close relatives, the neighbors, the freedmen, and the servants of him who received the petition, can be brought forward to us. And, therefore, I ask that you designate by name in the petition those whom you yourselves see, whom you know, whose penance you perceive is the nearest to satisfaction and, thus, you may address to us letters becoming to faith and discipline. I trust that you, most valiant and dearly beloved Brethren, are always well in the Lord and mindful of us. Farewell.

16. *Cyprian to the priests and deacons, his brethren, greeting.*[1]

(1) For a long time I have kept my patience, dearly beloved Brethren, as if our reserved silence would be profitable for quiet. But since the unbridled and defiant presumption of some attempts by its rashness to disturb both the honor of the martyrs and the modesty of the confessors and the tranquillity of all the people, I ought no longer to keep silence lest excessive taciturnity result equally in our danger and in that of the people. For what danger ought we not to fear from the displeasure of the Lord when some of the priests, mindful neither of the Gospel nor of their own station and considering

---

3 *libellos. Libellus,* used by Cyprian to designate petition signed by martyr asking for reinstatement of lapsed in the Church and to designate certificate purchased from magistrate to save person from actually sacrificing. Since this latter course gave the impression that the man had apostatized, it was definitely immoral. In some cases, those who received *libellos* of the second type from magistrates sought *libellos* of the first to be reinstated after their fall. I have translated the first as 'petition' and the second as 'certificate.'

1 250 A.D.

neither the future judgment of the Lord nor the bishop now placed over them, claim everything for themselves with abuse and contempt of their prelate—a thing which was never done at all under our predecessors?

(2) But would that they might claim all things for themselves without destroying the safety of our brethren! I could ignore and bear the insults to my episcopate as I have always ignored and borne them. But now it is not opportune to ignore them when our brotherhood is being deceived by some of you who, while they wish to be worthy of applause, without regard for restoring salvation rather do great injury to the lapsed. For, that it is a very great fault which the persecution has forced to be committed, even they themselves who have committed it know since our Lord and our Judge said: 'He who has acknowledged me before men, I also will acknowledge him before my Father, who is in heaven. But whoever disowns me, I will disown him.'[2] And again He said: 'All sins shall be forgiven to the sons of men and blasphemies. But whoever has blasphemed against the Holy Spirit does not have forgiveness, but is guilty of an everlasting sin.'[3] Likewise the Blessed Apostle said: 'You cannot drink the cup of the Lord and the cup of devils; you cannot be partakers of the table of the Lord and of the table of devils.'[4]

He who takes away these truths from our brethren deceives the wretched so that they who, by doing true penance, can satisfy God, the merciful Father, now by their prayers and their good works are led astray, so that they rather perish and they who can lift themselves up fall the more. For, although sinners do penance for a just time for the lesser sins and, according to the order of discipline, come to confession that they may receive the right to receive Communion through the imposition of hands of the bishop and of the clergy, now in an unpropitious time with a persecution still raging, with the

---
[2] Cf. Matt. 10.32, 33.
[3] Cf. Mark 3.28, 29.
[4] 1 Cor. 10.21.

peace of the Church itself not yet restored, they are admitted to Communion and there is an offering in their name. And, although penance has not yet been performed, confession has not yet been made, hands have not yet been imposed upon them by bishop and clergy, the Eucharist is given to them although it is written: 'Who eats the bread or drinks the cup of the Lord unworthily, will be guilty of the body and the blood of the Lord.'[5]

(3) But now those who have kept the law of the Scripture least are not the guilty. But guilty will they be who are over them and do not suggest these things to the brethren that, instructed by those placed over them, they should do all things with the fear of the Lord and with the circumspection given and ordained by Him. Finally, they expose the blessed martyrs to hatred and they involve the glorious servants of God in controversy with the bishop of God. For, although the former, mindful of our position, have sent letters to me and have asked that their desires be examined and peace be given, then—when our Mother herself has first received peace through the mercy of the Lord and the divine protection has brought us back to His Church—the latter, having taken away the honor which the blessed martyrs with the confessors have given us, having despised the law of the Lord and the circumspection which the same martyrs and confessors command to be kept, before the fear of persecution has been quenched, before our return, almost before the very death of the martyrs, are in communion with the lapsed; and they offer the Holy Sacrifice and give them the Eucharist, when even if the martyrs in the glow of glory, not contemplating Scripture, wish for anything more contrary to the law of the Lord, they ought to be admonished by priests and deacons who suggest it has always been done in the past.

(4) Thus the divine censure does not cease to castigate us by day or night. Besides the nightly visions, by the days also the innocent age of children among us is filled with the Holy

---
5 Cf. 1 Cor. 11.27.

Spirit, which in ecstasy sees with eyes and hears and speaks those things by which the Lord condescends to warn and instruct us. And you will hear all when the Lord, who ordered me to withdraw, will bring me back to you. In the meantime, let certain rash and incautious and boastful men who do not respect man among you at least fear God, knowing that, if they persist longer in the same matters, I shall use the admonition which the Lord orders me to use that, meanwhile, they may be prohibited from offering Mass, who will have to plead their cause before us and before the confessors themselves and before the whole people when, with the Lord permitting, we shall begin to be gathered again in the bosom of Mother Church. Concerning this, I have written letters to the martyrs and confessors and to the people, both of which I have ordered to be read to you. I trust that you, dearly beloved and ardently desired Brethren, are always well in the Lord and mindful of us. Farewell.

17. *Cyprian to the brethren abiding among the people, greeting.*[1]

(1) I know from myself, dearly beloved Brethren, that you are groaning and grieving over the ruins of our brethren because I myself groan for each one and grieve and suffer and feel equally with you what the Blessed Apostle says: 'Who is weak,' he says, 'and I am not weak? Who is made to stumble, and I am not inflamed?'[2] And again he has written in his epistle, saying: 'If one member suffers, the other members also suffer; and if one member glories, the other members rejoice.'[3] I suffer with, I grieve with our brethren who, having lapsed and fallen by the impetus of persecution, drawing part of our hearts with them, have brought a like sorrow on us with their wounds; the Divine Mercy is powerful to give healing to them.

---
1 250 A.D.
2 2 Cor. 11.29.
3 Cf. 1 Cor. 12.26.

Yet I think that we ought not to rush into things, nor to act incautiously and hurriedly in anything, lest, while peace is rashly usurped, the displeasure of divine indignation be more seriously aroused. The blessed martyrs have sent a letter to us concerning some, asking that their desires be examined. When, after peace has first been given to us all by the Lord, we shall begin to return to the Church, each one will be examined in your presence and with you judging.

(2) Yet I hear that some of the priests, not mindful of the Gospel, not considering what the martyrs have written to us, not reserving for the bishop the honor of his priesthood and of his see, have already begun to be in communion with the lapsed and to offer for them the Holy Sacrifice and to give them the Eucharist although they should attain to these things in order. For since in minor offenses which are not committed directly against God penance is done for a just time and confession is made when the life of the one who does penance has been investigated and since no one can come to Communion unless, first, hands have been imposed upon him by the bishop and the clergy, how much more in these exceedingly grievous and extreme sins ought all things to be observed cautiously and moderately according to the discipline of the Lord!

Priests and deacons, indeed, ought to have warned our people about this that they might protect the sheep entrusted to them and, with the divine teaching, instruct them in the way of obtaining salvation. I have known equally the calmness and the fear of our people; they would watch for the satisfaction and impetration of God if certain priests, attempting to oblige them, had not deceived them.

(3) Assuredly, therefore, rule yourselves each one and, by your advice and moderation, restrain the minds of the lapsed according to the divine precepts. Let no one pluck the unripe fruit at a time still unsuitable. Let no one entrust his shattered and damaged ship to the waves again before he has carefully repaired it for the deep. Let no one hasten to receive and to

put on the ripped tunic unless he has first seen it repaired by the skillful workman and has received it restored by the fuller.

Let them listen patiently, I beg, to our counsel. Let them await our return so that, when we come to you through the mercy of God, after having assembled our fellow bishops, many of us may be able to examine the letters and desires of the blessed martyrs according to the discipline of the Lord and in the presence of the confessors and with your decision. Concerning this I have written letters to the clergy and to the martyrs and confessors, both of which I have commanded to be read to you. I trust that you, dearly beloved and ardently desired Brethren, are always well in the Lord and mindful of us. Farewell.

18. Cyprian to the priests and deacons, his brethren, greeting.[1]

(1) I wonder that you, dearly beloved Brethren, have written nothing in answer to my many letters which I have frequently sent to you although both the advantage and the necessity of our brotherhood would be governed in this way if, instructed by you, we could investigate the plan for carrying out affairs. Yet since I see that there is not yet an opportunity to come to you and summer has already begun—a time which is disturbed with unremitting and serious illnesses—I think that our brethren must be relieved so that they who have received petitions from the martyrs and may be helped by their prerogative, if they should be seized with any injury and danger of illness when our presence is not expected, may make confession of their sin before whatever priest may be present or, if a priest has not been found and death begins to be imminent, before even a deacon that they may come to the Lord when hands have been imposed upon them in penance with the peace which, in letters sent to us, the martyrs have desired to be given.

---

[1] 250 A.D.

(2) Protect by your presence also the rest of the people who have lapsed and revive them by your solace that they may not withdraw from the faith and mercy of the Lord. For they who, meek and humble and truly doing penance, have persevered in good expectations so that the divine aid may look out for them will not be forsaken by the resource and help of the Lord. Let not your vigilance be wanting even to the catechumens if any have been overtaken by danger and appointed for death; let not the mercy of God be denied to those who implore divine grace. I trust that you, dearly beloved Brethren, are always well and mindful of us. Greet all the brotherhood in my name and urge them to be mindful of us. Farewell.

19. Cyprian to the priests and deacons, his brethren, greeting.[1]

(1) I have read your letter, dearly beloved Brethren, in which you wrote that your salutary advice has not been wanting to our brethren: that, when they have cast aside their rash haste, they should offer to God religious patience so that, when we come together through His mercy, we may be able to investigate all kinds of things according to ecclesiastical discipline, especially since it is written: 'Remember whence thou hast fallen, and repent.'[2] But he repents who, mindful of the divine precept, meek and patient and obedient to the priests of God by his compliance and just works, is worthy of the Lord.

(2) Yet since you have indicated that some are impetuous and are insisting on being received into communion immediately and you have desired me to give you a pattern for this matter, I believe that I have written fully enough about this matter in the last letter sent to you. For example, those who have received a petition from the martyrs and can be assisted by their help, with the Lord regarding their sins, if

---
1 250 A.D.
2 Cf. Apoc. 2.5.

they begin to be hard pressed by any illness and danger, when they have made confession and hands have been imposed upon them by you in penance with the peace promised to them by the martyrs, may be restored to the Lord.

But let the rest who, having received no petition from the martyrs, are stirring up hatred await first the public peace of the Church itself through the protection of the Lord since this is a case not of a few, nor of one church, nor of one province, but of the whole world. For this is fitting to the respect and to the discipline and to the life itself of all of us that we prelates, assembled with the clergy in the presence of the people who stand steadfast, to whom also honor must be given because of their faith and fear of the Lord, be able to dispose of all matters according to the religious obligation of a common council.

For the rest, how irreligious it is and how dangerous to impetuous men themselves that, although men made exiles and driven from their country and deprived of all their goods have not yet returned to the Church, some of the lapsed hasten to go before the confessors themselves and to enter the Church before them! If any are in a very great hurry, they have what they are asking in their own power since the time itself provides more than what they ask. The battle is still going on and the struggle is daily renewed. If they repent truly and steadfastly of the fault committed and ardor of faith prevails, he who cannot be put off may be crowned. I trust that you, dearly beloved Brethren, are always well and mindful of us. Greet all the brotherhood in my name and urge them to be mindful of us. Farewell.

20. *Cyprian to the priests and deacons, his brethren, abiding in Rome, greeting.*[1]

(1) Since I have learned, dearly beloved Brethren, that

---
1 250 A.D.

what has been done and is being done here by us is reported to you in a way not straightforward and accurate, I have considered it necessary to write this letter to you to present to you an account of our action and discipline and diligence. For as the commands of the Lord instruct, after the first attack of the disturbance had suddenly arisen, when the people with violent clamor had often demanded us in person, considering not so much my safety as public peace for the brethren, I withdrew for a time lest the sedition which had begun be further provoked through our indiscreet presence. Although absent in body, I have not been absent in spirit, or in action, or in my admonitions, so that I might at least, with what moderate ability I could, look out for our brethren according to the precepts of the Lord.

(2) And what I did, letters which I have transmitted to you—thirteen in number—sent on various occasions tell you. In them neither advice was wanting to the clergy, nor exhortation to the confessors, nor rebukes to the exiled when it was necessary, nor our appeals and persuasion to the whole brotherhood for beseeching the mercy of God, as far as, according to the law of faith and the fear of God, our moderate ability could accomplish at the suggestion of the Lord.

But after tortures came also, our speech penetrated the prison to strengthen and console them, whether, indeed, our brethren had already been tortured or were still shut up to be tortured. Likewise, when I had found out that those who had stained their hands and mouths by sacrilegious contacts or had polluted their consciences just as much with evil certificates were going to the martyrs in every direction and were also corrupting the confessors with troublesome and complaisant appeal, so that, without any discrimination and examination of each one, thousands of petitions were being given out daily contrary to the law of the Gospel, I sent letters by which I recalled the martyrs and confessors as much as possible by my counsel to the precepts of the Lord. Priests and deacons, likewise, were not wanting in the sacerdotal vigor of the priesthood so that some who had already begun to be in communion with the lapsed, too little mindful of discipline and precipitate with rash haste, were checked at our intervention. We composed the minds of the people also, as far as possible, and instructed them to observe ecclesiastical discipline.

(3) But afterward, when some of the lapsed, whether of their own accord or through another instigator, rushed forward with the bold demands to make an effort to extort with violent attack the peace promised to them by the martyrs and confessors, I wrote twice concerning this to the clergy, and I commanded the letters to be read to them to mitigate also the violence of those for a time that, if any should depart from the world after having received a petition from the martyrs, after they had made confession and had hands imposed in penance, they should be sent to the Lord with the peace promised to them by the martyrs. I did not give the law in this and I did not rashly appoint myself an authority.

But since it seemed fit both for honor to be given to the martyrs and for the attack of those who wished to disturb everything to be checked and, furthermore, since I had read your letter which you had recently sent to our clergy through Crementius, the subdeacon,[2] that some aid should be given to those who might, after their lapse, be seized with illness and, penitent, might desire communion, I thought that we ought to take a stand according to your advice lest our action which ought to be unified and to agree in all things should be in any way different. Even though they had received a petition from the martyrs, I plainly commanded the cases of the rest to be postponed and to be reserved until my return that, when peace has been given to us by the Lord, we many prelates may begin to assemble together and, after having communicated our plan to you, we may be able to dispose or to reform each one. I trust that you, dearly beloved Brethren, are always well.

---

2 Cf. Letter 8, n. 2.

21.¹ *Celerinus² to Lucian.*³

(1) When I wrote this to you, my dear Brother, I was rejoicing and sorrowful: rejoicing in that I heard that you had been tried for the Name of our Lord Jesus Christ, our Savior, and had confessed His Name before the magistrates of this world; but sorrowful in that, from the time when I accompanied you, I was never able to receive your letters. Even now recently, a twofold sadness has fallen on me because you knew that Montanus,⁴ our mutual brother, was coming to me from you from prison and you did not express to me anything concerning your safety or how things are with you. But this continually happens to the servants of God, especially to those who are appointed for the confession of Christ.

For I know, in fact, that everyone no longer pays attention to the affairs of the world since he is hoping for the heavenly crown. I said, in fact, that perchance you had forgotten to write to me. For if from the lowest place also I may be called 'yours' or 'brother,' if I have been worthy to hear myself named Celerinus, for all that when I also was in so glorious a confession, I was mindful of my oldest brethren and I reminded them in my letters that their former love was still with me and mine.

Yet I entreat, dearly Beloved, from the Lord that you may be washed in that Holy Blood, if you have suffered first, for the Name of our Lord Jesus Christ, before my letter reaches

---

1 250 A.D.
2 Celerinus, a confessor at Rome, apparently the same Celerinus ordained by Cyprian in December, 250, tortured before Decius, remained firm and was released. His letter to his friend, Lucian, to secure petitions of pardon for his two sisters shows a knowledge of Latin and a style quite inferior to Cyprian's.
3 Lucian, a rather imprudent, but very brave Carthaginian confessor, caused Cyprian much trouble by circulating to lapsed Christians petitions which asked that the latter be received back immediately into the Church because of the intercession of the martyrs. Lucian's granting of these pardons without discrimination was interfering with ecclesiastical discipline.
4 Montanus, a Christian imprisoned in Carthage under the Decian persecution, went to Rome to Celerinus on his release.

you in this world, or that, if it reaches you now, you may write back to me in answer to this. Thus may He crown you whose Name you have confessed! For I believe, indeed, although we shall not see each other in this world, yet that, in the future, we shall embrace each other in the presence of Christ. Pray that I also may be worthy to be crowned among your number.

(2) Yet I know that I am placed in great tribulation and I remember your former love day and night as if you were present with me. God alone knows. And, therefore, I entreat you to grant my desire and to grieve with me in the death of my sister who has fallen to Christ in this devastation. For she sacrificed and provoked our Lord, as it seems manifest to us. Because of her actions, weeping day and night in this season of Paschal joy, I have spent and, even to this day, am spending days full of tears in sackcloth and ashes until the help of our Lord Jesus Christ and the compassion of you and of those my lords who have been crowned, from whom you are about to ask it, may have come to the aid of so disastrous a shipwreck. For I remembered your former love that you may grieve with all for our sisters[5] whom you also knew well, that is, Numeria[6] and Candida,[7] in the face of whose sin we ought to be on guard since they regard us as brethren. For I believe that Christ, according to their repentance and the works which they have rendered to our exiled colleagues who came to us from you, from whom themselves you will hear of their works, that Christ, I believe, will now pardon them if you, His martyrs, entreat.

(3) For I have heard that you have undertaken the ministry of the glorious martyrs. Oh, happy you! Receive your wishes which you have always desired, even sleeping on the earth. You hoped to be put in prison for His Name; now

---

5 *sorore nostra* .... Other defects in text also including *cum omnes*.
6 Numeria, a sister of Celerinus, had bribed officers to be exempted from sacrificing. Benson states that her real name was Etecusa but that is doubtful. Even the form of the name is a problem.
7 Candida, another sister of Celerinus, had been weak enough to sacrifice during the persecution.

that has happened to you, as it is written: 'The Lord grant you according to your own heart!'[8] And now, made an overseer of God over those, the same authority has certified.[9]

I ask, therefore, Master, and entreat through our Lord Jesus Christ that you may refer to the rest of your colleagues, your brethren, my lords, and that you may entreat from them that whoever of you is first crowned should remit so great a sin for those our sisters, Numeria and Candida. For I have always called Etecusa herself this—God is Witness for us—because she counted out[10] gifts in order not to sacrifice, but she seems only to have ascended to the Three Fates[11] and then to have come down. I know, therefore, that she has not sacrificed. After their case had been heard recently, the leaders ordered them to be as they are in the meantime until a bishop should be appointed. But as far as possible, through your holy prayers and petitions in which we trust since you are friends as well as witnesses of Christ, we hope that you may be indulgent in all things.

(4) I entreat, therefore, dearly beloved Master Lucian, that you be mindful of me and that you grant my petition. Thus Christ grant that holy crown which He has given to you, not only for confession, but also for holiness, in which you have always run quickly and have always been an example and a witness of the saints, that you may refer to all my lords, your brethren, the confessors concerning this matter that they may receive help from you. For you ought to know this, my dear Brother, that I am not alone in seeking help for them, but also Statius[12] and Severianus,[13] and all the confessors who

---

8 Cf. Ps. 19.6.
9 Defect in text interferes with clarity.
10 *numeravit.*
11 Statue to the Three Fates, called Parcae, or birth spirits: Clotho, Lachesis, and Atropos, located in the Forum on the way to the Capitol. The statement may signify that the girl repented and did not go the whole way.
12 Statius, a confessor of Carthage in the Decian persecution, fled to Rome and was received by Numeria, who was trying to atone for her sin by hospitality to the refugees.
13 Severianus, a confessor of Carthage.

have come thence from you hither. To meet them, the women themselves went down to the harbor and supported them in the city because they ministered to sixty-five and even to this day they have protected them in all things. All are, indeed, with those women.

But I ought not to burden that holy heart of yours more since I know that you are exerting yourself to the full. With his sisters, Cornelia[14] and Emerita,[15] Macarius,[16] who is joyful about your glorious confession, and, indeed, that of all of the brethren, greets you, and Saturninus,[17] who also himself struggled with the devil, and who bravely confessed the Name of Christ, and who confessed bravely there in the punishment of the nails, and who especially asks and pleads with you for this favor. Your brethren, Calpurnius[18] and Mary,[19] and all the holy brethren, greet you. For you ought to know this, that I have written also to my lords, your brethren, a letter which I ask you to deign to read to them.

22.[1] *Lucian[2] to Celerinus,[3] his lord, if I be worthy to be called a colleague in Christ, greeting.*

(1) I have received your letter, dearly beloved Lord and Brother, in which you burdened me so much because of your burden that I almost lost a very great joy as I rejoiced to read the letter which for so long a time I hoped to read. In it you deigned to remember me according to the kindness of your

---

14 Cornelia, Roman Christian.
15 Emerita, her sister, a confessor.
16 Macarius, a Christian at Rome during the persecution, brother of Cornelia and Emerita, was one of the comrades of Maximus in accepting and later in rejecting Novatian.
17 Saturninus, a Carthaginian confessor, tortured, later went to Rome.
18 Calpurnius, Roman confessor.
19 Mary, Roman confessor.

---

1 250 A.D.
2 Cf. Letter 21, n. 3. The ungrammatical wording of parts of Lucian's letter makes it rather difficult to translate.
3 Cf. Letter 21, n. 2.

very great humility, who, writing to me said: 'If I be worthy to be called your brother,' of a man who confessed with fear the Name of God among more insignificant men. For you, by God's will, having confessed, have not only terrified but conquered the greater serpent[4] himself, the precursor of Antichrist, by that voice and those divine words through which I know that you are, as it were, lovers of the faith and men jealous for the discipline of Christ. In this I know and rejoice that you are engaged with eagerness.

Now, indeed, dearly Beloved, already to be numbered among the martyrs, you wished to burden us by your letter in which you gave the news about our sisters, for whom, would it could be done that we should remember them without so great a crime committed! We should not be oppressed with such great tears as we are now.

(2) You ought to know what has happened to us. When the blessed martyr Paul[5] was still in the body, he called me and said to me: 'Lucian, in the presence of Christ, I say to you that if anyone should seek peace from you after my departure, give it in my name.' But all of us also whom the Lord has deigned to summon together in such great tribulation have given peace, letters to all according to agreement. See, therefore, Brother, that what Paul recommended to me in part we, in all cases, agreed upon from the time when already before this tribulation we were ordered, according to the command of the emperor, to be killed by hunger and thirst; and we were shut up in two cells in such a way that nothing happened from the hunger and thirst. But the fire from the effect of our affliction was so intolerable that no one could bear it. But now we are established in full light itself.

And, therefore, dearly beloved Brother, greet Numeria[6] and

---

4 Emperor Decius.
5 Paul, a martyr of Carthage in 250, requested Lucian to establish a system of dispensations for the lapsed. Lucian's attempt to carry out the request posed a definite problem for the Carthaginian bishops.
6 Cf. Letter 21, n. 6.

Candida,[7] according to the direction of Paul and of the rest of the martyrs whose names I add: of Bassus[8] in the mine, Mappalicus[9] at the inquisition, Fortunio[10] in prison, Paul[11] after the inquisition, Fortunata,[12] Victorinus,[13] Victor,[14] Herennius,[15] Credula,[16] Hereda,[17] Donatus,[18] Firmus,[19] Venustus,[20] Fructus,[21] Julia,[22] Martial,[23] and Aristo,[24] who, by the will of God, died of hunger in prison, whose companions you will hear within a few days we are.

For now we have been shut up again eight days to the day on which I wrote you the letter. For before the eight days, for five days we received only a little bread and water rationed out. And, therefore, Brother, as here, when the Lord has begun to give peace to the Church itself, according to the direction of Paul and our discourse, after the case has been set before the bishop and they have made confession, I entreat that not only these women, but also those whom you know belong to our way of thinking, may have peace.

(3) All my colleagues greet you. Greet the confessors of the Lord who are there with you, whose names you have mentioned, among whom also are Saturninus[25] with his com-

---

7 Cf. Letter 21, n. 7.
8 Bassus belonged to a group of martyrs imprisoned with Aristo in Carthage, 250 A.D.
9 Cf. Letter 10, n. 5.
10 Fortunio, martyr with above.
11 Paul, martyr with Aristo.
12 Fortunata, martyr with same group.
13 Victorinus, martyr with Aristo.
14 Victor, martyr with above.
15 Herennius, martyr with above.
16 Credula, martyr with above.
17 Hereda, martyr with above.
18 Donatus, martyr with above.
19 Firmus, martyr with above.
20 Venustus, martyr with above.
21 Fructus, martyr with above.
22 Julia, martyr with above.
23 Martial, martyr with above.
24 Aristo, with the martyrs listed, was imprisoned with Lucian in Carthage. Mappalicus apparently died under torture; the other martyrs were victims of hunger, thirst, and crowding in prison.
25 Cf. Letter 21, n. 17.

panions, but also my colleague, and Maris,[26] Collecta,[27] and Emerita,[28] Calpurnius,[29] and Mary,[30] Sabina,[31] Spesina,[32] and the sisters, Januaria,[33] Dativa,[34] Donata.[35] We greet Saturus,[36] with his family, Bassianus,[37] and all the clergy, Uranius,[38] Alexius,[39] Quintianus,[40] Colonica;[41] and I ask for them all whose names I have not written because I was so weary. Therefore, they must pardon me. I trust that you, Alexius, and Getulicus,[42] and the silversmiths, and the sisters are well. My sisters, Januaria and Sophia,[43] whom I commend to you, greet you.

23.[1] *All the confessors to Pope[2] Cyprian, greeting.*

Know that all of us have given peace to those whose record of what they have done after the transgression was agreeable to you and we wish this plan to become known also to the other bishops through you. We trust that you have peace with the

---

26 Maris, confessor at Rome in Decian persecution, mentioned with Collecta and Emerita. Lucian may be confusing Maris and Collecta with Macarius and Cornelia.
27 Collecta, apparently Cornelia, cf. Letter 21, n. 14.
28 Cf. Letter 21, n. 15.
29 Cf. Letter 21, n. 18.
30 Cf. Letter 21, n. 19.
31 Sabina, Christian at Rome.
32 Spesina, Christian at Rome, Carthaginian.
33 Januaria, evidently a sister of Lucian, was another Carthaginian refugee, a Christian at Rome.
34 Dativa, another Carthaginian refugee, a Christian at Rome.
35 Donata, also Carthaginian refuge, a Christian at Rome.
36 Saturus, a Carthaginian confessor at Rome, a cleric, may be the man whom Cyprian ordained reader.
37 Cf. Letter 8, n. 11.
38 Uranius, Carthaginian refugee at Rome.
39 Alexius, Christian at Rome.
40 Quintianus, probably Carthaginian refugee.
41 Colonica, refugee with confessors at Rome.
42 Getulicus, Christian at Rome.
43 Sophia, sister of Lucian.

---

1 250 A.D.
2 Cf. Letter 8, n. 3.

holy martyrs. Lucian³ wrote this in the presence of an exorcist and a reader of the clergy.

24.¹ *Caldonius² to Cyprian and his fellow priests abiding in Carthage, greeting.*

The necessity of the time demands that we do not give peace rashly. But it seems that I ought to write to you that some of those who before sacrificed to the gods, when they were tried a second time, became exiles. They seem, therefore, to me to have wiped out their previous sin since they are losing their possessions and homes and, doing penance, are following Christ. Therefore, Felix,³ who ministered to the presbytery under Decimus⁴ and was next to me in chains (for I know this same Felix very well), and Victoria,⁵ his wife, and Lucius,⁶ being faithful, were banished; they left their goods which the state treasury has now confiscated. But also under the same persecution, a woman named Bona,⁷ who was dragged by her husband to sacrifice, who did not pollute⁸ her conscience, but as those holding her hands sacrificed, so she herself began to cry out against this: 'I have not done it; you have done it'; and thus she herself was banished.

When, therefore, all sought peace from me saying: 'We have regained the faith which we had lost; doing penance, we have publicly confessed Christ,' although it seems to me that they

---
3 Cf. Letter 21, n. 3.

1 250 A.D.
2 Caldonius, a bishop of an unknown African see, mentioned in several letters of Cyprian, was much trusted by the former and sent occasionally to perform special duties.
3 Felix, a lapsed Christian in Africa, later repented, was banished, and his goods were confiscated. An assistant to Decimus, he was married to Victoria, who, with Lucius, likewise fell and repented.
4 Decimus, priest whom Felix assisted.
5 Victoria, wife of Felix.
6 Lucius, a companion of Felix, denied the faith with him, repented, and was banished.
7 Bona, otherwise unknown.
8 *commiscuit*, perhaps a misreading for *comminxit*.

ought to receive peace, yet I have sent them to consult you lest I should seem to presume to do anything rashly. If, therefore, anything should be approved in the common judgment, write to me. Greet our people. Our people greet you. I trust that you most blessed ones are well.

25. *Cyprian[1] to Caldonius,[2] his brother, greeting.*

We have received your letter, dearly beloved Brother, much restrained and full of integrity and faith. We are not surprised that you, so well trained and versed in the Scriptures of the Lord, carry out everything carefully and deliberately. But you judged rightly that peace which they have regained for themselves by true penance and the glory of the confession of the Lord ought to be bestowed upon our brethren, justified by their speech by which before they had doomed themselves. Since, therefore, they have washed away all sin and wiped out the first stain by their later virtue, with the assistance of the Lord, they who, banished and despoiled of all their goods, have redeemed themselves and have begun to stand with Christ ought not to lie any longer, as it were, prostrate under the devil.

And would that others penitent also after their fall might be thus reformed to their former state! That you may know how we have settled those now pressing for and extorting peace rashly and importunely, I have sent a book to you with letters, in number, five, which I wrote to the clergy, and to the people, and to the martyrs also, and to the confessors. These letters, which have been sent out, have been pleasing to very many of our colleagues and they have written back that they also stand with us in the same judgment according to the Catholic faith. You will transmit this also to as many of our colleagues as you can that, among all, one action and

---
1 250 A.D.
2 Cf. Letter 24, n. 2.

one agreement may be held according to the precepts of the Lord. I trust that you, dearly beloved Brother, are always well.

26. *Cyprian to the priests and deacons, his brethren, greeting.*[1]

The Lord speaks and says: 'For whom shall I have respect except for the lowly and peaceful man who trembles at my words?'[2] Although we ought all to be this, then much more ought those to be such who must labor after a serious lapse to be able to merit the Lord by true penance and all humility. Yet I have read the letter[3] of all the confessors which they wished to be made known by me to all our colleagues also that peace given by themselves come to those 'whose record of what they have done after the transgression was agreeable to us.'

Since this matter attends the judgment and opinion of us all, I dare not prejudge and claim for myself a common decision. And, therefore, let the matter stand, in the meantime, according to the last letter which I wrote to you, a copy of which also I have already sent to many colleagues. They wrote at length that they were pleased at what we decided and that we ought not to depart from it for you until, after peace has been restored to us by the Lord, we may assemble together to examine the case of each one.

But that you may know both what Caldonius,[4] my colleague, wrote to me and what I wrote back to him, I have added a copy of both letters to my letter. I ask that you read all to our brethren that more and more they may be reconciled to patience and not add to their former crime yet another crime as long as they do not permit us to follow the Gospel nor to examine their causes according to the letter of all the confessors. I trust that you, dearly beloved Brethren, are well and mindful of us. Greet all the brotherhood.

---
1 250 A.D.
2 Cf. Isa. 66.2.
3 Letter 23.
4 Cf. Letter 24, n. 2.

27. *Cyprian to the priests and deacons, his brethren, abiding in Rome, greeting.*[1]

(1) Since I sent you the letter, dearly beloved Brethren, in which my action was explained and my method of discipline and of diligence, however small, was declared, another matter has come up which ought not itself to be concealed from you. For our brother, Lucian,[2] himself also one of the confessors, ardent, indeed, in faith and strong in courage, but much less established in the teachings of the Lord, has attempted certain things in a most imprudent manner, for a long time now appointing himself an authority that petitions written in his handwriting were given to many in crowds in the name of Paul,[3] whereas Mappalicus,[4] the martyr, cautious and modest, mindful of the law and of discipline, wrote no letter contrary to the Gospel but, moved only by filial piety, he requested that peace be given to his mother and to his sister who had lapsed; Saturninus,[5] also still confined in prison after torments, sent out no letter of this nature.

But Lucian, not only while Paul was still in prison gave out indiscriminately petitions written in his own hand in the name of Paul, but even after his death continued to do the same in his name, saying that he had been commanded to do this by Paul and not knowing that one must obey the Lord rather than a fellow prisoner. Many petitions, written in the handwriting of this same Lucian, have also been given in the name of Aurelius,[6] a youth who suffered tortures, because the latter did not know how to write.

(2) In order that this might be opposed as much as possible, I sent them the letters which I sent to you with an earlier epistle, in which I did not cease to entreat and to persuade

---
1 250 A.D.
2 Cf. Letter 21, n. 3.
3 Cf. Letter 22, n. 5.
4 Cf. Letter 10, n. 5.
5 Cf. Letter 21, n. 17.
6 Aurelius, a reader and confessor at Carthage under Cyprian, could not write.

them that the order of the law of the Lord and of the Gospel ought to be held. After these letters, as if something might be done more moderate and restrained, Lucian wrote a letter in the name of all the confessors in which almost every bond of faith and fear of God and command of the Lord and sanctity and strength of the Gospel were subverted. For he wrote in the name of all that they had all given peace and wished this plan to become known to the other bishops through me. I have sent you a copy of this letter. There was added plainly: 'Whose record of what they have done after the transgression was agreeable.' This matter stirs up greater animosity against us so that, when we have begun to hear and to investigate the case of each one, we may seem to deny to many what they all now boast they have received from the martyrs and confessors.

(3) Finally, the commencement of this sedition has already begun. For in several cities in our province an attack has been made upon the authorities by the multitude and, having terrified and subdued their leaders, who, by no means, had the power in courage of spirit and strength of faith to resist, they have compelled them to manifest the peace which they kept clamoring had once been given to all by the martyrs and confessors. Among us also certain turbulent individuals who were with difficulty restrained by us in the past and who were put off until our return, aroused by this letter as if by some torches, began to be more inflamed and to extort peace given to them. I have sent you a copy of what letters I wrote to the clergy regarding these men. And also what Caldonius,[7] a colleague, in his integrity and faith wrote to me and what I replied to him, I have sent you both to read.

I have also sent you copies of the letter of Celerinus,[8] a good and firm confessor, which he wrote to the same confessor, Lucian, and likewise what Lucian replied to him, that you may know our diligence is at work in all things and that you

---

7 Cf. Letter 24, n. 2.
8 Cf. Letter 21, n. 2.

may perceive by the truth itself how moderate and how circumspect both in humility and in fear for our mode of life and how reserved is Celerinus, the confessor. But Lucian, as I have said, is less skilled in knowledge of the Lord's teaching and unrestrained in his facility to let hatred for our moderate position remain.

For although the Lord said that nations are baptized in the Name of the Father and of the Son and of the Holy Spirit and that past sins are forgiven in baptism, this man, ignorant of the precept and of the law, commands peace to be given and sins to be forgiven in the name of Paul. And he says that this matter was entrusted to him by the former, as you will observe in the letter of the same Lucian written to Celerinus, in which he has not at all considered that martyrs do not make the Gospel, but that martyrs are made through the Gospel, inasmuch as the Apostle Paul, whom the Lord called a vessel of His election, wrote in his Epistle, saying: "I marvel that you are so quickly deserting him who called you to grace . . . to another gospel; which is not another, except in this respect, that there are some who trouble you and wish to pervert the gospel of Christ. But even if we or an angel from heaven should preach a gospel to you other than that which we have preached to you, let him be anathema!"[9]

(4) Your letter to the clergy which I received came at an opportune time, indeed, likewise those which the blessed confessors, Moses,[10] Maximus,[11] Nicostratus,[12] and the rest, sent

---

9 Cf. Gal. 1.6-9.
10 Moses, a leading member of the group of confessors about the time of the beginning of the Novatianist schism, with Nicostratus, Maximus, Rufinus, Urban, Sidonius, Macarius, and Celerinus, among the first confessors in the Decian persecution, imprisoned when Fabian was martyred, wrote urging the claims of discipline upon the Carthaginian confessors. After almost a year in prison, Moses died, a confessor and martyr.
11 Maximus, a Roman priest and confessor, took the lead after Moses' death; then he followed the heresy of Novatian. Later, reconciled to Cornelius, he became his strong supporter.
12 Nicostratus, a Roman deacon and confessor, was a fellow-sufferer of Moses and Maximus and like them a follower of Novatian. When they returned to the Catholic Church, he went with Novatus to Carthage to further the Novatianist cause. He was accused by Cornelius of giving the funds of the Roman Church to heretics.

to Saturninus and Aurelius and the rest, in which the full vigor of the Gospel and the strong discipline of the law of the Lord are contained. Your words have greatly helped us who labor here and struggle with all our strength of faith against the attack of hatred so that there might be gain from heaven; and before the letters which I last sent to you reached you, you declared to us that according to the law of the Gospel your judgment was firmly and unanimously with us. I trust that you, dearly beloved and ardently desired Brethren, are always well.

28. *Cyprian*[1] *to Moses*[2] *and Maximus,*[3] *the priests, and to the other confessors, his dearly beloved brethren, greeting.*

(1) I had learned a long time ago by hearsay of the glory of your faith and your fortitude, very brave and blessed Brethren, and I rejoiced greatly also and congratulated you especially because the extraordinary condescension of our Lord prepared you by the confession of His Name for the crown. For you, having become the chiefs and leaders, have moved the standards of the heavenly militia to the battle of our time. You have filled with your virtues the spiritual struggle which the Lord now wished to be waged. You have broken the first attacks of the rising war with immovable strength and unshaken stability. Thence have arisen happy beginnings of fighting. Thence have begun signs of conquering.

Here it occurred that martyrdoms were consummated through tortures, but he who, preceding in the encounter, going ahead has been made the example of valor to his brethren shares with the martyrs in honor. Thence, besides you have handed over the crowns woven by your hand and you have pledged your brethren in the Chalice of Salvation.

(2) To glorious beginnings of confession and omens of victorious warfare has been added the uninterrupted course

---
[1] 250 A.D. *sede vacante*. Death of Fabian.
[2] Cf. Letter 27, n. 10.
[3] Cf. Letter 27, n. 11.

of discipline which we have seen from the vigor of your letter which you lately sent to your colleagues, joined with you in the confession of the Lord, with solicitous urging that the holy precepts and life-giving commands of the Gospel, once entrusted to us, should be kept always with strong and steadfast observance. Behold another sublime step of your glory; behold again a double title for meriting of God with your confession: to stand with a firm step both in this line of battle which is attempting to destroy the Gospel and to drive back with the strength of faith those bringing impious hands to undermine the precepts of the Lord; to have afforded previously beginnings of virtues, and now to afford instruction for living.

The Lord after the Resurrection, sending the apostles, commands and says: 'All power in heaven and on earth has been given to me. Go, therefore, and make disciples of all nations, baptizing them in the name of the Father, and of the Son, and of the Holy Spirit, teaching them to observe all that I have commanded you.'[4] And the Apostle John, mindful of the command, afterward places it in his Epistle: 'In this,' he says, 'we understand that we know him, if we keep his commandments. He who says that he knows him, and does not keep his commandments, is a liar and the truth is not in him.'[5]

You suggest the keeping of these precepts; you observe the divine and celestial commands. This is to be a confessor of the Lord; this is to be a martyr of Christ, to keep the inviolate and solid strength of His voice in all things; it is not to become a martyr of the Lord and, at the same time, to attempt to destroy the precepts of the Lord. To use the honor which He has given to you against Him, as it were, to become a rebel with the very arms received from Him—this is to wish to confess Christ and to deny the Gospel of Christ.

I rejoice, therefore, in you, most brave and faithful Brethren, and as much as I congratulate the martyrs honored there

---
4 Matt. 28.18-20.
5 Cf. 1 John 2.3, 4.

because of the glory of their strength, so much do I equally congratulate you also even because of the crown of the discipline of the Lord. The Lord has poured out His condescension in a manifold kind of abundance; He has distributed the praises and spiritual glories of good soldiers in abundant variety. We are also sharers in your honor; we count your glory our glory whose times such great felicity has brightened that, in our age, it has been given to us to see the servants of God proved and soldiers of Christ crowned. I trust that you, very brave and blessed Brethren, are always well and mindful of us.

29. Cyprian to the priests and deacons, his brethren, greeting.[1]

Lest anything be concealed from your knowledge, dearly beloved Brethren, I have sent you a copy of both the letter which was written to me and that which I sent in response; and I believe that what I answered does not displease you. But I must now bring this before you in my letter that for an urgent reason I have sent a letter to the clergy who abide in the city. And whereas I ought to write through clerics, I know, on the other hand, that very many of our own are absent, that the few, in fact, who are there scarcely suffice for the daily work of the ministry; it was necessary to appoint some new ones to be sent out.

But know that I have made Saturus[2] a reader and Optatus,[3] the confessor, a subdeacon, men whom we had long ago in a common council appointed next to the clergy, either when we gave the reading to Saturus on Easter once and again or recently when we tested the readers diligently with the priest teachers; we appointed Optatus among the readers of the teachers of the catechumens, examining whether all things

---
[1] 250 A.D.
[2] Cf. Letter 22, n. 36.
[3] Optatus, Carthaginian confessor, after being reader and master of catechumens, was raised to the subdiaconate by Cyprian.

were fitting to them which ought to be in those who were preparing for the clergy. Therefore, nothing new has been done by me in your absence, but what had already begun long ago, in the common council of us all, was effected because of urgent necessity. I trust that you, dearly beloved Brethren, are always well and mindful of us. Greet the brotherhood. Farewell.

30. The priests and deacons abiding in Rome to Pope Cyprian, greeting.[1]

(1) Although the mind honorably conscious in itself and sustained by the vigor of evangelical discipline and made a true witness of itself according to the heavenly decrees is accustomed to be content with God alone as Judge and neither to seek the praises nor to dread the accusations of another, yet, they are worthy of a double praise who, although they know that they owe conscience to God, the only Judge, yet, desire that their actions be approved also by their brethren themselves. It is no wonder that you do this, Brother Cyprian, who, with your modesty and innate zeal, wished us to be found not so much judges as participants in your plan so that we might find praise with you in your accomplishments in that we approve of them and that we might be able to be joint heirs because also supporters of your good counsels. For we are all believed to have labored the same way in that we have all been discovered united by the same agreement of censure and discipline.

(2) For what is either more truly so fitting in peace or so necessary in a war of persecution than to preserve the due severity of the divine vigor? He who has relaxed this necessarily always wanders in an unstable course of things and is tossed about hither and thither by the various and uncertain storms of affairs and, as it were, with the helm of counsels snatched from his hands, he dashes the ship of the safety of

---
[1] 250 A.D.

the Church against the rocks so that it appears that not otherwise can the safety of the Church be looked out for unless, indeed, both they who act against it, as certain adverse waves, are repelled and the accustomed plan of discipline itself is always kept as a salutary helm in the storm.

Nor was this counsel now recently planned by us, nor have these unexpected protections against the wicked lately surprised us. But this is read of among us as the ancient severity, the ancient faith, the ancient discipline since the Apostle would not have revealed so great praise of us when he said: 'because your faith is proclaimed all over the world,'[2] if already this vigor had not borrowed the roots of faith from those times; it is a very great crime to have been unworthy of these praises and of glory. For it is less disgrace never to have approached the commendation of praise than to have fallen violently from the summit of praise. It is less criminal not to have been honored with a good testimony than to have lost the honor of good testimonies. It is less prejudicial to have remained ignoble without praise of valor than, becoming disinherited from faith, to have lost enduring praises. For these things which are revealed for the glory of another, unless they are preserved by anxious and careful labor, swell up to the odium of the greatest crime.

(3) That we are not saying this erroneously, our former letters have proved. In them, we have revealed to you our judgment in a clear exposition against those who had betrayed themselves as unfaithful by the unlawful public acknowledgment of the nefarious certificates as if, by this, they seemed to avoid those entangling snares of the devil. By this, they would not be less bound than if they had approached the nefarious altars by that very fact that they have attested this, but even against those who had acquired receipts although they had not been present when they were acquired, since they certainly had made themselves present by ordering that they should so be written down. For he who has ordered it to be

---
2 Rom. 1.8.

committed is not free from a heinous act; nor is he innocent of guilt by whose consent it is granted that a crime not committed be imputed to him publicly. And since the whole mystery of faith is known to be dependent on the confession of the Name of Christ, he who seeks false deceptions to excuse himself has denied Him and he who wishes to appear to have satisfied either the edicts or the laws proposed against the Gospel has already obeyed by the very fact that he wished to seem to have obeyed.

And, assuredly, even now we have made known our faith and unanimity against those who have also polluted their hands and mouths with unlawful sacrifices, having first polluted their own minds, whence also are polluted their very hands and mouths. For far be it from the Roman Church to relax its vigor with such profane facility and to dissolve the sinews of severity by the overthrown majesty of faith so that, when as yet the ruins of the subverted brethren are not only lying prostrate but are still falling, too quickly applied antidotes of communion assuredly may not prove an advantage and, through false mercy, new wounds may be added to the old wounds of sin so that repentance also may be snatched from the wretched for their greater downfall. For where can the medicine of pardon appear if even the doctor himself encourages dangers when repentance has been cut off, if he only covers the wound and does not allow the necessary antidotes of time to heal the scar? This is not to cure but, if we wish to speak the truth, to kill.

(4) Moreover, from those confessors also whom the dignity of their confession has up to now kept in prison and whom their faith has already crowned in confessing gloriously for the evangelical struggle, you have letters in accord with our letters in which they have advocated severity of ecclesiastical discipline and have withdrawn unlawful petitions from the shame of the Church. If they had not done this easily, they would not easily repair the ruins of evangelical discipline, especially since it would have been so fitting to no one else

to keep undiminished dignity with the uninterrupted course of evangelical strength than to those who had handed themselves over to furious men to be tortured and torn to pieces for the Gospel lest they deservedly lose the honor of martyrdom if, on the occasion of martyrdom, they had wished to be traitors to the Gospel. For he who does not guard what he has in that condition on which he possesses it, while he violates that on which he possesses it, loses that which he possessed.

(5) In this place, we ought to give and do give you very great thanks because you have illumined the darkness of their prison with your letters; because you have come to them in whatever way you could enter; because you have invigorated their souls, solid in their own faith and confession, by your consolations and letters; because, having followed with worthy praises their glorious deeds, you have stirred them up to a much more ardent longing for heavenly glory; because you have driven them forward; because, as we believe and hope, you have animated future victors with the strength of your correspondence so that, although this may seem to come solely from the faith of the confessors and from the divine favor, yet in their martyrdom they seem to have become in a way your debtors.

But that this speech may return again to the point from which it seemed to digress, you will have affixed also letters such as we sent to Sicily. And yet a greater necessity for the postponing of this affair falls upon us for whom since the death of Fabian,[3] a man of most noble memory, because of the difficulties of affairs and of the times, a bishop has not yet been chosen to regulate all these matters and to be able with authority and wisdom to have a plan for those who have lapsed.

And yet what you yourself also discussed in so important a business pleases us: first, to sustain the peace of the Church; then, when the gathering for counsel has been accomplished with the bishops, priests, deacons, confessors, and likewise with

---

[3] Fabian, Pope from 236 to 250, was martyred under Decius.

the laity who stand fast, to discuss a plan for the lapsed. For it seems extremely hateful and burdensome to us not to examine through many what seems to have been committed by many and for one to give a judgment when so great a crime is known to have existed scattered among many people since that cannot be a firm decree which will not seem to have had the agreement of the majority.

Look at almost the whole world devastated and at the remains and ruins of the destruction lying everywhere; therefore, counsel must be sought in proportion as the delinquency seems widely spread. Let not the remedy be less than the wound is; let not the cures be fewer than the ruins, that, as those who have fallen have fallen because they were careless with an exceedingly rash blindness, so those who try to settle this matter should use all moderation of counsels lest anything done as it ought not to be should be judged by all as of no effect.

(6) With one and the same counsel, therefore, and with the same prayers and weeping, let us ask peace, as much for ourselves, who up to now seem to have escaped the ruins of this time, as also for those who seem to have fallen upon these disasters of the time, begging the Divine Majesty for peace in the name of the Church. With mutual prayers, let us, in turn, aid, protect, fortify each other. Let us pray for the lapsed that they may be lifted up; let us pray for the persevering that they may not be tempted to their destruction; let us pray that those who are said to have fallen, recognizing the magnitude of their sin, may know enough not to desire a slight and hasty remedy. Let us pray for repentance that it may follow the effects of the pardon of the lapsed that, with the knowledge of their crime, they may wish to manifest patience with us for a time and that they may not stir up the unquiet state of the Church lest they themselves appear to have stirred up internal persecution for us and the fact that they were disturbed be added to the heap of their crimes.

For modesty is especially fitting for those in whose sins a

shameless mind is condemned. Let them knock, certainly, at the door but, assuredly, let them not break it down. Let them approach to the threshold of the Church but, assuredly, let them not leap across it. Let them watch at the gates of the heavenly camp, but armed with the modesty by which they recognize that they have been deserters. Let them resume the trumpet of their prayers, but let them not clamor with it in a warlike fashion. Let them arm themselves, indeed, with the weapons of modesty and let them resume the shield which they had cast away for the fear of death by denying their faith; let them believe themselves armed, but now as armed against the enemy, the devil, not against the Church which grieves for their fall. A modest petition will avail much for them, a moderate request, necessary humility, patience not idle. Let them send tears as messengers for their sorrows; let them employ the advocacy of prolonged groaning from their inmost heart, proving their sorrow and shame for the crime committed.

(7) Indeed, if they shudder at the magnitude of the infamy incurred, if they treat the deadly plague of their heart and of their conscience and the deep recesses of the serpentine wound with a truly healing hand, let them blush even to ask, unless again there is both greater danger and shame not to have sought the aid of peace. But, indeed, let all this be in the Sacrament, not merely in the law of the very demand itself, after a moderation of time has been granted, but with humble request and with subdued prayers, since also he who is entreated ought to be favorably impressed, not aroused to anger. And as the Divine Clemency ought to be contemplated, so also ought the Divine Censure to be contemplated; as it is written: 'I forgave thee all the debt, because thou didst entreat me,'[4] so it is written: 'Whoever disowns me before men, I in turn will disown him before my Father and before his angels.'[5]

For as God is indulgent, so, likewise, is He exacting about

---
4 Matt. 18.32.
5 Cf. Matt. 10.33. Luke 12.9 refers to the angels.

His commands and, indeed, diligent; and as He calls to the banquet, so also He casts out by hands and feet from the meeting of the Saints one not having on the wedding garments.[6] He has prepared heaven, but He has also prepared hell. He has prepared places of rest, but He has also prepared eternal torments. He has prepared the inaccessible light, but He has also prepared the vast and eternal darkness of everlasting night.

(8) Seeking to control this balance of moderation, we and many here, indeed, for a long time now, both with certain bishops near us and, indeed, within reach of us and those whom the heat of this persecution had driven far from other provinces lying at remote distances, thought that nothing should be altered before the consecration of a bishop.[7] But we believed that we should use proper measure moderately for the care of the lapsed that, in the meantime, while a bishop is awaited to be given by God to us, the cause of those who can sustain the delay of postponement may be kept in suspense. But the cause of those for whom the urgent approach of the end of their life cannot endure delay, when they have done penance and frequently confessed a detestation of their offenses, if with tears, if with groans, if with the weeping, grieving, and truly repentant they have produced the signs of such a spirit, when no hope of living remains, according to man, then, finally, cautiously and carefully, are they to be aided, with God Himself knowing what He would do with such and in what way He would examine the weight of judgment, yet with us caring anxiously that neither wicked men may praise our easy forgiveness, nor the truly penitent men accuse us, as it were, of harsh cruelty. We trust that you, dearly beloved and glorious Pope, are always well and mindful of us in the Lord.

---

6 Cf. Matt. 22.12-14.
7 A new Pope.

31.[1] *Moses*[2] *and Maximus,*[3] *the priests, and Nicostratus*[4] *and Rufinus*[5] *and the others who are with them, confessors, to Pope Cyprian, greeting.*

(1) To us abiding among various and multiple sorrows, Brother, on account of the present ruin of many throughout almost the whole world, this especial solace has come, in that we have been cheered by the receipt of your letter and have recognized alleviations of the sorrows of our grieving spirit. From this we can know already that the grace of Divine Providence perhaps has wished to keep us for so long a time shut up by the bonds of prison for no other reason than that, instructed and more strongly encouraged by your letter, we might be able to arrive at the destined crown with a more disposed prayer. For your letter has enlightened us as certain serenity in storm, as greatly desired tranquillity in a raging sea, as rest in labor, as safety in dangers and sorrows, as a bright and shining light in the thickest darknesses. Thus we drank it in with a thirsting soul and have received it with a hungry longing, that we may rejoice that we have been sufficiently fed and refreshed by it for the struggle with the enemy.

The Lord will bestow a reward upon you for this love of yours and will render to you the due recompense for this so very good work. For he who has encouraged others is not less worthy of the reward of the crown than he who has suffered; he who has taught is not less worthy of praise than he who has acted. He who has admonished is not less to be honored than he who has obeyed the exhorter, unless, indeed, a greater glory redounds to him who has instructed than to him who has shown himself a docile disciple. For the latter perchance would never have been able for what he did unless the former had taught.

---
1 250 A.D.
2 Cf. Letter 27, n. 10.
3 Cf. Letter 27, n. 11.
4 Cf. Letter 27, n. 12.
5 Rufinus, a Roman deacon and confessor, 250 A.D.

(2) We have felt, therefore, we shall say it again, Brother Cyprian, great joy, great solace, great alleviation, especially because you have described, I shall not say the glorious deaths of the martyrs, but their immortality with glorious and worthy praises. For such deaths had to be celebrated with such language that the deeds which were related might be told in such a manner as they were done. From your letter, therefore, we saw with our eyes those glorious triumphs of the martyrs and, in some way, as if we looked on, we followed them when they were seeking heaven and, as it were, we contemplated them abiding among angels and powers and heavenly dominations. And also we, in some way, heard with our ears the Lord before His Father, giving His promised testimony for them. This it is, therefore, which cheers our spirit day by day and inflames it to obtain the ranks of such great dignity.

(3) For what more glorious or more felicitous could happen to any man from the divine condescension than, undaunted before the very executioners, to confess the Lord God; than to confess Christ, the Son of God, among the various and refined tortures of the cruel secular power and even with the body twisted and racked and butchered and even dying yet with a free spirit; than, having abandoned the world, to have sought heaven; than, having left men behind, to stand among angels; than, breaking all worldly impediments, to present oneself already free in the sight of God; than to receive the heavenly kingdom without any delay; than to have been made a colleague in the Passion with Christ in the Name of Christ; than to have been made a judge of one's judge by the divine condescension; than to have brought back an unstained conscience from the confession of His Name; than not to have obeyed human and sacrilegious laws against faith; than to have proved the truth in a public testimony; than, by dying, to have overcome death itself which is feared by all; than to have gained immortality by death itself; than, torn to pieces by all the instruments of cruelty and racked by the very tortures themselves, to have overcome the tortures; than

to have struggled against all of the pains of a mutilated body with strength of spirit; than not to have shrunk from one's own blood flowing freely; than to have begun to love one's tortures because of faith; than to consider it the very misfortune of one's life to have lived?

(4) For to this battle, as if with a certain trumpet of His Gospel, the Lord incites us, saying: 'He who loves father or mother more than me is not worthy of me; and he who loves his soul more than me is not worthy of me, and he who does not take up his cross and follow me, is not worthy of me.'[6] And again: 'Blessed are they who have suffered persecution for justice' sake, for theirs is the kingdom of heaven. Blessed are you when they have persecuted you and held you in hatred. Rejoice and exult . . . for so did they persecute the prophets who were before you.'[7] And: 'Because you will stand before kings and governors. . . . And brother will hand over brother to death, and the father, the son . . . and he who has persevered even to the end, he will be saved.'[8] And: 'To the one who overcomes, I will give to sit upon my throne; as I also have overcome and have sat upon the throne of my Father.'[9] And the Apostle also says: 'Who shall separate us from the love of Christ? Shall tribulation, or distress, or persecution, or hunger, or nakedness, or danger, or the sword? Even as it is written, "For thy sake we are put to death all the day long. We are regarded as sheep for the slaughter." But in all these things we overcome because of him who has loved us.'[10]

(5) When we read these and other things of this nature collected in the Gospel, let us feel, as it were, certain torches set under us with the voice of the Lord to stir up our faith; already we do not shudder so much at, but also attack, the enemies of truth. And we have conquered the enemies of God already by this very fact that we have not yielded. And

---
6 Cf. Matt. 10.37, 38.
7 Cf. Matt. 5.10-12.
8 Cf. Matt. 10.18, 21, 22.
9 Cf. Apoc. 3.21.
10 Rom. 8.35-37.

we have overcome nefarious laws against truth. And if we have not yet shed our blood, but have been prepared to have shed it, let no one consider this delay of our postponement a clemency; it thwarts us; it is an impediment to glory; it postpones heaven; it keeps us away from the glorious sight of God. For in a struggle of this nature and in a battle of this kind in which faith is tried, it is not true clemency for a delay to have postponed martyrs.

Entreat, therefore, dearly beloved Cyprian, that the Lord may arm and enlighten us more and more by His grace from day to day more richly and willingly, that He may strengthen and fortify us by the strength of His power that, as the best General, He leads forth now to the field of the proposed combat His soldiers whom even up to now He has exercised and proved in the camp of prison. May He furnish divine arms for us, those weapons which do not know how to be conquered: the breastplate of justice which is never wont to be destroyed, the shield of faith which cannot be perforated, the helmet of salvation which cannot be broken, and the sword of the spirit which is not wont to be maimed. For to whom rather ought we to entrust our petition that he entreat for us than to such a glorious bishop so that destined victims[11] may seek help from the priest?

(6) Behold another joy of ours, that in the duty of your episcopal office, although in the meantime on account of the condition of the time you are removed from the brethren, yet you have not failed them, because you have frequently strengthened the confessors with your letters, because you have even furnished necessary expenses from your own just labors, because in all things you have shown yourself present in some way, because in no part of your office have you ever wavered as a deserter.

But we cannot be silent about what has stirred us up more forcibly to greater joy; in fact, we may describe it with all the testimony of our voice. For we have noticed that you have

---
11 Text: *hostiae destinati.*

rebuked fittingly and worthily with your censure those who, unmindful of their crimes, had extorted peace in your absence with a hurried and overeager desire from the priests and those who, without respect for the Gospel, had given away with the greatest of ease the holy of the Lord and the pearls[12] although so great a crime, spread also with incredible devastation throughout almost the whole world, ought not to be handled except, as you yourself write, cautiously and moderately, with the advice of all of the bishops, priests, deacons, confessors, and the faithful laity themselves being consulted, as you yourself also testify in your letters; lest, while we wish rashly to bring relief to the ruins, we may appear to prepare other greater ruins.

For where is fear of the Lord left if pardon is so easily granted to the sinners? Certainly, their souls must be preserved and must be nourished for the time of their maturity and they must be instructed concerning the Scriptures because they have committed so huge a sin and one greater than all. Let not their spirits be lifted up because they are many, but rather let them be reprimanded for this very reason because they are not few. Number is accustomed to contribute nothing to the extenuating of the shamefulness of sin; but shame, but modesty, but penitence, but discipline, but humility and subjection, but to have awaited the judgment of others regarding oneself, but to have sustained a sentence of others regarding one's own act—it is these which prove repentance. It is these which produce a scar over the inflicted wound. It is these which raise and lift up the ruins of a dejected spirit, which soothe and end the fiery disease of burning crimes. For the doctor will not give to the sick those things which are for healthy bodies, lest untimely food should not check the temperature of a raging fever, but augment it, perchance lest what could have earlier been healed through saving fasting would seem through impatience to have been put off longer by overloading the stomach with food.

---

12 Cf. Matt. 7.6.

(7) Hands contaminated with impious sacrifice, therefore, must be cleansed by good works; and wretched mouths polluted with heinous food must be purified by the words of true repentance; and the spirit must be renewed and preserved in the recesses of a faithful heart. Let frequent lamentations of the penitents be heard and, likewise, let faithful tears be shed from the eyes, that those very eyes which have looked evilly upon idols may wipe out with tears pleasing to God that which they had unlawfully committed. Nothing is necessary for diseases if not patience. Those who are ill contend with their pain and thus hope at last for health if they have overcome the pain by endurance. For that scar which a too hasty physician induces is not to be trusted and the healing is broken open at the first accident if remedies are not faithfully furnished for this very slowness. Quickly again is flame called back into fire unless the material of the whole fire is extinguished even to the last spark so that men of this nature should know justly that there is more to be looked for, even for themselves, from the very delay and that more trustworthy remedies are assured from the necessary postponements.

(8) Besides, where will it be that they who confess Christ are shut up in the custody of a squalid prison if they who have denied Him are without any hardship of faith? Where will it be that they are bound in the embrace of chains for the Name of God if they who have denied the confession of God are not without Communion? Where will it be that the imprisoned give up their glorious souls if they who have abandoned faith do not feel the magnitude of their dangers and sins? But if they feel an excessive impatience and demand an intolerable speed in receiving Communion, in vain do they utter those quarrelsome and hateful and not at all influential words against truth, outcries from a petulant and unrestrained mouth since, indeed, it was in their power to have retained in their own right what they are now compelled to ask with the need imposed by their own will. For the faith which could confess Christ could likewise be retained in Communion by Christ. We trust that you, Brother, are well and mindful of us.

32. *Cyprian to the priests and deacons, his brethren, greeting.*[1]

That you might know, dearly beloved Brethren, what letters I sent to the clergy acting at Rome and what they replied to me and what Moses[2] and Maximus,[3] the priests, and Nicostratus[4] and Rufinus,[5] the deacons, and the other confessors locked up with them in prison, likewise, answered to my letters, I have sent copies to you to be read. See to it as far as you can in your diligence that both our writings and the answers received to them may be known to our brethren.

But if, also, any bishops, my colleagues from foreign lands, or priests or deacons should be present or come later, let them hear all these things from you. And if they wish to transcribe copies of the letters and bring them to their people, let them have the opportunity for transcription.

And, as much as possible, I have ordered Saturus,[6] the reader, our brother, to make available to all individuals who desire it the opportunity of copying so that, in a certain manner, meanwhile, in setting in order the state of the Churches, one faithful agreement may be kept by all.

Concerning the other matters which must be looked after, as I have written also to very many of my colleagues, we shall treat more fully in a common council when we begin to assemble together, when the Lord permits. I trust that you, dearly beloved and ardently desired Brethren, are always well. Greet the brotherhood. Farewell.

Letter 33[1]

(1) Our Lord, whose precepts we ought to fear and to keep, assigning the honor of the bishop and the plan for His Church,

---

1 250 A.D. *sede vacante.*
2 Cf. Letter 27, n. 10.
3 Cf. Letter 27, n. 11.
4 Cf. Letter 27, n. 12.
5 Cf. Letter 31, n. 5.
6 Cf. Letter 22, n. 36.

1 250 A.D. The letter is addressed to the lapsed.

speaks in the Gospel and says to Peter: 'I say to thee that thou art Peter, and upon this rock I will build my Church, and the gates of hell shall not prevail against it. And I will give thee the keys of the kingdom of heaven; and whatever thou shalt bind on earth shall be bound also in heaven, and whatever thou shalt loose on earth shall be loosed also in heaven.'[2] Thus through the changes of times and successions, the ordination of bishops and the organization of the Church run through so that the Church is established upon the bishops and every action of the Church is governed through these same prelates.

Since this has been thus founded upon Divine Law, I marvel that some with bold rashness thus have so wished to write to me that they wrote letters in the name of the Church since the Church is established upon the bishop and upon the clergy and upon all of the faithful who stand. For far be it from the mercy of God and His invincible power to allow the number of the lapsed to be called the Church since it is written: 'He is not the God of the dead, but of the living.'[3] We hope, indeed, that all may be brought back to life, and we pray by our entreaties and our lamentations that they may be restored to their former status. But if some lapsed wish themselves to be the Church and if the Church is among them and in them is the Church, what remains but for us to ask them that they may deign to admit us into the Church? It behooves them, therefore, to be submissive and quiet and modest who, mindful of their sin, ought to satisfy God and not to send letters in the name of the Church, especially since they know that they are writing to the Church.

(2) But some of the lapsed have written to me, humble and mild and timid and God-fearing men who have also always labored gloriously and seriously in the Church and who have never ascribed their work to the Lord, knowing that He said: 'And, when you have done all these things, say,

---

2 Cf. Matt. 16.18, 19.
3 Matt. 22.32.

"We are unprofitable servants; we have done what it was our duty to do." [4] These men, who think about these matters, although they had also received a petition from the martyrs, yet, that satisfaction itself might be made to the Lord, praying, have written to me that they recognized their sin and were doing true penance and were not hastening rashly and importunely to peace, but were awaiting our presence, saying that peace itself would be sweeter to them if they should receive it in our presence. The Lord, who has deigned to show what such servants of this nature deserve of His bounty, is the Witness as to how I congratulated them.

Since I have received this letter and have now read that you have written otherwise, I ask you to express your desires and, whoever you are who have now sent this letter, to subscribe your names to the petition, and to send the petition with the name of each one to me. For this is to know beforehand to whom I have to write. I shall reply in my moderate ability of station and actions to the individual problems about which you have written. I trust that you, Brethren, are well and carry on quietly and tranquilly according to the discipline of the Lord. Farewell.

34. Cyprian to the priests and deacons, his brethren, greeting.[1]

(1) You have acted uprightly and according to discipline, dearly beloved Brethren, in that you have decided according to the counsel of my colleagues who were present that Communion should not be given to Gaius,[2] the priest from Dida,[3] and to his deacon. They, being in communion with the lapsed and offering their oblations, being caught frequently in their

---
[4] Cf. Luke 17.10.
[1] 250 A.D.
[2] Gaius, a priest who, with his deacon, was in communion with lapsed persons without ecclesiastical sanction, was excommunicated by the Carthaginian clergy and bishops including Cyprian.
[3] Dida or Didda, otherwise unknown, was probably a place near Carthage.

wicked errors and warned again and again by my colleagues not to do this, according to what you have written me, have persisted boldly in their presumption and audacity, deceiving certain brethren of our people, whose welfare we wish considered with every advantage and for whose salvation we provide, not with corrupt flattery, but with sincere faith, that they may entreat God with true repentance and lamentation and full sorrow for it is written: 'Remember whence thou hast fallen, and repent.'[4] And again the Divine Scripture says: 'Thus says the Lord: "When, converted, you lament, then you shall be saved and shall know where you were." '[5]

(2) But yet how can they lament and do penance whose lamentations and tears certain of the priests interrupt, so as to think that they must rashly be in communion with the former, not knowing that it is written: 'Those who call you blessed mislead you and disturb the path of your steps'?[6] Our salutary and true counsels deservedly avail nothing so long as the salutary truth is hindered by enticements and pernicious flattery, and the wounded and sick mind of the lapsed suffers what the weak and infirm also often suffer bodily in that, while they spurn healthful food and suitable drink as bitter and distasteful and long for those things which seem to be delightful and pleasant at the moment, they stir up destruction and death for themselves through heedlessness and intemperance and do not make progress toward their salvation by the true remedy of the healer while the sweet allurement of the enticer deceives them.

(3) Do you, therefore, deliberating faithfully and sanely, according to my letter, not withdraw from better counsels. But read this same letter also to my colleagues, if any either are present or may come in, that we may hold salutary counsel, unanimously and harmoniously, to protect and heal the wounds of the lapsed, for we intend to treat of everything most fully

---
[4] Cf. Apoc. 2.5.
[5] Cf. Isa. 30.15.
[6] Cf. Isa. 3.12.

when we begin to come together through the mercy of the Lord. Meanwhile, if any immoderate or impulsive person, either of our priests or deacons or of strangers, shall dare to have communion with the lapsed before our decision, let him be banished from our communion until he will declare the cause of his rashness before us all, when, the Lord permitting, we shall have come together.

(4) You also desired that I should write back what seems best to me concerning Philumenus[7] and Fortunatus,[8] subdeacons, and Favorinus,[9] an acolyte, who withdrew in the meantime and have now returned. I think that I alone ought not to give a decision in this matter, since many of the clergy are still absent and have not lately thought that they should seek their place again, and since this examination of each one must be discussed and investigated more fully, not only with my colleagues, but with the whole people themselves. For a matter which may constitute an example for the future regarding ministers of the Church must be weighed and judged with careful deliberation. Let them refrain, meanwhile, from the monthly collection, not as if they seem to be deprived of their ecclesiastical ministry, but that, with everything safe, they may be deferred until we are on hand. I trust that you, dearly beloved Brethren, are always well. Greet all the brotherhood. Farewell.

35. Cyprian to the priests and deacons abiding in Rome, his brethren, greeting.[1]

Both common love and reason demand, dearly beloved

---

[7] Philumenus, a Carthaginian subdeacon, lapsed, with subdeacon Fortunatus and acolyte Favorinus, in the Decian persecution, but returned to duty before the persecution was over. Cyprian, prohibiting them from the monthly distribution of clerical funds, reserved their case for the Council of 251.
[8] Fortunatus, mentioned in n. 7 above, was a subdeacon of Carthage.
[9] Favorinus, likewise mentioned in n. 7, was a Carthaginian acolyte.

[1] 250 A.D.

Brethren, that I should keep back nothing of those matters which are being carried on among us from your knowledge so that we may have common counsel for the advantage of the administration of the Church. For after I wrote a letter to you which I sent through Saturus,[2] the reader, and Optatus,[3] the subdeacon, our brethren, the rashness of some of the lapsed who refuse to do penance and to satisfy God was united. They wrote me a letter demanding, not that peace be given to themselves, but, as it were, claiming that it had already been given because they say that Paul[4] had given to all, as you will read in their letter, a copy of which I have sent you.

At the same time, that you may know what I replied briefly to them in the meantime, and what sort of letter I afterward wrote to the clergy, I have sent you a copy of this also. But if, besides, their recklessness has not been checked either by my letters or by yours nor restrained by salutary counsels, we shall do those things which the Lord, according to the Gospel, commanded us to do. I trust that you, dearly beloved Brethren, are always well. Farewell.

36. *The priests and deacons abiding in Rome to Pope Cyprian, greeting.*[1]

(1) When, Brother, we had carefully read your letter which you had sent by Fortunatus,[2] the subdeacon, we were stricken with double sorrow and perplexed with twofold grief because no rest at all was given to you in such great exigencies of the persecution, and the immoderate impudence of the lapsed brethren was observed by us extended even to the dangerous rashness of words. But although those things which we have

---

2 Cf. Letter 22, n. 36.
3 Cf. Letter 29, n. 3.
4 Cf. Letter 22, n. 5.

---

1 250 A.D.
2 Cf. Letter 34, n. 8.

mentioned afflicted us and our spirit greatly, yet your vigor and firmness, applied according to the discipline of the Gospel, moderated the grave weight of our sorrow since you both justly check the wickedness of some and, by exhorting to repentance, show the way of true salvation. We are, indeed, considerably surprised that they wished to rush so headlong into this matter as not so much to seek peace for themselves as to demand it so urgently and in so premature and unripe a time, nay rather, to say that they already have it in heaven.

If they have it, why do they seek what they have? But if, from the very fact that they seek it, it is proved that they do not have it, why do they not uphold the judgment of those from whom they thought that the peace which they certainly do not have ought to be sought? But if they believe that they have the prerogative of communion from another source, let them attempt to compare that with the Gospel that so, at last, it may be worth much if it is not at variance with the law of the Gospel. Besides, by what pact could that offer communion of the Gospel which seems fixed against the truth of the Gospel? For since every prerogative thus finally looks forward to the privilege of favor if it is not out of harmony with Him with whom it wishes to be associated, because this is out of harmony with Him with whom it wishes to be associated, it must necessarily lose the indulgence and privilege of association.

(2) Let them see, therefore, what they are attempting to do in this matter. For if they say, indeed, that the Gospel has decreed one thing, but the martyrs have asserted otherwise, they who crush the martyrs against the Gospel will be in danger from both sides. For both the majesty of the Gospel will seem broken and abandoned if it could have been overcome by the novelty of another decree and the glorious crown of confession will seem taken from the heads of the martyrs if they are found not to have gained from the preservation of the Gospel that whence they become martyrs, so that for no one is it rightly so fitting to decide nothing against the Gospel

more than for the one who labors to receive the name of martyr from the Gospel.

We should wish, moreover, to learn this. If martyrs become martyrs for no other reason than that, by not sacrificing, they may keep the peace of the Church even to the shedding of their blood, lest, overcome by the anguish of torture, they lose their salvation in losing peace, how do they believe that this salvation, which they thought that they themselves would not have if they had sacrificed, ought to be given to those who are said to have sacrificed, since they ought to preserve this law for others which they seemed to have placed first for themselves? In this business, we notice that they have brought forth against themselves the very thing which they thought they made for themselves. For if the martyrs thought that peace ought to be given to these, why did they themselves not give it? Why did they propose that those men should be referred to the bishop, as they themselves say? For he who orders something to be done can certainly do what he orders to be done. But, as we know, nay rather, as the matter speaks for itself and cries out, the holiest martyrs thought that a proper measure of modesty and of truth ought to be shown on both sides. For, because they were hard pressed by many, while they sent them to the bishop, they thought that they should look out for fitting modesty lest they should be disturbed further; and since they themselves did not give those communion, they judged that the integrity of the evangelical law must be kept undiminished.

(3) Yet you, Brother, never cease, of your charity, to restrain the souls of the lapsed and to offer the medicine of truth to the erring although the sick soul is accustomed to spurn the service of physicians. This wound of the lapsed is still fresh and, up to now, the injury is rising like a tumor. And, therefore, we are sure that in the space of a more protracted time, as the attack itself becomes older, they will like this, that they have been put off for true medicine, provided only that they are absent who might arm them for their

own danger and, perversely instructing, demand for them the deadly poisons of premature communion in place of the salutary remedies of delay.

For we do not believe that all would have dared so impudently to demand peace for themselves without the instigation of some persons. We have known the faith of the Church of Carthage; we have known its learning; we have known its humility. Therefore, indeed, we were astonished in that we noted certain things written rather harshly against you in a letter, since we had often experienced your mutual love and charity by many examples of reciprocal affection.

It is time, therefore, that they should do penance for the sin, that they should prove sorrow for their lapse, that they should show reserve, that they should manifest humility, that they should demonstrate modesty, that they should arouse the clemency of God toward themselves by their submission, and that they should draw divine mercy upon themselves by due honor to the bishop of God. How much better would have been the letter of those very men, if the prayers for them of those who stood fast had been aided by their own humility, since more easily is what is sought gained when he for whom it is asked is worthy to gain what is asked.

(4) But for what pertains to Privatus of Lambaesis,[3] you who wished to announce the matter to us as disturbing have acted according to your custom. For it becomes all of us to be on our guard for the body of the whole Church, whose members are scattered throughout all of the various provinces. But the fraud of the cunning man could not escape us even before we had your letter. For, when previously, from the throng of that very wickedness, a certain Futurus,[4] a standard-bearer of Privatus, had come and was trying fraudulently to obtain

---

3 Privatus Lambaesitanus, once Bishop of the city of Lambaesis in Numidia, condemned for heresy by ninety bishops at a Council held under Donatus, Cyprian's predecessor as Bishop of Carthage, in 240 A.D., visited Rome in 250 and Cyprian warned the Roman clergy about him. Privatus favored the party with the lax view regarding the *Lapsi*.
4 E. W. Benson questions the use of Futurus as a proper name in Africa. Pamelius thought that Futurus referred to Felicissimus.

letters from us, he did not conceal who he was nor did he obtain the letters which he wished. We trust that you are always well.

37. Cyprian[1] to Moses[2] and Maximus,[3] the priests, and the other confessors, his brethren, greeting.

(1) Celerinus,[4] a comrade of yours in faith and virtue and a soldier of God in glorious encounters, came here and represented you all equally and individually in our affections, dearly beloved Brethren. In his coming, we saw you all and, when he spoke of your charity toward me sweetly and often, we heard you in his words. I rejoice often and greatly when such things are brought from you through such men.

We, too, are in a certain way there with you in prison; we believe that we who cling so firmly to your hearts feel with you the distinctions of divine condescension. Your indivisible love joins us to your honor; the spirit does not allow love to be separated. Confession imprisons you there; disturbance, me. And we, indeed, mindful of you day and night, both when we offer prayer in the Sacrifices with many and when we petition apart in private prayers, beg the full favor of the Lord for your crowns and praises.

But our moderate ability is too weak to render a return to you. You, who, hoping already for only heavenly things and meditating only on things divine, ascend to loftier heights by the very delay of suffering and do not dissipate your glories with the long passage of time but increase them, give more when you are mindful of us in prayer. The first and only confession makes one blessed. You confess as often as you are asked to come out of prison and prefer the prison with faith and courage. Your praises are as numerous as the days; the

---
1 250 A.D.
2 Cf. Letter 27, n. 10.
3 Cf. Letter 27, n. 11.
4 Cf. Letter 21, n. 2.

increases of your merits are as many as the courses of the months. He who suffers immediately conquers once. But he who, remaining always in punishments, engages with tribulation and is not conquered is crowned daily.

(2) Let magistrates and consuls or proconsuls now go forth; let them glory in the standards of yearly dignity and in the twelve fasces. Behold heavenly dignity has been sealed in you with the fame of glory for a year and has already passed the revolving circle of the returning year in the long duration of victorious glory. The rising sun and the waning moon illuminate the world; but He who made the sun and the moon has been a greater light to you in prison, and, in your heart and mind, the brightness of Christ resplendent with that eternal and shining light has shone over the darkness of the penal place, horrible and fatal for others.

Through the changes of the months the winter has passed, but you, shut up by the winter of persecution, experience the time of winter. Spring temperature, joyful with roses and crowned with flowers, has succeeded winter, but for you roses and flowers from the delights of paradise were at hand and heavenly garlands crowned your head. Behold the summer is fruitful with the fertility of the harvests and the threshing-floor is filled with grain; but you who have sown glory are harvesting a crop of glory and, placed on the threshing-floor of the Lord, you see the chaff burned with unquenchable fire; you yourselves, as grains of wheat purified and precious harvest, already tried and found faithful, count the lodging of the prison as a granary. Nor is there wanting in the autumn the spiritual grace for performing the duties of the season. The harvest is pressed out of doors and the grape destined to fill the cups is trodden in the wine presses; you, rich clusters from the vineyard of the Lord and bunches with fruit already ripe, trodden by the persecution of worldly pressure, feel our wine press in the tormenting prison; you pour out blood in place of wine; brave for enduring suffering, you willingly drink the chalice of martyrdom. Thus the year passes among the servants of God. Thus the vicissitude of the seasons is celebrated with spiritual merits and heavenly rewards.

(3) Abundantly blessed are those of you who, passing through these footprints of glory, have already departed from the world and, having finished the journey of virtue and faith, have come to the embrace and to the kiss of the Lord, as the Lord Himself rejoices. But the glory is not less for those of you who, still engaged in the struggle and soon to follow the glories of your associates, have long carried on the fight and, with immovable and unshaken faith, steadfastly exhibit to God a daily spectacle by your virtues. The longer your fight, the more sublime your crown! The one struggle is but the heaping up of a manifold number of battles. With the firmness of an oak, you conquer hunger and you despise thirst and you tread underfoot the squalor of the prison and the horror of the penal cell.

Punishment is overcome there; torture is crushed. Death is not feared but hoped for, which, indeed, is conquered by the reward of immortality, so that he who has conquered should be honored with an eternity of life. What spirit must be in you now; how sublime and full must be the heart when such and so great matters are pondered, when nothing but the precepts of God and the rewards of Christ are thought of! The will is only God's there and, still remaining in the flesh, it is granted to you to live your life, not for the present world, but for the future.

(4) Now it is fitting, most blessed Brethren, for you to remember me so that, among your great and divine thoughts, you may also think of me in your heart and mind and I may be in your prayers and petitions when that voice of yours, illustrious by the purification of confession and praiseworthy for its holding to the course of honor, penetrates to the ears of God and, with heaven open to it, sent up from these parts of the conquered world to the world above, gains from the goodness of the Lord the favor which it asks.

For what do you ask from the mercy of the Lord which you

do not deserve to gain, you who have thus observed the commandments of the Lord, who have kept to the discipline of the Gospel with the sincere vigor of faith, who, standing bravely with the uncorrupted honor of virtue, with the precepts of the Lord, and with His apostles, have strengthened the wavering faith of many with the truth of your martyrdom? Truly witnesses of the Gospel and truly martyrs of Christ fixed in His roots, established with a firm foundation upon the rock, you have joined discipline with virtue; you have stirred up others to the fear of God; you have made your martyrdoms examples. I trust that you, most valiant and most blessed Brethren, are always well and mindful of us.

38. Cyprian to the priests and deacons and likewise all the people, greeting.[1]

(1) In the ordinations of clerics, dearly beloved Brethren, we are accustomed to consult you in advance and in common council to weigh the characters and merits of each one. But human testimonies must not be looked for when divine approbations precede. Aurelius,[2] our brother, an illustrious youth already tested by the Lord and dear to God, is still young in years, but advanced in the praise of virtue and faith, lesser in the talent of his age, but greater in honor; he has fought in a double struggle, twice confessed and twice glorious in the victory of his confession both when he conquered, having been sent into banishment in the course, and when he finally fought in a more violent struggle, conqueror and victor in the battle of suffering. As often as the adversary wished to provoke the servants of God, just as often this very alert and very brave soldier both fought and conquered. It was a small matter for him to have fought before under the eyes of the few when he was banished; he deserved to fight also in the forum

---
[1] 250 A.D.
[2] Cf. Letter 27, n. 6.

with more outstanding valor that, after he conquered both magistrates and proconsul, he might overcome tortures after exile.

I do not know which I ought to praise more in him, the glory of his wounds or the modesty of his character, the fact that he is renowned in the honor of courage or praiseworthy in the admiration of modesty. Thus he is both lifted up in dignity and abased in humility that it may be evident that he is preserved by divine inspiration to be an example to others regarding ecclesiastical discipline in which the servants of God should conquer in confession by their virtues; after confession they should be distinguished by their holiness of life.

(2) Such a one was deserving of the higher steps of clerical ordination and a greater promotion, not so considered for his years, but for his merits. But, in the meantime, it seemed right for him to start with the office of reading since nothing was more becoming also to the voice which confessed God with glorious praise than to sound Him forth through the celebrating of the divine readings, after the sublime words which bespoke martyrdom for Christ: to read the Gospel of Christ whence martyrs are made, to come to the pulpit after the scaffold; to have been conspicuous there to a multitude of the Gentiles, to be conspicuous here to the brethren; to have been heard there to the marvel of the people standing around, to be heard here to the joy of the brotherhood.

Know, therefore, dearly beloved Brethren, that he has been ordained by me and by colleagues who were present. I know that you both willingly esteem him and hope that as many as possible like him are being ordained in our Church. And since joy is always hastening, and rejoicing cannot brook delays, in the meantime, he reads for us on Sunday, that is, he is auspicious for peace while he dedicates the reading. Continue frequently in your prayers and aid our entreaties with your entreaties, that the mercy of God, favoring us may quickly return the bishop unharmed to his people and the martyr reader with the bishop. I trust that you, dearly beloved Brethren in God the Father and Christ Jesus, are always well.

39. Cyprian to the priests and deacons and all the people, his brethren, greeting.[1]

(1) Dearly beloved Brethren, we must recognize and welcome the divine benefits with which the Lord has condescended to glorify and to honor His Church in our times by giving respite to His good confessors and glorious martyrs that they who had sublimely confessed Christ should afterwards adorn the clergy with ecclesiastical ministries of Christ. Exult, therefore, and rejoice with us after you have read our letter in which my colleagues who were present and I refer to you our brother, Celerinus,[2] glorious alike for his courage and for his character, joined to our clergy, not by human favor but by divine condescension. When he was hesitating to consent, he was compelled by the admonition and encouragement of the Church itself in a vision in the night that he should not refuse. With our persuasion, this was granted to him and pressed upon him the more because it was not right nor fitting that he whom the Lord thus honored with the dignity of heavenly glory should be without ecclesiastical honor.

(2) He was first in the battle of our time; he was a leader in battle among the soldiers of Christ; he, at the violent beginnings of persecution, having an encounter with the very leader and author of the disturbance, while he conquered the adversary with the invincible firmness of his attack, made a way for conquering for the others, a victor with no small number of wounds, but triumphant by a miracle in the close and unrelenting punishments of the long struggle. For nineteen days in the custody of the prison, he was enclosed in durance and chains. But with his body placed in chains, his spirit remained

---
1 250 A.D.
2 Cf. Letter 21, n. 2

released and free. His flesh wasted away with the long duration of hunger and thirst, but God fed his soul, living on faith and virtue, with spiritual food. He lay among the tortures stronger than his tortures; confined, greater than those who confined him; prostrate, loftier than those who stand; bound, firmer than those who bound; judged, more sublime than those who judge; and although his feet were bound with cords, the helmeted serpent was both crushed and conquered.

The bright marks of his wounds shine in his glorious body; they stand out and appear clear tokens in the sinews of the man and in the limbs consumed by long wasting away. They are great, they are remarkable things which the brotherhood may hear of his courage and of his praises. And if anyone should appear like Thomas, who believes his ears not at all, the evidence of the eyes is not wanting that anyone may also see what he hears. In the servant of God, the glory of wounds made a victory; memory preserves the glory of the scars.

(3) Nor is this title of glories strange and new in our dearly beloved Celerinus. He is following the footprints of his kindred; he rivals his parents and relatives with a similar distinction of divine condescension. His grandmother, Celerina,[3] was long ago crowned with martyrdom. His paternal and his maternal uncles, likewise, Laurentine[4] and Egnatius,[5] themselves also formerly fighting in the worldly camp, but true and spiritual soldiers of God, while they cast down the devil by the confession of Christ, deserved the palms and crowns of the Lord by their glorious passion. We offer Sacrifices for them always, as you remember, as often as we celebrate the passions and days of the martyrs with an annual commemoration.

He, therefore, whom thus the dignity and generous nobility of his family stirred up by domestic examples of courage and faith, could be neither inferior to his ancestors nor less great.

---

3 Celerina, grandmother of Celerinus, a martyr at Rome.
4 Laurentine, uncle of Celerinus, also suffered martyrdom at Rome.
5 Egnatius (Ignatius), another uncle of Celerinus, also a martyr.

Now if it is a mark of praise and esteem in a worldly family to be a patrician, of how much greater praise and honor is it to become eminent in heavenly praise? I do not know whom I should rather call more blessed, whether it should be those of so famous a posterity or him from a glorious origin. The divine condescension so equally recurs and comes among them that the dignity of the offspring embellishes their crown and the sublimity of his birth illumines his glory.

(4) What else, dearly beloved Brethren, should we have assigned to him, who came to us with so great condescension of the Lord, illustrious with the testimony and the wonder of the very one who himself had persecuted him, but put him in the pulpit, that is, over the tribunal of the Church, supported in the loftiness of the higher place and conspicuous before the whole people for the shining brightness of his honor, to read the precepts and the Gospel of the Lord, which he bravely and faithfully follows? Let the voice which confessed the Lord daily among them be heard on the things which the Lord spoke.

Let there be seen whether there is a further step to which he can be advanced in the Church; there is nothing in which a confessor may be of greater help to his brethren than that, while the evangelical reading of the Gospel is heard from his lips, whoever hears may imitate the faith of the reader. He had to be joined in the reading with Aurelius,[6] with whom he has been joined in the association of divine honor, with whom he was united in all the distinctions of virtue and of praise. Both are alike and both similar to each other, as much sublime in glory as humble in modesty, as much advanced by the divine condescension as submissive in quiet and tranquillity, both offering alike examples of courage and of character to each one, fitting both for war and for peace, praiseworthy in the former for strength and in the latter for modesty.

(5) In such servants, the Lord rejoices; He glories in confessors of this kind, whose doctrine and conversation accom-

---
6 Cf. Letter 27, n. 6.

plish so much for the foreshadowing of glory that they offer an instruction of discipline to others. For this reason Christ wished them to be in the Church for a time; for this reason, He preserved them safe, snatched from the midst of death by a certain resurrection, so to speak, made in their regard that, since nothing is perceived by the brethren more sublime in honor, nothing more submissive in humility, the brotherhood, having followed eagerly, may accompany these same men.

Yet know that these have been appointed readers, meanwhile, because it was fitting that the lamp be placed upon the lamp-stand whence it may enlighten all and that glorious countenances be stationed upon a higher place where, seen by all those around, they may furnish an incentive to glory to the onlookers. Know, furthermore, that we have already planned the honor of priesthood for them both that the same ones may be honored with the priests in the collections and that they who will sit with us when they are older and more advanced may share the monthly distributions in fair quantities, although he who has surpassed age in the dignity of glory can be considered inferior in nothing except in the natural quality of age. I trust that you, dearly beloved and ardently desired Brethren, are always well.

40. Cyprian to the priests and deacons and all the people, his very dear and most beloved brethren, greeting.[1]

That which pertains, dearly beloved Brethren, both to the common joy and to the greatest glory of our Church must be announced to you. For you should know that we have been instructed and advised by divine honor that the priest, Numidicus,[2] should be appointed in the number of the Carthaginian

---
1 250 A.D.
2 Numidicus, an African confessor in the Decian persecution, left for dead after stoning, was rescued by his daughter, but his wife did not survive. Cyprian ordained him.

priests and that he, illustrious by the very bright light of his confession and sublime in the honor of courage and faith, should sit with us among the clergy. By his own encouragement, he sent before himself a glorious number of martyrs killed by stones and flames and, rejoicing, he saw his wife, clinging to his side, burned, nay rather, I should say preserved, together with the others. When his daughter afterward, with anxious deference of love, sought the body of her father, he himself half-burned and covered with stones and left for dead, found half-alive and dragged out and resuscitated, unwillingly remained away from the associates whom he himself had sent before.

But, as we see, this was the cause of his remaining: that the Lord might add him to our clergy and adorn with glorious bishops the number of our priests decreased through the lapse of some. And he will be promoted, indeed, when God permits, to a higher place in his religion when we come into your presence with the protection of the Lord. In the meantime, let what is indicated be done, that we may receive this gift of God with thanksgiving, hoping for many distinctions of the same kind from the mercy of the Lord, so that, with the strength of His Church renewed, He may make such gentle and humble men flourish in the honor of our assembly. I trust that you, dearly beloved and ardently desired Brethren, are always well.

41. Cyprian[1] to Caldonius[2] and Herculanus,[3] his colleagues, and also to Rogatian,[4] and Numidicus,[5] his fellow priests, greeting.

(1) I have been very much saddened, dearly beloved Breth-

---
[1] 251 A.D.
[2] Cf. Letter 24, n. 2.
[3] Herculanus, an African bishop and colleague of Caldonius in Cyprian's commission, active in various councils in Carthage.
[4] Cf. Letter 6, n. 3.
[5] Cf. Letter 40, n. 2.

ren, in receiving your letter that, although I have always proposed to myself and promised to keep all our brotherhood safe and to preserve our flock undiminished as charity demands, now you announce that Felicissimus[6] has been making many wicked and insidious threats, so that besides his frauds and rapines, concerning which I had learned much a long while ago, he has now also tried to drive a portion of the people against the bishop, that is, to separate the sheep from the shepherd and to withdraw the sons from the parent and to scatter the members of Christ. And although I sent you as my vicars to settle the needs of our brethren with these resources, to aid, with such an addition as might be sufficient, the desires of those who wished also to practice their professions, at the same time, likewise, to distinguish both their ages and their conditions and their merits, that even now I, upon whom the care devolves, hope to know all and to promote whoever are worthy and humble and gentle to the offices of ecclesiastical administration, that man has interfered so that no one should be aided and that those things which I had desired could not be distinguished by the consideration of your diligence; our brethren who had first approached to be aided he has also threatened with wicked power and violent terror that those who had wished to obey us would not be in communion with him in death.

(2) And yet after all these things, moved neither by the honor of my station, nor broken by your authority and presence, disturbing the quiet of the brethren with his instigation, he rushed forth with very many testifying with rash fury that he was the leader of the faction and the chief of the sedition. In this, indeed, I rejoice that very many brethren withdrew from his boldness and preferred to yield to you that they might remain with Mother Church and receive her stipends

---

6 Felicissimus, deacon of Carthage, chief agent of those who opposed Cyprian, himself charged with various crimes, threatened with excommunication those who accepted relief from Cyprian's vicars and favored easy readmission of the lapsed. He was excommunicated and later his party was dissolved.

from the bishop who dispenses them because, indeed, I know for certain also that others will make peace and will quickly withdraw from their rash error. Meanwhile, since Felicissimus threatened that those who had obeyed us, that is, those who were in communion, would not be in communion with him in death, let him receive the sentence which he has first spoken that he may know himself excommunicated by us since, to his frauds and rapines which we learned with the clearest evidence, he has added the crime of adultery, which our brethren, grave men, have announced that they have found out and have asserted that they will prove. With the permission of God, we shall learn all these things when we meet together with very many colleagues.

But let Augendus[7] also, who, thinking neither of the bishop nor of the Church, has allied himself likewise with that conspiracy, receive the sentence which he, revolutionary and indiscreet, draws upon himself if he further perseveres with the same man. But let whoever has joined himself to his conspiracy and the faction know that he who has preferred of his own accord to separate himself from the Church will not be in communion with us in the Church.

Read this, my letter, to our brethren and send it to the clergy in Carthage with the names added of those who have joined themselves to Felicissimus. I trust that you, dearly beloved Brethren, are always well.

---

7 Augendus, an associate of Felicissimus, excommunicated with him and others of the same party, was possibly the same Augendus mentioned as the deacon of Novatian sent to Carthage with Maximus.

42.[1] *Caldonius*[2] *with Herculanus*[3] *and Victor,*[4] *his colleagues, and likewise with Rogatian*[5] *and Numidicus,*[6] *priests to Cyprian, greeting.*

We have rejected from communion Felicissimus[7] and Augendus,[8] likewise Repostus[9] of the exiles, and Irene[10] of the Rutili, and Paula,[11] a dressmaker, a fact you ought to know from my note. We have also excommunicated Sophronius[12] and Soliassus,[13] himself a basket weaver[14] among the exiles.

43. Cyprian to all the people, greeting.[1]

(1) Although, dearly beloved Brethren, Virtius,[2] a very faithful and very upright priest, and also Rogatian[3] and Numidicus,[4] priests and confessors, illustrious by the glory of the divine condescension, and, moreover, the deacons, good men, also devoted to the ecclesiastical administration in all obedi-

---

1 251 A.D.
2 Cf. Letter 24, n. 2.
3 Cf. Letter 41, n. 3.
4 Victor, an African bishop associated with Caldonius in the commission of Cyprian, is probably the Victor referred to in Letter 4, n. 3.
5 Cf. Letter 6, n. 3.
6 Cf. Letter 40, n. 2.
7 Cf. Letter 41, n. 6.
8 Cf. Letter 41, n. 7.
9 Repostus, excommunicated with Felicissimus by Caldonius, is possibly also the lapsed African bishop who induced many of his people to follow him back into paganism.
10 Irene, one of the confessors who had shed blood *(Rutili),* was also a leading member of the party of Felicissimus and was excommunicated with him.
11 Paula, another adherent of Felicissimus, also excommunicated with him.
12 Sophronius, another of Felicissimus' excommunicated followers.
13 Soliassus, a banished confessor, also followed Felicissimus.
14 The meaning of *budinarium* not clear.

---

1 251 A.D.
2 Virtius, priest at Carthage, one of Cyprian's chief supporters in his absence.
3 Cf. Letter 6, n. 3.
4 Cf. Letter 40, n. 2.

ence, with the other ministers, render the full attentiveness of their presence to you and do not cease to strengthen each one with assiduous exhortations and to rule and to reform the minds of the lapsed with salutary counsels, yet I advise you as much as I can and I visit you in whatever way I can by my letters. I say letters, dearly beloved Brethren. For the malice and perfidy of certain priests have accomplished this, that I may not be allowed to come to you before Easter Day since, mindful of their conspiracy and retaining those old venoms against my episcopate, nay rather, against your suffrage and the judgment of God, they resume their old attack against us and they renew once more sacrilegious machinations with their accustomed treacheries. And, indeed, by the Providence of God, although we neither wished nor desired it, and, indeed, we overlooked it and said nothing, they have paid the penalty which they had deserved, so that, not cast off by us, they cast themselves off voluntarily; they themselves passed the sentence according to their consciences; following your divinely inspired suffrages, conspirators and impious men drove themselves of their own accord from the Church.

(2) Now it has appeared whence the faction of Felicissimus[5] had come, on what roots and with what strength it stood. These men formerly gave inducements and encouragements to certain confessors not to agree with their bishop, not to observe ecclesiastical discipline with faith and quiet according to the precepts of the Lord, not to keep the glory of their confession by incorrupt and unspotted conversation. And, lest it would have been too little to have corrupted the minds of some of the confessors and to have wished to arm a portion of the broken brotherhood against the priesthood of God, they have now turned with their poisoned deceit to the destruction of the lapsed to call away from the healing of their wound the weak and the injured, less fit and less firm, through the calamity of their ruin, for undertaking stronger counsels and, having neglected prayers and petitions with which the Lord must be

---
5 Cf. Letter 41, n. 6.

appeased by long and unremitting satisfaction, to invite them to deadly indiscretion by the fiction of a deceptive peace.

(3) But I pray you, Brethren, watch against the attacks of the devil and, solicitous for your own salvation, be on your guard more diligently against the deadly deceit. This is another persecution and it is another temptation and these five priests are none other than those five leaders who, by edict, were joined recently to the magistrates to undermine our faith, to turn aside the frail hearts of our brethren into deadly snares by the prevarication of the truth. That same plan now, that same subversion is brought forward again through the five priests joined to Felicissimus for the ruin of salvation, that God be not implored and that he who denied Christ plead not with the same Christ, whom he had denied, and that penance be taken away after the guilt of the crime, and that the Lord be not satisfied through the bishops and priests of the Lord, but, abandoning the priests of the Lord, that a new tradition of sacrilegious institution arise contrary to evangelical discipline. And, although once it pleased us, as well as the confessors and clerics of the city and, likewise, all the bishops established either in our province or across the sea, that nothing be altered regarding the case of the lapsed unless we all assembled together and, comparing counsels, fixed judgment, tempered alike with discipline and mercy, against this plan of yours there is rebellion and all priestly authority and power are destroyed by contentious conspiracies.

(4) What sufferings do I now endure, dearly beloved Brethren, because I myself cannot come to you for the present, because I myself cannot approach each of you, because I myself cannot encourage you according to the teaching of the Lord and of His Gospel! An exile of already two years was not sufficient and a sorrowful separation from your countenance and from your eyes, continual sorrow and groaning which rack me to pieces alone without you with continued lamentation, tears flowing by day and by night because it has not been possible for the priest whom you have made with such love and ardor to greet you and to cling to your embraces.

This greater sorrow is added to our languishing spirit, that in so great solicitude and necessity I myself cannot hasten to you, since we are on guard lest a greater tumult arise there at our coming through the threats and through the treacheries of the perfidious and lest, although the bishop ought to provide for peace and tranquillity in all things, he himself seem to have provided opportunity for sedition and to have provoked persecution once more. Yet hence, dearly beloved Brethren, hence I urge you and, likewise, I advise you not rashly to believe dangerous voices, not to give your consent easily to fallacious words, not to receive darkness for light, night for day, hunger for food, thirst for drink, poison for medicine, death for salvation. Let neither the age nor the authority of these who are re-echoing the old evil of the two elders deceive you; just as those attempted to corrupt and to violate the chaste Susanna,[6] so these also with adulterated doctrine attempt to corrupt the chastity of the Church and to do violence to evangelical truth.

(5) The Lord cries out and says: 'Listen not to the words of the false prophets because the visions of their hearts are deceiving them. They speak but not from the mouth of the Lord. They say to those who despise the word of the Lord: "Peace shall be yours." '[7] They who themselves have neither peace nor the Church are now offering peace; they who have withdrawn from the Church are permitting the bringing back and recalling of the lapsed. God is one and Christ, one and the Church, one and the Chair established upon Peter by the voice of the Lord, one. Another altar cannot be set up nor a new priesthood be made contrary to the one altar and the one priesthood. Whoever has gathered elsewhere scatters. Whatever is established by human madness so that the divine plan is violated is adulterous, is impious, is sacrilegious. Withdraw far from the contagion of men of this kind and avoid their speech as cancer[8] and pestilence by fleeing, since the Lord

---
6 Cf. Dan. 13.
7 Cf. Jer. 23.16,17.
8 Cf. 2 Tim. 2.17.

warns and says: 'They are blind guides of blind men. But if a blind man guide a blind man, they fall together into a pit.'⁹

They interrupt our prayers which day and night you pour forth with us to God that you may please Him with just satisfaction. They interrupt our tears, with which you wash away the crime of the sin committed. They interrupt the peace which you are asking truly and faithfully from the mercy of God. They do not know that it is written: 'And that prophet or that dreamer is he who has spoken to make you wander from the Lord, your God.'¹⁰

Let no one lead you astray from the paths of the Lord, Brethren. Let no one snatch you Christians from the Gospel of Christ; let no one take sons of the Church from the Church. Let them alone who wished to perish, perish by themselves; let them alone who have withdrawn from the Church remain outside the Church; let them alone who have rebelled against the bishops be without bishops; let them alone who, formerly, according to your opinions, now according to the judgments of God, deserved to undergo the sentence for their conspiracy and malignity undergo the punishments of their conspiracy.

(6) The Lord warns us in His Holy Gospel, saying: 'You nullify the commandment of God that you may keep your own tradition.'¹¹ Let them who reject the commandment of God and attempt to substitute their own tradition be courageously and firmly scorned by you. Let one fall be sufficient for the lapsed. Let no one cast down by his oppression those wishing to rise. Let no one prostrate more severely and overwhelm those fallen for whom we entreat that they may be lifted up by the hand and arm of God. Let no one turn aside from all hope of salvation those half-alive and praying that they may recover their former salvation. Let no one extinguish all the light of the way of salvation from the wavering because of the blackness of their lapse.

The Apostle instructs, saying: 'If anyone teaches otherwise

---
9 Cf. Matt. 15.14.
10 Cf. Deut. 13.5.
11 Mark 7.9.

and does not agree with the sound instruction of our Lord Jesus Christ and his doctrine, puffed up with stupidity, depart from such a one.'[12] And again he himself says: 'Let no one deceive you with empty words; for because of these things the wrath of God comes upon the children of stubbornness. Do not, then, become partakers with them.'[13] It is not fitting that you, after being deceived by idle words, begin to be sharers in their depravity. Withdraw from such, I beg you, and assent to our counsels, who daily pour forth continual prayers for you to the Lord, who wish you to be recalled to the Church through the clemency of the Lord, who pray for the fullest peace from God, first for the mother and then for her children.

Join also your prayers and petitions with our prayers and petitions; unite your tears with our weeping. Avoid the wolves who separate the sheep from the shepherd; avoid the poisonous tongue of the devil, who from the beginning of the world, always false and lying, lies to deceive, entices to harm, promises good to grant evil, promises life to destroy it. His words are now clear also and his poisons are manifest. He promises peace in order that it may not be possible to attain peace. He promises salvation that he who has transgressed may not come to salvation. He promises the Church when he is bringing this about: the complete destruction of the one who believes in him.

(7) Now is the time, dearly beloved Brethren, for you who stand bravely to persevere and to keep with everlasting firmness your glorious stability, which you kept in the persecution, and for you who are lapsed through the deceiving adversary to look out faithfully for your hope and peace in this second trial and, in order that the Lord may pardon you, not to withdraw from the priests of the Lord since it is written: 'And any man who has the insolence to refuse to listen to the priest or judge, whoever he may be in those days, that man shall die.'[14]

---
12 Cf. 1 Tim. 6.3,4.
13 Cf. Eph. 5.6,7.
14 Cf. Deut. 17.12.

This is the most recent and extreme temptation of this persecution, which itself will quickly pass, by the protection of the Lord, so that I may be presented to you after Easter Day with my colleagues. In their presence, according to your judgment also and the common counsel of us all, as it was once agreed, we shall be able to set in order and to investigate those matters which must be treated. But if anyone, refusing to do penance and to make satisfaction to God, should go over to the party of Felicissimus and his satellites and should join with the heretical faction, let him know that he cannot afterward return to the Church and be in communion with the bishops and the people of Christ. I trust that you, dearly beloved Brethren, are always well and persist in imploring the mercy of the Lord in constant prayers with us.

44. Cyprian[1] to Cornelius,[2] his brother, greeting.

(1) Maximus,[3] the priest, and Augendus,[4] the deacon, and a certain Machaeus,[5] and Longinus[6] have come to us, sent by Novatian,[7] dearly beloved Brother. But since we had learned also from the letters which they brought with them and from their speech and assertion that Novatian had been made bishop, we, disturbed by the depravity of an unlawful ordination and one made against the Catholic Church, thought that

---

1 251 A.D.
2 Pope Cornelius, successor of Fabian, favored a milder policy towards those who had received petitions than Cyprian and the African Church. Cornelius died September 14, 252, exactly six years earlier than Cyprian.
3 Cf. Letter 27, n. 11.
4 Cf. Letter 41, n. 7.
5 Machaeus, a Roman Novatianist sent with Augendus to Cyprian.
6 Longinus, another Roman Novatianist.
7 Novatian, called by the Greeks, Novatus, and by Cyprian, Novatianus, a follower of the Novatus who founded Novatianism, was converted as an adult and never confirmed. In spite of this, since he was a talented and influential man, he was admitted to the priesthood. Novatus of Carthage brought three bishops to consecrate Novatian, but Cyprian rejected him at once and a synod of sixty bishops at Rome excommunicated him. He established a separate Church and rebaptized his followers.

they should immediately be restrained from our communion. And when they had been refuted and restrained in what they attempted to claim stubbornly and pertinaciously, yet very many colleagues, who had come to me, and I awaited the coming of colleagues, Caldonius[8] and Fortunatus,[9] whom we had recently sent to you and to our fellow bishops who were present at your consecration, as special envoys that, when they came and reported the truth of the matter, with greater authority and clear proof, the depravity of the opposing party might be crushed through them. But our colleagues, Pompey[10] and Stephen,[11] arrived, who themselves also brought thence for our instruction according to their gravity and faith manifest signs and testimonies, so that it was not necessary for those who had come, sent by Novatian, to be heard further.

(2) When in the assembly they rushed forward also with hateful cries and turbulent clamors and demanded that the accusations which they said they brought and proved might be examined publicly by us and by the people, we said that it was not in keeping with our dignity to assemble to allow the honor of our colleague, already chosen and ordained, and approved by the praiseworthy opinion of many, to be discussed lightly any further by the evil voice of the envious. And since it was tedious to put in a letter in what they were refuted and checked and in what unlawful attempts they were exposed for having stirred up heresy, you will hear everything very fully from Primitivus,[12] our fellow priest, when he comes to you.

---

8 Cf. Letter 24, n. 2.
9 Fortunatus, a colleague of Caldonius in the embassy mentioned in this letter, may also be the Bishop of Thuccabor, near Carthage, who was present at Cyprian's synods.
10 Pompey, an African bishop in the second synod of Carthage, is probably the man mentioned here as present at Rome with Stephen for the consecrations of Cornelius and Novatian.
11 Stephen, another African bishop, with Pompey presented evidence to Cyprian about the unlawful consecration of Novatus or Novatian, as Cyprian called him.
12 Primitivus, a priest or bishop of Carthage, was sent to bring letter and details to Pope Cornelius for the Council of Carthage. He also brought back the answer of Cornelius.

(3) And lest the raging boldness of those men should ever cease, they are here attempting also to distract the members of Christ into factions of schism and to rend and to lacerate His body of the Catholic Church, so that, running about from door to door through the homes of many or from town to town through certain states, they seek comrades of their obstinacy and harsh error for themselves.

We have given them an answer once for all and we have not ceased to command them that, having put aside their pernicious dissension and wrangling, they should know it is an impious act to desert their Mother and that they should recognize and understand that, when a bishop has once been chosen and approved by the testimony and judgment of his colleagues and of the people, another can in no way be chosen. Therefore, if peacefully and faithfully they confess that they have looked out for themselves, if they confess that they are followers of the Gospel and of Christ, let them first return to the Church. I trust that you, dearly beloved Brother, are always well.

45. Cyprian[1] to Cornelius,[2] his brother, greeting.

(1) As it befitted the servants of God and especially just and peaceful priests, dearly beloved Brother, we had recently sent our colleagues, Caldonius[3] and Fortunatus,[4] to strive as far as possible, not only by the persuasion of our letters, but also by their presence and the counsel of all of you, to work together to reconcile the members of the broken body to the unity of the Catholic Church and to join the bond of Christian charity. But since the obstinate and inflexible pertinacity of the opposing party has not only refused the bosom and the embrace of its root and Mother, but, even with discord spreading

---
1 251 A.D.
2 Cf. Letter 44, n. 2.
3 Cf. Letter 24, n. 2.
4 Cf. Letter 44, n. 9.

gradually and breaking out again for the worse, it has appointed for itself a bishop and, against the mystery of the divine arrangement and of once transmitted Catholic unity, has made an adulterous and a contrary head outside the Church; having received your letter as well as those of our colleagues, likewise with the coming of Pompey[5] and Stephen,[6] our colleagues, good and very dear to us, by whom all these things have been asserted and approved for us firmly with mutual joy according to what the sanctity of divine tradition and of ecclesiastical institution equally with truth demands, we have directed our letter to you. Bringing these same matters, moreover, to individual colleagues throughout our province for their notice, we have also ordered that brethren must be sent back by these also with letters.

(2) And yet our mind and intention had already been revealed to the brethren and to the whole people in that place, when, having received letters recently from both sides, we read your letter and mentioned your ordination to the bishopric in the hearing of each one. Mindful of the common honor also and keeping the respect of sacerdotal dignity and sanctity, we have scorned those things which had been gathered from divers sources in a list which was sent out with criminal accusations, considering equally and pondering whether it ought to be read and heard in so great and so religious an assembly of the brethren with bishops of God sitting together and the altar erected. For those things which stir up scandal in the hearers with a discordant pen and confuse by uncertain opinion brethren situated far away and located across the sea should not easily be uttered nor recklessly and rashly be made public.

Let those look to it who, enslaved either by their anger or lust and heedless of the divine law and sanctity, are delighted to make a show of that which they cannot prove and, although they are not able to destroy and ruin innocence, they accom-

---
5 Cf. Letter 44, n. 10.
6 Cf. Letter 44, n. 11.

plish enough by evil rumor and false lying in spreading scandal; certainly, as it is fitting to prelates and to bishops, we must take heed that, when such things are written up by certain people, they should be rejected by us. For where will be what we learn and teach to have been written: 'Keep your tongue from evil and your lips from speaking guile'?[7] Again likewise: 'Your mouth has abounded with evil, and your tongue has framed deceits. Sitting you speak against your brother; and against your mother's son you lay scandal.'[8] Likewise what the Apostle says: 'Let no ill speech proceed from your mouth, but whatever is good for the edification of faith, that it may give grace to the hearers.'[9]

In turn, we show that these things ought to be done if, when such matters are drawn up by the calumnious rashness of some, we allow them to be read in our presence. And, therefore, dearly beloved Brother, when such writings against you had come to me even from a fellow priest living with you, I commanded to be read to the clergy and to the people those things which sounded forth a religious simplicity and which did not make much noise with any barkings of curses and of wranglings.

(3) But, because we desired the writings of our colleagues who had been present there at your ordination, we were not seeking something new, forgetful of old customs. For it would have been enough for you to announce in a letter which you had written that you were the bishop, if there had not been a contrary faction of the opposition which, with its criminal and calumnious comments, was disturbing alike the minds and hearts of our colleagues and of very many of the brethren. For the calming of this affair, we considered it necessary that the firm and solid authority of our colleagues who wrote to us should be provided.

They, proclaiming the testimonies of their letters fit to be

---

7 Ps. 33.14.
8 Cf. Ps. 49.19, 20.
9 Cf. Eph. 4.29.

compared also with the character of your life and teaching, have removed even from the malicious and from those rejoicing either in novelty or depravity of affairs all scruple of hesitation and of dispute; and, according to our counsel weighed with salutary reasoning, the minds of our brethren, which were wavering in this disturbance, have approved sincerely and firmly of your bishopric. For this Brother, we both work and ought especially to work that we may take care to preserve, as far as possible, the unity handed down by the Lord and through the apostles to us as their successors and that we may gather together in the Church which is among us the bleating and wandering sheep whom the perverse faction and the heretical temptation of some men are withdrawing from their mother, with those alone remaining without who have remained stubborn through their own obstinacy or madness and have refused to return to us; they themselves will render an account to the Lord of the division and separation made by them and of the Church abandoned.

(4) As far as this pertains to the priesthood of some and to the case of Felicissimus,[10] that you may know what has been done here, our colleagues have sent letters to you signed by their own hand, that, when you have heard them, you may learn from their letters both what they have judged and what they have pronounced. But you will do better, Brother, if you order copies of the letters which I had sent recently to you through Caldonius and Fortunatus, our colleagues, in accordance with our mutual affection, which I had written concerning the same Felicissimus and concerning his priests to the clergy there and also to the people, to be read to the brethren there; these, indeed, explain the ordination and plan of this matter, that both here and there the brotherhood may be instructed by us regarding all matters. But I have transmitted copies of the same now also through Mettius,[11] the

---
10 Cf. Letter 41, n. 6.
11 Mettius, a subdeacon, sent to Rome with Nicephorus by Cyprian.

subdeacon sent by me, and Nicephorus,[12] the acolyte. I trust that you, dearly beloved Brother, are always well.

46. Cyprian[1] to Maximus[2] and Nicostratus[3] and the other confessors, greeting.

(1) As you have learned frequently from my letters, dearly Beloved, both what honor for your confession and what love for your associated brotherhood I have expressed in my speech, believe, I beg you, and be content with these letters of mine in which I both write and take counsel simply and faithfully for you and your deeds and your praises. For I am oppressed and saddened and the intolerable sorrow of my stricken and almost prostrate spirit overwhelms me now that I have found out that you there, against the arrangement of God, against the law of the Gospel, against the unity of the Catholic Institution, have consented that another bishop should be made; that is, to do what is neither right by divine law nor lawful to do: to institute another Church to tear asunder the members of Christ, to lacerate with divisive rivalry the one mind and body of the flock of the Lord. I beseech you, therefore, that among you, at least, this unlawful rending of our brotherhood may not continue, but that, mindful both of your confession and of the divine tradition, you may return to the Mother whence you went forth, whence you have come to the glory of confession with the rejoicing of the same Mother.

(2) Do not think that you are thus defending the Gospel of Christ when you separate yourselves from the flock of Christ and from His peace and concord, especially since it is more fitting for good and glorious soldiers to stand within their own home camp and, placed within, to carry on and to pro-

---
12 Nicephorus, a Roman acolyte, with Mettius, brought news to Cyprian from Cornelius.

1 251 A.D.
2 Cf. Letter 27, n. 11.
3 Cf. Letter 27, n. 12.

vide for those matters which are to be treated in common. For since our unity and concord ought by no means to be torn because we cannot abandon the Church to go out and thus come to you, we beg and exhort you with what exhortations we can rather to return to Mother Church and to your own brotherhood. I trust that you, dearly beloved Brethren, are always well.

47. Cyprian[1] *to Cornelius,*[2] *his brother, greeting.*

I have considered it both a conscientious and a necessary duty, dearly beloved Brother, to write a short letter[3] to the confessors who are there and who, led astray by the obstinacy and depravity of Novatian[4] and Novatus,[5] have withdrawn from the Church, to exhort them by this, for the sake of our mutual affection, to return to their Mother, that is, to the Catholic Church. I have directed that this letter be read first to you by the subdeacon, Mettius,[6] lest anyone should pretend that I had written something other than what is contained in my letter. I have, however, instructed the same Mettius, sent by me to you, to carry out the matter according to your will and, if you think that this same letter should be entrusted to the confessors, only then to deliver it to them. I trust that you, dearly beloved Brother, are always well.

48. Cyprian[1] *to Cornelius,*[2] *his brother, greeting.*

(1) I have read your letter,[3] dearly beloved Brother, which

---
1 251 A.D.
2 Cf. Letter 44, n. 2.
3 Letter 46.
4 Cf. Letter 44, n. 7.
5 Cf. Letter 14, n. 11.
6 Cf. Letter 45, n. 11.

---
1 251 A.D.
2 Cf. Letter 44, n. 2.
3 We do not have this letter.

you sent by Primitivus,[4] our fellow priest, in which I learned that you were disturbed because, although letters to you were being directed from the Hadrumetine colony in the name of Polycarp,[5] yet after Liberalis[6] and I had come to that same place, letters began to be directed thither to the priests and to the deacons.

(2) In respect to this, we wish you to know and to believe for certain that it was done through no frivolity or insult or disrespect. But, although we many colleagues who had come together had decided that, since our fellow bishops, Caldonius[7] and Fortunatus,[8] had been sent as legates to you, everything in the meantime should be suspended until our same colleagues, having restored affairs there to peace or having ascertained their truth, should return to us; the priests and deacons who abide in Hadrumetum, in the absence of Polycarp, our fellow bishop, did not know what we had decided in common. But when we came just now and they had learned our purpose, they themselves also began to observe what others did so that the unanimity of the churches abiding there was in no way in question.

(3) Yet some persons sometimes disturb minds and spirits by their talk, through announcing certain things contrary to truth. For we, giving a plan to those who took ship lest they do so with any scandal, know that we have encouraged them to acknowledge and to keep the matrix and root of the Catholic Church. But since our province is widespread and even has Numidia and Mauritania attached to it, lest a schism made in Rome should confuse with uncertain rumor the minds of those far away, we determined—after we had learned the truth of the matter through the bishops, we had found greater authority to sanction your consecration—then, at last,

---

4 Cf. Letter 44, n. 12.
5 Polycarp, Bishop of Hadrumetum, was present at the First Council of Carthage and at several others.
6 Liberalis, African bishop of an unknown see, was also present with Cyprian at Hadrumetum at the Council of Carthage.
7 Cf. Letter 24, n. 2.
8 Cf. Letter 44, n. 9.

after all scruple had been cast out of the heart of everyone, that letters should certainly be sent, as they have been, by all placed there that all our colleagues might firmly approve and maintain you and your communion, that is, the unity and also the charity of the Catholic Church. That this, by divine inspiration, has come to pass and that our plan, by Divine Providence, has proceeded, we rejoice.

(4) For thus now both the truth and also the eminence of your episcopate have been established in the most open light and with the most manifest and firm approval so that from the replies of our colleagues who have thence sent letters to us and from the report and testimonies of our fellow bishops, Pompey[9] and Stephen[10] and Caldonius and Fortunatus, both the requisite beginning and the lawful manner and also the glorious innocence of your ordination might be known to all.

The Divine Protection will accomplish that we, at the same time with the rest of our colleagues, may administer this office also securely and firmly and that we may keep in the harmonious unanimity of the Catholic Church, so that the Lord, who condescends to elect and to appoint for Himself bishops in His Church, may protect those chosen and also appointed by His will and assistance, inspiring them in their government and supplying both vigor for restraining the insolence of the wicked and mildness for nourishing the repentance of the lapsed. I trust that you, dearly beloved Brother, are always well.

49.[1] *Cornelius*[2] *to Cyprian, his brother, greeting.*

(1) In proportion to the solicitude and anxiety which we sustained concerning those confessors who had been led astray and almost deceived and alienated from the Church by the

---
9 Cf. Letter 44, n. 10.
10 Cf. Letter 44, n. 11.
---
1 251 A.D.
2 Cf. Letter 44, n. 2.

treachery and malice of the sly and crafty man[3] were the great joy with which we were affected and the thanks we gave to Almighty God and to Christ, our Lord, when they, acknowledging their error and perceiving the poisonous cunning of the malicious man, as if of a serpent, came back, as they themselves confess from their heart with a sincere will, to the Church from which they had gone forth. And first, indeed, our brethren of approved faith, loving peace, hoping for unity, announced the pride of the former, the weakness of the latter. Yet faith was not sufficient to make us believe easily that the former had suddenly changed.

But afterward, Urban[4] and Sidonius,[5] the confessors, came to our fellow priests, affirming that Maximus,[6] the confessor and priest, equally with themselves wished to return to the Church. But since many things described by them had preceded, which you also learned from our fellow bishops and from my letters, so that faith might not rashly be placed in them, we determined to hear from their own mouth and confession those matters which they had entrusted to an embassy. When they had come and what they had done was being examined by the priests, recently because numerous letters filled with calumnies and curses had been sent in their names through all of the churches and they had disturbed almost all of the churches, they confessed that they had been deceived and had not known what was in those letters; they had merely signed them and, led astray by the slyness of the man, they had engaged in and had been the authors of schism and heresy so that they allowed hands to be placed upon him as if for the bishopric. When these and other matters had been charged to them, they begged that they might be effaced and banished from memory.

---

[3] Novatian.
[4] Urban, a Roman confessor in the Decian persecution of 250, was with Moses, Maximus, and other influential men.
[5] Sidonius, another confessor with Moses, Maximus, and Celerinus, was sent with Urban by Maximus to Cyprian.
[6] Cf. Letter 27, n. 11.

(2) When the full account had been related to me, I resolved to assemble the clergy—and even five bishops were present, who were also present today—that with steadfast counsel it might be determined with the agreement of all what ought to be observed in respect to their persons. And that you might know the reaction of all and the counsel of each, I resolved to bring to your notice our judgments, which you may read appended.

After these things had been done, Maximus, Urban, Sidonius, and a very great part of the brethren who had joined themselves to them, came to the presbytery desiring with the greatest entreaties that all of those things which had been done before might fall into oblivion and no mention be made of them and, accordingly, that it should be as if nothing had been done or said; and they, in turn, after all had been forgiven, would now offer to God a pure and clean heart, following the voice of the Evangelist: 'Blessed are the clean of heart, for they shall see God.'[7]

What followed was that all of this action had to be reported to the people that they might see these very men established in the Church, whom they had for so long seen and mourned as wandering and drifting. When their wish had been made known, a great crowd of the brotherhood assembled. There was one voice of all giving thanks to God, expressing joy of heart with tears, embracing them as if this day they had been liberated from the punishment of prison. And that I may point out their own words: 'We know,' they say, 'that Cornelius has been elected Bishop of the most holy Catholic Church by Almighty God and by Christ, our Lord. We confess our error. We have suffered imposture. We were deceived by treachery and misleading speech. For although we seemed to have had, as it were, a certain communion with a schismatical and heretical man, yet our heart has always been in the Church. For we are not ignorant that there is one God and that there is one Christ the Lord, whom we have con-

---
7 Cf. Matt. 5.8.

fessed, one Holy Spirit, and that there ought to be one bishop in the Catholic Church.' Who would not be moved by that acknowledgment of theirs to grant that what they had confessed before the power of the world, they might prove when established in the Church? Wherefore, we ordered Maximus, the priest, to resume his place. As for the rest, with the great approbation of the people, we have entrusted all things done before to Almighty God, in whose power all things are reserved.

(3) These things, therefore, dearly beloved Brother, we have transmitted to you in writing, at the very hour, at the very minute, and I have sent away at once Niceforus,[8] the acolyte, hastening to descend to sailing from the harbor so that, with no delay made, you might, as if present among that clergy and in that meeting of the people, give thanks with us likewise to Almighty God and to Christ, our Lord.

We believe, nay rather, we rely upon it for certain, that the others also who have been in this error will shortly return to the Church when they see that their advisers are acting with us. I think that you ought to send this letter to the other Churches, dearly beloved Brother, that all may know that the treachery and the prevarication of this schismatic and heretic are being rejected daily. Farewell, dearly beloved Brother.

50.[1] *Cornelius*[2] *to Cyprian, his brother, greeting.*

That nothing might be wanting to the future punishment of this wicked man, laid low by the powers of God, after Maximus[3] and Longinus[4] and Machaeus[5] had been expelled from thence, he has risen again; and as I indicated in a former

---
8 Niceforus (Cornelius' spelling); cf. Letter 45, n. 12.

---
1 251 A.D.
2 Cf. Letter 44, n. 2.
3 Cf. Letter 27, n. 11.
4 Cf. Letter 44, n. 6.
5 Cf. Letter 44, n. 5.

letter which I sent to you by Augendus,[6] the confessor, I think that Nicostratus[7] and Novatus[8] and Evaristus[9] and Primus[10] and Denis[11] have already come there. Let there be great care, therefore, that it be made known to all of our fellow bishops and brethren: that Nicostratus, guilty of many crimes, has not only committed frauds and rapines against his secular patroness, whose affairs he managed, but also—a matter which is reserved for perpetual punishment for him—he stole no small amount of the deposits of the Church; that Evaristus, indeed, was with the author of a schism and Zetus[12] was appointed bishop and successor in his place for the people over whom he had formerly presided. But Novatus represented here those things by his malice and inexplicable avarice which he has always shown before you; thus you may know what leaders and protectors this schismatic and heretic has always as his companions. Farewell, dearly beloved Brother.

51. Cyprian[1] to Cornelius,[2] his brother, greeting.

(1) We confess, dearly beloved Brother, that we both have given and are giving very great thanks without ceasing to God, the Father Almighty, and to His Christ, our Lord and Savior God, because the Church is so divinely protected that its unity and sanctity are not continually or wholly injured by the obstinacy of perfidy and heretical depravity. For we read your

---
6 Cf. Letter 41, n. 7.
7 Cf. Letter 27, n. 12.
8 Cf. Letter 14, n. 10.
9 Evaristus, an Italian bishop, probably one of those who consecrated Novatian. Pope Cornelius considered him one of the leaders of the Novatianist schism. He was deposed and was succeeded by Zetus. He accompanied Novatus to Carthage.
10 Primus, another follower of Novatian.
11 Denis (Dionysius), a Novatianist who went to Carthage with Nicostratus and Novatus.
12 Zetus, bishop who succeeded Evaristus when the latter was removed from his bishopric.

---
1 251 A.D.
2 Cf. Letter 44, n. 2.

letter and we received exultingly the very great joy of our common prayer that Maximus,[3] the priest, and Urban,[4] confessors, with Sidonius[5] and Macarius,[6] have returned to the Catholic Church, that is, having abandoned error and schism, nay rather, having deserted heretical madness, they have again sought with the healing of faith the home of unity and truth, that, whence they had set out for glory, thence they might return glorious, lest any who had confessed Christ afterward abandon the camp of Christ or any who had not been overcome in strength and courage be led astray from the faith of charity and of unity.

Behold the unimpaired and immaculate integrity of their praise! Behold the incorruptible and genuine dignity of these confessors to have withdrawn from deserters and traitors, to have abandoned the betrayers of faith and the attackers of the Catholic Church! Deservedly both the clergy and the people, all of the brotherhood, with the greatest joy received them when they returned, as you write, since, in the case of the confessors who preserve their glory and return to unity, there is no one who does not consider himself a partner and sharer of their glory.

(2) We can estimate the joy of this day from our own feelings. For if here the whole number of the brethren rejoiced at your letter which you sent about the confession of those men and with the greatest alacrity received this message of common congratulation, what must it have been there where the action itself and the instant joy were displayed under the eyes of all! For since the Lord in His Gospel says: 'There is the greatest joy in heaven over one sinner who repents,'[7] how much greater is the joy, both on earth and likewise in heaven, over the confessors who return to the Church of God with their own glory and with praise and who give others doing

---
3 Cf. Letter 27, n. 11.
4 Cf. Letter 49, n. 4.
5 Cf. Letter 49, n. 5.
6 Cf. Letter 21, n. 16.
7 Cf. Luke 15.7.

the same a way of returning by the faith and approval of their example!

For this error had led astray certain of our brethren because they thought they were following the communion of the confessors. Since their error has been removed, light has been infused into the hearts of all and the Catholic Church has been shown to be one, incapable of being rent or divided. Nor will anyone now be able easily to be deceived by the loquacious words of a raging schismatic since it has been proved that good and glorious soldiers of Christ could not for long be detained by the falsehood and faithlessness of others outside the Church. I trust that you, dearly beloved Brother, are always well.

52. Cyprian[1] to Cornelius,[2] his brother, greeting.

(1) You have acted both with diligence and love, dearly beloved Brother, in sending to us with haste Niceforus,[3] the acolyte, both to announce to us the glorious joy of the reconciled confessors and to instruct us very fully respecting the new and pernicious stratagems of Novatian[4] and Novatus[5] for attacking the Church of Christ. For, although this harmful faction of heretical depravity had reached here the day before, itself already doomed and destined to destroy the others who agreed to it, on the next day, Niceforus arrived with your letter. From this we both learned and began to teach and to instruct others: that Evaristus[6] from being a bishop no longer remained as a layman; a man banished from see and people and an exile from the Church of Christ, he wanders about far off through other provinces and, himself made a

---
1 251 A.D.
2 Cf. Letter 44, n. 2.
3 Cf. Letter 45, n. 12.
4 Cf. Letter 44, n. 7.
5 Cf. Letter 14, n. 11.
6 Cf. Letter 50, n. 9.

shipwreck of truth and faith, is stirring up certain ones like to himself to similar shipwrecks; that Nicostratus,[7] also having lost the diaconate of holy administration, having by sacrilegious fraud taken away the ecclesiastical revenues and having refused to give up the deposits of widows and orphans, not so much wished to come to Africa as to have fled thence from Rome because of the consciousness of his rapines and nefarious crimes.

And now a deserter and a fugitive from the Church as if to have changed the region were to change the man, he boasts and, furthermore, proclaims himself a confessor although he who has denied the Church of Christ cannot be said to be, or be, a confessor of Christ. For when Paul the Apostle says: 'For this cause a man shall leave his father and mother, . . . and the two shall become one flesh,' this is a great mystery— I mean in reference to Christ and to the Church;[8] when, I say, the blessed Apostle says this and is giving testimony with his holy voice to the unity, likewise, of Christ and the Church, cleaving with indivisible bonds, how can he who is not with the Spouse of Christ and in His Church be with Christ? Or how does he who has despoiled and defrauded the Church of Christ assume to himself the care of ruling or of governing the Church?

(2) For concerning Novatus, nothing thence needed to be reported to us since Novatus ought rather to be shown by us to you as always eager for novelties, raging with the rapacity of an insatiable avarice, inflated with the arrogance and stupidity of a haughty pride, always unfavorably known to the bishops here, always condemned by the voice of all of the bishops as a heretic and a traitor, always inquisitive to betray, for this reason, a flatterer to deceive, never faithful to love, a torch and a fire to kindle the flames of sedition, a whirlwind and tempest to make shipwrecks of faith, an enemy of quiet, an adversary of tranquillity, a foe of peace.

---
7 Cf. Letter 27, n. 12.
8 Eph. 5.31, 32.

Finally, when Novatus withdrew thence from you, that is, when the storm and whirlwind withdrew, there, in part, quiet came about and glorious and good confessors who had withdrawn from the Church at his instigation, after he had withdrawn from Rome, returned to the Church. He is the same Novatus, who first sowed the fire of discord among us, who separated some of the brethren here from the bishop, who, in the same persecution, was still another persecution of our people for perverting the minds of the brethren. He is the very one who, without my permission or knowledge, through his faction and soliciting, appointed Felicissimus,[9] his satellite, as deacon, and, with his upheaval at Rome, sailing also to overthrow the Church, threatened similar and very like things there, separating a part of the people from the clergy and rending the concord of a brotherhood well-united in itself and mutually loving. Since plainly, because of its greatness, Rome ought to precede Carthage,[10] he committed there greater and more serious misdeeds. He who had made a deacon here against the Church made a bishop there.

Let not anyone wonder at this in such men. Demented men are always carried away by their fury of evil and, after they have committed crimes, they are agitated by the very consciousness of a wicked mind. Nor can they who have not kept divine and ecclesiastical discipline either in the conduct of their work or in the peace of their manners remain in the Church of God. Orphans robbed by that wretch, widows defrauded, the moneys of the Church also withheld, demand from him these punishments which we see in his fury. His father also died of hunger in the street and afterwards was not buried by him in death. The womb of his wife was struck by his shoe and a delivery brought on with an abortion coming quickly after a parricide. And now he dares to condemn the hands of those who sacrifice although he himself is more guilty in his feet, by which his son who was being born was killed!

---
9 Cf. Letter 41, n. 6.
10 Note primacy given to Rome.

(3) He has now for a long time feared the common knowledge of his crimes. Because of this, he held it for certain that not only would he be cast out from the priesthood, but that he would be prohibited from communion. And, at the insistence of the brethren, the day of reckoning was drawing near on which his case would have been deliberated among us if the persecution had not come before. He, welcoming this with a certain desire of evading and of profiting from his condemnation, committed and stirred up all these things so that he who was considered to be cast out and excluded from the Church anticipated the judgment of the bishops by a voluntary withdrawal as if to have evaded the penalty were to have prevented the sentence.

(4) But, concerning the other brethren, over whom we grieve that they were led astray by him, we are taking pains that they may escape the destructive person of the crafty fellow, that they may evade the deadly traps of his instigating, that they may again seek the Church from which that man has deserved to be banished by the Providence of God. These, indeed, with the help of the Lord, can be received back through His mercy. For a man cannot perish unless it is clear that he must perish since the Lord says in His Gospel: 'Every plant that my heavenly Father has not planted will be rooted up.'[11] He alone who has not been planted according to the precepts and warnings of God, the Father, can withdraw from the Church; he alone, after the bishops have been abandoned, can remain in madness with schismatics and heretics. Assuredly, the mercy of God, the Father, and the forgiveness of Christ, our Lord, and our own patience will unite the rest to us. I trust that you, dearly beloved Brother, are always well.

---

11 Matt. 15.13.

53.¹ *Maximus,² Urban,³ Sidonius,⁴ and Macarius⁵ to brother Cyprian, greeting.*

We are certain, dearly beloved Brother, that you also rejoice with us in a similar prayer that we, after having had a council, looking out rather for the advantages and peace of the Church, having cast aside all matters and reserved them for the judgment of God, have made peace with Cornelius,⁶ our bishop, and likewise with the whole clergy. You ought to know most certainly from our letter that this was done with the joy also of the universal Church, with the charity also of all disposed to us. We pray that you, dearly beloved Brother, will be well for many years.

54. *Cyprian¹ to Maximus,² the priest, and likewise to Urban³ and Sidonius⁴ and Macarius,⁵ his brethren, greeting.*

(1) When I read your letter,⁶ dearly beloved Brethren, which you wrote to me concerning your return and concerning the peace of the Church and brotherly restoration, I confess that I rejoiced as much as I had rejoiced before when I learned the glory of your confession and, joyful, I received the heavenly and spiritual praise of your warfare. For this is another confession of both your faith and praise to confess that there is one Church, not to become a sharer in the error or rather depravity of another, to seek again the same camp

---
1 251 A.D.
2 Cf. Letter 27, n. 11.
3 Cf. Letter 49, n. 4.
4 Cf. Letter 49, n. 5.
5 Cf. Letter 21, n. 16.
6 Cf. Letter 44, n. 2.

---
1 Late 251 or 252 A.D.
2 Cf. Letter 27, n. 11.
3 Cf. Letter 49, n. 4
4 Cf. Letter 49, n. 5.
5 Cf. Letter 21, n. 16.
6 **Letter 53.**

whence you went forth, whence you leaped forth with the greatest strength to carry on the battle and to conquer the adversary. For trophies from the line of battle ought to have been brought back thither whence arms for the line of battle had been received lest the Church of Christ not retain the same glorious men whom Christ had prepared for glory.

Now, assuredly, you have kept in the peace of the Lord both the fitting tenor of your faith and the law of undivided charity and of concord; and you have given, by your return, an example of love and peace to others so that the truth of the Church and the unity of the Gospel and of the rite which were held by us might be joined also with your agreement and bond that confessors of Christ who had lived as praiseworthy authors of virtue and honor should not become leaders of error.

(2) Let others see how much they may congratulate you or how much among themselves each one may glory. I confess that I both congratulate you greatly and glory more than others in this your peaceful return and love. For you ought to hear simply what has been in my heart. I grieved vehemently and I was greatly distressed because I could not be in communion with those whom once I had begun to love. After schismatical and heretical error received you, going out from prison, the case was as if your glory had remained in prison. For there the honor of your name seemed to have been left behind when soldiers of Christ did not return to the Church from the prison into which they had formerly gone with the praise and congratulations of the Church.

(3) For although there seem to be tares in the Church, yet neither our faith nor our love ought to be hindered so that, because we see that there are tares in the Church, we ourselves should withdraw from the Church. We must labor only that we may become wheat that, when the wheat has begun to be gathered into the barns of the Lord, we may receive the reward for our work and labor. The Apostle says in his Epistle: 'But in a great house there are vessels not only of gold and

silver, but also of wood and clay; and some, indeed, are for honorable uses, but some for ignoble.'[7] Let us take pains and let us labor as much as we can that we may be vessels of gold or of silver. But to destroy vessels made of clay is granted to the Lord alone, to whom also the iron rod has been given.

The servant cannot be greater than his lord, nor can anyone claim for himself what the Father has assigned to the Son alone, that he should think that he can bring the spade for winnowing and purifying the threshing-floor or separate by human judgment all the tares from the wheat. That is proud obstinacy and sacrilegious presumption which depraved madness assumes to itself. And while certain ones always assume to themselves more than gentle justice demands, they perish from the Church and, while they insolently extol themselves, blinded by their own pride, they lose the light of truth. Because of this, we also, keeping moderation and contemplating the scales of the Lord and thinking of the goodness and mercy of God the Father, have long and frequently weighed what must be done, after having treated of this among ourselves with proper moderation.

(4) You may look into all of these matters thoroughly by reading the treatises[8] which I had read recently here and, for the sake of our mutual love, had sent to you likewise to be read, in which there is wanting neither the censure to reprove the lapsed, nor the medicine to heal them. Moreover, our moderate endowment has expressed as well as it can the unity of the Catholic Church. Now I trust that this treatise will please you more and more since you already read it in such a manner that you may approve and love because, what we have written in words, you fulfill in deeds when you return to the Church in the unity of love and peace. I trust that you, dearly beloved Brethren, are always well.

---

7 Cf. 2 Tim. 2.20.
8 *Concerning the Lapsed* and *Concerning the Unity of the Catholic Church.*

55. Cyprian[1] to Antonian,[2] his brother, greeting.

(1) I received your first letter, dearly beloved Brother, firmly maintaining the concord of the priestly college and adhering to the Catholic Church; in it you signified that you are not in communion with Novatian,[3] but are following our counsel and are holding one agreement with Cornelius,[4] our fellow bishop. You also wrote that I should forward a copy of this same letter to Cornelius, our colleague, that, casting aside all solicitude, he might know immediately that you are in communion with him, that is, with the Catholic Church.

(2) But, in fact, afterward there followed another letter of yours, sent through Quintus,[5] a fellow priest, in which I noticed that your mind, moved by the letter of Novatian, had begun to waver. For, although you had previously firmly fixed both your counsel and your consent, you desired in this letter that I should write back to you what heresy Novatian had introduced or for what reason Cornelius gives Communion to Trofimus[6] and those who sacrificed. If, indeed, you are attending to this because of anxious solicitude for the faith and, solicitous, you wish to find out the truth of a dubious matter, the solicitude of your hesitating mind, wavering in divine fear, is not to be reprehended.

(3) Since I see, nevertheless, that, after the first opinion of your letter, you have been disturbed afterward by the letter of Novatian, I maintain this, dearly beloved Brother, in the first

---

1 Late 251 or 252 A.D.
2 Antonian of Numidia, a bishop who wrote to Cyprian to pledge loyalty to Cyprian and to Cornelius in the case of Novatian, was later disturbed by the charges of Novatian against the Pope.
3 Cf. Letter 44, n. 7.
4 Cf. Letter 44, n. 2.
5 Quintus of Mauretania was the African bishop who transmitted to Cyprian the second letter of Antonian. This letter brought word of the latter's doubt about supporting Cornelius.
6 Trofimus, an Italian bishop, offered incense in the Decian persecution; his flock followed him in his lapse. Cornelius restored the bishop to lay communion because his influence brought his people back to the Church. Cyprian denied the rumor spread by the Novatianists that Trofimus was reinstated in his bishopric.

place: serious men and men once established with a firm foundation upon a rock are not disturbed, I do not say by a light breeze, but not even by wind or storm, lest a doubtful and uncertain mind be frequently agitated by various opinions as by certain gusts of onrushing winds and be changed from its own purpose with a certain reproof of levity. Lest the letter of Novatian should do this to you or to anyone else, I shall explain the account of the matter to you briefly, Brother, as you have desired.

And indeed first, since you seem moved by my action also, I must vindicate both my person and my cause before you lest anyone should think that I have withdrawn lightly from my purpose and that, although I defended evangelical vigor at first and at the beginnings, afterward I seem to have turned my mind from discipline and from my earlier judgment to think that peace should be made easy for those who have stained their conscience with certificates or have engaged in nefarious sacrifices. But neither of these things was done by me without a long-deliberated and well-pondered reason.

(4) For when the battle was still at hand and the struggle of a glorious contest was raging in the persecution, the forces of the soldiers had to be stirred up by every exhortation and complete ardor and, especially, the minds of the lapsed had to be animated by the trumpet call of our voices, as one might say, that they might follow the way of penance, not only with prayers and lamentations, but, since an occasion was given of repeating the struggle and of regaining salvation, reproved by my voice, they might be drawn rather to the ardor of confession and the glory of martyrdom. Finally, when the priests and deacons had written to me concerning some persons that they were immoderate and pressing hastily to be received into communion, replying to them in my letter, which is extant, I also added this: 'If any are in a very great hurry, they have what they are asking in their own power since the time itself provides more than what they ask. The battle is still going on and the struggle is daily renewed. If they repent truly and

steadfastly of the fault committed, and ardor of faith prevails, he who cannot be put off may be crowned.'[7] Yet concerning this, I have postponed what must be decided about the case of the lapsed so that, when quiet and tranquillity have been given and the Divine Mercy has permitted the bishops to assemble together in one place, then, when the advice from the conference of all has been communicated and weighed, we might decide what ought to be done. But, if anyone, before our council and before decision agreed by the advice of all, should wish to give Communion rashly to the lapsed, he should himself be held back from Communion.

(5) I wrote this very fully also to Rome to the clergy then still acting without a bishop and to the confessors, Maximus,[8] the priest, and the others held in custody, now joined with Cornelius in the Church; you may know what I wrote from their answer. For in their letter, they stated thus: 'And yet, what you yourself also discussed in so important a business pleases us: first, to sustain the peace of the Church; then, when the gathering for counsel has been accomplished with the bishops, priests, deacons, confessors, and likewise with the laity who stand fast, to discuss a plan for lapsed.'[9] It was added also with Novatian, then writing and reciting with his voice what he had written, and with the priest, Moses,[10] then still a confessor, but now, indeed, a martyr, subscribing, that peace should be given to the lapsed who were sick and about to die. This letter was sent to the whole world and was brought to the notice of all of the churches and of all of the brethren.

(6) Yet, according to what had been before decided, after the persecution had calmed down, when an opportunity for assembling together had been given, a goodly number of bishops whom their faith and the protection of the Lord kept whole and unharmed, we assembled together. And, after

---

7 Cf. Letter 19 before close, p. 53.
8 Cf. Letter 27, n. 11.
9 Cf. Letter 30, pp. 75-76.
10 Cf. Letter 27, n. 10.

Scripture had long been cited on both sides, we weighed a right mean with salutary moderation that neither hope of communion nor of peace should be totally denied to the lapsed lest they fail more through desperation and, since the Church was closed to them, they live like the heathen following the world; nor yet should evangelical censure be relaxed lest they rush to Communion rashly, but that repentance should endure for a time and that paternal clemency should be sought in sorrow, and that the situations and the wishes and necessities of each one should be examined according to what is contained in the treatise which, I trust, has come to you, in which separate headings of our decisions are drawn up.[11] And if the number of bishops in Africa should not seem sufficient, we also wrote about this matter to Rome to Cornelius, our colleague. He himself, after having held a council with very many fellow bishops, agreed to the same decision with us with equal gravity and salutary moderation.

(7) Concerning this, it has now been necessary to write to you that you may know that I have done nothing lightly but, according to what I had before stated in my letter, that I deferred everything to the common decision of our council and that I gave Communion to none of the lapsed previously since up to that point there was a way whereby the lapsed might not only receive pardon, but also a crown. Yet, afterward, as the concord of the college and the advantage of binding together the brethren and of healing their wound required, I submitted to the urgency of the times and thought that provision ought to be made for the salvation of the many. And I do not now depart from those decisions which pleased us together in our council by common agreement although many things are rumored about by the voices of many; and lies against the bishops of God, brought forth from the mouth of the devil to destroy the concord of Catholic unity, are tossed about everywhere. But it behooves you, as a good brother and a fellow priest of the same mind, not easily to receive what

---
11 Apparently lost encyclical.

evil men and apostates may say, but to weigh what your colleagues, modest and serious men, may do from the examination of our life and teaching.

(8) I come now at this time, dearly beloved Brother, to the character of Cornelius, our colleague, that with us you may know Cornelius more truly, not from the lie of malignant men and slanderers, but from the judgment of God who made him bishop, and from the testimony of his fellow bishops, whose whole number has agreed in the unanimity of concord throughout the whole world. For what recommends our dearly beloved Cornelius to God and to Christ and to His Church and also to all of his fellow bishops with laudable praise is that he did not attain the episcopate suddenly, but, having been promoted through all of the ecclesiastical offices and having often deserved well of the Lord in divine ministrations, he ascended to the sublime summit of the priesthood through all of the steps of religious service. Then, finally, he neither asked for nor desired the episcopate itself, nor, as others do, whom the swelling of arrogance and of their own pride puffs up, did he seize it, but, quiet otherwise and modest and such as those who are divinely chosen for this office are accustomed to be, by virtue of the modesty of his virginal continence and the humility of his innate and accustomed reverence, not only did he make no attempt to become bishop, as some do, but he himself suffered violence in being compelled to accept the episcopate.

And he was made bishop by very many of our colleagues, who were then present in the city of Rome, who sent to us concerning his ordination letters doing him honor both laudatory and glorious for the testimony of his praise. But Cornelius was made bishop by the judgment of God and of His Christ, by the testimony of almost all of the clergy, by the vote of the people who were then present, by the college of venerable bishops and good men, when no one had been made before him, when the place of Fabian,[12] that is, when the

---

[12] Cf. Letter 30, n. 3.

place of Peter and the position of the episcopal chair were vacant. Since this has been occupied both by the will of God and the confirmed agreement of all of us, it is necessary for whosoever now wishes to become bishop to become so outside; nor would he have ecclesiastical ordination who does not maintain the unity of the Church. Whosoever he may be, although boasting much about himself and claiming very much for himself, he is an impious man; he is a stranger; he is outside. And since, after the first, there cannot be a second, whosoever has been made after the one who ought to be alone is not now a second, but is none.

(9) Then, finally, after an episcopate neither secured by canvassing nor obtained by force, but undertaken through the will of God who makes bishops, what virtue there was in the very episcopate he had accepted, what strength of mind, what firmness of faith, which we ought with a simple heart both to observe completely and to praise that he sat intrepid in the episcopal chair in Rome at a time when a tyrant hostile to the bishops of God was threatening speakable and unspeakable horrors, at a time when he heard much more patiently and tolerantly that a rival leader was raised up against himself than that a bishop of God was established at Rome!

Is not this man, dearly beloved Brother, to be commended with the highest testimony of virtue and of faith? Is he not to be numbered among the glorious confessors and martyrs, who remained for so long a time expecting the murders of his body and the avengers of the raging tyrant, who, when Cornelius resisted, face to face, their deadly edicts and trampled under foot by the vigor of his faith their threats and tortures and torments, were to assault with a sword or crucify or burn with fire or mangle his interior organs and his members by some unheard of kind of punishment? For although the majesty and goodness of the protecting Lord shielded the appointed bishop, the one whom He wished to be appointed, yet, Cornelius, insomuch as it pertains to his devotion and fear, suffered whatever he could suffer and conquered first by his priesthood the tyrant afterwards overcome by arms and war.

(10) But do not wonder that certain dishonest and malignant statements are being bruited about concerning him since you know that this is always the work of the devil to injure the servants of God by lying and to destroy a glorious name with false reports so that they who shine out in the light of their conscience may become tarnished by the reports of others. But know that our colleagues have investigated and most certainly have found that he has been stained by no blemish of a certificate, as certain ones intimate, nor has he shared a sacrilegious Communion with bishops who have sacrificed, but he has joined with us only those whose cause has been heard and whose innocence has been established.

(11) And now concerning Trofimus also of whom you desired something to be written to you, the matter is not as rumor and the lying of the malignant have reported it to you. For, as our predecessors also often did, our dearly beloved brother yielded to necessity after our brethren had been assembled. And since a very large part of the people had withdrawn with Trofimus, when Trofimus now returned to the Church and made satisfaction and confessed with the penance of supplication his former error and, with full humility and satisfaction, recalled the brotherhood of the flock whom he had recently withdrawn, his prayers were heard. And not only Trofimus, but a very large number of the brethren who had been with Trofimus were readmitted into the Church of the Lord, all of whom would not have returned to the Church unless they had come in the company of Trofimus. Therefore, after the matter had been discussed there with very many of our colleagues, Trofimus was taken back, for whom the return of the brethren and the restored salvation of the many made satisfaction. Yet, Trofimus was admitted so that he might receive Communion as a layman, not according to what the letters of the malicious have reported to you, as if he usurped a place in the episcopate.

(12) Moreover, as for the fact that Cornelius is reported to you to be giving Communion generally to those who have

offered sacrifice, this also has come about through fictitious rumors of the apostates. For neither can they who leave us praise us, nor ought we expect to please them who, displeasing to us and rebellious against the Church, persist violently in enticing the brethren away from the Church. Wherefore, neither hear nor easily believe, dearly beloved Brother, anything they spread abroad concerning both Cornelius and us.

(13) If there are any who are stricken with infirmities, assistance is given to them in danger as it has been decided. Yet after they have been aided and peace has been given to them in danger, they cannot be suffocated by us, or destroyed by force, or be urged forward at our hands to the departure of death, as if, because peace is given to the dying, it is necessary for those who have received peace to die, although the token of divine affection and paternal lenity appears rather in this, that they who receive the pledge of life in the place given may also be kept for life after they have received peace. And, therefore, if after peace has been received, a reprieve is granted by God, no one ought to calumniate the bishops for this because it seemed right to them for the brethren to be aided in danger.

Nor should you think, dearly beloved Brother, as some do, that those with certificates ought to be considered in the same category with those who have sacrificed, since even among those very ones who have sacrificed frequently both the condition and the case are different. Nor must the one who rushed immediately forward of his own will to be the nefarious sacrifice and the one who, having long struggled and delayed, came finally by compulsion to this disastrous deed be considered in the same category; the one who betrayed both himself and his own people and the one who, himself approaching the crisis for all, protected his wife and children and whole household at the expense of his own danger; the one who drove immigrants or his friends to the evil deed and the one who spared immigrants and settlers and even received many brethren who were fleeing, banished and exiled, into his home and hospitality, showing and offering to the Lord many living and unharmed souls to pray for the one wounded.

(14) Since, therefore, among those who have sacrificed, the diversity is great, what lack of mercy there is and what bitter hardness to associate those with certificates with those who have sacrificed, when he to whom the certificate has been given may say: 'I had previously read and had learned from the bishop who instructed that one must not sacrifice to idols, that the servant of God ought not adore images, and, therefore, lest I should do that which was not lawful, when the opportunity of the certificate had been offered, which itself I should not have accepted unless the occasion had been indicated, either I went to the magistrate or I sent word with another going that I was a Christian, that it was not lawful for me to sacrifice, that I could not come to the altars of the devil, that I gave a bribe for this lest I should do what is not lawful.' Yet now, even he who has been stained by the certificate, after he has learned from our admonition that he ought not to have done this—although his hand is pure and his lips have been polluted with no contagion of the deadly food, yet his conscience has been polluted—weeps when he hears us and laments and is admonished now for that in which he has sinned; and, beguiled, not so much by sin as by error, he gives testimony that he is now instructed and prepared for the future.

(15) If we scorn the repentance of those who have, in some degree, the assurance of a bearable conscience, immediately they are drawn by the devil's invitation into heresy or schism with their wife and children, whom they had kept unharmed. And it will be charged against us on judgment day that we have not cared for the wounded sheep and have lost many innocent ones because of one wounded.[13] And, although the Lord, having left the ninety-nine whole, sought the one wandering and weary and, having found it, He Himself car-

---

13 Cf. Ezech. 34.4.

ried it back on His shoulders,[14] we not only do not seek out the weary, but we hinder them when they come; and, although false prophets do not cease to devastate and wound the flock of Christ, we give occasion to the dogs and wolves so that we lose through our harshness and inhumanity those whom a devastating persecution has not destroyed. And what will become, dearly beloved Brother, of what the Apostle says: 'I myself in all things please all men, not seeking what is profitable to myself but to the many, that they may be saved. Be imitators of me as I am of Christ'?[15] And again: 'To the weak I became weak, that I might gain the weak.'[16] And again: 'If one member suffers, the other members also suffer, and if one member glories, all the members also rejoice.'[17]

(16) Quite otherwise is the reasoning of the philosophers and of the Stoics, dearly beloved Brother, who say that all sins are equal and that a serious man ought not easily to be influenced. But there is a very great difference between Christians and philosophers. And, since the Apostle says: 'See to it that no one deceives you by philosophy and vain deceit,'[18] we must avoid those things which do not come from the clemency of God, but descend from the presumption of a too harsh philosophy. But we read in Scripture concerning Moses the saying: 'And Moses was a man exceedingly meek.'[19] And the Lord in His Gospel says: 'Be merciful even as your Father had mercy on you.'[20] And again: 'It is not the healthy who need a physician, but they who are sick.'[21] How can he practice medicine who says: 'I cure the healthy only for whom a doctor is not necessary.' We ought to offer our assistance, our healing remedy, to those who are wounded. Let us not think that they whom we see lying wounded by this destructive

---
14 Cf. Luke 15.4.
15 1 Cor. 10.33; 11.1.
16 1 Cor. 9.22.
17 Cf. 1 Cor. 12.26.
18 Col. 2.8.
19 Cf. Num. 12.3.
20 Cf. Luke 6.36.
21 Cf. Matt. 9.12.

persecution are dead, but rather half alive. If they had been completely dead, never afterward from these same men would both confessors and martyrs be made.

(17) But, since there is in them something which may be strengthened to faith by subsequent repentance and since strength is armed by repentance to virtue—which could not be armed, if anyone should fall away through despair; if, segregated from the Church harshly and cruelly, he should turn himself to pagan ways and to worldly works or, if, rejected by the Church, he should pass over to the heretics and schismatics whence, although he should afterwards have been killed for the Name, having been put out of the Church and divided from unity and from love, he could not be crowned in death—therefore, also, it seemed fitting, dearly beloved Brother, when the cases of each had been examined, for those who had received the certificates to be admitted meanwhile, for those who had sacrificed to be received at death because there is no confession among the dead, nor can anyone be compelled to repentance by us if the fruit of repentance should be taken away. If the battle should come first, he will be found strengthened by us, armed for the battle; but if infirmity should press hard before the battle, he dies with the solace of peace and of communion.

(18) For we do not prejudge since the Lord will come to judge so that, if He finds the repentance of the sinner full and just, then He may ratify whatever may have been decided by us here. But if anyone should deceive us with the pretense of repentance, God, who is not mocked and who sees the heart of man, will judge of those things which we have looked upon imperfectly and will correct the judgment of His servants, whereas we yet ought to remember, Brother, that it has been written: 'A brother helping his brother will be exalted.'[22] And the Apostle also said: 'Having in mind, each one, lest thou also be tempted. Bear one another's burdens, and so you will ful-

---

22 Cf. Prov. 18.19.

fill the law of Christ.'[23] Likewise, refuting the proud and breaking their arrogance, he states this is his Epistle: 'And let him who thinks he stands take heed lest he fall.'[24] And in another place he says: 'Who art thou to judge another's servant? To his own lord he stands or falls; but he will stand, for God is able to make him stand.'[25]

John also proves that Jesus Christ, our Lord, is Advocate and Intercessor for our sins, saying: 'My dear children, these things I write to you in order that you may not sin. And if anyone sins, we have an advocate with the Father, Jesus Christ the just; and he is a propitiation for our sins.'[26] And the Apostle Paul also stated in his Epistle: 'If when as yet we were sinners, Christ died for us, much more now that we are justified by His blood, shall we be saved through Him from the wrath.'[27]

(19) Meditating upon His goodness and clemency, we ought not to be so bitter, nor harsh, nor inhuman in encouraging the brethren, but to grieve with those who grieve, and to weep with those who weep, and to encourage them also as much as we can with the aid and solace of our love, and to be not so severe and pertinacious in blunting their repentance, nor, again, free and easy in rashly relaxing communication. Behold the wounded brother lies injured by the adversary in the line of battle. There, the devil attempts to kill the man whom he has wounded; here, Christ exhorts that the man whom He has redeemed should not be wholly lost. Which of these two do we assist? On whose side do we stand? Do we favor the devil that he may destroy and do we pass by the brother lying half dead as did the priest and Levite in the Gospel? Or, in truth, as bishops of God and of Christ, imitating what Christ both taught and did, do we snatch the

---

23 Cf. Gal. 6.1, 2.
24 Cf. 1 Cor. 10.12.
25 Rom. 14.4.
26 Cf. 1 John 2.1, 2.
27 Cf. Rom. 5.8, 9.

wounded from the jaws of his adversary? Do we save him cured for God, the Judge?

(20) Do not think, dear Brother, henceforth that either the courage of the brethren is diminished or that martyrdoms fail because repentance has been mitigated for the lapsed and because hope of reconciliation has been offered to the penitents. The strength of the truly believing remains constant and integrity persists stable and strong among those who fear and love God with their whole heart. For a time of penance is allowed by us even to adulterers and peace is given to them. Yet virginity does not, on that account, fail in the Church, nor does the glorious design of continency languish through the sins of others. The Church flourishes, crowned with so many virgins, and chastity and modesty keep the tenor of their glory; nor is the vigor of continency destroyed because penance and pardon are mitigated for adulterers.

It is one thing to stand for pardon; another to arrive at glory. It is one thing for one put in prison not to come out from there until he has 'paid the last penny';[28] another thing to receive immediately the reward of faith and virtue. It is one thing, tortured by long sorrow for sins, to be cleansed and purged for a time by fire; another thing to have purged all sins by suffering. It is one thing, finally, to wait on the day of judgment for the sentence of the Lord; another thing to be immediately crowned by the Lord.

(21) And, indeed, among our predecessors, some of the bishops here in our province thought that peace should not be given to adulterers and they shut off completely the opportunity for penance in the case of adultery. Yet they did not withdraw from the college of their fellow bishops, break the unity of the Catholic Church through the obstinacy either of their harshness or censure so that, because peace was given by some to adulterers, he who did not give it should be separated from the Church. While the bond of concord remains and the indivisible rite of the Catholic Church continues, each bishop

---
28 Cf. Matt. 5.26.

disposes and directs his own work as one who will render an account of his purpose to the Lord.

(22) But I wonder that some are so obstinate as to think that penance ought not to be allowed to the lapsed or as to consider that pardon ought to be denied to the penitent when it is written: 'Remember whence thou hast fallen and repent and do the former works.'[29] This is certainly said to him who, it is ascertained, has fallen and whom the Lord exhorts to rise again through works since it is written: 'Alms deliver . . . from death,'[30] and not certainly from that death which once the Blood of Christ extinguished and from which the water of salutary baptism and the grace of our Redeemer freed us, but from that which afterward creeps in through sins.

In another place, also, time is given for repentance and the Lord threatens the one who does not do penance: 'I have,' He says, 'many things against thee that thou sufferest thy wife Jezebel, who calls herself a prophetess, to teach, and to seduce my servants, to commit fornication, and to eat of things sacrificed to idols. And I gave her time that she might repent, and she does not want to repent of her fornication. Behold, I will cast her upon a bed, and those who commit fornication with her are in the greatest tribulation, unless they repent of their deeds.'[31]

The Lord certainly would not exhort to repentance if it were not because He promised pardon to the penitent. And in the Gospel: 'I say,' He says, 'to you, that so, there will be joy in heaven over one sinner who repents, more than over ninety-nine just who have no need of repentance.'[32] For since it is written: 'God did not make death, nor does He rejoice in the destruction of the living,'[33] certainly He, who wishes no one to perish, desires sinners to do penance and to return to life again through penance. And, therefore, through Joel,

---
29 Cf. Apoc. 2.5.
30 Tob. 4.11.
31 Cf. Apoc. 2.20-22.
32 Cf. Luke 15.7.
33 Wisd. 1.13.

the Prophet, He cries out and says: 'And now says the Lord, your God, return to me with your whole heart, at the same time with fasting, and weeping, and mourning; and rend your hearts, and not your garments, and return to the Lord, your God. For gracious and merciful is he, slow to anger, rich in kindness, and he softens the sentence against malice inflicted.'[34] In the Psalms we read, also, of the censure and of the clemency of God, at the same time, threatening and sparing, punishing that He may correct and saving when He has corrected. 'I will visit,' He says, 'their crime with a rod and their guilt with stripes. Yet my kindness I will not take from them.'[35]

(23) The Lord also in the Gospel, showing forth the mercy of God, the Father, says: 'What man is there among you, who, if his son asks for a loaf, will hand him a stone; or if he asks for a fish, will hand him a serpent? Therefore, if you, evil as you are, know how to give good gifts to your children, how much more will your heavenly Father give good things to those who ask Him!'[36] Here, the Lord compares the earthly father and the eternal and all embracing mercy of God, the Father. But if that wicked father on the earth, seriously offended by a sinful and evil son, yet if he sees the same one afterward reformed and, with the sins of his earlier life cast away, restored to sober and good living and to the discipline of innocence by the sorrow of repentance, rejoices and gives thanks and embraces with a prayer of fatherly exultation the one now received whom he had formerly cast out, how much more does the one and true Father, good, merciful, and loving, nay rather, Himself Goodness and Mercy and Love, rejoice in the repentance of His sons and not threaten angry punishment to the penitent or to the mourning or to the lamenting, but rather promise pardon and forgiveness?

Whence the Lord in the Gospel says the mournful are blessed[37] because he who mourns provokes mercy. He who is

---
34 Cf. Joel 2.12, 13.
35 Cf. Ps. 88.33, 34.
36 Cf. Matt. 7.9-11.
37 Cf. Matt. 5.5.

perverse and proud heaps up wrath against himself and the punishment of the coming judgment. And, therefore, dearly beloved Brother, we have decreed that those who do not do penance and testify to sorrow for their sins with their whole heart and with a manifest profession of their lamentation must be completely cut off from the hope of communion and of peace. If, in danger and in infirmity, they begin to plead, because, not repentance for their sin, but the warning of impending death, drives them to ask, he who has not reflected that he is destined to die is not worthy to receive solace in death.

(24) This, in truth, pertains to the person of Novatian, dearly beloved Brother, of whom you desired me to write to you as to what heresy he had introduced. Know that, in the first place, we ought not to be curious about what he is teaching since he is teaching outside. Whoever he is and whatever he is, he who is not in the Church of Christ is not a Christian. Although he may show off and declare openly his philosophy and eloquence with lofty words, he who has not kept brotherly love or ecclesiastical unity has lost even what he formerly had been. Unless, indeed, he seems to you to be a bishop who, after a bishop has been made in the Church by sixteen fellow bishops, struggles through ambition to be made a false and extraneous bishop by deserters! And, although there is one Church throughout the whole world divided by Christ into many members, also one episcopate diffused in a harmonious multitude of many bishops, that man, in spite of the tradition of God, in spite of the combined and everywhere joined unity of the Catholic Church, is attempting to make a human church and is sending his new apostles through very many cities to establish some fresh foundations of his own institution. And although long ago in all of the provinces and in each city, there are ordained bishops, senior in age, firm in faith, proved in trial, proscribed in persecution, that man dares to create other false bishops over and above them, as if he could either go through the whole world with the persistence of a new

attempt or destroy the structure of the ecclesiastical body by the sowing of his discord, not knowing that schismatics are always fervid at the outset, that, in truth, they cannot have increase and add to what they have begun illicitly, but immediately fail with their depraved rivalry.

But he could not keep the episcopate even if, made a bishop earlier, he withdrew from the body of his fellow bishops and from the unity of the Church since the Apostle admonishes us that we should mutually support one another lest we should withdraw from the unity which God has appointed and he says: 'Bearing with one another in love, taking sufficient care to preserve the unity of the Spirit in the bond of peace.'[38] He, therefore, who observes neither the unity of the Spirit nor the bond of peace, and separates himself from the bond of the Church and from the college of the bishops, can have neither the power nor the honor of a bishop since he has not wished either the unity or the peace of the episcopate.

(25) Then, finally, what a great swelling of avarice it is, what a great forgetfulness of humility and meekness, what a great boasting of his own arrogance that anyone should either dare or think he is able to do what the Lord did not allow to the apostles, that he should think that he can discern the tares from the grain, or, as if it were granted to him to bear the spade and to purge the threshing-floor, he should attempt to separate the chaff from the wheat and, although the Apostle says: 'But in a great house there are vessels not only of gold and silver, but of wood and clay,'[39] he should seem to choose the gold and silver vessels and to despise, indeed, to cast away, to condemn those of wood and clay since it is only in the day of the Lord that wooden vessels are to be burned by the fire of divine flame and those of clay are to be broken by Him to whom is given the iron rod.

(26) Or if he constitutes himself the scrutinizer and judge of the heart and of the reins, let him judge all things equally.

---

38 Cf. Eph. 4.2, 3.
39 2 Tim. 2.20.

And, since he knows that it is written: 'Behold, thou art cured. Sin no more, lest something worse befall thee,'[40] let him separate defrauders and adulterers from his side and from his company since the case of an adulterer is much more serious and much worse than that of the one who has received a certificate since the latter sinned under duress; the former, of his free will; the latter, thinking that it was enough for him that he did not sacrifice, has been deceived by error; the former, the destroyer of the marriage of another or the one, having entered a house of ill repute in the sewer and muddy whirlpool, has violated with base impurities a body sanctified and a temple of God, as the Apostle says: 'Every sin that a man commits is outside the body, but the immoral man sins against his own body.'[41] Yet even to these very men is penance granted and the hope of lamenting and of making satisfaction is left, according to the Apostle himself, saying: 'For I fear lest perhaps when I come to you, . . . I should mourn over many who sinned before and have not repented of the uncleannesses and immoralities and lusts that they practiced.'[42]

(27) Let not the new heretics flatter themselves in this that they say that they do not give Communion to idolaters when there are among them both adulterers and deceivers who are ensnared by the sin of idolatry, according to the Apostle, who says: 'For know this and understand, that no fornicator, or unclean person, or deceiver (for that is idolatry) has any inheritance in the kingdom of Christ and God.'[43] And again: 'Therefore mortify your members, which are on earth, putting off fornication and uncleanness and evil desire and cupidity (which are the service of idols). Because of these things the wrath of God comes.'[44]

For since our bodies are members of Christ and we are each a temple of God, whoever violates the temple of God by

---
40 John 5.14.
41 1 Cor. 6.18.
42 Cf. 2 Cor. 12.20, 21.
43 Cf. Eph. 5.5
44 Cf. Col. 3.5, 6.

adultery violates God, and he who does the will of the devil in committing sins serves demons and idols. For these evil deeds do not come from the Holy Spirit but, from the instigation of the adversary and from the unclean spirit of inborn concupiscence, they drive men to act against God and to serve the devil. Thus it happens that, if they say that one person is stained by the sin of another and if they contend by their own assertion that the idolatry of the guilty passes over to the one who is not guilty, they cannot be excused, according to their own saying, from the crime of idolatry since it is certain from the proof of the Apostle that the adulterers and deceivers to whom they give Communion are idolaters.

But for us, according to our faith and the form of divine preaching given to us, the rule of truth is adequate; everyone himself is held responsible for his own sin and one cannot be guilty for another since the Lord forewarns and says: 'The virtuous man's virtue shall be his own, and the wicked man's wickedness shall be his.'[45] And again: 'Fathers shall not die for their children and the children shall not die for their fathers. Every one shall die in his own sin.'[46] Reading, certainly, and holding this, we think that no one should be kept away from the fruit of satisfaction and from the hope of peace since we know, according to the faith of the Divine Scriptures, God Himself being the Author and Comforter, both that sinners are led to do penance and that pardon and forgiveness are not denied to the penitent.

(28) And, oh, mockery of deceived brotherhood! Oh, false deception of miserable mourners! Oh, inefficacious and vain tradition of heretical institution, to exhort to the repentance of satisfaction and to take away the healing from the satisfaction, to say to our brethren: 'Lament and shed tears and groan day and night and work frequently and diligently for washing away and purging your sin, but, after these things, you

---
45 Cf. Ezech. 18.20.
46 Cf. Deut. 24.16.

will die outside the Church! You will do whatever pertains to peace, but you will not receive the peace which you seek.' Who would not immediately perish? Who would not fail through despair itself? Who would not turn away his mind from the purpose of lamentation?

Do you think a farmer would be able to work if you said: 'Cultivate your field with all the skill of agriculture; press forward diligently in your husbandry, but you will reap no harvest; you will press no vintage; you will receive no fruit of your olive tree; you will pluck no apples from your trees'? Or if you should say to him whom you are urging to the control over and use of ships: 'Buy your material from the choicest woods, Brother; cover your vessel with very strong and select oak; take pains with the rudder, the ropes, the sails, that the ship may be made and equipped; but when you have done this, you will not see the fruit of its motions and voyages'?

(29) This is to shut up and to cut off the way of sorrow and the path of repentance so that, although the Lord God in the Scripture invites graciously those who return to Him and repent, through our hardness and cruelty, while the fruit of penance is cut off, the penance itself is taken away. But, if we find that no one ought to be prohibited from doing penance, to those entreating and imploring the mercy of the Lord, inasmuch as He is merciful and loving, peace can be given through His priests. The groans of those who mourn must be admitted and the fruit of repentance must not be denied to the sorrowful. And since in hell there is no confession and no confession can be made there, those who have repented with their whole heart and have asked ought to be received back, meantime, into the Church and to be kept in it for the Lord, who, when He comes to His Church, will judge concerning those certainly whom He will find therein. But apostates and deserters or adversaries and enemies who also lay waste the Church of Christ, even if they have been killed for His Name without, cannot be admitted, according to the

Apostle, to the peace of the Church since they have kept neither the unity of the Spirit nor of the Church.

(30) Meanwhile, dearly beloved Brother, I have described these few matters from many as briefly as I could, that by them I might both satisfy your desire and link you more and more to the society of our college and of our body. But, if you have an occasion and an opportunity of coming to us, we shall be able to confer upon many things in common and to treat more fully and fruitfully those things which may be done for salutary concord. I trust that you, dearly beloved Brother, are always well.

56. *Cyprian[1] to Fortunatus,[2] Ahymnus,[3] Optatus,[4] Privatian,[5] Donatulus,[6] and Felix,[7] his brethren, greeting.*

(1) You wrote to me, dearly beloved Brethren, that, when you were in the city of Capsa for the ordination of a bishop, Superius,[8] our brother and our colleague, reported to you that Ninus,[9] Clementian,[10] and Florus,[11] our brethren, who had previously been seized in the persecution and, having con-

---

1 252 A.D.
2 Fortunatus, African bishop from Capsa.
3 Ahymnus, bishop of Ausuaga, Africa, among those consulting Cyprian about restoration of Ninus, Clementian, and Florus, who had failed to stand in the Decian persecution. Cyprian reserved case for the next council.
4 Optatus, African bishop.
5 Privatian, African bishop.
6 Donatulus, African bishop of Capsa for whose consecration the five bishops had met.
7 Felix, African bishop. It is not known how many men of this name are concerned in the letters.
8 Superius, African bishop who introduced the problem of restoring lapsed who subsequently became confessors.
9 Ninus persevered with Florus and Clementian before the local magistrates, but broke down under torture before the proconsul. The case, first presented by Superius to six bishops at Çapsa, was referred to Cyprian who referred it to the Council. Cyprian favored restoration after three years of penance.
10 Clementian, colleague of Ninus.
11 Florus, colleague of Ninus and Clementian mentioned above.

fessed the Name of the Lord, had overcome the violence of the magistrates and the attack of the raging populace. Afterward, when they were tortured before the proconsul with excruciating torments, they were overcome by the force of the torments and, through the continued tortures, fell from the degree of glory to which they were tending in the full virtue of faith. Yet, after this grave lapse, brought about not through their free will but by compulsion, they have not ceased from doing penance throughout these three years. Concerning these, you thought that you ought to consult as to whether it would be right to admit them now to Communion.

(2) And, indeed, in respect to my own opinion, I think that the mercy of the Lord will not fail those who, it is known stood in the line of battle, confessed the Name of the Lord, overcame with the firmness of immovable faith the violence of the magistrates and the attack of the raging populace, suffered imprisonment, long resisted, in the midst of the threats of the proconsul and the fury of the people surrounding, torments which mangled and tortured by long repetition; that what seems overcome at the very last by the weakness of the flesh should be lifted up by the defense of their preceding merits; and that it should be sufficient for such men to have lost their glory; yet, we ought not to close to them the opportunity for pardon and deprive them of the love of their Father and of communion with us. For them we think that it can suffice to beg the clemency of the Lord because for three years continually and sorrowfully, as you write, they have lamented with the greatest sorrow of penance.

Certainly I think that peace is not being restored incautiously and rashly to those who, we see, did not fail at first in the bravery of their warfare or their battle, and, if the line of battle should also come again, they can repair their glory. For since it was decided in Council that those doing penance should be aided in the danger of sickness and peace given to them, assuredly, they ought to precede in receiving peace who, we see, did not fall through weakness of soul but, assembled in battle and wounded, were not able to endure to the end the crown of their confession through the weakness of the flesh, especially since it was not permitted to those who desired to die to be killed, but for so long a time, tortures lacerated weary men as they conquered, not their faith which is invincible, but they wore out their flesh which is weak.

(3) Yet, since you wrote that I should treat of this matter most fully with very many colleagues and since so important a subject demands greater and more deliberate counsel from the discussion of many and since now almost all, at this beginning of the Paschal season, are staying at home among their brethren, when they have satisfied their obligation of celebrating the festival among their own people and have begun to come to me, I shall treat with each one more fully that there may be a strong stand on this concerning which you sought advice and the firm judgment of many bishops pondered in the Council may be written back to you. I trust that you, dearly beloved Brethren, are always well.

57. *Cyprian*,[1] *Liberalis*,[2] *Caldonius*,[3] *Nicomedes*,[4] *Cecil*,[5] *Junius*,[6] *Marrutius*,[7] *Felix*,[8] *Successus*,[9] *Faustinus*,[10] *Fortunatus*,[11] *Victor*,[12] *Saturninus*,[13] *another Saturninus*,[14]

---

1 252 A.D.
2 Cf. Letter 48, n. 6.
3 Cf. Letter 24, n. 2.
4 Nicomedes, African bishop of Segermi, attended Synod of Carthage in 251 and 254 and the two synods concerning baptism.
5 Cf. Letter 4, n. 2.
6 Junius, African bishop who attended two councils of Cyprian.
7 Marrutius, African bishop who also attended councils.
8 Cf. Letter 56, n. 7.
9 Successus, bishop of Abbir Germaniciana in Africa, attended Cyprian's councils and was also martyred in 258 A.D. He is mentioned also in Letters 67, 70, and 80.
10 Faustinus, African bishop present at Cyprian's second Synod of Carthage.
11 Cf. Letter 44, n. 9.
12 Cf. Letter 4, n. 3. The references to Victor in the letters pose a problem as to the number of men involved. There were bishops of that name in Assurae, Octavum, and Gor. There were also priests and laymen.

Rogatian,[15] *Tertullus,*[16] *Lucian,*[17] *Sattius,*[18] *Secundinus,*[19] *another Saturninus,*[20] *Eutyches,*[21] *Ampius,*[22] *another Saturninus,*[23] *Aurelius,*[24] *Priscus,*[25] *Herculaneus,*[26] *Victoricus,*[27] *Quintus,*[28] *Honoratus,*[29] *Manthaneus,*[30] *Hortensian,*[31] *Verianus,*[32] *Iambus,*[33] *Donatus,*[34] *Pomponius,*[35] *Polycarp,*[36] *Demetrius,*[37] *another Donatus,*[38] *Privatian,*[39] *Fortunatus,*[40] *Rogatus,*[41] *and Monnulus,*[42] *to Cornelius,*[43] *their brother, greeting.*

[13] Saturninus, one of four bishops of the same name present at Cyprian's synod in 252 A.D. and at other councils.
[14] Cf. above.
[15] Cf. Letter 3, n. 2.
[16] Cf. Letter 4, n. 5.
[17] Lucian, African bishop who attended synod on baptism of heretics.
[18] Sattius, African bishop of Sicilibba, present at several councils.
[19] Secundinus, bishop also present at council concerning peace, is probably the Secundinus mentioned as attending a council on baptism and a martyr.
[20] Cf. above, n. 13.
[21] Eutyches, another bishop at Cyprian's synod concerning peace.
[22] Ampius, bishop listed as attending the second Council of Carthage in 252 A.D.
[23] Cf. above, n. 13.
[24] Aurelius, one of two bishops of the same name listed as attending several councils.
[25] Priscus, bishop of Africa, present at the council.
[26] Cf. Letter 41, n. 3.
[27] Victoricus, bishop of Thabraca in Numidia, present at several councils of Carthage.
[28] Quintus, African bishop present at council on baptism and at several other councils, answers questions of the Quintus probably referred to in Letter 55, n. 5.
[29] Honoratus, African bishop, present at several councils.
[30] Manthaneus, African bishop, present at second Synod of Carthage.
[31] Hortensian, African bishop, probably of Lares in Numidia, at Synod of Carthage.
[32] Verianus, African bishop, present at Synod of Carthage in 252 A.D.
[33] Iambus, African bishop of Germaniciana and confessor, present at several councils.
[34] Donatus, African bishop, present at Synod of Carthage on baptism, is mentioned also in Letter 70 with another bishop of the same name.
[35] Cf. Letter 4, n. 6.
[36] Cf. Letter 48, n. 5.
[37] Demetrius, African bishop, present at several synods.
[38] Cf. n. 34 above.
[39] Cf. Letter 56, n. 5.
[40] Cf. Letter 44, n. 9.
[41] Rogatus, African bishop at Synod of Carthage in 252 A.D.
[42] Monnulus, bishop of Girba, present at council in 252 A.D.
[43] Cf. Letter 44, n. 2.

(1) We, indeed, had decided long ago, dearly beloved Brother, after having mutually shared our counsel among ourselves, that they who, in the disturbance of the persecution, had been overthrown by the adversary and had lapsed and had defiled themselves with unlawful sacrifices should do full penance for a long time and, if the danger of sickness should press hard, they should receive peace under the thrust of death. For it was not right and the love of the Father and divine clemency did not permit the Church to be closed to those who knock and the help of the hope of salvation be denied to those who lament and supplicate so that, when they depart from the world, they should be sent forth to the Lord without Communion and peace; since He Himself permitted it and gave the law that what was bound on earth would be bound also in heaven,[44] but they who were first released here in the Church could be released there.

But, now, when we see again that the day of another persecution has begun to draw near and we are warned with frequent and constant signs that we should be armed and prepared for the struggle which the enemy is indicating to us, let us prepare with our exhortations the people entrusted to us by the divine condescension and let us assemble all, indeed, of the soldiers of Christ who desire arms and entreat battle within the camp of the Lord. With necessity compelling, we have decided that peace must be given to those who have not withdrawn from the Church of the Lord and have not ceased to do penance and to lament and to pray to the Lord from the first day of their fall, and that they ought to be armed and equipped for the battle which threatens.

(2) For we must conform to signs and just admonitions that the sheep should not be deserted in danger by their shepherds, but that the whole flock should be gathered together in one and the army of the Lord should be armed for the struggle of the heavenly army. For deservedly was the repentance of those who mourned put off for a longer time that help might be

---
44 Cf. Matt. 18.18.

given to the sick at death as long as quiet and tranquillity were present; this would allow us to put off the tears of those who grieved for a time and to give help to those close to dying in sickness. But now, in truth, peace is necessary, not for the sick, but for the strong; nor is Communion to be given by us to the dying but to the living that we should not leave unarmed and naked those whom we stir up and exhort to the battle, but should fortify them with the protection of the Blood and of the Body of Christ. And, since the Eucharist is appointed for this that it may be a safeguard for those receiving, let us arm with the protection of Divine Food those whom we wish to be safe against the adversary. For how do we teach or incite them to shed their blood for the confession of His Name if we deny the Blood of Christ to those who are about to fight? Or how do we make them fit for the chalice of martyrdom if we do not first admit them to drink the Chalice of the Lord in the Church by the right of Communion?

(3) There ought to be a difference, dearly beloved Brother, between those who either have apostatized and, having returned to the world which they had renounced, live as pagans or, having become deserters to the heretics, are daily taking up parricidal arms against the Church and between those who, not departing from the threshold of the Church and imploring continually and sorrowfully the divine solace of the Father also, confess that they are now prepared for the combat both to stand bravely and to fight for the Name of their Lord and for their own salvation.

At this time, we give peace, not to those who sleep, but to those who watch. We give peace, not for easy living, but for arms. We give peace, not for quiet, but for the line of battle. If, according to what we hear and wish and believe, they have stood forth bravely and laid prostrate the adversary with us in the assembly, we shall not repent having given peace so to such brave men. Nay rather, it is the great honor and glory of our episcopate that we have given peace to the martyrs, that we priests who daily celebrate the Sacrifices of God may prepare sacrifices and victims for God. But if—may the Lord avert it from our brethren—anyone of the lapsed should deceive us so as to seek peace by treachery and, in the time of impending battle, to receive Communion not ready to fight, he who conceals one thing in his heart and pronounces another with his voice deceives and tricks himself.

We see the appearance of each one insofar as it is granted to us to see and judge; we cannot scrutinize the heart and look into the mind. The Searcher and Witness of hidden things judges concerning these and He will come quickly and judge of the secret and hidden thoughts of the heart. But the evil ought not harm the good, but rather the evil ought to be aided by the good. Nor, therefore, must peace be denied to those about to undergo martyrdom because some will refuse to undergo it since, for this reason, peace must be given to all who are about to fight lest, through our ignorance, he who is to be crowned in battle should be the first to be passed over.

(4) Let not anyone say: 'He who receives martyrdom is baptized in his own blood and no peace from the bishop is necessary to him who is about to have the peace of his own glory and is about to receive a greater reward from the condescension of the Lord.' First of all, he who is not armed for the battle by the Church cannot be fit for martyrdom and his spirit, which the Eucharist received does not raise up and enkindle, is deficient. For the Lord in His Gospel says: 'But when they deliver you up, do not be anxious what you are to speak; for what you are to speak will be given you in that hour. For it is not you who are speaking, but the Spirit of your Father who speaks through you.'[45] But when He says that the Spirit of the Father speaks in those who are delivered up and set in the confession of His Name, how can he be found prepared or fit for that confession who first, not having received peace, has received the Spirit of the Father, who, strengthening His servants, Himself speaks and confesses in us?

---

45 Cf. Matt. 10.19, 20.

Then, finally, if anyone flees after having abandoned all of his things and, having found himself in hiding and in solitude, perchance falls among robbers or dies from fever or from weakness, will it not be imputed to us that so good a soldier who has left all his belongings and, having cast aside his home and his parents and his children, has preferred to follow his Lord, should die without peace and Communion? Will not either sluggish negligence or harsh cruelty be ascribed to us in the day of judgment because we pastors have not been willing to care for the sheep trusted and committed to us in peace nor to arm them in time of battle?

Would not the charge be brought against us by the Lord which He cries out and says through His prophet: 'Behold, you feed off their milk, and wear their wool and slaughter the fatlings, but the sheep you do not pasture. You did not strengthen the weak, nor heal the sick, nor bind up the injured. You did not bring back the strayed nor seek the lost; you weakened the strong with rigor. And my sheep were scattered, because there were no shepherds. And they became food for all the wild beasts with no one to look after them or to search for them. Thus saith the Lord God: I swear I am coming against these shepherds. And I will claim my sheep from them and put a stop to their shepherding my sheep so that they may no longer pasture themselves. And I will save my sheep from their mouths. And I will shepherd them in judgment.'[46]

(5) Lest, then, the sheep entrusted to us by the Lord be demanded back from our mouth by which we refuse peace, by which we oppose rather the harshness of human cruelty than the spirit of divine and fatherly love, it has seemed best to us, from the suggestion of the Holy Spirit and the warning of the Lord through many and clear visions, because the enemy is announced and shown to be threatening us, to assemble the soldiers of Christ within the camp and, after the case of each has been examined, to give peace to the lapsed,

---

46 Cf. Ezech. 34.3-6; 10-16.

nay rather, to supply arms to those about to fight. We believe that this will please you also in the contemplation of the mercy of the Father.

But if any one of our colleagues remains who thinks that peace should not be given to our brethren and sisters when the struggle is imminent, he will render an account in the day of judgment to the Lord either for his distressing censure or for his inhuman harshness. Because it was fitting to faith and love and solicitude, we made known those things which were in our conscience; the day of battle had approached; the violent enemy was pressing upon us quickly; the battle came not such as it was before, but more serious and graver by far; this was shown frequently to us by divine warning; concerning this we were frequently admonished by the providence and mercy of the Lord; with His help and goodness, we who trust in Him can be safe because He who in peace announces that there will be combat for His soldiers will give the victory to those fighting in union. We trust that you, dearly beloved Brother, are always well.

58. *Cyprian[1] to the people abiding in Thibaris,[2] greeting.*

(1) I had, indeed, thought, dearly beloved Brethren, and I had it in mind, if the condition of affairs and circumstances permitted, according to your frequently expressed desire, to come to you myself and, present there, strengthen the brotherhood with whatever little moderate power of exhortation I could. But since we are detained here by such pressing affairs that opportunity is not given to get away for long from this place and from the people over whom we are placed for a time through the divine favor, in the meantime, I have sent this letter to you as a substitute for me.

For since we are very often stimulated and urged by the

---
1 252 A.D.
2 Thibaris, modern Thibar, the see of Bishop Vincent.

condescension of the Lord instructing, we ought to bring to your knowledge also the solicitude of our exhortation. For you ought to know and to believe for certain and to hold that the day of persecution has begun to be over our heads and that the end of the world and the time of Antichrist have drawn near so that we may all stand ready for the battle and that we may think of nothing except the glory of eternal life and the crown of the confession of the Lord, and that we may not think that such things as are coming are as those things were which have passed. A severer and fiercer combat is now threatening for which, with an incorrupt faith and robust courage, the soldiers of Christ ought to prepare themselves, considering, therefore, that they daily drink the Chalice of the Blood of Christ so that they themselves may also be able to shed their blood for Christ.

For this is to wish to be found with Christ; this is to imitate what Christ taught and did, according to the Apostle John, who says: 'He who says that he abides in Christ, ought himself also to walk just as he walked.'[3] Likewise, the Apostle Paul exhorts and teaches, saying: 'We are sons of God. But if we are sons, we are heirs of God, but joint heirs with Christ, provided, however, we suffer with him that we may also be glorified with him.'[4]

(2) All of these matters must now be considered by us, that no one may desire anything from this already dying world, but may follow Christ, who both lives forever and vivifies His servants established in the faith of His Name. For the time has come, dearly beloved Brethren, which our Lord long ago foretold and taught was coming, saying: 'The hour is coming for everyone who kills you to think that he is offering worship to God. And this they will do because they have not known the Father nor me. But these things I have spoken to you, that when the time for them has come you may remember that I told you.'[5]

---
3 Cf. 1 John 2.6.
4 Cf. Rom. 8.16, 17.
5 Cf. John 16.2-4.

Let not anyone wonder that we are exhausted by unremitting persecutions and frequently driven by overpowering pressures, when the Lord predicted beforehand that these things would be at the end of the world and instructed our army by the teaching and encouragement of His words. Peter, also, His Apostle, taught that there would be persecutions that we might be tested and that we might, according to the just example of the just men who have preceded us, be joined even in death and suffering to the love of God. For he wrote in his Epistle, saying: 'Beloved, do not be startled at the trial by fire happening to you to prove you, nor do not fall away as if something strange were happening to you; but rejoice in all things in so far as you are partakers of the sufferings of Christ, that you may also rejoice in all things, with exultation in the revelation of his glory. If you are upbraided for the name of Christ, blessed will you be, because the name of the majesty and of the power of God rests upon you. That indeed, is blasphemed among them but is honored among us.'[6]

But the apostles taught us those things which they themselves also learned from the precepts of the Lord and from the heavenly commands, with the Lord Himself, indeed, strengthening us and saying: 'There is no one who has left house, or field, or parents, or brothers, or wife, or children, for the sake of the kingdom of God, who shall not receive seven times more in the present time, and in the age to come life everlasting.'[7] And again: 'Blessed,' He says, 'shall you be when men hate you, and when they shut you out, and expel you, and reject your name as evil because of the Son of Man. Rejoice on that day and exult, for behold your reward is great in heaven.'[8]

(3) The Lord wished us to rejoice and to exult in persecutions since, when persecutions are carried on, then crowns of faith are given; then the soldiers of God are tested; then the heavens lie open to the martyrs. For we have not given the

---
6 Cf. 1 Peter 4.12-14.
7 Cf. Luke 18.29, 30.
8 Cf. Luke 6.22, 23.

name to warfare in such a way that we ought to think only of peace and to draw back from and to refuse warfare since the Lord, the Master of humility and of endurance and of suffering, walked first in that very warfare so that, what He taught was to be done, He did first and He, who encourages us to suffer, Himself suffered first for us.

Let it be before your eyes, dearly beloved Brethren, that He, who alone received all judgment from the Father and who will come to judge, has already brought forth the sentence of His judgment and of His future trial, pronouncing and attesting that He will confess before His Father those who confess and that He will deny those who deny. If we could escape death, we might justly fear to die. But since it is necessary for a mortal to die, let us embrace the opportunity coming from the divine promise and condescension and let us go through the exit of death with the reward of immortality; let us for whom it is appointed to be crowned when we are killed not fear to be killed.

(3) Let not anyone be disturbed, dearly beloved Brethren, when he sees our people put to flight and scattered by the fear of persecution, because he does not see the brotherhood gathered together nor hear the bishops deliberating. All who are not allowed to kill but must be killed cannot be together then at the same time. Wherever, in these days, everyone of the brethren shall be separated from the flock, in the meantime as through the necessity of the time, in body, not in spirit, let him not be moved to the horror of this flight or, if he depart and hide, be terrified at the solitude of the desert place. He is not alone to whom Christ is a Companion in flight. He is not alone who, serving the temple of God wherever he may be, is not without God.

And if a robber has overpowered a fugitive in the solitude and in the mountains, if a wild beast has attacked him, if hunger or thirst or cold has afflicted him, or the tempest and storms have submerged him hastening through the seas in a precipitous voyage, Christ everywhere looks upon His soldier who fights because of the persecution for the honor of His Name and gives a reward to him when he dies, as He promised that He would give in the resurrection. Nor is the glory of martyrdom less not to have perished publicly and among many since the reason for perishing is for the sake of Christ. That Witness who approves and crowns martyrs suffices for the testimony of his martyrdom.

(5) Let us imitate, dearly beloved Brethren, the just Abel, who initiated martyrdoms since he was the first to be killed for justice. Let us imitate Abraham, the friend of God, who did not hesitate to offer with his own hands his son as a victim while he obeyed God with the faith of devotion. Let us imitate the three youths, Ananias, Azarias, Misael, who, neither terrified on account of age nor broken by captivity, after Judea had been subdued and Jerusalem captured, overcame the king in his own kingdom by the virtue of their faith. They, ordered to adore the statue which Nabuchodonosor, the king, had made, remained more steadfast than the threats of the king and flames, proclaiming and testifying to their faith in these words: 'King Nabuchodonosor: There is no need for us to defend ourselves before you in this matter. For our God, whom we serve, can save us from the white-hot furnace and he will save us from your hands. And if not, know that we will not serve your gods and worship the golden statue which you set up.'[9] They believed, according to their faith, that they could escape from him, but they added, 'And if not,' that the king might know that they could also die for God, whom they loved.

For this is the strength of virtue and of faith to believe and to know that God can free from present death and yet not to fear death, nor to yield, that faith may be proved more strongly. The incorrupt and invincible vigor of the Holy Spirit burst forth through their mouth that that might appear to be true which the Lord declared in His Gospel, saying: 'But when they deliver you up, do not be anxious what you are to speak; for what you are to speak will be given you in that hour. For it

---
9 Cf. Dan. 3.16-18.

is not you who are speaking, but the Spirit of your Father who speaks through you.'[10] He said that what we are able to speak and to answer is given and offered to us in that hour by Providence, that it is not we who speak but the Spirit of God the Father. Since He does not withdraw or separate from those who confess Him, He Himself both speaks and is crowned in us. And Daniel, thus, when he was being compelled to adore the idol Bel, whom then the people and the king worshiped, in claiming the honor of His God with full faith and liberty, broke forth, saying: 'I worship nothing except the Lord my God, who made heaven and earth.'[11]

(6) What of the oppressive torments of the blessed martyrs in the Machabees and the manifold punishments of the seven brothers and the mother comforting her children in punishments and dying herself also with the children? Do not the documents testify to great virtue and to faith and exhort us by their sufferings to the triumph of martyrdom? What of the prophets whom the Holy Spirit animated to the foreknowledge of the future? What of the apostles whom the Lord chose? When the just are killed on account of justice, have they not also taught us to die? The birth of Christ began immediately with the martyrdoms of the infants that for His Name those who were of two years of age and under were killed. An age not yet fit for battle was fit for the crown. That it might appear that the innocents are they who are killed because of Christ, innocent infancy was destroyed for His Name. It was shown that no one is free from the danger of persecution when even such as these suffered martyrdoms.

How serious a cause is it, in truth, for a servant of a Christian man[12] to be unwilling to suffer since the Lord first suffered, and for us to be unwilling to suffer for our sins since One who had no sin of His own suffered for us! The Son of God suffered that He might make us sons of God, and the son

---
10 Cf. Matt. 10.19, 20.
11 Cf. Dan. 14.4.
12 Hartel, p. 662, *hominis christiani*, but Bayard's *nominis christiani* [of a Christian name] seems more appropriate.

of man does not wish to suffer that he may continue to be a son of God! If we labor in the hatred of the world, Christ first sustained the hatred of the world. If we endure insults in this world, if flight, if torments, the Maker and Lord of this world experienced more serious burdens. He also admonishes us, saying: 'If the world,' He says, 'hates you, remember that it has hated me before you. If you were of the world, the world would love what is its own. But because you are not of the world and I have chosen you out of the world, therefore, the world hates you. Remember the word that I have spoken to you: No servant is greater than his master. If they have persecuted me, they will persecute you also.'[13] Our Lord and God also did whatever He taught so that the disciple who teaches and does not do cannot be excused.

(7) Let not anyone of you, dearly beloved Brethren, be so terrified by the fear of future persecution or the coming of the threatening Antichrist that he may not be found armed for all things by evangelical exhortations and heavenly precepts and warnings. Antichrist comes, but Christ overcomes. The enemy approaches and rages, but immediately the Lord, who will vindicate our sufferings and wounds, follows. The adversary is angry and threatens, but there is One, who can free from his hands. He whose wrath no one can evade is to be feared, Himself forewarning and saying: 'And do not be afraid of those who kill the body but cannot kill the soul. But rather be afraid of him who is able to kill both the body and soul in hell.'[14] And again: 'He who loves his life, loses it; and he who hates his life in this world, will keep it unto life everlasting.'[15] And the Apocalypse instructs and forewarns us saying: 'If anyone worships the beast and its image and receives a mark upon his forehead and upon his hand, he shall also drink of the wine of the wrath of God mixed in the cup of his wrath; and he shall be tormented with fire and brimstone in the sight of the holy angels and in the sight of the Lamb. And the

---

13 Cf. John 15.18-20.
14 Cf. Matt. 10.28.
15 Cf. John 12.25.

smoke of their torments will go up forever and ever; and they will rest neither day nor night, whoever worships the beast and its image.'[16]

(8) Men are tried and prepared for the secular combat and think it great glory of their honor if it happens to them to be crowned with the people looking on and the emperor present. Behold a sublime and a great and a glorious contest for the reward of the heavenly crown, that God looks upon us struggling and, casting His eyes upon those whom He has deigned to make sons, He enjoys the spectacle of our combat. God looks upon us fighting and battling in the assembly of faith; His angels look on, and Christ looks on. How great is the dignity of the glory, how great is the happiness to fight and to be crowned with God as Protector and Christ as Judge?

Let us be armed with all strength, dearly beloved Brethren, and let us be prepared for the struggle with mind incorrupt, faith whole, courage dedicated. Let the camp of God proceed to the line of battle which is indicated to us. Let upright men be armed that the upright may not lose what recently stood; and let lapsed men be armed that the lapsed also may receive back what he has lost. Let honor stimulate the upright; sorrow, the lapsed to battle. The Blessed Apostle teaches us to be armed and prepared, saying: 'For our wrestling is not against flesh and blood, but against the Powers and Principalities of this world and of this darkness, against the spiritual forces of wickedness on high. Therefore, put on complete armor that you may be able to resist in the most evil day, and stand in all things perfect, having girded your loins with truth, and having put on the breastplate of justice, and having your feet shod with the readiness of the gospel of peace, taking up the shield of faith, with which you may be able to quench all the fiery darts of the most wicked one, and the helmet of salvation and the sword of the spirit, that is, the word of God.'[17]

(9) Let us take these arms; let us fortify ourselves with

---
16 Cf. Apoc. 14.9-11.
17 Cf. Eph. 6.12-17.

spiritual and heavenly safeguards that we may be able to fight back and to resist the threats of the devil in that most evil day. Let us put on the breastplate of justice that our heart may be fortified and safe against the darts of the enemy. Let our feet be shod with the teaching of the Gospel and armed so that, when the serpent begins to be trampled upon and crushed by us, he may not be able to bite and throw us down. Let us carry bravely the shield of faith; with this protecting, whatever the enemy throws can be extinguished. Let us receive also a spiritual helmet for the protection of the head that ears may be fortified lest they hear deadly edicts; that eyes be fortified lest they see the detested images; that forehead be fortified that the sign of God may be preserved safe; that mouth be fortified that the victorious tongue may confess its Lord Christ. And let us arm with the sword of the Spirit the right hand that it may bravely reject the deadly sacrifices, that the hand[18] which, mindful of the Eucharist, receives the Body of the Lord may embrace Him, afterward to receive of the Lord the reward of the heavenly crowns.

(10) Oh, what and how great will be that day at its coming, dearly beloved Brethren, when the Lord begins to survey His people and to recognize with the examination of divine knowledge the merits of each individual, to cast into hell evildoers, and to condemn our persecutors with the perpetual fire of the penal flame, to present to us in truth the reward of faith and devotion! What will be the glory and how great will be the joy to be admitted to see God, to be honored to receive the joy of salvation and of the eternal light with Christ the Lord, your God, to greet Abraham and Isaac and Jacob and all of the patriarchs and apostles and prophets and martyrs, to rejoice with the just and with the friends of God

---

18 In the early Church, the priest put the Sacred Host in the right hand of the recipient who kissed it and put it into his own mouth. The faithful carried the Blessed Sacrament to their homes or upon long journeys. In the early days, the communicant could receive from priest, layman, or woman in case of necessity. The First Council of Nicaea required that the reception be from those with power to offer Sacrifice.

in the kingdom of heaven in the delight of immortality bestowed, to receive there what 'eye has not seen nor ear heard, nor has it entered into the heart of man.'[19]

The Apostle foretells that we receive even greater things than we perform or suffer here, saying: 'The sufferings of the present time are not worthy to be compared with the glory to come that will be revealed in us.'[20] When that revelation has come, when the brightness of God has shown round us, we shall be as blessed and joyful honored by the condescension of the Lord as they will remain guilty and miserable who, deserters of God or rebels against God, have done the will of the devil so that it is necessary for them to be tortured together with that one himself in inextinguishable fire.

(11) Let these points remain in your hearts, dearly beloved Brethren. Let this be the preparation of our arms, this our daily and nightly meditation, to have before our eyes and to consider always in our thought and senses the punishments of the wicked and the rewards and merits of the just, what the Lord threatens as punishment to those who deny Him, what He promises, on the contrary, as glory to those who confess Him. If the day of persecution comes upon us thinking and meditating upon these things, the soldier of Christ, trained by His precepts and warnings, does not shrink from the fight, but is prepared for the crown. I trust that you, dearly beloved Brethren, are always well.

59. *Cyprian*[1] *to Cornelius,*[2] *his brother, greeting.*

(1) I read your letter, dearly beloved Brother, which you sent by Saturus,[3] our brother, the acolyte, abundantly full of brotherly love and ecclesiastical discipline and of priestly cen-

---
19 1 Cor. 2.9.
20 Rom. 8.18.

---
1 252 A.D.
2 Cf. Letter 44, n. 2.
3 Cf. Letter 22, n. 36.

sure. In it you indicated that Felicissimus,[4] no new enemy of Christ, but one excommunicated long ago because of his many and most serious crimes and condemned, not only by my judgment, but also by that of very many of our fellow bishops, has been rejected by you there. And when he had come surrounded by a crowd and faction of desperate men, he was driven from the Church with the full vigor with which bishops ought to act. From this he was driven long ago with men like to himself by the majesty of God and by the severity of Christ, our Lord and Judge, lest the author of schism and of discord, the embezzler of money entrusted to him, the violator of virgins, the destroyer and the corrupter of many marriages, further desecrate also by the shame of his presence and by a disgraceful and incestuous contagion the Spouse of Christ, up to now incorrupt, holy, modest.

(2) But, assuredly, after I had read another letter which you added to the first, Brother, I was rather astonished when I had noticed that you were somewhat disturbed by the threats and terrors of those who had come there, when, according to what you wrote, they had approached you with the greatest desperation, threatening that, if you did not receive the letters which they bore, they would publicly read them aloud and would utter many base and ignoble things worthy of their mouth.

But if the matter is thus, dearly beloved Brother, that the boldness of the most wicked is feared and, what evil men cannot accomplish rightly and justly, they may perform with rashness and desperation, there is at stake the vigor of the episcopate and the sublime and divine power of governing the Church. We cannot any longer endure or even be Christians now if it has come to this, that we dread the threats and plots of incorrigible men. For both Gentiles and Jews threaten and heretics and all of those whose hearts and minds the devil has possessed testify daily with furious voice to their poisoned rage. Yet we must not, therefore, yield because they threaten;

---
4 Cf. Letter 41, n. 6.

nor, therefore, is the adversary and the enemy greater than Christ because he claims and assumes so much for himself in the world.

There ought to remain in us, dearly beloved Brother, immovable vigor of faith and stable and unbroken courage against all inroads and attacks of the overwhelming waves as we ought to resist with the firmness and strength of the rock lying in the way. Nor does it matter whence either terror or danger comes to a bishop, who lives exposed to terrors and to dangers and thus becomes glorious from those very terrors and dangers. For we ought not to think of and to look upon the single threats of the Gentiles or Jews when we see that the Lord Himself was hindered by brethren and betrayed by a man whom He Himself had chosen among the apostles, that, also, at the beginning of the world, no one but his brother killed Abel the just, and his hostile brother persecuted Jacob fleeing, and the boy Joseph was sold with his brethren doing the selling. We also read in the Gospel that it was foretold that it would be rather those of one's own household who would be enemies and that those who were first joined by the sacrament of unity would, in turn, betray their own.

It matters nothing who betrays or treats cruelly since God permits one to be betrayed and to be crowned. For it is no ignominy for us to suffer from the brethren what Christ suffered; nor is it glory to them to do what Judas did. But what presumption is theirs, what swelling and inflated and vain boasting is that of the threateners there in my absence to threaten me when here they have me present in their power. We do not fear their outcries with which they daily injure themselves and their own life; we do not dread their clubs and stones and swords which they brandish with parricidal words. As far as it is in them, such men are homicides before God. Yet they cannot kill unless the Lord permits them to kill. And although we all must die once, yet they slay us daily by their hatred and words and crimes.

(3) But not for that reason, dearly beloved Brother, must

ecclesiastical discipline be abandoned or episcopal censure be stilled because we are disturbed by their outcries or we shiver because of their terrors since the Divine Scripture answers and warns, saying: 'But he who presumes and is stiff-necked, a man taking pride in himself, he will accomplish nothing at all who has enlarged his mind like hell.'[5] And again: 'And fear not the words of a sinful man, for his glory will be as dung and worms: Today he is lifted up, and tomorrow he shall not be found, because he is returned into his earth, and his thought will come to nothing.'[6] And again: 'I saw a wicked man exalted and lifted up above the cedars of Libanus. And I passed by, and lo, he was no more; and I sought him, and his place was not found.'[7]

Exaltation and puffing up and arrogant and proud boasting do not spring from the teaching of Christ, who teaches humility, but from the spirit of Antichrist, whom the Lord rebukes through the prophet and says: 'But you said in your heart: "I will scale the heavens; above the stars of God I will set up my throne; I will take my seat in the high mountain over the high mountains in the North. I will ascend above the clouds. I will be like the Most High." '[8] And He added, saying: 'Yet down to the nether world you go to the recesses of the pit! And they that see you, they will stare at you.'[9]

Whence also the Divine Scripture in another place threatens a like punishment to such and says: 'For the day of the Lord of hosts is upon all that is unjust and proud and upon all that is high and lofty.'[10] By his mouth, therefore, and by his words, each one immediately is discovered; and whether he has Christ in his heart or, in truth, Antichrist is revealed in his speaking, according to what the Lord in His Gospel says: 'You brood of vipers, how can you speak good things, when you are evil? For

---

5 Cf. Hab. 2.5.
6 Cf. 1 Mach. 2.62, 63.
7 Cf. Ps. 36.35, 36.
8 Cf. Isa. 14.13, 14.
9 Cf. Isa. 14.15, 16.
10 Cf. Isa. 2.12.

out of the abundance of the heart the mouth speaks. The good man from his good treasure brings forth good things; and the evil man from his evil treasure brings forth evil things.'[11]

Whence also is that rich sinner who implores help from Lazarus, placed in Abraham's bosom and situated in a cool place, while he, destined to be tortured in torments, is burning in the fires of the consuming flame; among all the parts of his body, his mouth and his tongue especially pay the penalty because, perchance, he sinned more by his tongue and by his mouth.

(4) For since it is written: 'The evil-tongued will not possess the kingdom of God,'[12] and again the Lord in His Gospel says: 'Whoever says to his brother, "Raca," and whoever says, "Thou fool," shall be liable to the fire of Gehenna,'[13] how can they evade the censure of the Lord, the Avenger—they who utter lavishly such things not only to their brethren, but to the bishops to whom such great honor is given through the condescension of God—that whoever also did not obey His bishop, who judges here for a time would be immediately killed? In Deuteronomy, the Lord God speaks, saying: 'And any man who has the insolence to refuse to listen to the priest or judge, whoever he may be in those days, that man shall die. ... And all the people on hearing of it, shall fear, and never again be so insolent.'[14]

Likewise, God says to Samuel when he was spurned by the Jews: 'They have not rejected thee, but they have rejected me.'[15] And the Lord also says in the Gospel: 'He who hears you, hears me and him who sent me; and he who rejects you, rejects me and him who sent me.'[16] And when He had cleansed the leper, 'Go,' he said, 'and show thyself to the priest.'[17] And when afterward, at the time of His Passion, He had received

---

11 Matt. 12.34, 35.
12 Cf. 1 Cor. 6.10.
13 Cf. Matt. 5.22.
14 Cf. Deut. 17.12, 13.
15 Cf. 1 Kings 8.7.
16 Cf. Luke 10.16.
17 Cf. Matt. 8.4.

a blow from the servant of the priest and when he had said to Him: 'Is that the way thou dost answer the high priest?'[18] the Lord answered nothing contumeliously against the high priest; nor did He detract at all from the honor of the priest, but asserting and showing rather His own innocence: 'If I have spoken ill,' He said, 'bear witness to the evil; but if well, why dost thou strike me?'[19]

Likewise, in the Acts of the Apostles afterward, the blessed Apostle Paul, when it had been said to him: 'Dost thou attack God's high priest by insulting?'[20] although, with the Lord crucified, these had begun to be sacrilegious and impious and bloodthirsty and no longer retained anything of their priestly honor and authority—yet Paul, thinking of that name itself, although empty and, as one might say, the shadow of the priest, said: 'I did not know, brethren, that he was the high priest; for it is written, "Thou shalt not speak evil of a ruler of thy people." '[21]

(5) When these so great and so many examples are before us in which the sacerdotal authority and power are strengthened by divine condescension, of what sorts do you think that those are who, enemies of the bishops and rebels against the Catholic Church, are terrified neither by the threat of the Lord, who forewarns, nor by the vengeance of the coming judgment? Nor from elsewhere have heresies sprung up nor have schisms been born than from this, that there is no obedience to the bishop of God and no one in the Church is thought to be for the time the bishop and for the time judge in the place of Christ.

If, according to the divine teaching, the whole brotherhood would obey him, no one would ever move against the assembly of bishops; no one, after the divine judgment, after the suffrage of the people, after the consent of the fellow bishops, would make himself judge, not now of the bishops, but of

---
18 John 18.22.
19 John 18.23.
20 Cf. Acts 23.4.
21 Acts 23.5.

God. No one would rend the Church of Christ by the destruction of its unity; no one pleasing himself and boastful would establish a new heresy separately without, unless anyone is of such sacrilegious rashness and of such lost mind as to think that a bishop is made without the judgment of God although the Lord in His Gospel says: 'Are not two sparrows sold for a farthing? And not one of them falls to the ground without your Father's leave.'[22]

Since He says that not the least things are done without the will of God, does anyone think that the highest and greatest things in the Church of God are done without either God's knowledge or permission? And will His bishops, that is, His dispensers, have been ordained without His approval? This is not to have the faith by which we live; this is not to give honor to God at whose nod and will we know and believe that all things are ruled and governed. Undoubtedly, bishops are made without the will of God, but these are they who are made outside of the Church, who are made contrary to the disposition and tradition of the Gospel, as the Lord Himself asserts and says in the Twelve Prophets: 'They made themselves a king, but not by my authority.'[23] And again: 'Their sacrifices will be like mourners' bread: all that eat it will be defiled.'[24] And through Isaia also, the Holy Spirit cries out and says: 'Woe to you, rebellious children; the Lord says these things; you carry out plans that are not mine, and you have an agreement not inspired by me, to add sins upon sins.'[25]

(6) As for the rest—for I speak provoked, I speak grieving, I speak compelled—when a bishop is appointed in the place of one deceased, when he is chosen by the suffrage of the whole people in peace, when He is protected by the help of God in persecution, joined faithfully to all his colleagues, already approved by his people in a four-year episcopate, serving discipline in peace, proscribed in a disturbance, with the name

---
22 Cf. Matt. 10.29.
23 Cf. Osee 8.4.
24 Cf. Osee 9.4.
25 Cf. Isa. 30.1.

of his bishopric attached and added, so many times sought for the lion in the circus, honored in the amphitheater by the testimony of the Lord's condescension, in these very days in which I have written this letter to you, demanded again by the clamor of the people for the lion in the circus on account of the sacrifices which, by the proposed edict, the people were ordered to celebrate; when such a one, dearly beloved Brother, seems to be impugned by certain desperate men both lost and excommunicated from the Church, it is clear who is impugning. It certainly is not Christ, who both appoints and protects priests, but he who is the adversary of Christ and the personal enemy of His Church for this purpose persecutes with his malice the leader of the Church that, when the ruler has been taken away, he may move more atrociously and violently for the shipwreck of the Church.

(7) This ought not, dearly beloved Brother, to disturb any faithful man mindful of the Gospel and retaining the commands of the Apostle, who forewarns, if, in the last days, certain men, proud and contumacious and enemies of the bishops of God, either withdraw from the Church or act against the Church, since both the Lord and His apostles foretold beforehand that there would be such. Nor let anyone wonder that the servant in charge should be deserted by some when His disciples abandoned the Lord Himself, who worked wonders and the greatest miracles and showed forth the virtues of God the Father by the testimony of His deeds. And yet He did not reproach nor gravely threaten those who were leaving, but, rather, having turned to His apostles, said: 'Do you also wish to go away?'[26] respecting, indeed, the law by which a man, left to his own liberty and settled in his own free will, seeks for himself either death or salvation.

Yet Peter, upon whom the Church was established by the same Lord, speaking one for all and answering with the voice of the Church, says: 'Lord, to whom shall we go? Thou hast the word of everlasting life, and we believe and we know that

---
26 John 6.68.

thou art the Christ, the Son of the living God,'[27] signifying, doubtless, and showing that those who withdrew from Christ perished through their own fault; yet the Church, which believes in Christ and which holds that which it has once learned, never withdraws from Him at all, and they who remain in the House of God are the Church. We see that they who are not a plantation planted, in truth, by God the Father are not made firm with the stability of grain, but are as the chaff tossed in the air by the spirit of a scattering enemy; concerning these also John in his Epistle says: 'They have gone forth from us, but they were not of us. For if they had been of us, they would have continued with us.'[28]

Paul also warns us when the evil perish from the Church not to be moved nor to diminish our faith because of treacherous ones who are leaving. 'For what,' he says, 'if some of them have fallen from faith? Will their unbelief make void the fidelity of God? By no means! For God is true, but every man is a liar.'[29]

(8) As for us, it befits our conscience, Brother, to pay attention lest anyone perish from the Church through our fault. But if anyone of his own accord and through his own fault should perish and should be unwilling to do penance and to return to the Church, we who have looked out for his salvation shall be guiltless in the day of judgment; those only who refused to be healed by the salutary nature of our advice shall remain in punishment. The reproaches of the wicked ought not to move us to withdraw from the straight way and from the certain rule since the Apostle instructs, saying: 'If I were trying to please men, I should not be a servant of Christ.'[30] The thing that matters is whether one wishes to be worthy of men or of God. If one pleases men, God is offended. But if we strive for this and labor to be able to please God, we ought to scorn both human reproaches and insults.

27 Cf. John 6.69, 70.
28 1 John 2.19.
29 Cf. Rom. 3.3, 4
30 Cf. Gal. 1.10.

(9) But I did not write immediately to you concerning Fortunatus,[31] that false bishop appointed also by a few inveterate heretics, dearly beloved Brother, because the matter was not such that it ought to be brought to your notice hurriedly at once, as if it were great or dreadful to be endured, especially since you already knew sufficiently the name of Fortunatus. He is one of five priests who long ago fled from the Church and recently were excommunicated by the sentence of many of our fellow bishops, many and most serious men, who wrote letters to you about this affair last year. Likewise, you would recognize Felicissimus, the standard-bearer of sedition, who himself is also included in the same letters of our fellow bishops written to you earlier. He was not only excommunicated by them here, but was recently driven from the Church by you there. Since I was confident that these matters were in your knowledge and I knew, for certain, were fixed in your memory and discipline, I did not think it necessary for the follies of the heretics to be announced to you quickly and urgently. For it ought not to belong to the majesty and, likewise, to the dignity of the Catholic Church that it should be threatened by the audacity of heretics and schismatics in its midst. For the party of Novatian[32] is said also to have made a false bishop there of Maximus,[33] the priest, recently sent to us as a legate by Novatian and now rejected from our communion.

Yet, I had not written to you about this because all these are esteemed lightly by us, and I had sent you recently the names of the bishops appointed here who, upright and sound, are in charge of the brethren in the Catholic Church. We agreed by all means, therefore, to write to you concerning the counsel of us all so that a short way of dissolving error and of seeing the truth might be made and that you and our colleagues might know to whom to write and from whom, in

---
31 Cf. Letter 14, n. 10.
32 Cf. Letter 44, n. 7.
33 Maximus, African lapsed schismatic with Felicissimus, made Novatianist bishop of Carthage.

return, you ought to receive letters. But if anyone except those whom we have included in our letter should dare to write to you, you would know him to be stained either by sacrifice or by a certificate or to be one of the heretics, perverse, doubtless, and profane.

Yet, having found an opportunity through a man of my household and cleric, I wrote to you also concerning this Fortunatus through Felician,[34] the acolyte, whom you had sent with Perseus,[35] our colleague, among other things which had to be brought to your notice from this place. But while this Felician, our brother, was either delayed by the wind or detained by us for receiving other letters, he was outstripped by Felicissimus, hastening to you. For thus always do evil deeds hasten as if to prevail over the innocent by their haste.

(10) But through Felician, I indicated to you, Brother, that Privatus,[36] a heretic of long standing, had come to Carthage into the colony of Lambaesis, fully condemned by the sentence of ninety bishops, also our predecessors, many years previously for many and grave crimes, a fact, also, which, noted most emphatically by the letter of Fabian[37] and Donatus,[38] has not been concealed from your knowledge. When he said he wished to plead his cause before us in the council which we had the last Ides of May and was not admitted, he made that Fortunatus a false bishop for himself worthy of his college.

And a certain Felix,[39] whom he himself had formerly appointed a false bishop outside the Church in heresy, had come there with him also. But Jovinus[40] and Maximus were with

---

34 Felician, an acolyte of Rome sent to Cyprian by Cornelius. His delay in returning to the Pope with the news of the party of Felicissimus was a disadvantage to Cornelius.
35 Perseus, bishop sent from Rome to Carthage with Felician.
36 Cf. Letter 36, n. 3.
37 Cf. Letter 30, n. 3.
38 Donatus, predecessor of Cyprian in see of Carthage, was one of a council of ninety bishops who condemned Privatus of Lambaesis for heresy.
39 Felix, false bishop with Privatus.
40 Jovinus, African lapsed schismatic.

the heretic Privatus as companions, condemned by the sentence of nine of our colleagues on account of the nefarious sacrifices and crimes proved against them and again also excommunicated by many of us in the council last year. Joined with these four, moreover, was Repostus[41] of Sutunurca, who not only fell himself under the persecution, but cast down by sacrilegious persuasion a very great part of his people. These five, with a few either of those who had sacrificed or were conscious of evil in themselves, appointed Fortunatus as a false bishop for themselves that, for crimes agreeing together, the ruler should be such as those who are being ruled.

(11) Hence, you may already know the other lies, also, dearly beloved Brother, which desperate and abandoned men have spread abroad there, that, although from those who had sacrificed or were heretics there were not more than five false bishops who came to Carthage and appointed Fortunatus for themselves an ally of their madness, yet, these very ones, as sons of the devil and full of lying, dared, as you write, to boast that there were twenty-five bishops present. That lie they had spread before here among our brethren saying that twenty-five bishops would come from Numidia to make a bishop for themselves.

After they were detected and confused in this lie of theirs, with only five abandoned men coming together and excommunicated by us, they sailed to Rome with the reward of their lies as if truth could not sail after them to convict their lying tongues by the proof of the certain fact. And this is true madness, Brother, not to think or to know that lies do not deceive for a long time and that the night is only so long as until the day breaks but that, when the day has come in its brightness and the sun has appeared, the darkness and the blackness yield to light and the outrages which are committed during the night cease.

Finally, if you were to ask their names of them, they would

---

41 Repostus, lapsed bishop of Africa, probably of Tuburnuc or Tuburnica, which Hartel lists as Sutunurcensis. Cf. Letter 42, n. 9.

have none or they would name themselves falsely. There is such a scarcity of evildoers among them even that for them not twenty-five can be assembled from those who offered sacrifice or were heretics. And yet, the number is inflated by lying to deceive the ears of the simple and of the absent as though, even if this number were true, either the Church might be conquered by the heretics or justice overcome by the unjust.

(12) Nor is it necessary for me, dearly beloved Brother, to do like things now with them and to mention in my report what they have done up to now and are now doing since we must consider what bishops of God ought to say and to write. Sorrow ought not to speak among us so much as shame and I should not seem provoked to bring together abusive words rather than crimes and sins. I am remaining silent, consequently, about the frauds inflicted upon the Church. I pass over the conspiracies and adulteries and various kinds of sins. Concerning the crime of those men, that one I think should not be concealed in which it is not my cause, nor that of men, but of God, that immediately from the first day of the persecution, when the recent crimes of the delinquents were inflamed and not only the altars of the devil, but even the very hands and mouths of the lapsed were smoking from the unspeakable sacrifices, they did not cease to be in communion with the lapsed and to obstruct the penance to be done.

God cries out: 'Whoever sacrifices to the gods, except to the Lord alone, shall be doomed.'[42] And the Lord in the Gospel says: 'Whoever disowns me, I will disown him.'[43] And in another place, divine indignation and wrath are not silent, saying: 'To these you poured out libations and to these brought offerings. Shall I not be angry at these things? says the Lord.'[44] And they interpose lest God, who Himself testifies that He is angry, be asked! They interpose lest Christ, who confesses that He disowns them who disown Him, be entreated with prayers and satisfactions.

---
42 Cf. Exod. 22.20.
43 Cf. Matt. 10.33.
44 Cf. Isa. 57.6.

(13) In this time of persecution, we have sent letters concerning this very matter and we have not been heard. A council, great in numbers, having been held, we decreed, not only by our agreement, but by our threat that the brethren should do penance, that no one should give peace rashly to those who do not do penance. And those men, sacrilegious against God, reckless with impious fury against the bishops of God, withdrawing from the Church and bearing parricidal arms against the Church, struggle hard that the malice of the devil may achieve its own end lest the Divine Clemency cure the wounded in His Church.

They corrupt the penance of the miserable with the fraud of their lies lest anyone satisfy an offended God, lest anyone who blushed before or feared to be a Christian afterward seek Christ, lest anyone who had gone out from the Church return to the Church. Pains are taken that sins may not be redeemed by just satisfactions and lamentations, that wounds be not washed clean with tears. True peace is taken away with the lie of false peace; the salutary embrace of the mother is shut out by the preventing stepmother lest there be heard from the heart and mouth the weeping and groans of the lapsed.

The lapsed, moreover, are compelled to this to bring insults upon bishops with their tongues and mouth with which they sinned before in the Capitol. They insult with contumelies and malicious voices the confessors and virgins and the just who were especially outstanding in the praise of the faith and glorious in the Church. By them, indeed, not so much do our modesty and humility and uprightness fall as their own hope and life are injured. For it is not he who hears who is miserable but he who gives the insult. It is not he who is struck by a brother but he who strikes a brother who is a sinner in the law. And when the evil are attacking the innocent, they who believe they are inflicting it suffer the injury.

Finally, here their mind is stricken and the spirit sluggish and the sense strange. Not to recognize sins lest penance follow is the wrath of God as it is written: 'And the Lord gave to them the spirit of a deep sleep,'[45] lest they actually return and be cured and be healed by their lamentations and just satisfactions after their sins. The Apostle Paul in his Epistle states and says: 'For they have not received the love of truth that they might be saved. Therefore God will send them a misleading influence that they may believe falsehood, that all may be judged who have not believed the truth, but have preferred wickedness.'[46]

The first degree of felicity is not to sin; the second, to recognize the sins committed. In the former, innocence runs upright and unimpaired to save; in the latter, there follows the remedy to cure. They have lost both of these by offending God in that both the grace which is gained from the sanctification of baptism is lost and the penance through which the fault is cured is not exacted. Or do you think, Brother, that crimes against God are light matters, small and of little moment, because through them the majesty of an offended God is not sought, because the wrath and fire and day of the Lord are not feared, because, with Antichrist at hand, the faith of a militant people is disarmed while vigor and the fear of Christ are taken away?

Let the laity see to it in what way they may be cured. A greater labor falls upon the bishops in serving and in attending to the majesty of God lest we seem to neglect anything in this respect since the Lord admonishes and says: 'And now, O priests, this commandment is for you. If you do not listen, and if you do not lay it to heart, to give glory to my name, says the Lord: I will send a curse upon you, and I will curse your blessing.'[47]

Is honor, therefore, given to God when the majesty and censure of God are despised in such a way that, although He says that He is indignant and angry at those sacrificing and although He threatens eternal punishments and perpetual tor-

---
45 Cf. Isa. 29.10.
46 Cf. 2 Thess. 2.10-12.
47 Cf. Mal. 2.1, 2.

tures, it is proposed by the sacrilegious and also said: 'Let not the wrath of God be considered; let not the judgment of the Lord be feared; let there not be any knocking at the Church of Christ; but, when penance has been taken away and no confession of sin made, when bishops have been despised and cast under foot, let peace be proclaimed by priests with false words and, lest the lapsed rise or those placed without return to the Church, let communion be offered to those not in communion'?

(14) It was not even sufficient for those to have withdrawn from the Gospel, to have taken away the hope of satisfaction and of penance from the lapsed, to have removed from every sense and fruit of penance those involved in fraud or stained with adulteries or polluted by the disastrous contagion of the sacrifices lest they entreat God, lest they make a confession of their crimes in the Church, to have constituted without for themselves outside the Church and against the Church an assembly of a perditious faction in order that there might come together there a mob of those accomplices with themselves and unwilling also to entreat and to satisfy God.

After these things, with a false bishop appointed for themselves by the heretics, they dare to sail and to bring letters from the heretics and blasphemers to the Chair of Peter and to the principal Church whence sacerdotal unity has sprung, and not to think that those are the Romans whose faith was praised by the Apostle preaching; to them perfidy cannot have access. But what was the cause of their coming and announcing that a false bishop had been made against the bishops? Either what they did pleases them and they persevere in their guilt or, if it displeases them and they withdraw, they know whence they should return. For since it was decided by all of us and is equally fair and just that the case of each one be heard there where the crime was committed and that a portion of the flock be entrusted to each pastor which each one should rule and govern, as one who will render an account of his actions to the Lord, those over whom we have charge ought not to be running around or destroying the united harmony of the bishops by their crafty and deceitful rashness, but to plead their case there where they may be able to have both accusers and witnesses of their crime, unless, to a few desperate and abandoned men, the authority of the bishops appointed in Africa, who have already passed judgment upon them and have recently condemned with the gravity of their judgment the conscience of those bound with the many snares of sins, seems too little. The case of these men is now known; sentence has now been passed concerning them. It is not proper that the censure of the bishops be rejected with the lightness of the fickle and inconstant mind since the Lord teaches and says: 'Let your speech be, "Yes, yes:" "No, no." '[48]

(15) If the number of those who judged concerning these last year is computed with priests and deacons, more were then present at the judgment and the trial than are those same ones who now seem to be joined with Fortunatus. For you ought to know, dearly beloved Brother, that he was deserted by almost all immediately after he was made a false bishop by the heretics. For those to whom in the past time deceptions were offered and false words uttered in that they were saying that they were about to return to the Church immediately, after they saw that a false bishop had been made there, learned that they had been tricked and deceived. They are both daily coming and knocking at the Church; yet an account of these must be rendered to the Lord by us anxiously pondering and carefully weighing who ought to be received and admitted to the Church. For either their crimes so prevent some or their brethren so obstinately and firmly fight against them that they cannot be immediately received to the scandal and danger of very many. For some spoiled objects must not be collected in such a way that those which are whole and sound may be infected; nor is the shepherd helpful and experienced who so mingles the diseased and infected sheep with the flock that he contaminates the whole flock with the affliction of the persistent evil. Do not pay attention to their number. For one

---
48 Matt. 5.37.

man fearing God is better than one thousand impious sons, as the Lord spoke through the prophet, saying: 'Son, rejoice not in wicked offspring, many though they be, . . . since they have not the fear of the Lord.'[49]

Oh, if you could, dearly beloved Brother, be with us here when these depraved and perverse men return from schism, you would see what labor I have in persuading patience to our brethren that, calming the sorrow of their souls, they may consent to receiving and caring for the evildoers. For as they rejoice and are glad when those less offensive and less guilty return, so, on the contrary, do they groan and are reluctant as often as the incorrigible and the wanton, and those contaminated either by adulteries or by sacrifices and, after these offenses, are still proud, so return to the Church as to corrupt the good dispositions within. With difficulty I persuade the people, nay rather, extort from them that such be readmitted. And the grief of the brotherhood is made more just from the fact that one and another, in spite of the opposition and of the objection of the people, having been received by my willingness, yet have remained worse than they had been before and that they have not been able to respect the faith of penance because they had not come with true penance.

(16) But what should I say concerning those rascals who, sent as legates by the false bishop Fortunatus, have now sailed to you with Felicissimus, guilty of all crimes, bearing to you letters as false as he himself is false whose letters they bear, as complicated with sins as their conscience, as execrable as their life, as base, so that, although they were in the Church, such men ought to have been excommunicated from the Church?

Finally, since they know their own conscience, they do not dare to come to approach the threshold of the Church, but, without, they run through the province circumventing and defrauding the brethren and, when sufficiently known to all and shut out on all sides because of their evil deeds, they

---
49 Cf. Sir. (Ecclus.) 16.1, 2.

sail there to you also. For they cannot have the face to approach and to take a stand among us since the crimes which are alleged against them by the brethren are most bitter and serious. If they wish to submit to our judgment, let them come. Finally, if there can be any excuse or defense for them, let us see what sense of reparation they have, what fruit of penance they bring.

For the Church here is not closed to anyone; nor is the Bishop refused to anyone. Our patience and willingness and sympathy are ready for those who come to us. I pray that all will return to the Church; I pray that all of our fellow soldiers will be enclosed together within the camp of Christ and the abode of God the Father. I pardon all things. I ignore many things in the zeal and pledge of gathering together the brotherhood. Even those things which have been committed against God, I examine not with the full judgment of religion. I myself am almost negligent in remitting sins much more than I ought. I embrace with prompt and full love those returning with repentance, confessing their sin with simple and humble satisfaction.

(17) But if there are any who think that they can return to the Church without prayers, but with threats, or think that they can make an entrance for themselves, not by lamentations and reparations, but by terrors, let them certainly consider that the Church of the Lord remains closed against such and that the camp of Christ, invincible and brave and fortified by the protecting Lord, does not yield to threats. The bishop of God, holding the Gospel, can be killed as observing the precepts of Christ; he cannot be conquered.

Zacharia, the high priest of God, suggests and gives to us examples of virtue and of faith. When he could not be terrified by threats and stoning, he was killed in the temple of God, crying out and saying the same thing which we shout also against heretics and say: 'Thus saith the Lord: You have forsaken the ways of the Lord and the Lord will forsake you.'[50]

---
50 Cf. 2 Par. 24.20.

For, because a few rash and wicked man have abandoned the heavenly and life-giving ways of the Lord and are cast aside by the Holy Spirit for not doing holy things, we ought not, therefore, to be unmindful of the divine tradition that we should believe that the crimes of the madmen are greater than the judgments of the bishops or that we should think human efforts can prevail more in resisting than Divine Protection prevails in protecting.

(18) Is it for this, dearly beloved Brother, that the dignity of the Catholic Church must be set aside and the faithful and incorrupt majesty of the people placed within and also the episcopal authority and power, that heretics appointed without the Church should say that they wish to judge concerning a bishop of the Church; the wounded, concerning the healthy; the injured, concerning the whole; the lapsed, concerning the upright; the guilty, concerning the judge; the sacrilegious, concerning the bishop? What more remains than for the Church to yield to the Capitol and, when the bishops withdraw and remove the altar of the Lord, for statues and idols with their altars to pass over into the sacred and venerated assembly of our clergy and for a greater and fuller opportunity of declaiming against us and of rebuking to be offered to Novatian if those who have sacrificed and denied Christ publicly are asked and admitted not only without acts of penance, but, in addition, have even begun to dominate by the power of their terror?

If they demand peace, let them put aside their arms. If they are making satisfaction, why should they threaten? Or if they threaten, let them know that they are not feared by the bishops of God. And not even when Antichrist has begun to come, will he enter the Church because he is threatening or will it yield to his arms and violence because he declares publicly that he will carry off those who resist. The heretics arm us while they think that we are terrified by their threat; nor do they cast us on our faces, but rather they lift up and inflame while they make peace itself worse than persecution for the brethren. And we wish, indeed, that they may not fill up with the crime of which they speak in their madness lest those who sin with perfidious and cruel words also sin in deeds. We pray and we entreat God, whom those men do not cease to provoke and exasperate, that they may soften their hearts, that they may return to health of mind when this madness has been put aside, that their hearts, filled with the darkness of sin, may recognize the light of repentance and that they may rather seek that the intercession and prayers of the bishop be poured out for themselves than that they themselves shed the blood of the bishop.

But if they remain in their madness and persevere cruelly in these threats and parricidal plots of theirs, no bishop of God is so infirm, so low and abject, so weak with the madness of human mediocrity that he will not struggle, with the divine assistance, against God's enemies and adversaries, whose humility and weakness will not be animated by the vigor and strength of the protecting Lord. It makes no difference to us either by whom or when we perish, we who are destined to receive the reward for our death and blood from the Lord; their condition is to be bewailed and lamented whom the devil so blinds that, not thinking of the eternal tortures of hell, they attempt to imitate the coming of the Antichrist who is already drawing near.

(19) And although I know, dearly beloved Brother, that from the mutual love which we owe and entertain for each other, you always read my letters to that most exemplary clergy remaining with you and to that very holy and very great number of the people, yet, I now advise and beg you to do at my request what you have always done with the others willingly and honorably that, after this my letter has been read, if any contagion of poisoned speech and wicked sowing has crept in, it may be cast out from the ears and hearts of the brethren, and an upright and sincere love may be cleansed from all the sordid stains of heretical detraction.

(20) For the rest, let our dearly beloved brethren shun

bravely and avoid the words and speech of those 'whose speech spreads like a cancer,'[51] as the Apostle says: 'Evil companionships corrupt good morals,'[52] and again: 'A factious man avoid after one admonition, knowing that such a one is perverted and sins and is self-condemned.'[53] And the Holy Spirit speaks through Solomon: 'A scoundrel,' he says, 'carries evil in his mouth and on his lips he builds a scorching fire.'[54] Likewise, he warns again, saying: 'Hedge round your ears with thorns; hear not a wicked tongue.'[55] And again: 'The evil man gives heed to the language of the wicked; but the just man does not hearken to lying lips.'[56]

Although I know that our brotherhood there, certainly fortified by your providence and sufficiently cautious because of its own vigilance, cannot be taken nor deceived by the poisons of the heretics, so much do the divine teachings and precepts prevail among them according as the fear of the Lord is in them, yet, from our abundance, either our solicitude or our charity urged me to write these things to you lest they have any business with such men, lest they mingle with the evil for any entertainments or talks; and let us be as separated from them as they are fled from the Church since it is written: 'But if he despise the Church, let him be to thee as the heathen and the publican.'[57]

And the blessed Apostle not so much warns us, but he orders us to withdraw from such: 'And we charge you,' he says, 'in the name of our Lord Jesus Christ, to withdraw yourselves from every brother who lives irregularly, and not according to the tradition which they have received from us.'[58] There can be no fellowship between faith and perfidy. He who is not with Christ, who is an adversary of Christ, who is

---
51 Cf. 2 Tim. 2.17.
52 1 Cor. 15.33.
53 Cf. Titus 3.11.
54 Cf. Prov. 16.27.
55 Cf. Sir. (Ecclus.) 28.24.
56 Cf. Prov. 17.4.
57 Cf. Matt. 18.17.
58 Cf. 2 Thess. 3.6.

an enemy of His unity and peace, cannot be united with us. If they come with prayers and reparations, let them be heard. If they assail with curses and threats, let them be rejected. I trust that you, dearly beloved Brother, are always well.

60. *Cyprian*[1] *to Cornelius,*[2] *his brother, greeting.*

(1) We have learned, dearly beloved Brother, the glorious testimonies of your faith and virtue and we have received the honor of your confession so exultingly that we think ourselves also sharers and allies in your merits and praises. For, since we have one Church and a united mind and indivisible concord, what bishop does not exult in the praises of his fellow bishop as if they were his own or what brotherhood everywhere does not rejoice in the joy of its brethren?

It cannot be adequately expressed how great was the exultation here and how great was the joy when we had learned such favorable and enduring news about you that you had stood forth as a leader of confession for the brethren there and also that the confession of the leader had increased from the agreement of the brethren; that, while you precede to glory, you have made many companions of glory and you have persuaded the people to become confessors while you were first prepared to confess for all, so that we do not find what we ought first to praise in you, whether your prompt and stable faith or your inseparable love of the brethren. The courage of the bishop who leads the way is publicly approved; the unity of the brethren who follow has been shown. While among you there is one mind and one voice, the whole Roman Church has confessed.

(2) The faith which the blessed Apostle foretold of you, dearly beloved Brother, has shone brightly. He even then foresaw in spirit this praise of courage and firmness of strength

---
[1] 252 A.D.
[2] Cf. Letter 44, n. 2.

and, testifying to your merits with the commendation of future deeds, while in praising the parents, he challenges the sons. While you are so unanimous, while you are brave, you have given great examples of unity and strength to the rest of the brethren. You have taught mightily to fear God, firmly to adhere to Christ; you have taught the people to be joined to their bishops in danger, brethren not to be separated from brethren in persecution, that a united harmony not only can in no way be overcome but, at the same time, whatever is asked by all, the God of peace grants to peacemakers.

The adversary had sprung forth to disturb the camp of Christ by violent terror. But with the same force by which he had come, by the same force was he repulsed and he found as much bravery and strength as he had brought fear and terror. He had believed that he could again supplant the servants of God and, according to his usual custom, strike them as beginners and unskilled as if less prepared and less cautious. Having attacked one at first, he had attempted, as the wolf, to separate a sheep from the flock, as the hawk, to separate a dove from the line of those flying, for he who has not sufficient strength against all seeks to circumvent the solitude of individuals. But, beaten back by the faith and, likewise, by the vigor of the united army, he has learned that the soldiers of Christ are on the watch, that they already stand serious and armed for the combat, that they cannot be conquered, that they are able to die, and that, in this very matter, they are invincible because they do not fear to die. They do not even fight against those who are attacking since it is not granted to the innocent to kill even the aggressor, but promptly to deliver up their souls and blood that, since so much malice and cruelty are rampant in the world, they may more quickly withdraw from the malicious and the cruel.

What a glorious spectacle in the eyes of God was that, what a joy of His Church in the sight of His Christ that, not individual soldiers, but the whole camp went forth at once for that fight which the enemy had attempted to bring! For it is evident that all would have come if they could have heard since everyone who heard came hastening and rushed up. How many of the lapsed were there restored by a glorious confession! The brave remained standing and, with the very sorrow of penance, were made stronger for the battle so that it appeared that those who had been recently agitated and had trembled with fear of the new and unaccustomed thing returned to themselves afterwards. They strengthened their true faith and strength based upon the fear of God constantly and firmly for all suffering; no longer do they stand for the pardon of crime, but for a crown for their suffering.

(3) What does Novatian[3] say to these things, dearly beloved Brother? Does he now lay aside his error? Or rather, as it is the custom of madmen, by our very good deeds and fortunes has he become more inflamed to fury? And the greater and greater the glory of faith and love grow here, does the madness of his zeal and dissension break out more violently there? Does the wretched man not cure his wound but, in addition, does he wound both himself and his followers more seriously making noise with his tongue to the danger of his brethren and hurling the darts of his poisoned eloquence, hard rather with the depravity of secular philosophy than peaceful with the gentleness of divine wisdom, a deserter of the Church, an enemy of mercy, a killer of penance, a teacher of pride, a corrupter of truth, a destroyer of charity?

Does he recognize now who is a bishop of God, what is the Church and home of Christ, who are the servants of God whom the devil has infested, who are the Christians whom Antichrist impugns? For he does not seek those whom he has already subdued or delighted to destroy, those whom he has long made his own. The enemy and foe of the Church despises and ignores as captives and slaves those whom he has led out and alienated from the Church. He continues to challenge those in whom he sees that Christ lives.

(4) And yet even if anyone of such men should be arrested,

---
3 Cf. Letter 44, n. 7.

it is not as if he should be enticed into the confession of the Name since it is evident, if such were killed outside the Church, there would not be the crown of faith, but rather the punishment of treachery; they would not live among the united in the House of God who, we see, have withdrawn from the peaceful and divine home in the fury of discord.

(5) We exhort you openly as much as we can, dearly beloved Brother, in the mutual charity with which we cling to one another that, since we are instructed by the providence of the Lord warning us and are admonished by the salutary counsels of the divine mercy that our day of struggle and of agony is approaching, we should not cease to be present with daily fastings and prayers with all of the people. Let us apply ourselves to unceasing lamentations and frequent intercessions. For these are our heavenly arms which enable us to remain steadfast and to persevere bravely; these are the spiritual defenses and the divine weapons which protect.

Let us be mindful of each other in turn, agreeing and united, and, on both sides, let us always pray for each other. Let us relieve burdens and anxieties with mutual charity and, if one of us should die first according to a swiftness decreed by the divine condescension, let our love persevere in the presence of the Lord and let not prayer for our brethren and sisters cease before the mercy of the Father. I trust that you, dearly beloved Brother, are always well.

61. *Cyprian[1] with his colleagues to Lucius,[2] his brother, greeting.*

(1) And recently, indeed, we congratulated you, dearly beloved Brother, when the divine condescension appointed you for the double honor of confessor, likewise, and of bishop in

---
1 253 A.D.
2 Lucius, Pope after Cornelius from c. June 25, 253 to c. March 5, 254, maintained views of Cornelius and Cyprian on the lapsed.

the administration of His Church. But now no less do we congratulate you and your companions and the whole brotherhood because the benign and abundant protection of the Lord has brought it about that you return to His people finally with the same glory and with your praises that the shepherd might be returned to feed the flock, and the pilot to govern the ship, and the ruler to rule the people, and that it might appear that your banishment was so arranged according to the divine plan, not that a bishop, banished and driven away, should be wanting to the Church, but that he should return to the Church greater.

(2) For there was not less dignity of martyrdom in the three youths because, when death had been frustrated, they came forth safe from the fiery furnace,[3] or Daniel, because he who had been cast to the lions for booty, not consumed, remained in his praises, lived protected by the Lord for glory.[4] Among the confessors of Christ, martyrdoms deferred do not lessen the merit of confession, but show the greatness of the divine protection. We see represented in you what the brave and illustrious youths preached in the presence of the king: that they were prepared, indeed, to burn in the flames rather than serve his gods or adore the image which he had made, yet that God, whom they worshiped and whom we also worship, was powerful to draw them out of the furnace of fire and free them from the hands of the king and from present punishments.

We find this now accomplished in the faith of your confession and in the protection of the Lord in your behalf that, when you were prepared and ready to undergo all torment, yet the Lord withdrew you from punishment and preserved you for the Church. The dignity of his confession has not decreased for the bishop in your return but rather the episcopal authority has increased that there may attend the altar of God a bishop who exhorts his people, not by words but by deeds, to

---
3 Cf. Dan. 3.
4 Cf. Dan. 6.

undertake the arms of confession and to accept martyrdom, and, with Antichrist imminent, prepares soldiers for battle, not alone by the incitement of his voice and words, but by the example of his faith and virtue.

(3) We know, dearly beloved Brother, and with the whole light of our heart we perceive the salutary and holy counsels of the divine Majesty, whence the sudden persecution recently sprang up there, whence the secular power suddenly broke forth against the Church of Christ, Bishop Cornelius,[5] the blessed martyr, and all of you, that, for confounding and repressing the heretics, the Lord might show what the Church is, what one bishop is His, chosen by the divine ordination, what priests were joined with the bishop in the sacerdotal honor, what united and true people of Christ were joined with the love of the flock of the Lord, who were those whom the enemy would torture, and, on the contrary, who were those whom the devil would spare as his own. For the adversary of Christ does not follow or attack any but the camp and soldiers of Christ. He despises and passes over the heretics once prostrate and made his own; he seeks to cast down those whom he sees to be standing.

(4) And would that the opportunity were now given, dearly beloved Brother, that we who love you with mutual charity might be present there at your return so that we ourselves also might share, present with the others, the most joyful fruit of your coming. What will be the exultation of all of the brethren there! What will be the meeting and embracing of all of the individuals meeting together! Scarcely will the mouths of those embracing be satisfied with kisses; scarcely will the faces and eyes of the people be satiated with seeing in the joy of your arrival! The brotherhood there is beginning to realize of what nature and how great is the joy which will follow with Christ coming. Because His coming has quickly approached, a certain foreshadowing of it has already gone before among you that, as John, His percursor and herald, com-

---

5 Cf. Letter 44, n. 2.

ing ahead preached that Christ had come, so now, with the bishop returning as confessor and priest of the Lord, it appears as if the Lord also is returning.

My colleagues and I and all of the brotherhood send this letter to you for us in our place, dearly beloved Brother, and, expressing our joy to you through a letter, we show forth the faithful allegiance of love, here also in our sacrifices and in our prayers not ceasing to give thanks to God the Father and to Christ, His Son, our Lord, and likewise to pray and to beseech that He, who has brought this about and is perfecting it, may guard you doing His work and accomplish in you the glorious crown of your confession. And He has perhaps brought you back for this, lest your glory remain hidden if the martyrdom of your confession had been consummated in exile. For the victim which offers to the brotherhood an example of courage and of faith ought to be immolated in the presence of the brethren. We trust that you, dearly beloved Brother, are always well.

62. *Cyprian[1] to Januarius,[2] Maximus,[3] Proculus,[4] Victor,[5] Modianus,[6] Nemesianus,[7] Nampulus,[8] and Honoratus,[9] his brethren, greeting.*

(1) With the greatest groaning of our spirit and not without tears, we have read your letter, dearly beloved Brethren, which, because of the solicitude of your love, you sent to us concern-

---

1 253 A.D.
2 Januarius, one of eight Numidian bishops to whom Cyprian sends aid for captive Christians in 253, probably bishop of Lambaesis, successor of deposed Privatus.
3 Maximus, Numidian bishop.
4 Proculus, Numidian bishop.
5 Cf. Letter 4, n. 3, and Letter 57, n. 12. This Victor is probably bishop of Octavum.
6 Modianus, Numidian bishop.
7 Nemesianus, bishop of Thubunae, one of the nine sent into the mines in Sigua and commemorated as martyrs in Africa.
8 Nampulus, Numidian bishop.
9 Honoratus, Numidian bishop.

ing the captivity of our brethren and sisters. For who would not grieve in cases of this nature or who would not consider the sorrow of his brother as his own since the Apostle Paul speaks and says: 'If one member suffers, the other members also suffer, and if one member glories, the other members also rejoice.'[10] And in another place he says: 'Who is weak and I am not weak?'[11] Wherefore now also the captivity of our brethren must be thought of as our captivity and the sorrow of those in danger must be accounted as our sorrow since, you may be sure, there is one body of our unity; and, not only love, but also religion ought to incite us and to encourage us to redeem the members of our brethren.

(2) For since the Apostle Paul says a second time: 'Do you not know that you are the temple of God and that the Spirit of God dwells in you?'[12] even though charity impelled us not at all to bring assistance to the brethren, yet we must consider in this place that it was the temples of God which were captured and that we ought not by long delay and neglect of their sorrow to allow the temples of God to be captured for a long time, but to work with the strength which we can and to bring it about speedily by our obedience that we may be deserving of Christ, our Judge and our Lord God. For since the Apostle Paul says: 'As many of you as have been baptized into Christ, have put on Christ,'[13] Christ must be contemplated in our captured brethren and He, who redeemed us from the danger of death, must be redeemed from the danger of captivity, that He, who delivered us from the jaws of the devil, now Himself, who remains and dwells among us, who redeemed us by the Cross and Blood, must be delivered from the hands of barbarians and redeemed by a sum of money. He, therefore, allows these things to be done in the meantime that our faith may be tried as to whether each one of us would do

---

10 Cf. 1 Cor. 12.26.
11 2 Cor. 11.29.
12 1 Cor. 3.16.
13 Cf. Gal. 3.27.

for another what he would wish to be done for himself if he himself were held captive among the barbarians.

For who would not, mindful of humanity and urged by mutual love, if he is a father, think that his sons are now there; if he is a husband, consider, with sorrow equally and love of marriage bond, his wife held captive there? How great truly is the common grief and torture for all of us at the danger of the virgins who are held there, for whom we should lament not so much the loss of their freedom as that of their honor? Nor must we weep over the chains of the barbarians so much as the defilements of the seducers and of the brothels, lest members dedicated to Christ and devoted to the eternal honor of continence should be stained in their modest virtue by the contagion of the lust of those insulting them.

(3) Our brotherhood here, thinking over all of those matters according to your letter and sorrowfully examining them, all promptly and freely and generously have collected a sum of money for the brethren, always, indeed, eager for the work of God according to the strength of their faith, now aroused so much the more to the salutary work by the contemplation of so great sorrow. For since the Lord in His Gospel says: 'I was sick and you visited me,'[14] with how much greater reward for our work will He say: 'I was a captive and you redeemed me.' And since He says again: 'I was in prison and you came to me,'[15] how much more is it when He begins to say: 'I was in the prison of captivity and, shut up and bound among the barbarians, I was prostrate and from that prison of servitude you freed me,' you who will receive a reward from the Lord when the day of judgment comes.

Finally, we give greatest thanks to you because you wished us to be sharers of your solicitude and of so good and necessary a work that you offered to us fertile fields in which to cast the seeds of our hope, expecting the harvest of most abundant fruits which accrue from this heavenly and salutary operation.

---
14 Cf. Matt. 25.36.
15 Cf. *ibid.*

But we have sent one hundred thousand sesterces, which have been collected here in the Church over which, by the favor of the Lord, we preside, from a collection of the clergy and people residing among us, which you will dispense there according to your diligence.

(4) And we pray, indeed, that nothing like that may happen in the future and that our brethren, protected by the majesty of the Lord, may be kept safe from perils of this nature. Yet if, to test the love of our spirit and to try the faith of our heart, something like that should happen, do not hesitate to tell us about it in your letters, considering it certain and knowing that our Church and the whole brotherhood here are begging with prayers that such a thing may not happen again. If it does happen, willingly and generously will they bestow assistance. But that you may have in mind in your prayers our brethren and sisters who have promptly and willingly contributed to this so necessary work that they may always work and that you, in return, may intercede for them in the sacrifices and prayers of good work, I have supplied the names of each. And I have also added the names of our colleagues and of our bishops, who, when they were also themselves then present, contributed according to their resources in their own name and that of their people. And besides I have also indicated and sent our own amount and their small sums. You ought to remember in your prayers and orations all of these according to what faith and charity demand. We trust that you, dearly beloved Brethren, are always well in the Lord and mindful of us.

63. Cyprian[1] to brother Cecil,[2] greeting.

(1) Although I know, dearly beloved Brother, that very many bishops placed by the divine condescension in charge of

---
1 253 A.D.
2 Cf. Letter 4, n. 2.

the Churches of the Lord in the whole world keep the order of evangelical truth and of the tradition of the Lord and do not depart by human and novel institution from that which Christ, the Master, both taught and did, yet since certain ones, either through ignorance or through simplicity, in consecrating the Chalice of the Lord and in ministering to the people, do not do that which Jesus Christ, our Lord and God, the Author and Teacher of this Sacrifice, did and taught, I consider it a matter of obligation and necessity as well to write to you a letter concerning this that, if anyone is still held captive in this error, when he has the light of truth, he may return to the root and origin of the tradition of the Lord.

Do not think, dearly beloved Brother, that we thus boldly presume, of our own human will or that of another, to write to you since we consider always with humble and modest moderation our own mediocrity. But when something is clearly prescribed by God's inspiration and command, it is necessary for the faithful servant to obey the Lord, excused by all because he who is compelled to fear an offense for the Lord unless he does what he is commanded is assuming nothing arrogantly to himself.

(2) But know that we have been warned in offering the Chalice that the tradition of the Lord must be observed and that nothing should be done otherwise by us than what the Lord first did for us, that the Chalice which is offered in His Commemoration should be offered mixed with wine. For when Christ says: 'I am the true vine,'[3] the Blood of Christ is, indeed, not water, but wine. Nor can His Blood, by which we are redeemed and vivified, which is foretold by the testimony and pledge of all of the Scriptures, be seen to be in the Chalice when wine, wherein the Blood of Christ is shown, is wanting to the Chalice.

(3) For we find, also, in Genesis concerning the sacrament that Noe anticipated this same thing and projected the figure of the Passion of the Lord there because he drank wine, be-

---
3 John 15.1.

cause he was inebriated, because he was made naked in his home, because he was reclining with his thighs naked and exposed, because that nakedness of the father was noticed by his second son and reported outside, but covered by the other two, the oldest and the youngest, and other things which it is not necessary to follow up since it is sufficient to comprehend this alone: that Noe, showing forth a type of future truth, drank not water, but wine, and so expressed the figure of the Passion of the Lord.[4]

(4) Likewise, in the priest Melchisedec, we see the Sacrament of the Sacrifice of the Lord prefigured according to what the Divine Scripture testifies and says: 'And Melchisedec, the king of Salem, brought out bread and wine, for he was a priest of the most high God and he blessed Abraham.'[5] But that Melchisedec portrayed a type of Christ, the Holy Spirit declares in the Psalms, saying in the Person of the Father to the Son: 'Before the day star . . . I have begotten you. . . . You are a priest forever according to the order of Melchisedec.'[6] This order, indeed, is this coming from that sacrifice and thence descending because Melchisedec was a priest of the most high God, because he offered bread, because he blessed Abraham. For who is more a priest of the most high God than our Lord Jesus Christ, who offered Sacrifice to God the Father and offered the very same thing which Melchisedec had offered, bread and wine, that is, actually, His Body and Blood.

And with respect to Abraham, that blessing going before extended to our people. For if Abraham believed God and it was imputed to him for justice, whoever, assuredly, believes in God and lives by faith is found a just man and is shown blessed already in the faithful Abraham and justified as the blessed Apostle Paul proves, saying: ' "Abraham believed God, and it was credited to him as justice." You know, therefore, that they who are of faith are the sons of Abraham. But the

---

4 Cf. Gen. 9.20-27.
5 Cf. Gen. 14.18, 19.
6 Ps. 109.3, 4.

Scriptures, foreseeing that God would justify the Gentiles by faith, announced to Abraham beforehand that all the nations would be blessed in him. Therefore, those who are of faith are blessed with faithful Abraham.'[7] Whence in the Gospel we find that sons are raised to Abraham from stones, that is, collected from the Gentiles.[8] And when the Lord praised Zachaeus, He answered and said: 'Today salvation has come to this house, since he, too, is a son of Abraham.'[9]

That, therefore, in Genesis through the priest Melchisedec the blessing should be ceremoniously celebrated in respect to Abraham, the image of the sacrifice goes before, appointed actually in the bread and wine. Accomplishing and fulfilling this action, the Lord offered bread and a chalice mixed with wine and He, who is the Plenitude, fulfilled the truth of the prefigured image.

(5) But also the Holy Spirit through Solomon shows forth the type of the Sacrifice of the Lord, making mention of the Immolated Victim and of the bread and wine and also of the altar and of the apostles. 'Wisdom,' he says, 'has built a house and she has set up seven columns. She has slain her victims, mixed her wine in a chalice, and has spread her table. And she has sent her servants, inviting with the highest commendation to the chalice, saying: "Let whoever is simple turn in to me; and to those who lack understanding, she said: 'Come and eat of my food, and drink the wine which I have mixed for you.' " '[10] He declares the wine is mixed, that is, he announces in a prophetic voice that the Chalice of the Lord is mixed with water and wine, that it may appear that what had been foretold before was accomplished in the Passion of the Lord.

(6) In the blessing of Juda, also, this same thing is signified when the figure of Christ is also expressed there that He should have to be praised and adored by his brethren, that He should press down the backs of enemies departing and

---
7 Cf. Gal. 3.6-9.
8 Cf. Matt. 3.9.
9 Luke 19.9.
10 Cf. Prov. 9.1-5.

fleeing, with the hands with which He bore the cross and conquered death, and that He Himself is the Lion of the tribe of Juda and reclines sleeping in His Passion and arises and is Himself the Hope of the Gentiles. To these things, the Divine Scripture adds and says: 'He shall wash his garment in wine and his robe in the blood of the grape.'[11] But when the blood of the grape is mentioned, what else is shown forth but the wine of the Chalice, the Blood of the Lord?

(7) And does not, also, the Holy Spirit, speaking in Isaia, testify this same thing concerning the Passion of the Lord, saying: 'Why are your vestments red and your garments as from treading the wine press full and well-trodden?'[12] For can water make vestments red or is it water which is trodden by the feet in the wine press or forced out by the press? The mention of wine is placed there, indeed, that in the wine the Blood of the Lord may be known and that which was afterward manifested in the Chalice of the Lord might be foretold by the prophets who announced it. The treading and pressing of the wine press are also spoken of since wine cannot be prepared for drinking in any other way unless the cluster of grapes is first trodden and pressed. Thus, we could not drink the Blood of Christ unless Christ had first been trodden upon and pressed and unless He had first drunk the Chalice by which He should drink to the believers.

(8) But as often as water alone is named in the Holy Scriptures, baptism is preached as we see signified in Isaia. 'Remember not the events of the past,' he says, 'the things of long ago consider not; see, I am doing new things which now will spring forth and you will know them. In the desert I make a way, in the wasteland, rivers . . . for my chosen people to drink, my people whom I won that they might announce my virtues.'[13] God announced there through the prophet that among the Gentiles, in places which before had been without

---
11 Cf. Gen. 49.11.
12 Cf. Isa. 63.2.
13 Cf. Isa. 43.18-21.

water, rivers should afterwards abound and should provide water for the elect people of God, that is, those made the sons of God through the regeneration of baptism.

Likewise, again, it is foretold and predicted before that the Jews, if they should thirst and seek Christ, would drink among us, that is, they would obtain the grace of baptism. 'If they have thirsted,' he said, 'in the deserts, he will give them water; he will bring forth water out of the rock for them, and the rock will be split and the water will gush out, and my people will drink.'[14] This is fulfilled in the Gospel when Christ, who is the Rock, is pierced by the blow of the lance in His Passion. And He, indeed, warning us again of what was before predicted by the prophet, cries out and says: 'If anyone thirst, let him come and drink. He who believes in me, as the Scripture says, "From within him there shall flow rivers of living water." '[15]

And that it might be the more manifest that the Lord is speaking there not of the Chalice, but of baptism, Scripture adds, saying: 'He said this, however, of the Spirit whom they who believed in him were to receive.'[16] But through baptism the Holy Spirit is received and thus, to the baptized and to those who have received the Holy Spirit, it is granted to drink the Chalice of the Lord. But let it disturb no one that, when the Divine Scripture is speaking of baptism, it says that we are thirsty and we drink since the Lord also in the Gospel says: 'Blessed are they who thirst and hunger for justice,'[17] because what is received with an avid and thirsty desire is drunk more fully and profitably. Likewise, in another place, the Lord speaks to the Samaritan woman, saying: 'Everyone who drinks of this water will thirst again. He, however, who drinks of the water that I will give shall never thirst.'[18] And by this, indeed, is signified the baptism of the saving water,

---
14 Cf. Isa. 48.21.
15 Cf. John 7.37, 38.
16 John 7.39.
17 Cf. Matt. 5.6.
18 John 4.13, 14.

which once it is received, assuredly, is not repeated; as for the rest, the Chalice of the Lord is always both thirsted for and drunk in the Church.

(9) There is no need for very many arguments, dearly beloved Brother, to prove that baptism is signified always by the appellation of water and, thus, we ought to know since the Lord, when He came, manifested the truth of baptism and of the Chalice; He taught that faithful water, the water of everlasting life, is given in baptism to the believers; He taught, in truth, by the example of His teaching power that the Chalice is mingled with the union of wine and of water. For taking the Chalice on the day of His Passion, He blessed it and gave it to His Disciples, saying: 'All of you drink of this; for this is the blood of the covenant, which is being shed for many unto the forgiveness of sins. I say to you, I will not drink henceforth of this fruit of the vine, until that day when I shall drink it new with you in the kingdom of my Father.'[19] In this part, we find that the Chalice which the Lord offered was mixed and that He called Blood what had been wine.

Whence it appears that the Blood of Christ is not offered if wine is lacking in the Chalice and that the Sacrifice of the Lord is not celebrated with lawful sanctification unless the Oblation and our Sacrifice correspond to the Passion. But in what way shall we drink the new wine of the creature of the vine with Christ in the kingdom of the Father if we do not offer the wine of Christ in the Sacrifice of God the Father and do not mingle the Chalice of the Lord according to the teaching of the Lord?

(10) The blessed Apostle Paul, moreover, elected by God and sent and appointed as a preacher of evangelical truth, writes these same things in his Epistle, saying: 'The Lord Jesus, on the night in which he was betrayed, took bread and gave thanks and broke and said, "This is my body which is for you; do this in remembrance of me." In like manner also he took the cup, after he had supped, saying, "This cup is the new

---
19 Cf. Matt. 26.27-29.

covenant in my blood; do this as often as you drink it, in remembrance of me. For as often as you shall eat this bread and drink the cup, you proclaim the death of the Lord, until he comes." '[20]

But if this is taught by the Lord and the same is confirmed and handed down by His Apostle, that as often as we drink in commemoration of the Lord, we should do this which the Lord did, we find that what was commanded is not observed by us unless we do the same things which the Lord did and, mixing the Chalice in like manner, we do not withdraw from the divine teaching. But that we must not depart at all from the evangelical teachings and that the disciples ought also to observe and do those same things which the Master taught and did, the blessed Apostle teaches more resolutely and strongly in another place, saying: 'I marvel that you are so quickly deserting him who called you to grace . . . to another gospel; which is not another, except in this respect that there are some who trouble you, and wish to pervert the gospel of Christ. But even if we or an angel from heaven should preach a gospel to you other than that which we have preached to you, let him be anathema! As we have said before, so now I say again: If anyone preach a gospel to you other than that which you have received, let him be anathema!'[21]

(11) Since, therefore, neither the Apostle himself nor an angel from heaven can announce otherwise or teach anything else than that which Christ once taught and His apostles preached, I marvel, indeed, whence this practice has come, contrary alike to both evangelical and apostolic discipline, that water, which alone cannot represent the Blood of Christ, is offered in some places in the Chalice of the Lord. The Holy Spirit is not quiet about the Sacrament of this matter in the Psalms, when He makes mention of the Chalice of the Lord and says: 'Your chalice which inebriates, how excellent it is!'[22]

---

20 Cf. 1 Cor. 11.23-26.
21 Cf. Gal. 1.6-9.
22 Cf. Ps. 22.5

But the Chalice which inebriates is assuredly mixed with wine. For water cannot inebriate anyone.

But thus the Chalice of the Lord inebriates as Noe drinking wine in Genesis also was inebriated. But because the inebriation of the Chalice and of the Blood of the Lord is not such as the inebriation coming from worldly wine, when the Holy Spirit says in the Psalms: 'Your chalice which inebriates,' he adds, 'how excellent it is!' because, actually, the Chalice of the Lord so inebriates that it makes sober, that it raises minds to spiritual wisdom, that from this taste of the world each one comes to the knowledge of God and, as the mind is relaxed by that common wine and the soul is relaxed and all sadness is cast away, so, when the Blood of the Lord and the lifegiving cup have been drunk, the memory of the old man is cast aside and there is induced forgetfulness of former worldly conversation and the sorrowful and sad heart which was formerly pressed down with distressing sins is now relaxed by the joy of the divine mercy. This then, at last, can delight the one who drinks in the Church of the Lord if what is drunk keeps to the truth of the Lord.

(12) How perverse it is, in truth, and how contrary that, although the Lord made wine from water at the marriage, we should make water from wine, when the Sacrament of this matter ought to warn and instruct us that in the Sacrifices of the Lord we should rather offer wine. For, since among the Jews spiritual grace was wanting, the wine failed also; for the vineyard of the Lord of hosts is the House of Israel.

But Christ, who teaches and shows that the people of the Gentiles were coming into that place which the Jews had lost and that we were arriving afterward through the merit of faith, made wine from water, that is, He showed that the people of the Gentiles rather would resort together and come to the nuptials of Christ and of His Church when the Jews were leaving. For the Divine Scripture declares in the Apocalypse that the waters signify the peoples, saying: 'The waters that thou sawest on which that harlot sits, are peoples and crowds and nations of the heathen and tongues.'[23] We perceive that this is actually, also, contained in the Sacrament of the Chalice.

(13) For, because Christ, who bore our sins, also bore us all, we see that people are signified in the water, but in the wine the Blood of Christ is shown. But when water is mixed with wine in the Chalice, the people are united to Christ, and the multitude of the believers is bound and joined to Him in whom they believe. This association and mingling of water and wine are so mixed in the Chalice of the Lord that the mixture cannot mutually be separated. Whence nothing can separate the Church, that is, the multitude established faithfully and firmly in the Church, persevering in that which it has believed, from Christ as long as it clings and remains in undivided love.

But thus, in the consecrating of the Chalice of the Lord, water alone cannot be offered, nor can wine alone. For, if anyone offers wine alone, the Blood of Christ begins to be without us. If, in truth, the water is alone, the people begin to be without Christ. But when both are mixed and, in the union, are joined to each other and mingled together, then the spiritual and heavenly Sacrament is completed. Thus, in truth, the Chalice of the Lord is not water alone, or wine alone, unless both are mixed together, just as flour alone or water alone cannot be the Body of the Lord unless both have been united and joined and made solid in the structure of one bread. By this Sacrament itself, our people are shown to be united; just as many grains collected in one and united and mixed form one bread, so in Christ, who is the heavenly Bread, we may know is one Body, to which our number is joined and united.

(14) There is no reason, dearly beloved Brother, for anyone to think that the custom of certain ones should be followed, if any in the past have thought that water alone should be offered in the Chalice of the Lord; for we must seek whom they themselves have followed. For, if in the

---
23 Cf. Apoc. 17.15.

Sacrifice which Christ offered, no one is to be followed but Christ Himself, certainly we ought to obey and to do what Christ did and what He commanded to be done since He Himself says in the Gospel: 'If you have done what I command you, no longer do I call you servants, but friends.'[24] And that Christ alone ought to be obeyed, His Father even states from heaven, saying: 'This is my dearly beloved Son, in whom I am well pleased; hear him.'[25]

Wherefore, if Christ alone is to be heard, we ought not to attend to what anyone else before us thought ought to be done, but what Christ, who is before all, did first. Neither ought we to follow the custom of men, but the truth of God since through Isaia, the prophet, God speaks and says: 'But in vain do they worship me, teaching the precepts and doctrines of men.'[26] And again in His Gospel, the Lord repeats this same thing, saying: 'You make void the commandment of God to choose your tradition.'[27] But in another place, He states and says: 'Whoever does away with one of these least commandments, and so teaches men, shall be called least in the kingdom of heaven.'[28]

But if it is not allowed to break the least of the commandments of the Lord, how much more important is it not to infringe upon matters which are so great, so tremendous, so closely connected to the very Sacrament of the Passion of the Lord and of our Redemption, or in any way to change for human tradition what has been divinely instituted? For, if Christ Jesus, our Lord and God, is Himself the High Priest of God the Father and first offered Himself as a Sacrifice to His Father and commanded this to be done in commemoration of Himself, certainly the priest who imitates that which Christ did and then offers the true and full Sacrifice in the Church of God the Father, if he thus begins to offer according to what

---
24 Cf. John 15.14, 15.
25 Cf. Matt. 17.5.
26 Cf. Isa. 29.13.
27 Cf. Mark 7.13.
28 Cf. Matt. 5.19.

he sees Christ Himself offered, performs truly in the place of Christ.

(15) Otherwise, all of the discipline of religion and of truth is subverted unless that which is prescribed spiritually is kept faithfully, unless in the Morning Sacrifice that which each one fears is that he should be redolent of the Blood of Christ through the savor of the wine. Thus, therefore, the brotherhood begins also to be kept back from the Passion of Christ in persecutions while it learns in the Oblations to be ashamed about His Blood and Bloodshed. But, in turn, the Lord in the Gospel says: 'Whoever is ashamed of me . . . of him will the Son of Man be ashamed.'[29] And the Apostle also speaks, saying: 'If I were trying to please men, I should not be a servant of Christ.'[30] For how can we who blush to drink the Blood of Christ shed our blood for Christ?

(16) Or is anyone enticed by this contemplation that, although water alone seems to be offered in the morning, yet, when we come to dinner, we offer a mixed Chalice? But when we dine, we cannot call the people to our banquet that we may celebrate the truth of the Sacrament with all of the brotherhood present. But, in fact, the Lord offered the mixed Chalice not in the morning but after dinner. Ought we then to celebrate the Sacrifice of the Lord after dinner so that by repeated Sacrifices we may offer the mixed Chalice? It was fitting for Christ to offer the Sacrifice about evening of the day that the very hour might show the setting and evening of the world as it is written in Exodus: 'And the whole multitude of the children of Israel shall slaughter it in the evening.'[31] And again in the Psalms: 'The lifting up of my hands as evening sacrifice.'[32] But we celebrate the Resurrection of the Lord in the morning.

(17) And since we make mention of His Passion in all Sacrifices, for the Passion of the Lord is, indeed, the Sacrifice

---
29 Cf. Mark 8.38.
30 Cf. Gal. 1.10.
31 Cf. Exod. 12.6.
32 Cf. Ps. 140.2.

which we offer, we ought to do nothing other than what He did. For Scripture says that, as often as we offer the Chalice in the commemoration of the Lord and of His Passion,[33] we should do that which it is certain the Lord did. And, dearly beloved Brother, let him look to it, if anyone of our predecessors either through ignorance or through simplicity did not observe this and did not keep that which the Lord taught us to do by His example and by His teaching. Pardon from the mercy of the Lord may be given to his simplicity. It cannot, in truth, be forgiven in us, who now are admonished and instructed by the Lord to offer the Chalice of the Lord mixed with wine, according to what the Lord offered, and to direct letters to our colleagues concerning this matter also, that everywhere the evangelical law and the tradition of the Lord should be kept and that there should be no departure from that which Christ both taught and did.

(18) For what else is it further to disdain those things and to persevere in the former error than to run into the rebuke of the Lord, who threatens in the Psalm and says: 'Why do you declare my justices, and profess my covenant with your mouth for you have hated discipline and cast my words behind you? If you saw a thief, you kept pace with him, and with adulterers you threw in your lot.'[34] For to declare the justices and the covenant of the Lord and not to do the same thing which the Lord did, what else is that but to cast aside His words and to despise the discipline of the Lord and to commit, not earthly, but spiritual robberies and adulteries? For he who steals from evangelical truth the words and deeds of our Lord both corrupts and adulterates the divine teaching, as it is written in Jeremia: 'What has the straw to do with the wheat?' he says, '. . . Therefore behold I am against the prophets, says the Lord, who steal my words everyone from his neighbor . . . and lead my people astray by their lies and

---

33 Cf. 1 Cor. 11.26.
34 Cf. Ps. 49.16-18.

by their errors.'³⁵ Likewise in another place in the same man: 'She played the harlot with wood and stone. And with all this, she did not return to me.'³⁶

We ought to observe religiously and fearfully and solicitously to beware that this robbery and adultery should not even now fall upon us. For if we are bishops of God and of Christ, I do not find anyone we ought to follow more than God and Christ since He Himself in His Gospel emphatically says: 'I am the light of the world. He who follows me will not walk in the darkness, but will have the light of life.'³⁷ Lest we walk, therefore, in darkness, we ought to follow Christ and to observe His precepts since He Himself in another place, sending His apostles, said: 'All power in heaven and on earth has been given to me. Go, therefore, and make disciples of all nations, baptizing them in the name of the Father, and of the Son, and of the Holy Spirit, teaching them to observe all that I have commanded you.'³⁸

Wherefore, if we wish to walk in the light of Christ, let us not depart from His precepts and admonitions, giving thanks, that, while He instructs us for the future as to what we should do, He forgives us for the past because we have sinned through simplicity. And since already His second coming is drawing near to us, more and more His kind and great condescension enlightens our hearts with the light of truth.

(19) It is, therefore, fitting to our religion and to our fear of God, both for the peace and for the office of our bishopric, dearly beloved Brother, to keep the truth of the tradition of the Lord in mixing and in offering the Chalice of the Lord and to correct what seems to have been an earlier error among certain people, according to the admonition of the Lord, that, when He begins to come in His brightness and heavenly majesty, He may find that we are holding firmly to what He

---
35 Cf. Jer. 23.28, 30, 32.
36 Cf. Jer. 3.9, 10.
37 Cf. John 8.12.
38 Cf. Matt. 28.18-20.

advised us, observing what He taught, doing what He did. I trust that you, dearly beloved Brother, are always well.

64. Cyprian[1] *and other colleagues who were present at the council, in number sixty-six, to Fidus,*[2] *their brother, greeting.*

(1) We have read your letter, dearly beloved Brother, in which you indicated concerning Victor,[3] formerly a priest, that, before he had done full penance and had made satisfaction to the Lord God against whom he had sinned, Therapius,[4] our colleague, rashly gave him peace after an insufficient time and with headlong haste. This matter disturbed us sufficiently in that it was a departure from the authority of our decree, that, before the legitimate and full time of satisfaction, both without the petition and against the conscience of the people, with no infirmity pressing and no necessity compelling, peace was granted to him. But after having weighed judgment among ourselves for a time, it was sufficient to reprimand our colleague, Therapius, for what he did so rashly and to instruct him that he should not do such a thing for anyone else. Yet we did not think that peace once granted by a bishop of God in whatever way should be taken away and, on account of this, we have granted this Victor the right to make use of the communion granted.

(2) But as for what pertains to the case of infants who, you said, ought not to be baptized within the second or third day after they were born and that the law of ancient circumcision

---

1 253 A.D.
2 Fidus, African bishop who complained to Cyprian about Therapius' premature action in reinstating the lapsed priest, Victor, stated also that he did not think infants should be baptized within two or three days of birth.
3 Victor, a lapsed African priest prematurely received back into communion as a layman.
4 Therapius, African bishop of Bulla, probably a confessor, censured for too hasty reinstatement of lapsed priests.

must be considered, that you thought that he who was born should not be baptized and sanctified within eight days, we thought far otherwise in our council. For in this matter, no one agrees with what you thought ought to be done, but we all judge that the mercy and grace of God must be denied to no man born.

For since the Lord in His Gospel says: 'The Son of Man did not come to destroy men's lives, but to save,'[5] as far as we can, if it can be done, no soul must be lost. For what is lacking to him who has once been formed in the womb by the hands of God? For us and to our eyes, those who are newly born seem to receive the increase according to the worldly course of days. As for the rest, whatever things have been made by God have been perfected by the work and majesty of God, the Maker.

(3) The faith of the Divine Scripture declares to us, finally, that there is one equality of the divine gift among all, whether infants or older persons, when Eliseus, calling upon God, so prostrated himself over the widow's infant son, who lay dead, that head was applied to head, and face to face, and the members of the prostrate Eliseus were over each of the members of the child and the feet touched the feet.[6] If this matter is thought of according to the quality of our birth and of our body, an infant could not be made equal to an adult prostrate over him; nor could the small members cling and stretch out to the larger. But, thereby is expressed the divine and spiritual equality because all men are alike and equal since they have been made once by God, and our age can have discrimination according to the world in growth of body, but not according to God, unless, indeed, grace itself which is given to the baptized is considered greater or lesser according to the age of those who receive it since the Holy Spirit offers to all, not according to measure, but according to love and fatherly mercy equal for all. For God does not make such a distinction of

---
5 Cf. Luke 9.56.
6 Cf. 4 Kings 4.32-35.

person or of age since He offers Himself as a Father to all to obtain celestial grace with balanced equality.

(4) Inasmuch as you have said also that the foot of the infant in the first days after his birth is not clean, that each one of us shudders at the thought of kissing it, we do not think that this ought to be an impediment to the giving of heavenly grace. For it is written: 'For the clean all things are clean.'[7] Nor ought anyone of us to shudder at what God has deigned to make. For although a child is as yet of recent birth, yet he is not such that anyone ought to shudder to kiss him in giving him grace and restoring him to peace since, in the kiss of the infant, each one of us ought to think in accordance with his religion of the hands of God themselves still fresh, which we kiss in a certain manner in this human being newly formed and lately born, when we embrace that which God has made.

For, because the eighth day was kept in the Judaic carnal circumcision, that was a pledge prefigured in the shadow and in the image, but it was fulfilled with truth with the coming of Christ. For, because the eighth day, that is, the first day after the Sabbath, was to be that on which the Lord rose and vivified us and gave us a spiritual circumcision, this octave day, that is the first after the Sabbath, and Sunday, has come forth as a prefiguring. The image ceased with the coming of the truth afterwards and with the giving to us of the spiritual circumcision.

(5) Because of this, we think that no one should be prevented from gaining grace according to that law which has already been made: that spiritual circumcision ought not to be hindered by a carnal circumcision, but that all, indeed, should be admitted to the grace of Christ, since Peter also in the Acts of the Apostles speaks and says: 'God has told me that I should not call any man common and unclean.'[8] Otherwise, if anything could hinder men from the gaining of grace,

---

[7] Titus 1.15.
[8] Cf. Acts 10.28.

much more could the more serious sins hinder adults, both those more exalted and those of a more advanced age. But, in turn, if, in the case of the greatest sinners and those sinning much against God, when afterward they believe, the remission of their sins is granted and no one is prevented from baptism and grace, how much more should an infant not be prohibited, who, recently born, has not sinned at all, except that, born carnally according to Adam, he has contracted the contagion of the first death from the first nativity. He approaches more easily from this very fact to receive the remission of sins because those which are remitted are not his own sins, but the sins of another.

And, therefore, dearly beloved Brother, this was our decision in the council that no one ought to be cut off by us from baptism and from the grace of God, who is merciful and kind and loving to all. Since this must be observed and maintained towards all, we think it ought to be even more observed regarding infants themselves and the newly born who deserve more, for this very reason, from our help and from the divine mercy because immediately at the very beginning of their birth, wailing and weeping, they can do nothing but plead. We trust that you, dearly beloved Brother, are always well.

65. Cyprian[1] to Epictetus,[2] his brother, and to the people abiding at Assurae, greeting.

(1) I was gravely and painfully moved, dearly beloved Brethren, because I learned that Fortunatian,[3] formerly bishop among you, after the serious lapse of his ruin, is wishing now to act as if he were upright and has begun to claim the episcopate for himself. This matter has saddened me, first, be-

---
1 253 A.D.
2 Epictetus, successor of Fortunatian as bishop of Assurae.
3 Fortunatian, lapsed bishop of Assurae, tried to resume his office without penance although the most he could have received with penance was reinstatement in the lay state.

cause of the man himself who, poor wretch, either totally blinded by the darkness of the devil or deceived by the sacrilegious persuasion of certain persons, although he ought to make satisfaction and exert himself to supplicate the Lord day and night with tears and prayers and entreaties, still dares to claim as his own the priesthood which he has betrayed, as if to approach the altar of God from the shrines of the devil were right or would not provoke greater wrath and indignation of the Lord upon himself in the day of judgment since he who could not be a leader of faith and of courage to the brethren appears as a teacher of perfidy and boldness and rashness; and he who did not teach the brethren to stand bravely in battle teaches those who were conquered and prostrate not to petition although the Lord says: 'To these you poured out libations, and to these you offered sacrifice. Shall I not be angry at these things?'[4] And in another place: 'Whoever sacrifices to the gods, except to the Lord alone, shall be doomed.'[5]

Likewise, the Lord again speaks and says: 'They worship that which their fingers have made. And man is abased and man is brought low, and I will not forgive them.'[6] In the Apocalypse also, we read of the wrath of the Lord, who threatens and says: 'If anyone worships the beast and its image and receives a mark upon his forehead and upon his hand, he also shall drink of the wine of the wrath of God, mixed in the cup of his wrath; and he shall be tormented with fire and brimstone in the sight of the holy angels and in the sight of the Lamb. And the smoke of their torments will go up forever and ever; and they will rest neither day nor night, they who worship the beast and its image.'[7]

(2) Since, therefore, the Lord threatens these torments, these punishments in the day of judgment, to those who obey the devil and sacrifice to idols, how does he think that he

---
4 Cf. Isa. 57.6.
5 Cf. Exod. 22.19.
6 Cf. Isa. 2.8, 9.
7 Cf. Apoc. 14.9-11.

who has obeyed and served the priests of the devil can act as bishop of God or how does he think that his hand, which was captive to sacrilege and crime, can be transferred to the Sacrifice of God and the prayer of the Lord when, in the Divine Scriptures, God prohibits from approaching the Sacrifice priests found even in lighter crime? And in Leviticus, He says: 'The man who has a defect and stains shall not come forward to offer up gifts to God.'[8]

Likewise in Exodus: 'The priests, too, who approach the Lord God must be sanctified lest perhaps the Lord abandon them.'[9] And again: 'And those who approach the altar of the Holy One to minister will not bring sin upon themselves lest they die.'[10] They, therefore, who have brought grave sins upon themselves, that is, who have offered sacrilegious sacrifices by sacrificing to idols, cannot claim the priesthood of God for themselves, nor can they offer any prayer for the brethren in His sight since it is written in the Gospel: 'God does not hear the sinner; but if anyone has worshipped God and done his will, him he hears.'[11] However, the profound blackness of violent darkness has so blinded the hearts of certain persons that they admit no light from the life-giving precepts but, once turned away from the right path of the true journey, they are carried along headlong into the abyss by the blackness and error of their crimes.

(3) It is not strange if they who have denied the Lord now reject our counsels or the precepts of the Lord. They desire the donations and the offerings and the money over which, earlier, insatiable, they brooded and even now they gaze longingly both at the banquets and the feasts, the intoxication of which, recently surviving, belched forth crudely for days, now openly confirming that before they served not religion but rather their stomachs and profit with unholy cupidity.

Whence we both perceive and believe that censure itself has

---
[8] Cf. Lev. 21.17.
[9] Cf. Exod. 19.22.
[10] Cf. Exod. 28.43.
[11] Cf. John 9.31.

come from the examination of God, lest they should any longer persevere in standing before the altar and contracting the shame of the incestuous, the faith of the perfidious, the religion of the sacrilegious, the divine actions of the earthly, and the holy actions of the sacrilegious. That such should not return again to the desecration of the altar and to the pollution of the brethren, we must be vigilant with all of our strength; lest they still attempt to act as bishops who, cast down to the extremities of death, have rushed beyond the lapsed laymen with a weight of greater ruin, with all our vigor, we must struggle as far as we can to restrain them from this boldness of their sin.

(4) But if this insane madness has persevered among the mad and, at the departure of the Holy Spirit, that blindness which has begun has remained in its night, there will be a plan by us to separate each of the brethren from the error of these men and, lest any fall into the nets of error, to separate them from contagion of these men since the Oblation cannot be consecrated there where the Holy Spirit is not; nor does the Lord reward for his prayers and entreaties anyone who himself has dishonored the Lord.

But if Fortunatian, either unmindful of his sin through the blindness of the devil or made a minister and servant of the devil to deceive the brotherhood, remains in this fury of his, endeavor as far as you can and, in this blackness of the raging devil, recall the minds of the brethren from error lest they easily consent to the madness of another, lest they themselves become sharers in the crimes of the desperate; but untainted, let them hold the uninterrupted course of their salvation and the perpetual vigor of their integrity preserved and guarded by themselves.

(5) Let not the lapsed, in truth, thinking over the magnitude of their offense, cease from begging the Lord and let them not abandon the Catholic Church, which is the one and only one established by the Lord; but, not delaying in reparations and beseeching the mercy of the Lord, let them knock

at the door of the Church that they may be received there where they were and may return to Christ from whom they have withdrawn. Let them not hear those who deceive themselves by false and deadly seduction since it is written: 'Let no one lead you astray with empty words; for because of these things the wrath of God comes upon the children of disobedience. Do not, then, become partakers with them.'[12]

Therefore, let no one associate with those who are obstinate and do not fear God and withdraw completely from the Church. But if anyone has been impatient in asking the Lord, who has been offended, and does not wish to obey us, but has followed wicked and abandoned men, it will be imputed to him when the day of judgment comes. For how will he who both before this has denied Christ and now also the Church of Christ and, not obeying the sound and untainted and living bishops, has shown himself as a comrade and associate of the dying be able to entreat the Lord in that day? I trust that you, dearly beloved Brethren, are always well.

66. Cyprian,[1] also known as Thascius, to Florentius,[2] his brother, also known as Puppian, greeting.

(1) I had believed finally, Brother, that you were already converted to penance because in the past you had given heed to or you had rashly believed concerning us such unspeakable, such base, and such detestable things even for the pagans. But I notice again even now in your letter that you are still the same as you were before, that you believe the same things concerning us, and that you are persisting in that which you believed, and, lest the dignity of your excellence and martyrdom be stained by communion with us, you are inquiring diligently into our actions and you are unwilling for God, who makes

---
12 Eph. 5.6, 7.

---
1 254 A.D.
2 Florentius Puppian, bishop and confessor in the Decian persecution.

bishops, to be Judge afterwards, I should not say of me—for what am I?—but to judge concerning the judgment of God and of Christ.

This is not to believe in God; this is to be a rebel against Christ and against His Gospel so that, although He says: 'Are not two sparrows sold for a farthing? And not one of them falls to the ground without your Father's leave,'[3] and His majesty and truth prove that even the least things are not done without the knowledge and permission of God, you think that bishops of God are ordained in the Church without His knowledge. For to believe that those who are ordained are unworthy and impure, what else is it but to contend that His bishops are not appointed in the Church by God nor through God?

(2) Or do you think that my testimony of myself is greater than that of God since the Lord Himself teaches and says that the testimony is not true if anyone is witness of himself because each one certainly favors himself and no one brings out matters which are hostile and unfavorable against himself. Let the faith of truth be sincere, certainly, if in our praises another is the eulogist and the witness. 'If I bear witness concerning myself,' He says, 'my witness is not true. For there is another who is a witness concerning me.'[4]

But, if the Lord Himself, who will come afterward to judge all things, thus was unwilling to be believed on His own witness, but preferred to be approved by the judgment and witness of God the Father, how much the more ought His servants, who are not only approved by the testimony and judgment of God, but even are glorified by it, to observe this. And now the falsehood of enemies and of evil men has prevailed, however, with you against the divine decree, against our conscience relying upon the strength of its faith, as if among the lapsed and profane and those placed outside of the Church, from whose breasts the Holy Spirit has withdrawn,

---

[3] Cf. Matt. 10.29.
[4] Cf. John 5.31, 32.

there could be anything else but a depraved mind and a false tongue and hateful poison and sacrilegious lies. He who believes them will, of necessity, be found with them when the day of judgment comes.

(3) But as to the fact that you have said that priests ought to be humble since both the Lord and His apostles were humble, both all the brethren and the Gentiles also know best and love my humility and you also knew and loved it when you were still in the Church and were in communion with me. But which of us is far from humility, I, who daily serve the brethren and receive benignly and with desire and joy each one who comes to the Church, or you, who appoint yourself bishop of a bishop and judge of a judge given for the time by God? And yet the Lord God says in Deuteronomy: 'And any man who has the insolence to refuse to listen to the priest or judge, whoever he may be in those days, that man shall die. . . . And all the people on hearing of it, shall fear, and never again be so insolent.'[5] And again He speaks to Samuel and says: 'They have not rejected thee, but they have rejected me.'[6]

And again the Lord in the Gospel, when it was said to Him: 'Is that the way thou dost answer the high priest?' guarding and teaching that the sacerdotal honor ought to be respected, said nothing against the High Priest, but only vindicating His own innocence, answered, saying: 'If I have spoken ill, bear witness to the evil; but if well, why dost thou strike me?'[7] Likewise, the blessed Apostle, when it had been said to him: 'Dost thou insult the high priest?' spoke nothing insulting against the priest when he could have constantly lashed out against those who had crucified God and had destroyed the Lord and Christ and the Temple and the priesthood, but thinking very much upon the false and despoiled priests as the shade, however light, of the priestly name, said: 'I did

---
5 Cf. Deut. 17.12, 13.
6 Cf. 1 Kings 8.7.
7 John 18.23.

not know, brethren, that he was the high priest; for it is written, "Thou shalt not speak evil of a ruler of thy people." [8]

(4) Unless, indeed, I was a bishop to you before the persecution when you were in communion with me and I have ceased to be a bishop after the persecution! For the persecution which came carried you to the greatest sublimity of martyrdom; but it afflicted me with the burden of proscription when it was publicly read: *'If anyone keeps and possesses the goods of Cecil Cyprian, Bishop of the Christians,'* that even those who did not believe in God's appointing a bishop might at least believe in the devil's proscribing a bishop.

I do not boast of these matters, but, sorrowing, I mention them since you appoint yourself judge of God and of Christ, who says to the apostles and thus to all of those placed in charge who now succeed to the apostles by delegated ordination: 'He who hears you, hears me; and he who hears me, hears him who sent me; and he who rejects you, rejects me and him who sent me.'[9]

(5) For whence do heresies and schisms arise and appear? It is at the time that the bishop who is one and is in charge in the Church is despised by the proud presumption of some and the man honored by the condescension of God is considered unworthy by men. For what swelling of pride is this, what arrogance of mind, what boasting of spirit to call prelates and bishops to one's own judicial examination? And unless we have been justified by you and absolved by your statement, behold for six years already the brotherhood have not had a bishop, nor the people a leader, nor the flock a shepherd, nor the Church a ruler, nor Christ a bishop, nor God a priest!

Let Puppian come to help and express his decision; let him report for acceptance the judgment of God and of Christ lest so great a number of the faithful who have been summoned away under us seem to have expired without the hope of salvation and of peace, lest a new multitude of the faithful be

---
8 Cf. Acts 23.4, 5.
9 Cf. Luke 10.16.

judged to have gained no grace of baptism and of the Holy Spirit, lest peace given to so many lapsed and penitent and our communion granted by examination be cast away by the authority of your judgment. Promise once to deign to report about us also and to strengthen our episcopate by the vigor of your knowledge, that God and His Christ may be able to thank you that, through you there, a bishop and ruler has been restored equally to the people and to their altar!

(6) The bees have a king and the flocks keep their leader and their faith; mercenaries obey their legal purchaser with the full allegiance of humility. How much simpler and better than you are the brute herds and the mute animals and the plunderers although they are raving and bloodthirsty with their swords and in arms! There the leader is known and feared, one whom Divine Decree has not appointed, but upon whom a wicked faction and a harmful band agree.

(7) You have said sensibly that the scruple into which you have fallen must be removed from your mind. You have fallen, but through your irreligious credulity. You have fallen, but by your sacrilegious mind and will. You willingly hear now impure, then impious, now abominable thoughts against your brother, against the bishop, and you believe freely. You defend the lies of others as if your own and personal and you do not remember that it is written: 'Hedge in thy ears with thorns, hear not a wicked tongue.'[10] And again: 'The evil man gives heed to the tongue of the wicked, the just man, however, does not use his lips for lies.'[11] Why have not the martyrs, filled with the Holy Spirit and already near to the sight of God and of His Christ by their suffering, fallen into this scruple? Recognizing the bishop of God and appealing to him, they addressed a letter from prison to Bishop Cyprian.

Why have not so many fellow bishops, my colleagues, fallen into this scruple, who, when they withdrew from our midst, were either proscribed or were seized and cast into prison and

---

10 Cf. Sir. (Ecclus.) 28.24.
11 Cf. Prov. 17.4.

chains or who, relegated to exile, set out to the Lord on a glorious journey or who were punished in certain places and received the heavenly crowns from the glorification of the Lord? Why have not so many confessors of this our people who are with us and entrusted to us by the condescension of God fallen into this scruple, questioned and tortured and glorious in the memory of their outstanding wounds and scars, so many chaste virgins, so many praiseworthy widows, finally, of the whole Church united throughout the whole world with us in the bond of unity? Perchance all of these communicating with me, according to what you write, have been polluted by our polluted mouth and have lost the hope of eternal life by the contagion of our communion. Puppian alone, upright, inviolate, holy, modest, who did not wish to have anything to do with us, will dwell alone in paradise and in the kingdom of heaven!

(8) You have written also that on account of me the Church now has part of its members scattered although the whole people of the Church have been both collected together and united and joined in indivisible harmony among themselves. Only those have remained without who would have had to be excommunicated if they were within. God, the Protector and Guardian of His people, does not allow the grain to be plundered from his barn, but only the chaff can be separated from the Church since the Apostle also says: 'For what if some of them have fallen from faith? Will their unbelief make void the fidelity of God? By no means! For God is true, but every man is a liar.'[12]

And the Lord also in the Gospel, when the disciples abandoned Him speaking, having turned to the Twelve, said: ' "Do you also wish to go away?" Peter answered Him, saying: "Lord, to whom shall we go? Thou hast words of everlasting life, and we believe and we know that thou art the Son of the living God." '[13] There speaks Peter, upon whom the Church

---
12 Cf. Rom. 3.3, 4.
13 Cf. John 6.68-70.

had been built, teaching in the name of the Church and showing that, although the stubborn and proud multitude of those unwilling to obey withdraw, yet the Church does not withdraw from Christ, and the people united to their bishop and the flock clinging to their shepherd are the Church. Whence you ought to know that the bishop is in the Church and the Church is in the bishop and, if there is anyone who is not with the bishop, he is not in the Church. And, in vain, they flatter themselves who creep up not having peace with the priests of God and they believe they are in communion secretly with certain ones when the Church which is one, Catholic, is not divided nor rent, but is certainly united and joined, in turn, by the solder of the bishops adhering to one another.

(9) And, therefore, Brother, if you think of the majesty of God, who ordains priests of Christ, if you look at length upon Christ, who, by His will and Godhead and presence, governs both the leaders themselves and the Church with the leaders, if you believe concerning the innocence of the bishops, not by human hate, but by divine judgment, if you begin to do penance even late for your rashness and pride and insolence, if you give satisfaction most fully to the Lord and to His Christ, whom I serve and to whom I offer the Sacrifices with a pure and unspotted mouth equally in persecution and unceasingly in peace, we shall be able to have a plan for you to be in communion although the respect and fear of the divine censure yet remain among us. And first, I shall consult my Lord as to whether He may permit peace to be given to you and you to be admitted to the communion of His Church with His permission and admonition.

(10) For I remember what has already been made known to me, nay rather, what is commanded to the respectful and fearing servant also by the Lord's divine authority. Among the other things which He deigned to show and to reveal, He also imparted this: 'And so who does not believe Christ making the priest will begin to believe afterwards Christ avenging the priest.'

And yet I know that dreams seem ridiculous and visions absurd to certain people, but especially to those who prefer to believe against the priests rather than believe the priest. But nothing is strange since His brethren said of Joseph: 'Behold, here comes that dreamer. Come now, therefore, let us kill him.'[14] And the dreamer afterward accomplished what he had dreamed and the killers and the sellers were confused so that they who, at first, had not believed his words afterward believed his deeds.

But of these things which you have done either in persecution or in peace, it is foolish for me to wish to judge you, especially since you have already appointed yourself judge over us. I have written back to you according to both the upright conscience of my mind and my confidence in my Lord and God. You have my letter and I yours. Each will be read out in the day of judgment before the tribunal of Christ.

67. Cyprian,[1] Cecil,[2] Primus,[3] Polycarp,[4] Nicomedes,[5] Lucilian,[6] Successus,[7] Sedatus,[8] Fortunatus,[9] Januarius,[10] Secundinus,[11] Pomponius,[12] Honoratus,[13] Victor,[14] Aurelius,[15] Sattius,[16] Peter,[17] another Januarius,[18] Saturn-

---

14 Cf. Gen. 37.19, 20.

---

1 254 A.D.
2 Cf. Letter 4, n. 2.
3 Primus, bishop of Misgirpa, present at several councils.
4 Cf. Letter 48, n. 5.
5 Cf. Letter 57, n. 4.
6 Lucilian in Hartel, but Lucian in Bayard and in Benson's list of the bishops at the Fourth Council of Carthage in 254 A.D., bishop at several councils.
7 Cf. Letter 57, n. 9.
8 Cf. Letter 4, n. 4.
9 Cf. Letter 44, n. 9.
10 Januarius, bishop of Africa, present at council concerning Basilides.
11 Cf. Letter 57, n. 19.
12 Cf. Letter 4, n. 6.
13 Cf. Letter 57, n. 29.
14 Cf. Letter 4, n. 3, and Letter 57, n. 12.
15 Cf. Letter 57, n. 24.
16 Cf. Letter 57, n. 18.
17 Peter, African bishop, present at council of 254 A.D.
18 Another Januarius, bishop of Africa, also at council.

LETTERS   231

inus,[19] another Aurelius,[20] Venantius,[21] Quietus,[22] Rogatian,[23] Tenax,[24] Felix,[25] Faustus,[26] Quintus,[27] another Saturninus,[28] Lucius,[29] Vincent,[30] Libosus,[31] Geminius,[32] Marcellus,[33] Iambus,[34] Adelphius,[35] Victoricus,[36] and Paul,[37] to Felix,[38] the priest, and the people abiding at Legio[39] and Asturica,[40] and likewise to Aelius,[41] the deacon, and the people abiding at Emerita,[42] brethren in the Lord, greeting.

(1) When we had come together, dearly beloved Brethren, we read your letter which you sent to us through Felix[43] and

---

19 Cf. Letter 57, n. 13.
20 Cf. Letter 57, n. 24.
21 Venantius, African bishop of Thinisa, present at several councils.
22 Quietus, African bishop, present at councils in 254 and 256 A.D. He may be the Mauretanian bishop of Buruc.
23 Cf. Letter 3, n. 2.
24 Tenax, African bishop, present at councils in 254 and 256 A.D.
25 Cf. Letter 56, n. 7.
26 Faustus, bishop of Timida Regia, present at council of 254.
27 Cf. Letter 57, n. 28.
28 Cf. Letter 57, n. 13.
29 Lucius, African bishop, probably of Membrasa, present at council. Name also of other African bishops.
30 Vincent, African bishop of Thibaris, present at councils in 254 and 256 A.D.
31 Libosus, African bishop of Vaga, present at council.
32 Cf. Letter 1, n. 4.
33 Marcellus, African bishop at council in 254 A.D.
34 Cf. Letter 57, n. 33.
35 Adelphius, African bishop at council.
36 Cf. Letter 57, n. 27.
37 Paul, African bishop at Synod of Carthage 254 A.D., possibly bishop of Obba in Mauretania, listed as attending synod in 256 A.D.
38 Felix, priest in Spain, addressed by Cyprian and the council. The outcome of the matter discussed seems uncertain.
39 Legio or Leon and Asturica or Astorga in Spain formed the province of the fallen bishop. The inhabitants of these places appointed the priest Felix to appeal to Carthage for support and for a decision.
40 Cf. n. 39 above.
41 Aelius, the deacon of Emerita or Merida, was also appointed to compose an appeal to Carthage against having the lapsed bishops resume their sees.
42 Emerita or Merida in Spain, place from which the inhabitants appealed to Carthage and received a reply from Cyprian and the council.
43 Felix, priest ordained as bishop to replace Basilides after the latter's lapse. He and Sabinus were the successors of the two fallen bishops, Basilides and Martial.

Sabinus,[44] our fellow bishops, in the integrity of your faith and fear of the Lord, signifying that Basilides[45] and Martial,[46] contaminated by the certificates of idolatry and bound by the consciousness of heinous deeds, ought not to govern the bishopric and administer the priesthood of God. And you desired that an answer be sent to you in regard to these matters and that your just and necessary solicitude be relieved by either the solace or by the aid of our decision.

But, in fact, not so much our counsels as the divine precepts answer this desire of yours, by which, for a long time, there has been entrusted by the voice of heaven and prescribed by the law of God who and what kinds of men ought to serve at the altar and celebrate the Divine Sacrifices. For in Exodus, God speaks to Moses and warns, saying: 'The priests who approach the Lord God must be sanctified lest perhaps the Lord abandon them.'[47] And again: 'And when they approach the altar of the Holy One to minister, they will not bring sin upon themselves lest they die.'[48] Likewise in Leviticus, the Lord instructs and says: 'The man in whom there is blemish and imperfection shall not come forward to offer gifts to God.'[49]

(2) Since these things have been foretold and manifested to us, it is necessary for our obedience to serve the divine commands. Distinction of person cannot be admitted in affairs of this nature; human indulgence cannot bestow anything

---

44 Sabinus, bishop of Emerita, successor of Felix Martial, who was guilty of receiving certificates in the Decian persecution, was chosen by the bishops in the presence of the people.
45 Basilides, stained by the certificate and his blasphemies against God, first resigned his bishopric voluntarily and begged to be received into communion as a layman and then tried to deceive Pope Stephen into restoring him to his see.
46 Martial, Spanish bishop of Merida, who was weak enough to accept certificate in persecution of Decius, later with Basilides visited Rome to ask Stephen for restoration to his see. Felix and Aelius appealed to Cyprian. The Synod of Carthage in 254 supported Sabinus and Felix and considered that Stephen had been deceived.
47 Cf. Exod. 19.22.
48 Cf. Exod. 30.20, 21.
49 Cf. Lev. 21.17.

upon anyone when the divine prescription intervenes and prescribes a law. For we ought not to be unmindful of what the Lord, reproving and angry, spoke through Isaia, the prophet, to the Jews, because they had despised divine precepts and were following human doctrines. 'This people,' he said, 'honors me with their lips, but their heart is far separated from me. In vain, moreover, they honor me, teaching the commandments and doctrines of men.'[50] The Lord, likewise, repeats the same thing in His Gospel and says: 'You nullify the commandment of God, that you may keep your own tradition!'[51]

Having these matters before our eyes and carefully and religiously considering in the ordinations of bishops, we ought to choose none but spotless and upright priests who, offering Sacrifices holily and worthily to God, may be able to be heard in the prayers which they offer for the safety of the people of the Lord since it is written: 'God does not hear the sinner; but if anyone is a worshipper of God, and does His will, him he hears.'[52] Because of this, it is necessary, with full diligence and sincere examination, that they be chosen for the priesthood of God who, it is certain, may be heard by God.

(3) Let not the people flatter themselves as if they could be safe from contagion of sin, communicating with a sinful priest and yielding their obedience to the unjust and unlawful episcopacy of their leader, when the Divine Censure threatens through the Prophet Osee and says: 'Their sacrifices shall be like the bread of mourning: all who eat them shall be defiled,'[53] teaching obviously and showing that all are, indeed, involved in sin who have been contaminated by the sacrifice of a blasphemous and unjust priest.

We find that also made clear in Numbers when Core and Dathan and Abiron claimed for themselves the liberty of

---

50 Cf. Isa. 29.13.
51 Mark 7.9.
52 Cf. John 9.31.
53 Cf. Osee 9.4.

sacrificing in opposition to Aaron, the priest. There also, the Lord teaches through Moses that the people should be separated from them lest they be bound by the same guilt with the criminals and contaminate themselves by the same crime. 'Keep away,' he says, 'from the tents of most shameless wicked men, and do not touch anything that is theirs, lest you perish at the same time in their sin.'[54] Because of this, a people who obey the precepts of the Lord and fear God ought to separate themselves from a sinful leader and should not take part in the sacrifices of a sacrilegious bishop, especially since they themselves have the power either of electing worthy bishops or of refusing the unworthy.

(4) We see that this very fact also comes from divine authority, that a bishop be chosen in the presence of the people before the eyes of all and that he be approved as worthy and fit by public judgment and testimony as, in Numbers, God teaches Moses, saying: 'Take Aaron, your brother, and his son, Eleazar, and place them in the mountain before the whole synagogue. And strip Aaron of his garment and put it on his son, Eleazar, and let Aaron die and be laid there.'[55] The Lord orders the bishop to be appointed before the whole synagogue, that is, He instructs and shows that priestly ordinations ought not to be performed except with the knowledge of the people present that, in the presence of the people, either the crimes of the evil doers may be revealed or the merits of the good may be proclaimed and that the ordination which has been examined by the suffrage and judgment of all may be just and lawful. This is observed afterwards according to divine teachings in the Acts of the Apostles. When Peter is speaking to the people concerning the bishop to be ordained in the place of Judas, it says: 'Peter stood up in the midst of the disciples for the multitude was together.'[56] But we notice that the apostles observed this, not only in the ordination of

---

54 Cf. Num. 16.26.
55 Cf. Num. 20.25, 26.
56 Cf. Acts 1.15.

bishops and of priests, but also in the ordinations of deacons. Concerning this very thing, in their Acts, it is also written: 'The Twelve called together the multitude of the disciples,' it says, 'and spoke to them.'⁵⁷

This matter was, therefore, carried on so diligently and cautiously with the whole people assembled that no unworthy man should attain to the ministry of the altar or to the priestly rank. For the fact that sometimes unworthy men are ordained, not according to the will of God, but according to human presumption, and that these things which do not come from a legitimate and just ordination are displeasing to God, God Himself makes known through the Prophet Osee, saying: 'They made themselves a king but not by me.'⁵⁸

(5) Because of this, we must preserve diligently and keep of the divine traditions and apostolic observance what is kept among us also and through almost all of the provinces that, for the celebrations of ordinations with suitable ceremony for that people for whom a prelate is ordained, all the nearest bishops of the same province should assemble also and a bishop should be chosen in the presence of the people, who know most fully the life of each one and perceive the actions of each from his manner of living. We see this done among you also in the ordination of our colleague, Sabinus, that, from the suffrage of all of the brotherhood and from the judgment of the bishops who had all assembled at the moment and had written to you a letter concerning him, the bishopric was conferred upon him and hands were imposed upon him in the place of Basilides.

We cannot rescind this ordination, valid according to the law, because Basilides, after his crimes had been detected and laid bare by the confession of his own conscience, hastening to Rome, to solicit for himself unjustly to be reinstated in the bishopric from which he had rightly been deposed, deceived

---

57 Cf. Acts 6.2.
58 Cf. Osee 8.4.

our colleague, Stephen,⁵⁹ who is far away and unacquainted with the truth of the matter presented. The result of this is that the sins of Basilides are not so much wiped out as made even greater, that to his former sins he has added also the crime of falsehood and of fraud. Nor is the former, who was negligently taken by surprise, so much to be blamed as the latter, who fraudently deceived, is to be condemned. But if Basilides, however, could deceive men, he cannot deceive God since it is written: 'God is not mocked.'⁶⁰ But neither can this fallacy profit Martial anything since he himself, involved also in grave sins, ought not to hold the bishopric since the Apostle warns and says: 'For a bishop must be blameless as being the steward of God.'⁶¹

(6) Wherefore, since, as you write, dearly beloved Brethren, and as Felix and Sabinus, our colleagues, had asserted and also another Felix from Caesaraugusta,⁶² a lover of the faith and defender of the truth, indicates in his letter, Basilides and Martial have been contaminated with the abominable certificate of idolatry. Basilides, moreover, in addition to this, besides the stain of the certificate, when he was lying ill, blasphemed against God and confessed that he had blasphemed and, putting aside his bishopric of his own will because of the stain on his conscience, turned to the doing of penance, beseeching God and considering himself fortunate if he should be allowed to be in communion as a layman. Martial also, besides frequenting the shameful and vile banquets of the pagans for a long time in the college and placing his sons in the same college according to the custom of the foreign pagans and burying them with foreigners in a profane sepulchre, has

---

59 Stephen, Pope from May 12, 254 A.D. to Aug. 2, 257 A.D., apparently supported Basilides when the latter repented having resigned his see and wished to regain it. Cyprian's relations with Stephen were rather strained because of Cyprian's view that heretics coming into the Church needed to be rebaptized. The question was particularly pertinent because of the Novatian heresy.
60 Gal. 6.7.
61 Titus 1.7.
62 Another Felix from Caesaraugusta (Caesar Augusta, Saragossa) wrote to Cyprian and other bishops concerning Basilides.

also attested publicly in acts in the presence of the ducenarian procurator that he yielded to idolatry and that he denied Christ.

And since there are many other grave crimes also in which Basilides and Martial are implicated, in vain do such men attempt to usurp the episcopate since it is clearer that men of this type cannot be in charge of the Church of Christ or offer Sacrifices to God especially since, already long ago now with us and with all of the bishops appointed, indeed, in the whole world, Cornelius,[63] our colleague, a bishop, peaceful and just and honored by the condescension of the Lord with martyrdom also, decreed that men of this type could, indeed, be admitted to the performance of penance, but that they were to be excluded from clerical ordination and from the episcopal honor.

(7) Let it not disturb you, dearly beloved Brethren, if among certain ones in recent times either uncertain faith wavers or feeble fear of God is vacillating or peaceful harmony does not last. These things have been predicted as about to come at the end of the world. And by the voice of the Lord and by the statement of the apostles it is foretold that, when the world is already drawing near to the end and Antichrist is approaching, the good will also fail and the evil and perverse, in truth, will prevail.

(8) Yet not even in the last times has either evangelical vigor so fallen in the Church of God or the strength of Christian virtue or of faith so languished that there does not remain a portion of priests which has not at all succumbed to the ruins of affairs and the shipwrecks of faith, but, strong and stable, it guards the honor of the Divine Majesty and the priestly dignity with the full observance of fear.

We remember and we hold in mind that, although others yielded and succumbed, it was granted to Mattathias to have bravely vindicated the laws of God, to Helias to have stood and sublimely struggled with the Jews, failing and with-

---
63 Cf. Letter 44, n. 2.

drawing from the divine religion, to Daniel, deterred neither by the solitude of a strange region nor the threat of assiduous persecution, frequently and bravely to have rendered glorious testimonies, likewise to the three youths, broken neither by years nor threats, to have faithfully resisted against the Babylonian fires and to have overcome the victorious king in their very captivity. The number either of prevaricators or of traitors should see who now in the Church have begun to rise against the Church and to overthrow faith, likewise, and truth. There remain among very many a sincere mind and upright religion and a soul devoted only to its Lord and God. The treachery of others does not reduce their Christian faith to ruin, but, rather, it excites it and exalts it to glory, according to what the blessed Apostle exhorts and says: 'For what if some of them have fallen from faith? Will their unbelief make void the fidelity of God? By no means! For God is true, but every man is a liar.'[64] But if every man is a liar and God alone is true, what else ought we servants and bishops of God especially to do except to reject human errors and lies and to remain in the truth of God, obeying the precepts of the Lord?

(9) Wherefore, although there are some of our colleagues, dearly beloved Brethren, who think that God-made discipline ought to be ignored and who are in communion rashly with Basilides and Martial, this matter ought not to disturb our faith since the Holy Spirit in the Psalms threatens such, saying: 'You, however, have hated discipline and cast my words behind you. If you saw a thief, you kept pace with him, and with adulterers you threw in your lot.'[65] He shows that they who have been associated with the delinquent become sharers and partakers in the crimes of others.

But also Paul, the Apostle, writes and says the same thing: 'Whisperers, detractors, hateful to God, unjust, proud, boasting of themselves, plotters of evil; . . . Although they have

---
64 Cf. Rom. 3.3, 4.
65 Cf. Ps. 49.17, 18.

known the justice of God, they have not understood that those who practice such things are deserving of death. Not only do they do such evils but they consent to those who do them. Since they do such,' he says, 'they are deserving of death.'⁶⁶ He makes clear and proves that not only those who do evil are worthy of death and come to punishment, but also those who agree to those doing such things, who, while, in unlawful communion, they mix with the evil and sinners and those not doing penance, are polluted by the contacts of the guilty and, as they are joined in guilt, so they are not separated in punishment.

Because of this, dearly beloved Brethren, we praise equally and we approve the God-fearing solicitude of your integrity and faith and, as far as we can, we encourage it with our letters that you should not mingle in sacrilegious communion with contaminated and stained bishops, but that you should keep the whole and sincere firmness of your faith with a religious fear. I trust that you, dearly beloved Brethren, are always well.

68. Cyprian[1] to Stephen,[2] his brother, greeting.

(1) Our colleague, Faustinus,[3] abiding at Lyons, dearly beloved Brother, has written me time and again to mention matters which I know have likewise been reported to you as well by him as by the rest of our fellow bishops abiding in the same province: that Marcian,[4] abiding at Arles, has joined himself to Novatian[5] and has withdrawn from the truth of the Catholic Church and from the assembly of our body and

---

66 Cf. Rom. 1.30, 32.

1 254 A.D.
2 Cf. Letter 67, n. 59.
3 Faustinus, bishop of Lyons.
4 Marcian, bishop of Arles and follower of Novatian, refused to readmit the lapsed.
5 Cf. Letter 44, n. 7.

bishopric, holding the most stubborn depravity of heretical presumption that the solaces and aids of divine mercy and of paternal tenderness should be closed to the servants of God who repent and grieve and knock at the Church with tears and lamentation and sorrow, and that the wounded should not be admitted for the curing of their wounds but, left without hope of peace and of communion, they should be cast out as prey for the wolves and as plunder for the devil.

It is our duty to watch out and to provide a remedy for this situation, dearly beloved Brother, who thinking upon the divine clemency and holding the weight of governing the Church, show such censure of vigor to sinners that, yet, we do not withhold the medicine of divine goodness and of mercy from uplifting the lapsed and from curing the wounded.

(2) Wherefore, you ought to send a very full letter to our fellow bishops abiding in Gaul that they should no longer allow Marcian, stubborn and proud and hostile to divine mercy and to fraternal salvation, to insult our assembly because he does not yet seem to be excommunicated by us. He, for a long time now, has boasted and told abroad that, giving attention to Novatian and following his perversity, he has separated himself from our communion although Novation himself, whom he follows, was formerly excommunicated and judged an enemy of the Church. And when he had sent envoys to us in Africa hoping to be admitted to our communion, from this place from the Council of the many bishops who were assembled, he received the sentence that he was excommunicated and that he could not begin to be received into communion by any one of us. When Cornelius[6] was the bishop of the Catholic Church, ordained according to the judgment of God and to the suffrage of the clergy and of the laity, he attempted to erect a profane altar and to build a sacrilegious chair and to offer sacrilegious sacrifices against the true bishop. Then if he wished to come to his senses and to return to the discretion of a sane mind, he should do penance and return

---

6 Cf. Letter 44, n. 2.

as a suppliant to the Church. How vain it is, dearly beloved Brother, that, when Novatian has been recently rejected and refuted and excommunicated by the bishops of God in the whole world, we should now allow his sycophants to mock us and to judge concerning the majesty and dignity of the Church!

(3) Let letters be sent by you to the province and to the people abiding at Arles by which, after Marcian has been excommunicated, another may be substituted in his place and the flock of Christ which is despised today, scattered by that man and wounded, may be reassembled. Let it be sufficient that many of our brethren have died there in recent years without peace. Assuredly, let relief come to the rest who remain alive and groan both day and night and, beseeching the divine and paternal mercy, ask the solace of our help. For that reason, therefore, dearly beloved Brother, is the large body of bishops joined by the bond of mutual concord and the chain of unity so that, if anyone of our college should attempt to engage in heresy and wound and lay waste the flock of Christ, the others, as useful and merciful shepherds, should assist and should assemble the sheep of the Lord into the flock.

For, indeed, if any port on the sea begins to be difficult and dangerous to ships because of its broken fortifications, do not those sailing direct their ships to other neighboring ports where the access would be safe and the entrance advantageous and the station secure? Or if, on the way, some inn would begin to be beseiged and held by bandits so that each one who entered would be captured by the molestation of the besiegers there, should not those passing to and fro, when this matter had been made known, seek other safer inns to be found on the journey, where hospices are trustworthy and shelters safe for passersby? It is necessary for this situation to exist among us, dearly beloved Brother, that we may receive to ourselves with prompt and benign humanity our brethren who, having avoided the rocks of Marcian, seek the saving gates of the Church and that we may offer an inn to the travelers such as the one in the Gospel, in which those wounded and injured by robbers may be received and tended and protected by the innkeeper.

(4) For what is a greater or better occupation for bishops than with diligent solicitude and salutary healing to provide for protecting and saving the sheep since the Lord speaks and says: 'You did not strengthen the weak nor heal the sick nor console the sorrowing. You did not bring back the strayed nor seek the lost. . . . And my sheep were scattered there, because there were no shepherds, and they became food for all the beasts of the field. . . . And there was no one to look after them or to call them back. . . . Thus says the Lord God: Behold I myself am coming against the shepherds and I will claim my sheep from their hands and put a stop to their shepherding my sheep and they may no longer pasture them. And I will deliver them from their mouth. . . . And I will shepherd them with judgment.'[7]

Since, therefore, the Lord thus threatens such shepherds through whom the sheep of the Lord are neglected and perish, what else ought we to do, dearly beloved Brother, but to show full diligence in collecting and restoring the sheep of Christ and to apply the medicine of paternal piety to care for the wounds of the lapsed since the Lord also in the Gospel warns and says: 'It is not the healthy who need a physician, but they who are sick.'[8] For although we shepherds are many, yet we feed one flock; and all of the sheep whom Christ sought by His Blood and Passion we ought to collect and to cherish and not to allow our suppliant and grieving brothers to be cruelly despised and to be trodden under foot by the proud presumption of certain ones since it is written: 'The man, however, who is stiff-necked, boastful of himself, will accomplish

---

7 Cf. Ezech. 34.4-6, 10, 16.
8 Matt. 9.12.

nothing at all, who has opened his desire like the nether world.'⁹

And the Lord in the Gospel blames and condemns all of this nature, saying: 'You are they who declare yourselves just in the sight of men, but God knows your heart; for that which is exalted in the sight of men is an abomination before God.'¹⁰ He says that those who please themselves are accursed and detestable, who, boasting and proud, assume anything arrogantly to themselves. Since Marcian has begun to be of that number and, joining himself to Novatian, has shown himself an adversary of mercy and of pity, let him not speak sentence, but accept it; let him not act as if he himself judged concerning the college of bishops since he himself has been judged by all of the bishops.

(5) For the glorious honor of our predecessors, the blessed martyrs, Cornelius and Lucius,¹¹ must be preserved. Since we honor their memory, how much more, dearly beloved Brother, ought you who have been made their vicar and successor to honor it and to preserve it with your dignity and authority. For they, full of the Spirit of the Lord and appointed for a glorious martyrdom, decreed that peace should be given to the lapsed and signified by their letters that, when penance has been performed, the reward of communion and of peace must not be denied.

All of us everywhere and altogether have decreed this thing. For there could not be diverse opinions among us in whom there is one spirit and, therefore, it is evident that he whom we see to think differently does not keep the truth of the Holy Spirit with the others. Let us know plainly who has been substituted in place of Marcian in Arles that we may know to whom to direct our brethren and to whom we should write. I trust that you, dearly beloved Brother, are always well.

---
9 Cf. Hab. 2.5.
10 Luke 16.15.
11 Immediate predecessors of Stephen in the papacy. Cf. Letters 44, n. 2, and 61, n. 2.

244   SAINT CYPRIAN

69. Cyprian[1] *to Magnus,*[2] *his son, greeting.*

(1) With your conscientious diligence, you have consulted our poor intelligence, dearly beloved Son, as to whether, among other heretics, they also who come from Novatian[3] ought, after his profane washing, to be baptized and sanctified in the Catholic Church with the legitimate and true and only baptism of the Church. Concerning this matter, as much as the capacity of our faith and the holiness and truth of the Divine Scriptures suggest, we say that all heretics and schismatics altogether have no power or right. Because of this, Novatian neither ought to be nor can be made an exception because he himself, abiding outside of the Church and acting against the peace and love of Christ, should be considered among adversaries and antichrists.

For when our Lord Jesus Christ stated in His Gospel that His enemies were those who were not with Him, He did not point out any particular sort as heretics, but showed that all, indeed, who were not with Him and who, not collecting with Him, were scattering His flock, were His adversaries, saying: 'He who is not with me is against me; and he who does not gather with me scatters.'[4] Likewise, the blessed Apostle John himself did not point out any heresy or schism, nor did he propose any especially separate, but he called antichrists all who had gone out from the Church and were acting against the Church, saying: 'You have heard that Antichrist is coming, so now many antichrists have been made; whence we know that it is the last hour. They have gone forth from us, but they were not of us. For if they had been of us, they would have continued with us.'[5] Whence it appears that all are adversaries of the Lord and antichrists who, it is evident,

---
1 255 A.D.
2 Magnus, African Christian whom Cyprian advises on the two problems of Novatianist and clinical baptism.
3 Cf. Letter 44, n. 7.
4 Luke 11.23.
5 Cf. 1 John 2.18, 19.

have withdrawn from charity and from the unity of the Catholic Church.

In addition also, the Lord asserts in His Gospel and says: 'But if he despise even the Church, let him be to thee as the heathen and the publican.'[6] But if they who despise the Church are considered as the heathen and the publicans, much more certainly is it necessary for rebels and enemies, who erect false altars and unlawful priesthoods and sacrilegious sacrifices and false names, to be considered among the heathen and the publicans, since they who sin less and are only despisers of the Church are judged as heathen and publicans in the judgment of the Lord.

(2) That the Church is one, the Holy Spirit declares in the Canticle of Canticles, saying in the person of Christ: 'One is my dove, my perfect one; she is the only one of her mother, the chosen of her parent.'[7] Concerning this again, He says furthermore: 'An enclosed garden is my sister, my bride . . . a fountain sealed. . . . a well of living water.'[8] But if the garden enclosed is the spouse of Christ, which is the Church, a thing enclosed cannot lie open to outsiders and profane men. And if the fountain is sealed, there is no access to the fountain to anyone placed outside either to drink or to be sealed therewith. The well of living water, also, if it is one, is the same which is within; he who is situated outside cannot be vivified and sanctified by that water of which it is granted only to those who are within to have all use and drink.

And Peter, showing that there is one Church and that those alone who are in the Church can be baptized, asserted and said: 'In the ark of Noe, a few, that is, eight souls of men were saved through water. Its counterpart, Baptism, will now save you also,'[9] proving and testifying that one ark of Noe was the type of the one Church. If, in that baptism of the purged and purified world, he who was not in the ark of Noe could

---
6 Cf. Matt. 18.17.
7 Cant. 6.8.
8 Cf. Cant. 4.12, 15.
9 Cf. 1 Peter 3.20, 21.

then be saved by water, he who is not in the Church to which alone baptism has been granted can now be vivified through baptism!

But Paul, making this same matter clearer and more open, in addition, writes to the Ephesians and says: 'Christ loved the Church, and delivered himself up for her, that he might sanctify her, cleansing her in the bath of water.'[10] But if there is one Church which is loved by Christ and that alone is purged by His washing, how can he who is not in the Church either be loved by Christ or washed or purged by His washing?

(3) Because of this, since the Church alone has the life-giving water and the power of baptizing and of cleansing men, he who says with Novatian that anyone can be baptized and sanctified must first show and teach that Novatian is in the Church or presides over the Church. For the Church is one and what is one cannot be both within and without. For if it is with Novatian, it was not with Cornelius. If it was, in truth, with Cornelius, who succeeded Bishop Fabian[11] by a legitimate ordination and whom the Lord also glorified beyond the honor of the bishopric with martyrdom, Novatian is not in the Church; nor can he be counted as a bishop, who, succeeding to no one and despising evangelical and apostolic tradition, has sprung from himself. For he who was not ordained in the Church can neither have nor keep the Church in any way.

(4) But the faith of the Divine Scripture manifests that the Church is not outside and that it cannot be rent or divided against itself, but that it holds the unity of an inseparable and indivisible house since it is written concerning the rite of the Passover and of the Lamb, which Lamb signifies Christ: 'It shall be eaten in one house; you shall not take any of its flesh outside the house.'[12] We also see this expressed concerning Rahab, who herself also signified a type of the Church, to whom it was entrusted and said: 'Gather your father and

---

10 Cf. Eph. 5.25, 26.
11 Cf. Letter 30, n. 3.
12 Exod. 12.46.

your mother and your brothers and all the house of your father to yourself into your house. And whosoever shall go out of the door of your house, he will be responsible for himself.'[13]

In this mystery it is declared that in one house alone, that is, in the Church, there ought to be assembled together those who will live and escape from the destruction of the world. But whoever will go out from the elect gathered together, that is, if anyone whoever, having found grace in the Church, has withdrawn and departed from the Church, he will be responsible, that is, the fact that he may perish will be imputed to him. The Apostle Paul explains this, teaching and instructing that a heretic must be avoided as perverse and a sinner and condemned by himself.[14] For this is the man who will be responsible for himself, not cast out by the bishop, but having fled from the Church of his own will, with heretical presumption condemned by himself.

(5) And, therefore, the Lord, suggesting to us the unity coming from divine authority, asserts and says: 'I and the Father are one.'[15] Recalling His Church to that unity, He again says: 'And there shall be one fold and one shepherd.'[16] But if there is one flock, how can he who is not in the number of the flock be numbered in the flock? Or, when the true shepherd remains and presides in the Church of God after a valid ordination, how can he be considered as a shepherd who, succeeding no one but beginning from himself, has become foreign and strange, an enemy of the peace of the Lord and of divine unity, not living in the house of God, that is, in the Church of God, in which none live except the peaceful and those of one mind, since the Holy Spirit speaks in the Psalms and says: 'God makes men of one mind to dwell in a house'?[17]

Finally, the very Sacrifices of the Lord declare that Christian unanimity is bound to itself with a firm and inseparable char-

---

13 Cf. Jos. 2.18, 19.
14 Cf. Titus 3.10, 11.
15 John 10.30.
16 John 10.16.
17 Cf. Ps. 67.7.

ity. For when the Lord calls Bread made from the union of many grains His Body, He indicates our people whom He bore united; and when He calls Wine pressed from the clusters of grapes and many small berries and gathered in one His Blood, He, likewise, signifies our flock joined by the mixture of a united multitude. If Novatian is joined to this Bread of the Lord, if he himself is also united to the Chalice of Christ, he may also be able to seem to have the grace of the one ecclesiastical baptism if it is established that he holds the unity of the Church.

(6) Finally, how inseparable is the sacrament of unity and how hopeless are they and what greatest perdition they seek for themselves from the indignation of God—they who make a schism and, after having abandoned their bishop, appoint for themselves another false bishop from without—the Divine Scripture declares in the Book of Kings, when from the tribe of Juda and Benjamin ten tribes were separated and, abandoning their king, appointed themselves another from without. 'And the Lord was offended,' it says, 'at all the seed of Israel and afflicted them and delivered them up to plunder till he cast them away from his face because Israel was rent from the house of David, and they made Jeroboam son of Nabat their king.'[18] It said that the Lord was offended and gave them over to perdition because they had been dispersed from unity and had appointed another king for themselves.

And so great indignation of the Lord remained against those who had made the schism that, even when the man of God had been sent to Jeroboam to upbraid him for his sins and to foretell future vengeance, he was forbidden also to eat bread and to drink water among them. Since he had not heeded this and had dined contrary to the precept of God, he was immediately stricken by the majesty of divine censure, whence, upon his return, he was killed on the journey by the attack and bite of a lion. And does anyone of you dare to say that the life-giving water of baptism and heavenly grace can be

---
18 Cf. 4 Kings 17.20, 21.

common with schismatics with whom neither earthly food nor worldly drink ought to be common?

Moreover, the Lord satisfies us in His Gospel and reveals a greater light of understanding that the same men who then had separated themselves from the tribe of Juda and Benjamin and, after having abandoned Jerusalem, had withdrawn to Samaria, should be reputed among the profane and the Gentiles. For when He first sent His disciples upon the ministry of salvation, He commanded and said: 'Do not go in the direction of the Gentiles, nor enter the town of the Samaritans.'[19] Sending first to the Jews, He orders the Gentiles to be passed over as yet; but, adding that the city of the Samaritans, where there were schismatics, ought to be omitted, He shows that the schismatics were in the same category as the Gentiles.

(7) But if anyone objects—to say that Novatian holds the same law as the Catholic Church holds, baptizes with the same symbol with which we baptize, knows the same God the Father, the same Christ the Son, the same Holy Spirit, and, because of this, can usurp the power of baptizing because he seems not to differ from us in the questioning of baptism— let whoever thinks that this must be objected know first that there is not one law of symbol for us and the schismatics nor the same questioning. For when they say: 'Do you believe in the remission of sins and life everlasting through the Holy Church?' they lie by their questioning because they do not have a Church. Then, also, by their voice they themselves confess that the remission of sins cannot be given except by the Holy Church, which, not having, they show that sins cannot be remitted there.

(8) But that they are said to know the same God the Father, the same Christ the Son, the same Holy Spirit as we cannot help such men. For Core and Dathan and Abiron also knew the same God with the priest, Aaron, and Moses. Living under the same law and religion, they called upon the one and true God who must be adored and invoked. Yet, because,

---
19 Matt. 10.5.

having transgressed the ministry of their place against Aaron, the priest who had assumed the legitimate priesthood by the condescension and the ordination of the Lord, they claimed for themselves the privilege of sacrificing, stricken from heaven, they paid the penalty immediately for their unlawful attempts. Sacrifices offered irreligiously and illegally against the law of the divine decree could not be approved and be profitable.

That the very thuribles, also, in which incense had been offered unlawfully, should not be used again among the priests but should rather show forth the remembrance of the divine indignation and vengeance for the correction of posterity, by the order of the Lord, they were brought forth and burned and purged by fire into ductile plates and were affixed to the altar, according to what the Divine Scripture says. 'A reminder,' it says 'to the children of Israel that no layman who is not a descendant of Aaron should approach to offer incense before the Lord, lest he be as Core.'[20]

And yet those men had not made a schism nor, having gone out, had they rebelled against the priests of God impudently and hostilely. But now these who rend the Church, rebels also against the peace and unity of Christ, are attempting to erect a throne for themselves and to assume the primacy and to claim the liberty of baptizing and of sacrificing. How can they who are struggling against God for what is not lawful to them accomplish what they do or gain anything from God for their unlawful attempts? Wherefore, they who support Novatian or other schismatics of the same kind contend in vain that anyone can be baptized and sanctified by a salutary baptism when it is evident that the one baptizing has not the permission for baptizing.

(9) And that it may be better known what is the divine censure against boldness of this nature, we find that in so great a crime, not only the leaders and authors, but also the sharers; are destined for punishment unless they have separated themselves from the communion of the wicked since the

---
20 Cf. Num. 17.5.

Lord warns and says through Moses: 'Keep away from the tents of these most wicked men and do not touch anything that is theirs lest you perish likewise in their sins.'[21] And the Lord fulfilled what He had threatened by Moses, that whoever had not separated himself from Core and Dathan and Abiron immediately paid the penalty for his impious communion. By this example it is shown and proved that all who have mixed themselves with irreligious rashness with schismatics against prelates and bishops will be liable both for the guilt and the punishment, just as also, through the Prophet Osee, the Holy Spirit states and says: 'Their sacrifices will be like the bread of mourning; all who eat it shall be made unclean,'[22] teaching, indeed, and showing completely that all who were contaminated by the sin of those men were united with the leaders in their torture.

(10) For what can be the merits before God for them on whom punishments are divinely inflicted? Or how can such men who, as enemies of bishops, attempt to usurp those things which are foreign to them and illegal and granted to them by no law justify and sanctify the baptized? Yet we do not wonder that such men are disputing according to their depravity. It is necessary for each one of them to claim what he does, nor do the conquered yield easily although they know that what they are doing is not allowed. That is to be wondered at, nay rather, to be indignant at, and to be deplored that Christians are assisting antichrists and that prevaricators of the faith and betrayers of the Church stand within the very Church itself against the Church. Since these, indeed, stubborn and indocile as they are in other matters, yet confess this, that all either heretics or schismatics do not have the Holy Spirit and, therefore, can baptize but they cannot give the Holy Spirit, in that very matter they are held by us that we may show that those who do not have the Holy Spirit cannot baptize at all.

---
21 Cf. Num. 16.26.
22 Cf. Osee 9.4.

(11) For since in baptism his sins are forgiven for each one, the Lord proves and declares in His Gospel that sins can be forgiven through them alone who have the Holy Spirit. For, after the Resurrection, sending His disciples, He spoke to them and said: ' "As the Father has sent me, I also send you." When he had said this, he breathed upon them, and said to them, "Receive the Holy Spirit; whose sins you shall forgive, they are forgiven him; and whose you shall retain, they are retained." '[23] In this place, He shows that he alone who has the Holy Spirit can baptize and give the remission of sins.

Finally, John, who was to baptize Christ our Lord Himself, previously had received the Holy Spirit when he was still in his mother's womb, so that it might be certain and manifest that only those who have the Holy Spirit can baptize. Therefore, let those who defend heretics or schismatics answer us whether they have the Holy Spirit or whether they have not. If they have, why are hands placed upon the ones baptized there when they come to us to receive the Spirit since He would have already been received there if He could have been given?

But if all heretics and schismatics from without do not give the Holy Spirit and, therefore, hands are imposed by us that here He may be received because there He is not and cannot be given, it is clear that the remission of sins cannot be given through those men who, it is certain, do not have the Holy Spirit. And, therefore, that, according to the divine plan and the evangelical truth, they may be able to obtain the remission of sins and to be sanctified and to become the temples of God, all who come from adversaries and antichrists to the Church of Christ must, indeed, be baptized in the baptism of the Church.

(12) You have asked also, dearly beloved Son, what I thought about those who gain the grace of God in infirmity and illness, as to whether they are to be considered as legitimate Christians because they have not been bathed in the

---
23 Cf. John 20.21-23.

water of salvation, but sprinkled with it. In this matter, our reserve and moderation prejudge no one so that each one should perceive what he thinks best and should act according to his conscience. We, as far as our poor ability conceives of the problem, think that the divine benefits can in nothing be mutilated or weakened and that nothing else can occur there when, with full and complete faith of both the giver and of the receiver, there is received what is drawn from the divine gifts. For in the life-giving sacrament, the contagion of sins is not so washed away as the uncleanness of skin and of body in a carnal and worldly bath that there is need of saltpeter and also other aids and a tub and a pool in which the puny body can be washed and cleansed. In another fashion is the soul of the believer washed; in another fashion is the mind of man cleansed through the merits of faith. In the salutary Sacraments, when necessity compels and when God bestows His pardon, divine benefits are conferred completely upon the believers.

Nor ought it to disturb anyone whether the sick are sprinkled or drenched when they receive the grace of the Lord since the Holy Spirit speaks through the Prophet Ezechiel and says: 'And I will sprinkle clean water upon you and you shall be cleansed from all your impurities and from all your idols. And I will cleanse you. And I will give you a new heart and place a new spirit within you.'[24] Again in Numbers: 'And the man who shall be unclean until the evening shall be purified on the third day and on the seventh, and he shall be cleansed. But if he is not purified on the third day and on the seventh day, he will not be clean, and his soul will be exterminated from Israel because the water of sprinkling has not been sprinkled over him.'[25] And again: 'And the Lord spoke to Moses, saying: "Take the Levites from among the children of Israel and purify them. This is what you shall do to them to purify them. Sprinkle them with the water of

---
24 Cf. Ezech. 36.25, 26.
25 Cf. Num. 19.8, 12, 13.

purification." '[26] And again: 'The water of sprinkling is a purification.'[27] From this it appears that the sprinkling with water is also equal to the life-giving bath and, when these things are done in the Church, when the faith of both the recipient and of the minister is unblemished, everything is present and can be accomplished and consummated through the Majesty of the Lord and the truth of faith.

(13) But, in turn, as to the fact that certain ones call those who have gained the grace of Christ by this salutary water and lawful faith not Christians, but patients,[28] I do not find whence they take this name unless, perchance, those who have read also many hidden things in Hippocrates[29] and Soranus[30] have taken these patients[31] from them. For I, who know the patient of the Gospel, know that to that paralytic and infirm man, who lay on a bed through the long passage of his age, his infirmity hindered not at all his arriving at heavenly strength most fully. Not only was he raised by the mercy of the Lord from his bed, but he himself, when his strength was restored and repaired, picked up his own bed.

And, therefore, as far as it is given to us to understand by faith and to perceive, this is my opinion, that whoever has gained divine grace in the Church by the law and right of faith is judged a legitimate Christian. Or if any think that those have gained nothing from this because they have been only sprinkled by the life-giving water, if they are vain and empty, let them not be deceived that, if they overcome the inconvenience of their sickness and become well, they should be baptized. But if they who have already been sanctified by an ecclesiastical baptism cannot be baptized, why are they scandalized in their faith and in the mercy of the Lord? Or, have they obtained, indeed, the grace of the Lord, but in a

---

26 Cf. Num. 8.5-7.
27 Cf. Num. 19.9.
28 *clinicos*.
29 Hippocrates, Greek physician, father of medicine, c. 460-377 B.C.
30 Soranus, Greek physician, fl. 98-138 A.D., also wrote a biography of Hippocrates.
31 *istos clinicos*.

shorter and lesser measure of the divine gift and of the Holy Spirit, that they should be considered as Christians in a way, but not such that they should be considered with the rest?

(14) Nay, rather, the Holy Spirit is not given from a measure, but is poured out completely upon the believer. For if the day is born to all equally, and if the sun shines upon all with equal and similar light, how much more does Christ, the Sun and the True Day, bestow equally in His Church the light of eternal life with equal measure! We see that the pledge of this equality is celebrated in Exodus, when the manna from heaven fell and, with a prefiguring of the future, showed the nourishment of heavenly bread and the food of the coming Christ. For there, without distinction either of sex or of age, a measure was collected for each equally.

Whence it appears that the mercy of Christ and the heavenly grace following after are divided among all equally; without regard for sex, without discrimination of age, without respect of persons, the gift of spiritual grace is poured forth upon all of the people of God. Assuredly, that same spiritual grace which is received equally in baptism by the believers afterward either diminishes or increases in our manner of living and in our action as, in the Gospel, the seed of the Lord is sowed equally, but, according to the variety of the soil, some is taken away; some brings forth an abundant supply, either thirtyfold or sixtyfold or one hundredfold with abundant fruit. But still, when each one is called to the penny reward, why is it that what has been evenly distributed by God is lessened by human interpretation?

(15) But if anyone is disturbed in this that certain of those who are baptized while ill are still tempted by unclean spirits, let him know that the wickedness of the devil remains strong all the way up to the saving water, but, in true baptism, it loses all the virus of its malice. This example we see in the King Pharao, who, having resisted for a while and having delayed in his perfidy for so long a time, could resist and prevail until he came to the water; when he had come thither,

he was both conquered and destroyed. The blessed Apostle Paul declares that the sea was a pledge of baptism, saying: 'For I would not have you ignorant, brethren, that our fathers were all under the cloud, and all passed through the sea, and all were baptized in Moses and in the cloud and in the sea.'[32] And he added, saying: 'Now all these things came to pass as examples to us.'[33]

This is being carried out even today that through exorcists, by means of the human voice and the divine power, the devil is lashed out and burned out and tortured and, although he says often that he is going out and leaving the man of God, yet he deceives in what he has said and does what was first done through Pharoa with the same lying of obstinacy and of fraud. Yet when it comes to the water of salvation and to the sanctification of baptism, we ought to know and to trust that the devil is oppressed there and that the man dedicated to God is freed by the divine mercy. For if scorpions and serpents which prevail in dry land, when hurled into water can prevail or retain their poison, evil spirits, also, which are called scorpions and serpents, and yet are trodden under foot by the power given through us by the Lord, can remain in the body of man, in whom, baptized and after that sanctified, the Holy Spirit begins to dwell.

(16) We have found out this finally also through the things themselves: that with urgent necessity in illness those who are baptized and have gained grace are freed from the unclean spirit by which formerly they were urged on and live praiseworthy and approved in the Church and accomplish much through each day in the increase of heavenly grace through an increase of faith; and that, on the contrary, often some of those who are baptized in good health, if afterward they begin to sin, are distressed by the return of the unclean spirit; that it is manifest that the devil is excluded in baptism by the faith

---

32 1 Cor. 10.1, 2.
33 Cf. 1 Cor. 10.6.

of the believer; and that he returns afterward if faith should fail.

Unless it seems just to some people that those who are polluted among adversaries and antichrists by profane water outside the Church should be considered baptized! But those who are baptized in the Church seem to have gained less of mercy and of divine grace, and so great honor should be considered for the heretics that, when they come, they should not be questioned as to whether they were bathed or sprinkled, whether they were patient or peripatetic; but among us there is detraction from the whole truth of faith and its majesty and sanctity are taken away from ecclesiastical baptism.

(17) I have written an answer to your letter, dearly beloved Son, as far as my moderate ability availed and I have shown as well as possible, prescribing for no one, that every prelate, who will render an account of his actions to the Lord, should decide what he thinks best, according to what the blessed Apostle Paul writes in his Epistle to the Romans and says: 'Every one of us will render an account for himself. Therefore let us not judge one another.'[34] I trust that you, dearly beloved Son, are always well.

---

34 Cf. Rom. 14.12, 13.

70. *Cyprian,[1] Liberalis,[2] Caldonius,[3] Junius,[4] Primus,[5] Cecil,[6] Polycarp,[7] Nicomedes,[8] Felix,[9] Marrutius,[10] Successus,[11] Lucian,[12] Honoratus,[13] Fortunatus,[14] Victor,[15] Donatus,[16] Lucius,[17] Herculanus,[18] Pomponius,[19] Demetrius,[20] Quintus,[21] Saturninus,[22] Mark,[23] another Saturninus,[24] another Donatus,[25] Rogatian,[26] Sedatus,[27] Tertullus,[28] Hortensian,[29] still another Saturninus,[30] Sattius,[31] to Januarius,[32] Saturninus,[33] Maximus,[34] Victor,[35] another Victor,[36] Cassius,[37] Proculus,[38] Modianus,[39] Cittinus,[40] Gargilius,[41]*

1 255 A.D.
2 Cf. Letter 48, n. 6.
3 Cf. Letter 24, n. 2.
4 Cf. Letter 57, n. 6.
5 Cf. Letter 67, n. 3.
6 Cf. Letter 4, n. 2.
7 Cf. Letter 48, n. 5.
8 Cf. Letter 57, n. 4.
9 Cf. Letter 56, n. 7.
10 Cf. Letter 57, n. 7.
11 Cf. Letter 57, n. 9.
12 Cf. Letter 57, n. 17.
13 Cf. Letter 57, n. 29.
14 Cf. Letter 44, n. 9.
15 Cf. Letter 4, n. 3, and Letter 57, n. 12.
16 Cf. Letter 57, n. 34.
17 Lucius, African bishop, perhaps of Ausafa or of Membrasa. Cf. Letter 67, n. 29.
18 Cf. Letter 41, n. 3.
19 Cf. Letter 4, n. 6.
20 Cf. Letter 57, n. 37.
21 Cf. Letter 57, n. 28.
22 Cf. Letter 57, n. 13.
23 Mark, African bishop of Macthar, present at synod.
24 Cf. Letter 57, n. 13.
25 Cf. Letter 57, n. 34.
26 Cf. Letter 3, n. 2. Two bishops of this name attended the council.
27 Cf. Letter 4, n. 4.
28 Cf. Letter 4, n. 5.
29 Cf. Letter 57, n. 31.
30 Cf. Letter 57, n. 13.
31 Cf. Letter 57, n. 18.
32 Cf. Letter 62, n. 2.
33 Cf. Letter 57, n. 13.
34 Cf. Letter 62, n. 3.
35 Cf. Letter 57, n. 12, probably another Numidian bishop.
36 Cf. n. 35 above.
37 Cassius, Numidian bishop of Macomades near Cirta.
38 Cf. Letter 62, n. 4.
39 Cf. Letter 62, n. 6.

Eutychianus,[42] *another Gargilius,*[43] *another Saturninus,*[44] *Nemesianus,*[45] *Nampulus,*[46] *Antonian,*[47] *Rogatian,*[48] *Honoratus,*[49] *their brethren, greeting.*

(1) When we were together in council,[50] dearly beloved Brethren, we read your letter which you wrote concerning those who seem baptized among heretics and schismatics, as to whether they ought to be baptized when they come to the Catholic Church, which is one. Concerning this matter, although you yourselves there hold the truth and firmness of the Catholic rule, yet, because you thought that we ought to be consulted in accordance with our mutual love, we express our judgment, which is not new, but we join with you with a like agreement in one already decreed by our predecessors long ago and observed by us, judging plainly and holding for certain that no one can be baptized outside, without the Church, since there is one baptism appointed in the Holy Church. And it is written in the words of the Lord: 'They have forsaken me, the source of living water; and they have dug themselves broken cisterns, that cannot hold water.'[51] And again the Divine Scripture warns and says: 'Abstain from strange water and do not drink from a strange fountain.'[52]

But the water ought to be first cleansed and sanctified by the bishop that it may be able to wash away in its baptism the sins of the man who is baptized since the Lord says through Ezechiel: 'And I will sprinkle clean water upon you, and you

---

40 Cittinus, Numidian bishop.
41 Gargilius, Numidian bishop.
42 Eutychianus, Numidian bishop.
43 Another Gargilius, another Numidian bishop.
44 Cf. Letter 57, n. 13.
45 Cf. Letter 62, n. 7.
46 Cf. Letter 62, n. 8.
47 Cf. Letter 55, n. 2.
48 Rogatian, one of the bishops at the council. Cf. n. 47 above. It is difficult to distinguish these bishops with the same name.
49 Cf. n. 13 above. This is the second Honoratus mentioned in the letter.
50 Council of 255.
51 Cf. Jer. 2.13.
52 Cf. Prov. 9.18, LXX.

shall be cleansed from all your impurities and from all your idols. And I will cleanse you. And I will give you a new heart and place a new spirit within you.'[53] But how can he who is himself unclean and with whom the Holy Spirit is not cleanse and sanctify water since the Lord says in Numbers: 'Whatever the unclean person touches will be unclean.'[54] Or how can one who baptizes grant to another the remission of sins who, himself outside the Church, cannot put aside his own sins?

(2) But the very question which is used in baptism is a witness of the truth. For when we say: 'Do you believe in eternal life and the remission of sins through the Holy Church?' we know that the remission of sins is not given except in the Church. But among the heretics where the Church is not, sins are not forgiven. They who agree with the heretics, therefore, either change the questioning or vindicate the truth unless they claim the Church for those who, they contend, have baptism.

It is necessary also for him who is baptized to be anointed that, having received chrism, that is anointing, he can be anointed of God and have in himself the grace of Christ. But, in turn, it is by the Eucharist that the oil by which the baptized are anointed is sanctified on the altar. But he who has neither altar nor Church cannot sanctify the creature of oil. Thus neither can spiritual anointing be had among the heretics since it is evident that oil cannot be sanctified among them, nor the Eucharist be held among them at all. But we ought to know and remember that it is written: 'Let not the oil of the sinner anoint my head.'[55] Before in the Psalms, the Holy Spirit warned of this lest any going astray and wandering from the path of truth should be anointed among the heretics and adversaries of Christ.

But what prayer can the sacrilegious and sinful priest make on behalf of the baptized since it is written: 'God does not

---

53 Cf. Ezech. 36.25, 26.
54 Cf. Num. 19.22.
55 Cf. Ps. 140.5.

hear the sinner; but if anyone is a worshipper of God, and does his will, him he hears'?[56] But who can give what he himself does not have or how can he accomplish spiritual deeds who himself has lost the Holy Spirit? And, therefore, he who comes ignorant to the Church must be baptized and renewed that he may be sanctified within through the holy ones since it is written: 'Be holy, for I am also holy, says the Lord.'[57] Thus he who has been seduced into error and baptized without may put this aside also in the true and ecclesiastical baptism because a man coming to God, while he seeks the bishop, runs into a sacrilegious one by the fraud of error.

(3) As for the rest, it is to approve of the baptisms of heretics and schismatics to agree to it that they have baptized. For part cannot be void and part be valid there. If one could baptize, he could also give the Holy Spirit. But if he cannot give the Holy Spirit because, established outside, he is not with the Holy Spirit, he cannot baptize the one who comes since baptism is also one, and the Holy Spirit is one, and the Church founded by Christ our Lord upon Peter in the origin and established plan of unity is also one.

Thus it happens that, since all things are useless and false among those men, none of those things which they have done ought to be approved by us. For how can that be ratified and firm with the Lord which those do who the Lord says in His Gospel are His enemies and adversaries, stating: 'He who is not with me is against me; and he who does not gather with me scatters.'[58] And the blessed Apostle John, also keeping the commands and precepts of the Lord, put in his Epistle: 'You have heard that Antichrist is coming, so now many antichrists have been made; whence we know that it is the last hour. They have gone forth from us, but they were not of us. For if they had been of us, they would have continued with us.'[59]

Whence we also ought to assemble and to consider whether

---
56 Cf. John 9.31.
57 Cf. Lev. 19.2.
58 Luke 11.23.
59 Cf. 1 John 2.18, 19.

they who are the adversaries of the Lord and have been called antichrists can give the grace of Christ. Wherefore, we who are with the Lord and hold the unity of the Lord and administer His priesthood in the Church according to His condescension ought to repudiate and to reject and to consider as impious whatever His adversaries and antichrists do. And we ought to give through all of the Sacraments of divine grace the truth of unity and faith to those who, coming from error and depravity, recognize the true faith of the one Church. We trust that you, dearly beloved Brethren, are always well.

71. Cyprian[1] to Quintus,[2] his brother, greeting.

(1) Lucian,[3] our fellow priest, brought word to me, dearly beloved Brother, that you desired us to make known to you what we judge concerning these who seem baptized by heretics and schismatics. Concerning this matter, that you may know what we very many fellow bishops with priests who were present in a council[4] decided recently, I have sent to you a copy of the same letter. For I do not know by what presumption certain of our colleagues are led to think that they who have been baptized by heretics ought not to be baptized when they come to us because they say that there is one baptism which, indeed, is one in the Catholic Church because the Church is one and there cannot be baptism outside of the Church. For since there cannot be two baptisms, if the heretics truly baptize, they themselves have baptism. And whoever grants to them the protection of his authority yields to them and consents that an enemy and adversary of Christ would seem to have the power of washing and of purifying and of sanctifying men.

But we say that those who come thence are not rebaptized

---
1 255 A.D.
2 Cf. Letter 55, n. 5.
3 Lucian, African priest who delivered Quintus' letter to Cyprian.
4 255 A.D. Cyprian's Fifth Council of Carthage, first on baptism.

among us, but baptized. For they cannot receive anything there where there is nothing, but they come to us that they may receive here where there are both grace and all truth because both grace and truth are one. But again, certain of our colleagues prefer to give honor to heretics rather than to agree with us and, while, by the assertion of one baptism, they are unwilling to baptize those who come, thus they either themselves make two baptisms while they say that there is baptism among heretics or, certainly, what is more serious, they hasten to place before and to prefer the stained and profaned baptism of heretics to the true and one and legitimate baptism of the Catholic Church, not considering that it is written: 'He that is baptized by one dead, . . . what does his washing avail?'[5] But it is clear that those who are not in the Church of Christ are counted among the dead and that another cannot be vivified by one who himself is not living since there is one Church, which has followed the grace of eternal life and lives forever and vivifies the people of God.

(2) And they say that, in this, they are following ancient custom although, among the ancient heresies, there were as yet the first beginnings of schisms whenever these were there who withdrew from the Church and had been baptized in it first, it was not necessary to baptize them when they returned to the Church and did penance. We still practice this today, that it is sufficient to impose hands in penance upon those who, it is evident, have been baptized and have gone from us to the heretics if afterward, having recognized their sin and put aside their error, they return to truth and to their mother, that, because he had once been a sheep, the shepherd receives this wandering and straying sheep back into his sheepfold.

But if he who comes from the heretics was not first baptized in the Church, but comes as a stranger and a pagan completely, he must be baptized that he may become a sheep because there is one water in the Holy Church which makes sheep. And, therefore, because nothing can be common to

---

5 Sir. (Ecclus.) 34.30.

lying and to truth, to darkness and to light, to death and to immortality, to Antichrist and to Christ, we ought to hold through all things the unity of the Catholic Church and not to yield in anything to the enemies of faith and of truth.

(3) But one must not prescribe from custom but overcome by reason. For neither did Peter, whom the Lord chose first and on whom He built His Church, when Paul later disagreed with him concerning circumcision claim anything for himself insolently nor assume anything arrogantly, as to say that he held the primacy and ought to be obeyed by both the young and by the newcomers. He did not despise Paul because he had first been a persecutor of the Church, but admitted the counsel of truth and agreed easily to the legitimate reason which Paul asserted, showing, indeed, a lesson to us both of concord and of patience that we should not stubbornly love our own way, but we should rather consider as ours these ideas which are suggested at any time usefully and safely by our brethren and colleagues if they are true and lawful.

Paul, also, foreseeing this matter and looking out for concord and peace faithfully, wrote in his Epistle, saying: 'Let either two or three prophets speak, and let the rest act as judges. If anything is revealed to another sitting by, let the first keep silence.'[6] In this part, he taught and showed that many things are revealed for the better to individuals and that each one ought not to strive obstinately for that which he once learned and held, but that if anything better or more useful should exist, to embrace it willingly. For we are not conquered when better things are offered to us, but we are instructed, especially in these matters which pertain to the unity of the Church and to the truth of our hope and of our faith, that we bishops of God and prelates of His Church by His own condescension may know that the remission of sins cannot be given except in the Church and that the adversaries of Christ cannot claim anything of His grace for themselves.

---

6 Cf. 1 Cor. 14.29, 30.

(4) Agrippinus,[7] also, a man of happy memory, with the rest of his fellow bishops who were at that time governing the Church of the Lord in the African province and Numidia, decided and confirmed this, indeed, with the deliberate examination of the common council. We also have followed the religious and lawful decision of these men, salutary to faith and fitting to the Catholic Church. And that you may know what letters we have written about this matter, according to our mutual love, we have sent a copy of these to your notice as well as to that of our fellow bishops who are there. I trust that you, dearly beloved Brother, are always well.

72. *Cyprian*[1] *and others to Stephen,*[2] *their brother, greeting.*

(1) To settle certain matters and to investigate them by the examination of a common council, we thought it necessary, dearly beloved Brother, to summon and to proclaim a council with very many bishops assembled together; in this, indeed, many matters were brought forth and examined. But it was especially necessary to write to you and to confer with your dignity and wisdom concerning a matter which pertains greatly to sacerdotal authority and to the unity as well as to the dignity of the Catholic Church, coming from the ordination of the divine arrangement: that those who have been dyed[3] outside without the Church and stained by the touch of profane water among heretics and schismatics, when they come to us and to the Church which is one, ought to be baptized because it is not enough to impose hands upon them to receive the Holy Spirit unless they also receive the baptism of the Church.

For then, at last, they can be fully sanctified and be the sons

---

[7] Agrippinus, a predecessor of Cyprian in the see of Carthage, called the First Council of Carthage c. 215-217 A.D. This decided to rebaptize heretics.

[1] 255 A.D.
[2] Cf. Letter 67, n. 59.
[3] *tincti*. Although the word is used to refer to baptism, in this context with *maculati*, perhaps 'dipped' or 'dyed' is closer to Cyprian's thought.

of God if they are born of each sacrament since it is written: 'Unless a man be born of water and the Spirit, he cannot enter into the kingdom of God.'[4] For we find in the Acts of the Apostles that this was kept by the apostles and observed with the truth of salutary faith that, when, in the home of Cornelius, the Centurion, the Holy Spirit had descended upon the Gentiles who were there, burning with the fervor of faith, believing in the Lord with their whole heart, whereby filled, they blessed God in various tongues, nonetheless the blessed Apostle Peter, mindful of the divine precept and of the Gospel, taught that those same men who had already been filled with the Holy Spirit should be baptized, that nothing should seem to be omitted that they might keep the apostolic teaching through all of the divine precepts and the law of the Gospel. It has recently been expressed carefully in a letter which was written about this matter to Quintus,[5] our colleague abiding in Mauretania, that that is not baptism, moreover, which the heretics use, nor can anyone among them who struggles against Christ advance through the grace of Christ; it is, likewise, in the letter which our colleagues wrote before to fellow bishops presiding in Numidia; of both of these, I have submitted a copy.

(2) We add plainly and join, dearly beloved Brother, with common consent and authority that, even if any priests or deacons have been first ordained in the Catholic Church and afterwards have stood against the Church as perfidious men and rebels, or, among heretics, have been promoted by false bishops and antichrists by profane ordination, contrary to the will of Christ, and have attempted to offer in opposition to the one and divine altar false and sacrilegious sacrifices without, they also should be received when they return, upon this condition, that they should receive Communion as laymen and consider it sufficient that they who have remained the enemies of peace are admitted to peace. When they return, they ought

---
4 Cf. John 3.5.
5 Cf. Letter 55, n. 5.

not to retain among us the arms of ordination and of honor with which they have rebelled against us.

For bishops and ministers who serve the altar and the sacrifices ought to be upright and unstained since the Lord in Leviticus speaks and says: 'The man in whom there is stain and vice shall not draw near to offer gifts to the Lord.'[6] Likewise in Exodus, He teaches the same lessons and says: 'The priests, too, who approach the Lord God must be sanctified, lest perhaps the Lord abandon them.'[7] And again: 'And when they approach the altar of the Holy One to minister they will not bring sin upon themselves lest they die.'[8] But what sin can be greater, or what stain more deforming, than to have stood against Christ, than to have scattered His Church, which He prepared and established by His Blood, than, forgetful of evangelical peace and love, to have fought against the united and peaceful people of God with the madness of hostile discord?

And although these are the very men who later return to the Church, yet they cannot restore and bring back with them those who, seduced by them and overtaken by death without, have perished out of the Church without communion and peace, whose souls at the day of judgment will be required at the hands of these very men who were the authors and leaders of perdition. And, therefore, it is sufficient for pardon to be given to such men when they return, for their perfidy ought not to be promoted in the home of faith. For what shall we keep for the good and innocent and those who have not left the Church if we honor those who have withdrawn from us and have stood against the Church?

(3) We have brought these matters to your knowledge, dearly beloved Brother, for the sake of our common honor and our unaffected love, believing also that those things which are equally good and true are pleasing to you in accordance with

---
6 Cf. Lev. 21.21.
7 Cf. Exod. 19.22.
8 Cf. Exod. 28.43.

the truth of your religion and faith. As for the rest, we know that certain ones are unwilling to put aside what they have imbibed once and do not easily change their position but, while guarding among colleagues the bond of peace and concord, retain certain fixed ideas which they have once decided upon. In this matter, we do not apply force to anyone, nor do we give any law since each prelate has, in the administration of the Church, the free will of his own volition as one who will render an account of his action to his Lord. We trust that you, dearly beloved Brother, are always well.

73. Cyprian[1] to Jubaian,[2] his brother, greeting.

(1) You have written to me, dear Brother, desiring that the thought of my mind be signified to you as to what I judge concerning the baptism of heretics, who, placed outside and established out of the Church, claim for themselves a matter neither within their right nor within their power. We can neither ratify this nor consider it lawful since it is evident that this is illicit among them. And since we have already expressed in our letter,[3] what is our decision on this matter, to make a compendium for you, I have sent a copy of this same letter to you concerning what we decreed in the council when many were gathered together, what, likewise, I wrote back to our colleague, Quintus,[4] afterward when he inquired concerning the same matter.

And now also when we had assembled as many from the province of Africa as from Numidia,[5] bishops to the number of seventy-one, we confirmed this matter again with our decision, deciding that there is one baptism which is established

---

[1] 256 A.D.
[2] Jubaian, Mauretanian bishop who disagreed with Cyprian's views on baptism. Cyprian's answer was read at the council in 256 A.D.
[3] Letter 70.
[4] Letter 71.
[5] The Numidian bishops agreed with Cyprian and the other bishops of Africa regarding the need for baptizing those who came from heresy.

in the Catholic Church and that through this those coming to us from adulterous and profane water are not rebaptized, but baptized by us, and that they must be washed and sanctified by the truth of the saving water.

(2) Nor does what you explained in your letter disturb us, dearly beloved Brother, that the followers of Novatian[6] are rebaptizing those whom they entice away from us since what the enemies of the Church are doing does not pertain at all to us, provided we ourselves keep the honor of our power and the firmness of reason and truth. For Novatian, according to the custom of monkeys, which, although they are not men, imitate men, wishes to claim the authority and truth of the Catholic Church for himself when he himself is not in the Church, nay rather, remains up to this point a rebel and an enemy against the Church. For, knowing that there is one baptism, he claims this one for himself that he may say that the Church is with him and that he may make us heretics.

But we who hold the head and root of the one Church know for certain and we believe that nothing is allowed to him outside of the Church and that baptism which is one is with us, in which he himself was first baptized when he held the reason and the truth of the divine unity. But if Novatian thinks that those baptized in the Church must be rebaptized outside, out of the Church, he ought to begin with himself as the first to be rebaptized with a strange and heretical baptism since he, after the Church, nay rather, contrary to the Church, thinks that others must be baptized without.

But what is the reason that, because Novatian dares to do this, we should think it must not be done? What then? Because Novatian also usurps the honor of the episcopal throne, should we, therefore, renounce the throne? And because Novatian attempts to erect an altar and to offer sacrifices wrongfully, should we withdraw from the altar and sacrifices lest we seem to celebrate like and similar sacrifices with him? It is alike vain and stupid that, because Novatian claims for him-

---
6 Cf. Letter 44, n. 7.

self outside of the Church the image of truth, the Church should abandon truth.

(3) But among us it is no new or sudden thing for us to think that they who come from the heretics to the Church must be baptized, since the years are already many and the time is long from which, under Agrippinus,[7] a man of happy memory, many bishops assembling together decided this, and, from that day forth to this, so many thousand of heretics in our provinces, being converted to the Church, have not spurned or delayed but reasonably and freely embraced it that they might gain the grace of the life-giving fountain and of saving baptism. For it is not difficult for a teacher to make known true and lawful matters to him who, after having found out the depraved heresy and the ecclesiastical truth, comes for this that he may learn, learns for this that he may live. Let us not give to the heretics the stupidity of our support and agreement and they will promptly and freely follow the truth.

(4) Because I have found plainly in the letter of which you sent me a copy that it is written that what must be sought is not who baptized, since he who was baptized could receive the remission of sins according to his belief, I thought that this subject should not be passed by, especially since in the same letter I noticed that mention is made even of Marcion,[8] that he says that those coming from himself ought not to be baptized because they seem already to have been baptized in the Name of Jesus Christ.

We ought to consider, likewise, the faith of those who believe without as to whether they can gain any grace according to that same faith. For if there is one faith for both us and the heretics, there can also be one grace. If the Patripassians,[9]

---

7 Cf. Letter 71, n. 7.
8 Marcion, one of the most influential of second century heretics, adherent of Cerdo, made Christianity the starting point of his Gnostic sect.
9 Patripassians (Western name for those following the Sabellian heresy) identify the Father and Son as one person under two different names.

the Anthropians,[10] the Valentinians,[11] the Appelletians,[12] the Ophites,[13] the Marcionites,[14] and the other pests of heretics, and swords and poisons for overthrowing the truth, confess the same Father, the same Son, the same Holy Spirit, the same Church, it can be that there also baptism is one if faith is also one.

(5) But lest it be tedious to review all of the heresies and to think over either the ineptitudes or the insanities of each one since it does not delight us to say that which it is a shame or a horror to know, let us examine about Marcion alone, of whom mention was made in the letter sent to us by you, as to whether the method of his baptism can stand. For the Lord after the Resurrection, sending His disciples, instructs and teaches how they ought to baptize, saying: 'All power in heaven and on earth has been given to me. Go, therefore, and make disciples of all nations, baptizing them in the name of the Father, and of the Son, and of the Holy Spirit.'[15] He makes known the Trinity in whose Sacrament people were to be baptized. Does Marcion believe in this Trinity? Does he claim the same God the Father, the Creator, as we do? Does he recognize the same Son Christ, born of the Virgin Mary, who was the Word made Flesh, who bore our sins, who conquered death by dying, who first began the resurrection of the body through Himself and showed to His disciples that He had risen in the same Body?

But faith is far otherwise with Marcion and with the other heretics. Nay rather, there is nothing among them except perfidy and blasphemy and contention hostile to sanity and to truth. How, therefore, can he who is baptized with them seem to have gained the remission of sins and the grace of the

---
10 Anthropians, other heretics in Africa.
11 Valentinians, a Gnostic sect.
12 Apelletians or Appelletians, followers of Apelles, a Gnostic, the most famous of Marcion's disciples.
13 Ophites, a Gnostic sect in which the symbol of the serpent, abhorred by others, was an object of reverence.
14 Marcionites, followers of Marcion's Gnostic sect.
15 Matt. 28.18, 19.

divine mercy through his faith who does not have the truth of faith itself? For if, as it seems to some, anyone could receive anything outside, without the Church, according to his faith, assuredly he has received what he believed. But one believing the false could not receive the true, but rather he received adulterated and profane things according to what he believed.

(6) Jeremia, the prophet, censures in detail this subject of profane and adulterous baptism, saying: 'Why do those who grieve me prevail? My wound is incurable; when shall I be healed? When this is done, it is become for me as treacherous water not having faith.'[16] The Holy Spirit makes mention through the prophet of treacherous water also not having faith. What is this treacherous and faithless water? Assuredly it is that which asserts falsely the image of baptism and frustrates the grace of faith by its shadowy simulation.

But if, according to depraved faith, anyone could be baptized without and could gain the remission of his sins according to that same faith, he could, likewise, receive the Holy Spirit and it is not necessary for hands to be placed upon him when he comes that he may receive and be signed with the Holy Spirit. For either one could accomplish both by his faith without or he who had been without received neither of them.

(7) But it is clear when and through whom the remission of sins can be given, which is certainly given in baptism. For the Lord first gave to Peter, upon whom He built the Church and whence He instituted and showed the origin of unity, that same power that what he had absolved upon earth might be absolved. And after the Resurrection, He also speaks to the apostles, saying: ' "As the Father has sent me, I also send you." When he had said this, he breathed upon them and said to them, "Receive the Holy Spirit; whose sins you shall forgive, they are forgiven him and whose you shall retain, they are retained." '[17] Whence we know that only in the Church with

---

16 Cf. Jer. 15.18.
17 Cf. John 20.21-23.

prelates established by evangelical law and the ordination of the Lord is it lawful to baptize and to give the remission of sins; but, without, nothing can be either bound or absolved where there is no one who can either bind or absolve.

(8) Nor do we propose this, dearly beloved Brother, without the authority of the Divine Scripture when we say that by certain law and proper ordination all things are divinely appointed and that no one can usurp anything which is not of his own right and power for himself against bishops and priests. For Core, also, and Dathan and Abiron attempted to usurp for themselves the right of sacrificing against Moses and Aaron, the priest; yet they did not do unpunished what they dared unlawfully.[18] And the sons of Aaron, who placed a strange fire upon the altar, immediately were destroyed in the sight of the angry Lord.[19] That punishment awaits those who bring a strange water to a false baptism that the divine censure may avenge and punish heretics for doing that against the Church which is lawful only for the Church alone.

(9) But some say this: that for those who had been baptized in Samaria, at the coming of the Apostles Peter and John, only as hands were imposed upon them did they receive the Holy Spirit; yet they were not rebaptized. This situation, dear Brother, we see does not at all pertain to the present case. For those who had believed in Samaria had believed in the true faith and had been baptized within by the deacon, Philip, whom the same Apostles had sent, in the Church, which is one and to which alone it is permitted to give the grace of baptism and to absolve sins.[20] And, therefore, it was not necessary for those who had received legitimate and ecclesiastical baptism to be baptized again, but only that which was lacking was supplied by Peter and John, after having prayed for them and imposed hands upon them that the Holy Spirit should be invoked and infused into them.

---

18 Cf. Num. 16.35.
19 Cf. Lev. 10.1-3.
20 Cf. Acts. 8.14-17.

This now also is being done among us that those who are baptized in the Church are offered to the bishops of the Church and, through our prayer and the imposition of hands, may receive the Holy Spirit and be signed with the seal of the Lord.

(10) It is not, therefore, for us to judge, dearly beloved Brother, that we ought to yield to the heretics and to think that baptism, which has been given to the one and only Church alone, should be betrayed. It is the duty of a good soldier to defend the camp of his commander against rebels and enemies. It is the duty of the glorious leader to carry out the commissions entrusted to him. It is written: 'The Lord, your God, is a jealous God.'[21] We who have received the spirit of God ought to have the zeal of divine faith, by which zeal Phinees, meritorious, pleased God and softened the wrath of the angry One toward the people about to perish.[22] Why do we who have known only one Christ and His one Church consider for acceptance matters adulterous and strange, hostile to the divine unity?

The Church, expressing the image of Paradise,[23] encloses on the inside fruitful trees within its walls from which what does not make good fruit is cut off and cast into the fire. It waters these trees with four rivers, that is, with the four Gospels, from which it bestows the grace of baptism by the salutary and heavenly inundation. Can he who is not inside the Church water from the fountains of the Church? Can he who, perverse and condemned by himself and banished beyond the fountains of Paradise, has dried up and has failed with the dryness of eternal thirst bestow upon anyone the healthful and salutary drinks of Paradise?

(11) The Lord cries out that whoever thirsts should come and drink from the rivers of living water which have flowed from within Him.[24] Whither is he who thirsts to come? Will it

---
21 Cf. Deut. 4.24.
22 Cf. Num. 25.7-13.
23 Cf. Gen. 2.8.
24 Cf. John 7.37,38.

be to the heretics where the fountain and river of living water are not at all or to the Church, which is one and has been established by the voice of the Lord upon one who has received its keys? She is the one who keeps and possesses all the power of her Spouse the Lord. In her we preside; for her honor and unity we fight; we defend her grace and glory equally with faithful devotion. We water the thirsting people of God with the divine permission; we guard the boundaries of the life-giving fountains. If we hold the law of our possession, if we recognize the sacrament of unity, why do we appear as prevaricators of truth; why as betrayers of unity? The water of the Church, faithful and salutary and holy, cannot be corrupted and adulterated, just as the Church herself is also incorrupt and chaste and pure.

If heretics are devoted to the Church and are established in the Church, they can use her baptism and her other salutary goods. But if they are not in the Church, nay rather, if they are acting against the Church, how can they baptize with the baptism of the Church?

(12) It is not a small and slight matter granted to heretics when their baptism is considered accepted by us since thence begin all origin of faith and the salutary entrance to the hope of eternal life and the divine condescension in purifying and vivifying the servants of God. For if anyone could be baptized by heretics, he could certainly also obtain the remission of sins. If he obtained the remission of sins, he was also sanctified; if he was sanctified, he became a temple of God; if he became a temple of God, I ask of which God? If of the Creator, he could not be because he did not believe in Him. If of Christ, he who denies that Christ is God cannot become His temple. If of the Holy Spirit, because the Three are one, how can the Holy Spirit be pleased with him who is an enemy either of the Son or of the Father?

(13) Accordingly, in vain do some who are conquered by reason oppose custom to us as if custom were greater than truth or as if it ought not to be followed in spiritual matters

because it was revealed better by the Holy Spirit. For one who errs through simplicity can be pardoned as the blessed Apostle said concerning himself: 'For I formerly,' he said, 'was a blasphemer and persecutor and a bitter adversary; but I obtained mercy because I acted ignorantly.'[25] But after inspiration and revelation granted, he who continues foreknowing and understanding in that in which he had erred sins without pardon for ignorance. For he struggles with presumption and even a certain obstinacy when he is overcome by reason. Let not anyone say: 'We follow that which we have received from the apostles,' since the apostles handed down nothing if not one Church and one baptism, which is not established except in the same Church. And we find that no one, when he had been baptized among the heretics, was admitted in the same baptism and communicated by the apostles lest the apostles seem to have approved the baptism of heretics.

(14) For some say this as if what the Apostle Paul said pertained to the rights of heretics: 'Provided only that in every way, whether in pretense or in truth, Christ is being proclaimed';[26] we find this also that nothing can avail for their defense who support and applaud heretics. For Paul was not speaking of heretics or of their baptism in his Epistle that he may be shown to have stated anything which pertains to this matter. He was speaking concerning brethren either walking out of order and against the discipline of the Church or serving evangelical truth from the fear of the Lord.[27] And he stated that some of those spoke the Word of the Lord constantly and intrepidly, but some engaged in hatred and dissension; that some observed benevolent charity toward him, but others had evil dissension; but he himself patiently was enduring all things provided either in truth or through favorable moment the Name of Christ which Paul preached should come to the attention of very many and that the sow-

---

25 Cf. 1 Tim. 1.13.
26 Phil. 1.18.
27 Cf. Phil. 1.12-20.

ing of the word, as yet new and unpolished, might increase with the preaching of the speakers.

It is one thing, moreover, for those who are within the Church to speak of the Name of Christ; it is another for those who are without and act against the Church to baptize in the Name of Christ. Wherefore, let not him who supports the heretics quote that which Paul stated concerning the brethren, but let him show if he thought that anything ought to be granted to a heretic or if he approved either their faith and baptism or if he decided that perfidious and blasphemous men could receive the remission of sins outside of the Church.

(15) But if we consider what the apostles thought about heretics, we shall find that in all of their Epistles they execrate and abominate the sacrilegious depravity of the heretics. For, since they say: 'Their speech spreads like a cancer,'[28] how can this speech, which as a cancer passes imperceptibly to the ears of the hearers, give the remission of sins? And since they say that there is nothing in common between justice and iniquity, no communion between light and darkness,[29] how can the darkness illuminate or iniquity justify? And since they say that they are not from God, but from the spirit of Antichrist,[30] how do they who are enemies of God and whose breasts the spirit of Antichrist fills carry on both spiritual and divine affairs? But, if, having abandoned the errors of human contention, we return to the evangelical authority and to the apostolic tradition with sincere and upright faith, we know that they are allowed nothing toward ecclesiastical and salutary grace who, scattering and fighting against the Church of Christ, are called adversaries by Christ Himself and antichrists by His apostles.

(16) But it is not right that anyone should bring forward the Name of Christ to circumvent Christian truth so as to say: 'Wherever and however men are baptized in the Name of

---

28 2 Tim. 2.17.
29 Cf. 2 Cor. 6.14.
30 Cf. 1 John 4.3.

Jesus Christ, they receive the grace of baptism' when Christ Himself speaks and says: 'Not everyone who says to me, "Lord, Lord" shall enter the kingdom of heaven.'[31] And again He forewarns and instructs lest anyone easily be deceived in His Name by false prophets and false christs. 'For many,' He says, 'will come in my name, saying, "I am Christ," and they will lead many astray.'[32] And afterwards, He added, saying: 'Be on your guard, therefore; behold, I have told you all things beforehand.'[33] Whence it appears that those things which are tossed about in the Name of Christ ought not to be received and accepted immediately, but those which are performed in the truth of Christ.

(17) For, because, in the gospels and in the epistles of the apostles, the name of Jesus Christ is inserted for the remission of sins, it is not in such a way as if the Son alone could profit anyone without the Father or against the Father, but that it might be shown to the Jews, who boasted that they had the Father, that the Father would profit them nothing unless they believed in the Son whom He had sent. For they who knew God the Creator, the Father, ought likewise to know Christ the Son—nor could they applaud and encourage themselves for the Father alone without the recognition of His Son, who also said: 'No one comes to the Father but through me.'[34] But He Himself shows the same thing, that it is the knowledge of the Two which saves, saying: 'This is everlasting life, that they may know thee, the only true God and Jesus Christ, whom thou hast sent.'[35] Since, therefore, from the preaching and testimony of Christ Himself, the Father, who sent, must be known first, then, finally, Christ, who has been sent, and there cannot be any hope of salvation except in the knowledge of these Two at the same time, how, when God the Father has not been known, nay rather, has been blasphemed, are they

---

31 Matt. 7.21.
32 Cf. Mark 13.6.
33 Mark 13.23.
34 John 14.6.
35 Cf. John 17.3.

who are said to have been baptized among the heretics in the Name of Christ considered to have gained the remission of their sins?

For there was one rule for the Jews under the apostles, another condition for the Gentiles. The former, because they had already received the most ancient baptism of the law and of Moses, had to be baptized also in the Name of Jesus Christ, according to what Peter in the Acts of the Apostles tells to them and says: 'Repent and be baptized every one of you in the name of the Lord Jesus Christ for the forgiveness of your sins; and you will receive the gift of the Holy Spirit. For to you is the promise and to your children and to all, even those whom the Lord our God calls.'[36] Peter makes mention of Jesus Christ, not as if the Father should be omitted, but that the Son might also be joined to the Father.

(18) Finally, when after the Resurrection, the apostles are being sent to the Gentiles by the Lord, they are ordered to baptize the Gentiles in the Name of the Father and of the Son and of the Holy Spirit. How, therefore, do some say that a Gentile baptized without, outside the Church, nay rather, and against the Church, provided it be in the Name of Jesus Christ, wherever it be and whatever it be, can obtain the remission of sins when Christ Himself orders the Gentiles to be baptized in the complete and united Trinity?

Unless, indeed, although he who denies Christ is denied by Christ, he who denies His Father, whom Christ Himself confessed, is not denied, and he who blasphemes against Him whom Christ declared His Lord and God is rewarded by Christ and gains the remission of sins and the sanctification of baptism! But by what power can he who denies God, the Father of Christ, gain the remission of sins in baptism since Christ received that very power by which we are baptized and sanctified from the same Father, whom He called greater, from whom He sought to be glorified, whose will He fulfilled

---

36 Cf. Acts 2.38, 39.

even to the obedience of drinking the Chalice and of undergoing death?

What is it, therefore, other than to become a sharer with blaspheming heretics to wish to maintain and to assert that one who blasphemes seriously and sins against the Father and the Lord and God of Christ can obtain the remission of sins in the Name of Christ? What, then, is that argument that he who denies the Son does not have the Father, but he who denies the Father is considered to have the Son although the Son Himself attests and says: 'No one can come to me unless he is enabled to do so by my Father.'[37] That it may be clear that no remission of sins can be received in baptism from the Son which it has not pleased the Father to have given, He repeats the same thing especially, in addition, and says: 'Every plant that my heavenly Father has not planted will be rooted up.'[38]

(19) But if the followers of Christ do not wish to learn from Christ what veneration and honor are due to the Name of the Father, certainly let them learn from earthly and worldly examples, and let them know that Christ has stated, not without the greatest reproaching: 'The children of this world are more prudent than the children of the light.'[39] In this world, if anyone has uttered an insult to the father of another, if, abusive and bold, he has wounded his honor and reputation with a scurrilous tongue, the son is indignant and angry and attempts to avenge with all his strength the injury of his wounded father. Do you think that Christ gives impunity to impious and sacrilegious men and to those blaspheming against His Father and forgives them their sins in baptism who, it is evident, as baptized men heap up the same maledictions against the person of the Father and sin with the unceasing wickedness of a blaspheming tongue? Can a Christian, a servant of God, either conceive this in his mind or believe it in

---
37 John 6.66.
38 Matt. 15.13.
39 Cf. Luke 16.8.

faith or utter it in speech? And what will become of the divine precepts of the law which say: 'Honor father and mother'?[40] Unless, indeed, the name of father which is prescribed to be honored among men is to be violated with impunity in the case of God! And what will become of that which Christ Himself states in the Gospel and says: 'Let him who curses father or mother be put to death,'[41] unless He, who commands those who curse earthly parents to be punished and killed, Himself vivifies slanderers against the heavenly and spiritual Father and enemies of Mother Church?

A damnable and detestable thing is absolutely asserted by some, namely, that He who threatens the one who has blasphemed against the Holy Spirit that he will be guilty of an everlasting sin—the same One—is said to sanctify with a salutary baptism blasphemers against God the Father. And now do those who think that they must be in communion with such who come into the Church without baptism consider that they are not communicating in sins of others, nay rather, with eternal sins, in admitting without baptism those who can cast aside the sins of their blasphemies only in baptism?

(20) How vain and perverse it is, furthermore, that, when the heretics themselves, having repudiated and abandoned either the error or the wickedness in which they previously had been, acknowledge the truth of the Church, we should mutilate the laws and sacraments of the same truth and say to those who come and do penance that they have gained the remission of sins when they confess that they have sinned and because of that are coming to gain the pardon of the Church! Therefore, dearly beloved Brother, we ought both firmly to hold and to teach the faith and truth of the Catholic Church and to show through all of the evangelical and apostolic precepts the plan of the divine dispensation and unity.

(21) Can the power of baptism be greater or more powerful than confession, than suffering, that whoever confesses Christ

---
40 Cf. Exod. 20.12.
41 Matt. 15.4, but quoted from Exod. 21.17.

before men is baptized as in his own blood? And yet, this baptism does not avail the heretic although, having confessed Christ, he should have been killed outside of the Church, unless patrons and advocates of the heretics say that the heretics killed in the false confession of Christ are martyrs and, against the testimony of the Apostle, who says that these can accomplish nothing even though they are burned and killed,[42] assign the glory and the crown of suffering to them.

But, if the baptism of public confession and of blood cannot avail the heretic anything to salvation because there is no salvation out of the Church, how much less does it accomplish for him if, in secret places and in the caves of robbers, bathed by the contagion of adulterous waters, he has not so much revealed his former sins, but besides, rather added new and greater ones? Therefore, baptism cannot be common to us and to the heretics with whom neither God the Father, nor Christ the Son, nor the Holy Spirit, nor faith, nor the Church itself, are common. And, therefore, they who come to the Church from heresy ought to be baptized that they who are prepared by the legitimate and true and only baptism of the Holy Church for the kingdom of God by divine regeneration may be born again in both Sacraments since it is written: 'Unless a man be born again of water and the Spirit, he cannot enter into the kingdom of God.'[43]

(22) In this place some, as if they could escape by human argument the truth of the preaching of the Gospel, bring forward the catechumens to us, as to whether any of these, before he is baptized in the Church, should be seized and killed for the confession of the Name, should lose the hope of salvation and the reward of confession because he has not been born again of water first. Let men of this nature, partisans and promoters of the heretics, know, therefore, first, that those catechumens hold the upright faith and truth of the Church and advance to the warfare against the devil from the Divine

---

[42] Cf. 1 Cor. 13.3.
[43] John 3.5.

Camp with the full and sincere knowledge of God the Father and of Christ and of the Holy Spirit. Then they are not deprived of the Sacrament of baptism, nay rather, they are baptized with the most glorious and greatest baptism of blood, concerning which the Lord also said that He had another baptism to be baptized with.[44]

But the same Lord declares in the Gospel that they are baptized in their own blood and are consumed, sanctified by their suffering, and that they receive the grace of the divine promise when He speaks to the robber believing and confessing in His own Passion and promises that he will be with Him in Paradise.[45] Wherefore, we who are set over truth and faith ought not to deceive and lead astray those who come to faith and to truth and, doing penance, ask that sins be forgiven them, but to teach them, corrected by us and reformed for the kingdom of heaven with heavenly disciplines.

(23) But someone says: 'What, therefore, will become of those who, in the past, coming to the Church from heresy were admitted without baptism?' The Lord is powerful in His mercy to grant indulgence and not to separate from the gifts of His Church those who, admitted to the Church through simplicity, are dead. Yet because there was error at one time, there must not always be error since it is more fitting for wise and God-fearing men to follow the revealed and perceived truth willingly and unhesitatingly than, stubbornly and obstinately, to struggle for the heretics against brethren and against bishops.

(24) Let not anyone think that heretics, from the fact that baptism is set before them, as if scandalized by the name of a second baptism, are being hindered from coming to the Church. Nay rather, by this very fact, they are driven to the necessity of coming when the testimony of truth has been shown and proved to them. For, if they see that it is decided upon and decreed by our judgment and decision that the

---
44 Cf. Luke 12.50.
45 Cf. Luke 23.43.

baptism by which they are baptized there is considered just and legitimate, they will think also that they possess rightly and justly the Church and other gifts of the Church. There will be no reason for their coming to us when they, having baptism, seem also to have the rest.

But, in turn, when they know that there is no baptism without and that remission of sins cannot be given outside the Church, they will hasten to us more eagerly and promptly and implore the gifts and presents of Mother Church, certain that they cannot at all attain to the true promise of divine grace unless they first come to the truth of the Church. Nor will heretics refuse to be baptized among us with the legitimate and true baptism of the Church when they have learned from us that they who had already been baptized by the baptism of John were also baptized by Paul, as we read in the Acts of the Apostles.

(25) And now among some of us the seized baptism of the heretics is claimed as if, by a certain distaste for rebaptizing, it is considered contrary to divine law to baptize after the enemies of God although we find that they were baptized whom John had baptized,[46] that John, considered as greater among the prophets, that one filled with divine grace even in his mother's womb, that one made illustrious by the spirit and virtue of Elias, who was not an adversary of the Lord, but His precursor and preacher, who proclaimed the Lord, not only in words, but also pointed Him out to the eyes, who baptized Christ Himself, through whom others are baptized.

But if, on that account, a heretic could obtain the right of baptism because he first baptized, baptism will no longer belong to the one possessing it, but to the one seizing it. And since the Church and baptism cannot be separated from one another and divided at all, he who could first seize baptism, likewise also, has seized the Church and to him you who, having been anticipated, begin to be hindmost, begin to seem a heretic, who by yielding and giving way have relinquished

---
46 Cf. Matt. 3.11.

the right which you had received. But how dangerous it is in divine affairs that anyone should abandon his right and power, Holy Scripture declares when, in Genesis, Esau thence lost his birthright and could not afterwards recover that which he had once given up.[47]

(26) We have written these facts to you briefly, according to our moderate ability, dearly beloved Brother, prescribing to no one or prejudging no one, that each of the bishops should do what he thinks best, having the free power of his judgment. As far as possible, we are not disputing on account of heretics with our colleagues and fellow bishops with whom we are keeping the divine concord and the peace of the Lord, especially since the Apostle also says: 'But if anyone is thought to be contentious—we have no such custom, neither has the church of God.'[48] We preserve patiently and gently charity of soul, the honor of our college, the bond of faith, the concord of the priesthood. Because of this we have even now written a pamphlet concerning the good of patience, as far as our moderate ability was able with the permission and inspiration of the Lord, which we have sent to you for the sake of our mutual love. I trust that you, dearly beloved Brother, are always well.

74. Cyprian[1] to Pompey,[2] his brother, greeting.

(1) Although we expressed fully those things which must be said about the baptizing of heretics in the letters of which I sent you copies, dearly beloved Brother, yet, since you desired that what Stephen,[3] our brother, replied to our letters be brought to your notice, I have sent you a copy of his answer. When you have read this, you will notice more and more his

---
47 Cf. Gen. 27.
48 Cf. 1 Cor. 11.16.

---
1 256 A.D.
2 Cf. Letter 44, n. 10.
3 Cf. Letter 67, n. 59.

error, who is attempting to support the cause of the heretics against Christians and against the Church of God. For among other matters, either arrogant or irrelevant or self-contradictory, which he has written rather clumsily and without foresight, he even added this to say: 'If any, therefore, come to you from any heresy whatever, let nothing be done contrary to what has been handed down, namely, that hands should be imposed upon them in penance since the heretics themselves properly do not baptize those who come to them from each other but only receive them in communion.'

(2) He forbade to be baptized in the Church 'one coming from any heresy whatever,' that is, he judged that the baptism of all heretics is just and lawful. And although the individual heresies have individual baptisms and different sins, he, having communion with the baptism of all, has kept the sins of all heaped up in his bosom. And he taught 'nothing is to be done contrary to what has been handed down,' as if he would innovate who, holding unity, claims one baptism for the one Church and not he, indeed, who, forgetful of unity, usurps the lies and contagions of profane baptism. 'Let nothing be done,' he says, 'contrary to what has been handed down.' Whence is that tradition? Is it one coming from the authority of the Lord and of the Gospel or from the commands and epistles of the apostles?

For God testifies that those things which are written must be done and warns us, saying to Josue, son of Nun: 'The Book of the Law will not depart from your mouth and you will meditate upon it day and night that you may observe carefully all that is written in it.'[4] Likewise, the Lord, sending His apostles, commands the Gentiles to be baptized and to be taught to observe all things whatsoever He has taught.[5] If, therefore, it is either taught in the gospel or contained in the epistles of the apostles that 'those coming from whatever

---
4 Cf. Jos. 1.8.
5 Cf. Matt. 28.20.

heresy' should not be baptized, but only 'hands placed upon them in penance,' let this divine and holy tradition be observed.

But if heretics everywhere are called nothing else but adversaries and antichrists, if they are declared persons to be avoided as perverted and self-condemned,[6] why is it that they should seem not to be condemned by us—they who, it is evident from the apostolic testimony, have been condemned by themselves?—so that no one ought to defame the apostles as if they approved of the baptism of heretics or were in communion with them without the baptism of the Church when the apostles wrote such things concerning the heretics, and this when the sharper heretical plagues had not yet broken out and Marcion of Pontus[7] had not as yet emerged from Pontus, whose master Cerdo[8] came to Rome under Hyginus, the Bishop,[9] who was the ninth in the City? Marcion, having followed the former, with other involvements loaded more impudently to his crime, began to blaspheme more defiantly against God the Father and Creator and armed, with sacrilegious arms, the heretical madness more wickedly and more seriously rebelling against the Church.

(3) But if it is evident that more and worse heresies have arisen afterward, and if nowhere, not even in the past, was it taught or written that hands only should be imposed upon the heretic in penance and thus he should be admitted to communion, and if there is only one baptism, which is among us and within and is granted to the Church alone through the divine condescension, what is this obstinacy or what is this presumption to place human tradition before the divine plan and not to notice that God is offended and angered as often as human tradition subverts and disregards the divine precepts, as He cries and says through Isaia, the prophet: 'This people

---

6 Cf. Titus 3.11.
7 Cf. Letter 73, n. 8.
8 Cerdo, a Gnostic teacher of the first half of the second century, predecessor of Marcion, went to Rome during the papacy of Hyginus, alternated between repentance and reversion to his own teachings.
9 Hyginus, Pope from c. 137-141 A.D.

honors me with their lips, but their heart is far separated from me. In vain, moreover, they honor me, teaching the commandments and doctrines of men'[10]?

The Lord in the Gospel, likewise, rebuking in a similar manner and reproving, asserts and says: 'You nullify the commandment of God, that you may keep your own tradition.'[11] Mindful of this precept, the blessed Apostle Paul himself warns also and instructs, saying: 'If anyone teaches otherwise and does not agree with the sound instruction of our Lord Jesus Christ and his doctrine, puffed up with stupidity and knowing nothing, depart from such a one.'[12]

(4) Surely an illustrious and legitimate tradition which should offer suitable authority for us is proposed by the teaching of Stephen, our brother! For in the same place in his letter he added and granted: 'Since the heretics themselves properly do not baptize those who come to them from each other but only receive them in communion'! To this depth of evils has the Church of God and the Spouse of Christ sunk, that it follows the examples of heretics, that, for the celebration of the heavenly sacraments, light should borrow discipline from darkness and Christians do what antichrists do! But what blindness of soul, what depravity is it to be unwilling to recognize the unity of faith which comes from God the Father and from the tradition of Jesus Christ, our Lord and our God? For if, therefore, the Church is not with the heretics because it is one and cannot be divided and if, therefore, the Holy Spirit is not there because He is one and He cannot be with the profane and the strangers, certainly baptism, also, which stands firmly in the same unity, cannot be with the heretics because it can be separated neither from the Church nor from the Holy Spirit.

(5) Or if they assign the efficacy of baptism to the majesty of the Name so that they who are baptized in the Name of

---

10 Cf. Isa. 29.13.
11 Mark 7.9.
12 Cf. 1 Tim. 6.3, 4.

Jesus Christ, anywhere and in any way it may be, are considered renewed and sanctified, why, in the Name of the same Christ, are not hands imposed upon the baptized there for him to receive the Holy Spirit? Why does not the same majesty of the same Name which they contend was valid for the sanctification of baptism prevail for the imposition of hands? For, if he who was born outside the Church can be made a temple of God, why cannot the Holy Spirit also be infused into the temple for whoever, after his sins have been made manifest, has been sanctified in baptism and reformed spiritually to the new man has become fit to receive the Holy Spirit since the Apostle says: 'As many soever of you as have been baptized into Christ, have put on Christ'?[13]

He who, baptized among the heretics, can put on Christ, can much more receive the Holy Spirit whom Christ sent. Otherwise, He who has been sent will be greater than He who sends, that the one baptized without should, indeed, begin to have put on Christ, but should not have been able to receive the Holy Spirit, as if either Christ could be put on without the Spirit or the Spirit separated from Christ. It is also stupid for them to say that, although the second nativity, by which we are born in Christ through the washing of regeneration, is spiritual, anyone can be born spiritually among the heretics where they say the Spirit is not. For water alone cannot cleanse sins and sanctify man unless he also has the Holy Spirit. Wherefore, it is necessary either for them to concede that the Spirit is there where they say there is baptism or that there is no baptism where the Spirit is not because there can be no baptism without the Spirit.

(6) But what is it to assert and to contend that they who have not been born in the Church can be sons of God? For the blessed Apostle makes manifest and proves that it is baptism in which the old man dies and the new man is born, saying: 'He saved us through the bath of regeneration.'[14] But,

---
13 Cf. Gal. 3.27.
14 Titus 3.5.

if regeneration is in the bath, that is, in baptism, how can a heresy, which is not the spouse of Christ, generate sons to God through Christ? For it is the Church alone which, joined and united to Christ, spiritually generates sons, according to the same Apostle again saying: 'Christ loved the Church, and delivered himself up for her, that he might sanctify her, cleansing her in the bath of water.'[15] If this, therefore, is the beloved and the Spouse who alone is sanctified by Christ and alone is cleansed by His bath, it is clear that heresy, which is not the spouse of Christ, can neither be cleansed nor sanctified by His bath, cannot generate sons to God.

(7) But, furthermore, not through the imposition of hands is anyone born again when he receives the Holy Spirit, but in baptism, that he, already born, may receive the Spirit as it happened in the first man, Adam. God formed him first; then He breathed upon his face the breath of life. For the Spirit cannot be received unless he who receives it has existence. But since the nativity of Christians is in baptism, but the generation and sanctification of baptism are with the Spouse of Christ alone, who can bring forth spiritually and generate sons to God, where and of whom and to whom was he born who is not a son of the Church so that anyone might have God for Father before he has the Church for Mother?

Although, in truth, no heresy at all nor even any schism can have the sanctification of salutary baptism without, to such an extent has the harsh obstinacy of Stephen, our brother, broken out that he contends that sons of God are born even from the baptism of Marcion, likewise of Valentine,[16] and of Appelles,[17] and of the rest of the blasphemers against God the Father, and he says that the remission of sins is given there in the Name of Jesus Christ where there is blasphemy against the Father and against Christ the Lord God!

(8) In this place, we must consider, dearly beloved Brother,

---
15 Cf. Eph. 5.25, 26.
16 Valentine, founder of Valentinians, who changed doctrines of Gnostic heresy to suit his own system.
17 Apelles or Appelles, a Gnostic follower of Marcion.

for the sake of the faith and religion of the sacerdotal office which we exercise, whether the account of a bishop of God who asserts and approves and considers acceptable the baptism of blasphemers can be satisfactory when the Lord threatens and says: 'And now, O priests, this commandment is for you. If you do not hear and if you do not lay it to heart to give glory to my Name, says the Lord God Omnipotent, I will send a curse upon you and of your blessing I will make a curse.'[18] Does he who is in communion with the baptism of Marcion give glory to God? Does he who thinks that the remission of sins is granted among those who blaspheme against God give glory to God? Does he who asserts that sons of God are born of an adultress and a fornicatress without give glory to God? Does he who, not holding the unity and truth coming from the Divine Law, defends heresies against the Church give glory to God? Does he who, as a friend of heretics and an enemy of Christians, thinks that bishops of God protecting the truth of Christ and the unity of the Christ ought to be excommunicated give glory to God?

If glory is thus given to God, if the fear and discipline of God are thus preserved by his worshipers and bishops, let us cast aside our arms; let us surrender into captivity; let us hand over to the devil the ordination of the Gospel, the decree of Christ, the majesty of God; let the sacraments of the divine warfare be cast aside; let the standards of the heavenly camp be given up; let the Church succumb and yield to heretics, light to darkness, faith to perfidy, hope to despair, reason to error, immortality to death, love to hatred, truth to lying, Christ to Antichrist!

Deservedly thus, from day to day, schisms and heresies arise; they grow more frequently and more fruitfully, as, sprouting with serpentine locks against the Church of God, they exhibit the poison of their venom with greater force while authority and strength are offered to them by the support of certain ones, while their baptism is defended, while faith, while truth

---
18 Cf. Mal. 2.1, 2.

is betrayed, while that which is done without, against the Church, is defended within, in the very Church itself.

(9) But if there is among us, dearly beloved Brother, the fear of God, if the tenor of faith prevails, if we observe the precepts of Christ, if we protect the incorrupt and inviolate sanctity of His Spouse, if the words of the Lord abide in our minds and hearts when He says: 'Do you think when the Son of Man comes, he will find faith on the earth?'[19] as faithful soldiers of God who fight for God with faith and sincere religion, let us with faithful valor preserve by divine help the camp entrusted to us. Nor ought custom which has crept in among some hinder us from letting truth prevail and conquer. For custom without truth is the antiquity of error. Because of this, having abandoned error, let us follow truth, knowing that in Esdras also truth conquers as it is written: 'Truth abides and grows strong to eternity and lives and lasts forever and ever. With it there is no accepting of persons or differences, but it does what is just, nor is there any evil in its judgment but the strength, and the kingdom, and the majesty, and the power of all ages. Blessed be the God of truth.'[20] Christ, showing us this truth, says in His Gospel: 'I am . . . the truth.'[21] Because of this, if we are in Christ and have Christ in us and if we abide in truth and truth abides in us, let us hold those things which are true.

(10) But it happens by the practice of presumption and of insolence that each one defends more his own depraved and false views than he consents to the rights and truths of another. Foreseeing this matter, the blessed Apostle Paul writes to Timothy and warns that the bishop ought not to be quarrelsome, or contentious, but gentle and teachable.[22] But he who is meek and mild in the patience of learning is teachable. For bishops ought not only to teach, but also to learn because he

---
19 Cf. Luke 18.8.
20 Cf. 3 Esd. 4.38-40. This is not in the Confraternity translation, but the Latin is given in the Appendix of the Latin Vulgate.
21 John 14.6.
22 Cf. 2 Tim. 2.24.

who grows daily and profits by learning better things teaches better.

But the same Apostle Paul teaches the same thing also warning, for instance: 'If anything better is revealed to another sitting by, let the first keep silence.'[23] But there is a short way among religious and simple minds both to cast aside error and to find and to elicit truth. For, if we revert to the head and origin of the divine tradition, human error ceases and, when the plan of the heavenly sacraments has been perceived, whatever lay hid in obscurity under the gloom and cloud of darkness is opened into the light of truth. For example, if a conduit bringing water, which before flowed abundantly and freely, suddenly should fail, do we not go to the fountain that there the reason for the failure may be known: whether the water dried up at the head from dried up streams or whether, in truth, rushing forth whole and full thence, it ceased in the middle of its course as if it was caused by the fault of an interrupted or leaking conduit so that the constant water did not flow continually and perpetually, but when the conduit has been repaired and strengthened, the collected water may be presented for the use and drink of the city with the same fruitfulness and plenty with which it issues forth from the fountain?

And this bishops of God ought to do now, observing the divine precepts, that, if truth has wavered or vacillated in anything, we should return both to the divine origin and to the evangelical and apostolical tradition and thence the reason for our acts should arise whence both our order and our origin have arisen.

(11) For it has been handed down to us that there is one God and one Christ and one hope and one faith and one Church and one baptism appointed only in one Church; anyone who has departed from this unity must of necessity be found with heretics; while he vindicates these against the Church, he impugns the sacrament of divine tradition. We

---
23 Cf. 1 Cor. 14.30.

see the sacrament of this unity expressed also in the Canticle of Canticles in the person of Christ, who says: 'An enclosed garden is my sister, my bride, . . . a fountain sealed . . . a well of living water, a paradise with the fruit of the orchard.'[24] But if His Church is a garden enclosed and a fountain sealed, how can anyone who is not in the Church enter into this same garden or drink from its fountain?

Likewise Peter, himself also showing and vindicating unity, commanded and warned that we can be saved through the one baptism alone of the one Church. 'In the ark of Noe,' he says, 'a few, that is, eight souls of men were saved through water. Its counterpart, Baptism, will now save you also.'[25] In this brief and spiritual summary, he manifested the sacrament of unity for, as in that baptism of the world by which the ancient iniquity was purged, he who was not in the Ark of Noe could not be saved through water, so now he cannot seem to be saved through baptism who has not been baptized in the Church, which has been established in the unity of the Lord as the sacrament of the one Ark.

(12) Thus it is observed and held by us, dearly beloved Brother, after having explored and examined the truth, that all who are converted to the Church from any heresy whatsoever should be baptized by the one and lawful baptism of the Church, with the exception of those who had been baptized in the Church first and then afterwards had gone over to the heretics. For these ought to be received, when they return, through the imposition of hands only, after penance has been performed, and to be restored by the Shepherd to the sheepfold whence they have gone astray. I trust that you, dearly beloved brother, are always well.

---

24 Cf. Cant. 4.12, 15.
25 Cf. 1 Peter 3.20, 21.

75.[1] *Firmilian*[2] *to Cyprian, his brother in the Lord, greeting.*

(1) We have received through Rogatian,[3] our dearly beloved deacon, sent by you, the letter which you wrote to us, dearly beloved Brother, and we gave the greatest thanks to God for this because it has happened that we who are separated from one another in the body are so joined in the spirit as if we were not only occupying the same region but dwelling together in the very same house. And it is fitting to say this because the spiritual house of God is one. 'For in the last days,' it says, 'the mountain of the Lord and the house of God shall be established above the tops of the mountains.'[4] Those who come together in this are united with joy according to what is asked in this Psalm from the Lord to dwell in the house of God through all of the days of life. Whence it is manifested in another place also that there is among the saints a great love of will to assemble together. 'Behold,' it says, 'how good and how pleasant it is where brethren dwell at one!'[5]

(2) For union and peace and concord provide the greatest pleasure, not only to men who believe and know the truth, but also to the heavenly angels themselves for whom the divine discourse says there is joy over one sinner who repents[6] and returns to the bond of unity. But, certainly, this would not be said of the angels who hold conversation in heaven unless they themselves who rejoice in our union were also united to us, as, on the contrary, they are certainly saddened when they see the different minds and the divided wills of some as if they not only do not invoke the one and the same

---

1 256 A.D.
2 Firmilian, bishop of Caesarea in Cappodocia, one of the great bishops of the time, upheld Cyprian, whose letter to him has been lost.
3 Rogatian, Carthaginian deacon sent with letter to Firmilian in 256 A.D. by Cyprian.
4 Cf. Isa. 2.2.
5 Cf. Ps. 132.1.
6 Cf. Luke 15.7.

God together but, separated and divided from one another here, can have no intercourse or common speech.

But we may give thanks to Stephen[7] for this only, because through his unkindness it has now been brought about that we receive the proof of your faith and wisdom. But even if we have received this grace of benefit because of Stephen, Stephen has not presently engaged in anything worthy of favor and grace. For Judas also cannot seem worthy by his perfidy and betrayal which he wickedly committed against the Savior as if he himself provided the cause of so great benefits that through him the world and the people of the Gentiles might be liberated by the Passion of the Lord.

(3) But let these things which have been done by Stephen be passed over, in the meantime, lest, while we remember his audacity and insolence, from matters carried on wickedly by him we bring a more prolonged sorrow for ourselves. But, learning from you what you have decided according to the rule of truth and the wisdom of Christ about this matter of which there is now a question, we have rejoiced with great joy and have given thanks to God because we have found in brethren situated so far away so great a unanimity of faith and of truth with us. For the grace of God is powerful to join and unite with the bond of charity and of unity even those things which seem to be divided by a vaster space of lands, according to the way that the divine power formerly united in the bond of unity Ezechiel and Daniel, later in age, separated by an interval of time from Job and Noe, who were among the first, but, although they had been separated by long periods, yet they felt the same divine inspiration.

And we notice this now in you, that you who are separated by very vast regions from us yet prove that you are joined with us in inclination and in spirit. This whole thing has been accomplished through the Divine Unity. For since the Lord, who dwells in us, is One and the Same, He joins and unites His own everywhere in the bond of unity. Whence the sound

---

[7] Cf. Letter 67, n. 59.

of them who were sent by the Lord, running quickly with the spirit of unity, has gone forth into the whole world; as, on the contrary, nothing avails certain others very close and united to each other in body if they disagree in spirit and mind since souls which have separated themselves from the unity of God cannot at all be united. 'For behold,' it says, 'they who withdraw from you shall perish.'[8] But such will receive the judgment of the Lord as they deserve who forsake the words of Him, who prayed the Father for unity and said: 'Father, grant that even as I and thou are one, so also they may be in us.'[9]

(4) Assuredly, we have received those things which were written by you as if they were our own; we do not read them hurriedly, but we have committed them, often repeated, to memory. Nor is it prejudicial to salutary use either to repeat the same things to confirm the truth or to add certain things to accumulate proof. But if anything has been added by us, it is not so added as if too little had been said by you, but because the divine speech surpasses human nature and the soul cannot conceive the whole and perfect. Therefore, also, so great is the number of prophets that the manifold and Divine Wisdom may be distributed through many. Whence the first who speaks in prophecy is instructed also to be silent if something has been revealed to a second.[10]

For this reason, it happens necessarily among us that, through the years, we older men and prelates assemble together to dispose of those matters which have been entrusted to our care, that, if there are any more important matters, they may be set right in the common council, that a healing remedy may be sought through penance for brethren lapsed and wounded by the devil after the salutary water of baptism, not as if they are gaining the remission of sins from us, but that through us they may be converted to the knowledge of their sins and may be compelled to satisfy the Lord more fully.

---
8 Cf. Ps. 72.27.
9 Cf. John 17.21.
10 Cf. 1 Cor. 14.30.

(5) But since that legate sent by you was hastening to return to you and wintertime was at hand, we wrote as much as we could in reply to your letter. And, indeed, as much as it pertains to what Stephen said, as if the apostles prohibited those who come from heresy to be baptized and handed this down to be observed by posterity, you responded most fully that no one is so stupid as to believe that the apostles handed this down since it is certainly evident that these very detestable and execrable heresies arose later since even Marcion,[11] the disciple of Cerdo,[12] is found late after the apostles and a long time after from them to have brought about a sacrilegious tradition against God. Appelles[13] also, consenting to his blasphemy, added many other new and graver matters hostile to faith and truth. But also the time of Valentine[14] and Basilides[15] was manifest because they themselves, after the apostles and a long period after, rebelled against the Church of God with their wicked lies.

It is evident, also, that the other heretics afterward introduced their wicked sects and perverse inventions as each one was led by error. It is clear that all of these were condemned by themselves and spoke an inexcusable sentence against themselves before the day of judgment. What else does he do who confirms their baptism than to judge himself with those very men and condemn himself by becoming a sharer in such activities?

(6) But that they who are at Rome do not observe in all respects those things which were handed down from the beginning and in vain pretend the authority of the apostles, anyone may know also from the fact that regarding the days of Easter to be celebrated and regarding many other mysteries of divine matter he may see that there are some diver-

---

11 Cf. Letter 73, n. 8.
12 Cf. Letter 74, n. 8.
13 Cf. Letter 74, n. 17.
14 Cf. Letter 74, n. 16.
15 Basilides, the founder of one of the Gnostic sects in the early second century.

sities among them and that all things there are not observed equally which are observed at Jerusalem, according as also, in very many other provinces, many things vary according to the diversity of places and of men. And yet, on account of this, there has been no withdrawal at all from the peace and unity of the Catholic Church.

Now Stephen has dared to do this, breaking the peace against you which his predecessors have always kept with you with mutual love and honor, now even disgracing Peter and Paul, the blessed Apostles, as if they themselves, who in their Epistles cursed heretics and warned us that we should avoid them, handed this down. Whence it appears that this is a human tradition which justifies heretics and maintains that they have baptism which belongs only to the Church alone.

(7) But you have also answered well to that part in which Stephen said in his epistle that the heretics themselves also agree regarding baptism and that they do not baptize those who come to them from one another, but only receive them into communion as if we should do this also. In this place, although you have already proved that it is sufficiently ridiculous for anyone to follow the erring, yet we add over and above, that it is not strange if the heretics do this, who, although they disagree in certain minor matters, yet in that which is the greatest, hold one and the same agreement to blaspheme the Creator, who invent for themselves certain dreams and phantasms of an unknown God. In any case, it is a consequence of this that they thus agree in the emptiness of their baptism as they consent to repudiate the truth of Divinity.

Concerning these, since it is tedious to answer the claim of each, either wicked or superfluous, it is sufficient to say briefly in a short way that those who do not hold the Father, the True Lord, cannot possess the truth either of the Son or of the Holy Spirit. According to this, they also who are called Cataphrygians[16] and attempt to usurp new prophecies can

---

16 Cataphrygians, a name for the followers of Montanus.

have neither the Father, nor the Son, because they do not have the Holy Spirit. From whom, if we seek what Christ they preach, they will answer that they preach Him who sent the Spirit speaking through Montanus[17] and Prisca.[18] In whom, when we notice that there was not the spirit of truth but of error, we know that those who claim the false prophecy of those men against the faith of Christ cannot have Christ.

But the other heretics also, if they have torn themselves from the Church of God, can have no power or grace since all power and grace have been appointed in the Church where elders preside who possess the power both of baptizing and of imposing hands and of ordaining. For as it is not lawful for a heretic to ordain nor to impose hands, so it is not lawful for him to baptize nor to do anything holily and spiritually since he is a stranger to spiritual and deifying sanctity. All of this, a while ago in Iconium, which is a place in Phrygia, we confirmed when we were assembled together with those who came together from Galatia and Cilicia and other nearby regions to be held firmly against the heretics and vindicated when there was doubt among certain people about this matter.

(8) And since Stephen and those who agree with him contend that the remission of sins and a second birth can proceed from the baptism of heretics, among whom even they themselves confess that the Holy Spirit is not, let them consider and know that there cannot be spiritual birth without the Spirit. According to this, the blessed Apostle Paul also baptized again with a spiritual baptism and thus imposed hands upon those who had been baptized by John before the Holy Spirit had been sent by the Lord that they might receive the Holy Spirit.

But what is the reason that, when we see that Paul baptized his own disciples again after the baptism of John, we hesitate

---

17 Montanus, originator of a second-century schism which was widespread for many years, claimed to be an inspired mouthpiece of the Holy Spirit.
18 Prisca or Priscilla, Montanist prophetess and devoted disciple of Montanus.

to baptize those who come to the Church from heresy after their unlawful and profane baptism unless Paul was inferior to the bishops of these times that they, indeed, through the imposition of hands alone, can give the Holy Spirit to the heretics who come but Paul was not fit to give the Holy Spirit by the imposition of hands to those baptized by John unless he had first baptized them with the baptism of the Church!

(9) That is absurd also for them to think that it is not necessary to inquire who it is who has baptized because he who has been baptized may have received grace by the invocation of the Trinity of Names of the Father and of the Son and of the Holy Spirit. This, then, will be the wisdom which Paul writes is in those who are mature,[19] that he who is mature in the Church and wise may either defend this or believe that this bare invocation of Names suffices for the remission of sins and the sanctification of baptism since they doubtless avail when both he who baptizes has the Holy Spirit and baptism itself is not conferred without the Spirit.

But they say that whoever in any way is baptized without may obtain grace by his disposition and faith. This in itself, without doubt, is ridiculous as if either a depraved mind could draw to itself from heaven the sanctification of the just or a false faith, the truth of the believers. But that not all who invoke the Name of Christ can be heard and can gain their request for any grace the Lord Himself makes clear, saying: 'Many will come in my name, saying: "I am Christ"; and they will lead many astray.'[20] There is no difference, finally, between a false prophet and a heretic. For, as the former deceives in the Name of God or of Christ, so the latter deceives in the sacrament of baptism. Each strives by a lie to deceive the wills of men.

(10) But I wish to tell you also about an episode which happened among us pertaining to this very matter. For, al-

---
19 Cf. 1 Cor. 2.6.
20 Cf. Mark 13.6.

most twenty-two years ago, in the times after the Emperor Alexander, many conflicts and struggles happened on this occasion both in common to all men and privately to Christians. There were, likewise, many and frequent earthquakes so that they destroyed many things through Cappadocia and through Pontus; certain cities, likewise, drawn back into the abyss, were swallowed up by the opening of the cracking earth so that from this a severe persecution was also begun against us for the Name; this, having suddenly sprung up after the long peace of the age past, from the unthought of and unaccustomed evil was made more terrible for disturbing our people. Serenian[21] was then governor in our province, a bitter and harsh persecutor.

But when the faithful placed in this disturbance were fleeing both hither and thither from fear of persecution and abandoning their native lands and going over into other parts of the regions (for there was an opportunity of going over there because that persecution was not yet through the whole world, but was local), suddenly, on this occasion, a certain woman appeared who, having been in ecstasy, presented herself as a prophet and acted as if thus filled with the Holy Spirit. But she was so carried along by the force of the principal devils that for a long time, accomplishing certain wonderful and portentous deeds, she disturbed and deceived the brotherhood and promised that she would cause the earth to be shaken, not that the demon had so great power that he would be able to move the earth or to cause the elements to tremble by his power, but that sometimes the evil spirit, foreseeing and knowing that there would be an earthquake, pretended that he would do what he saw was about to be done.

By these lies and boastings, he so led astray the minds of individuals that they obeyed him and followed whithersoever he taught and led. He also made that woman in raw winter go through the rough snow with bare feet and not be the least troubled or injured from that walking. She said also that she

---

21 Serenian, persecuting governor of the province in 236 A.D.

was hastening into Judea and Jerusalem, feigning as if she had come thence. Here, indeed, she deceived one of the priests, Rusticus,[22] and, likewise, another deacon so that they had intercourse with the same woman; this was discovered a short time after. For, suddenly, one of the exorcists appeared to her, a man approved, having also always spent his life well in regard to religious discipline, who, stirred up by the exhortation also of many of the brethren who themselves were strong and praiseworthy in the faith, raised himself against that evil spirit to conquer it which by subtle deceit also had predicted shortly before that a certain adverse and unbelieving assailant would come. Yet that exorcist, inspired by the grace of God, bravely resisted and revealed it to be a most wicked spirit which before was thought holy.

And that woman who earlier, through the tricks and deceits of the devil, was attempting many things for the deception of the faithful, among other things by which she had deceived very many also frequently dared this, that, with an invocation not considered invalid, she pretended to sanctify the bread and to celebrate the Eucharist and she offered the Sacrifice to the Lord, not without the rite of the customary commendation; usurping the accustomed and lawful words of interrogation, she also baptized many that nothing might seem to differ from ecclesiastical rule.

(11) What, then, shall we say of her baptism, by which a most wicked demon baptized through a woman? Do Stephen and those who agree with him approve of this also, especially since neither the symbol of the Trinity nor the lawful and ecclesiastical interrogation was lacking? Can it be believed that either the remission of sins was given or the regeneration of the life-giving font was accomplished rightly when all things, although in the image of truth, were nevertheless accomplished by the devil? Unless they who justify the baptism of heretics contend that the demon also gave the grace of baptism in the Name of the Father and of the Son and of the Holy

---
22 Rusticus, priest deceived by evil woman.

Spirit! Among them, without doubt, there is the same error; it is the very fallacy of the devils since the Holy Spirit is not at all among them.

(12) What is it, furthermore, that Stephen wishes: that the presence and holiness of Christ be present to those who are baptized among the heretics? For, if the Apostle does not lie when he says: 'As many soever of you as have been baptized into Christ, have put on Christ,'[23] assuredly, he who was baptized in Christ there put on Christ. But, if he has put on Christ, he could receive also the Holy Spirit, who was sent by Christ, and in vain are hands imposed upon him to receive the Holy Spirit when he comes back unless they separate the Spirit from Christ so that Christ is, indeed, among the heretics, but the Holy Spirit is not there.

(13) But let us review briefly also the other matters which have been discussed copiously and fully by you, especially since our dearly beloved deacon, Rogatian, is hastening to you. For it follows that they who defend the heretics must be asked by us whether their baptism is carnal or spiritual. For, if it is carnal, they differ not at all from the baptism of the Jews, which they use in such a way that, by it, as if in a common and vulgar font, only dirt is washed away. But, if it is spiritual, how can baptism be spiritual among those among whom the Holy Spirit is not? And thus, the water with which they are baptized is only a carnal washing for them, not the sacrament of baptism.

(14) But if the baptism of heretics can have the regeneration of the second birth, they who are baptized among them must not be considered heretics, but sons of God because the second birth, which is baptism, generates sons of God. But, if the Spouse of Christ, which is the Catholic Church, is one, it is she herself alone who generates sons to God. For there are not many spouses of Christ since the Apostle says: 'I betrothed you to one spouse to present a holy virgin to Christ.'[24]

---
23 Cf. Gal. 3.27.
24 Cf. 2 Cor. 11.2.

And: 'Hear, O daughter, and see, and turn your ear, and forget your people because the king has desired your beauty';[25] and: 'Come from Lebanon, my bride, you shall come and you shall pass by from the beginning of faith';[26] and: 'I have come to my garden, my sister, my bride.'[27] We see that one person is everywhere proposed because the spouse is also one.

But the synagogue of the heretics is not one with us because the spouse is not an adulteress and a fornicator. Whence she cannot bear children for God unless, indeed, according to what it seems to Stephen, heresy, indeed, brings forth and abandons and the Church receives those who have been abandoned and nourishes as her own those whom she has not herself brought forth although she cannot be the mother of strange children! And, therefore, Christ, our Lord, manifesting that His Spouse is one and declaring the sacrament of His unity, says: 'He who is not with me is against me; and he who does not gather with me scatters.'[28] For if Christ is with us, but the heretics are not with us, certainly, the heretics are against Christ; and if we gather with Christ, but the heretics do not gather with us, without doubt, they scatter.

(15) But neither must we pass over what has necessarily been said by you, that the Church, according to the Canticle of Canticles, is a garden enclosed and a fountain sealed, a paradise with the fruit of the fruit trees.[29] But they who have never entered into this garden and have not seen the Paradise planted by God the Creator, how can they offer to anyone the living water of the salutary washing from the fountain which is enclosed within and is sealed with the divine seal?

And since, in truth, the ark of Noe was nothing else but the sacrament of the Church of Christ, which then saved only those who were within the ark, whereas all without were perishing, clearly we are instructed to have regard for the

---
25 Cf. Ps. 44.11, 12.
26 Cf. Cant. 4.8.
27 Cant. 5.1.
28 Luke 11.23.
29 Cf. Cant. 4.12, 13.

unity of the Church, as Peter stated, saying: 'As its counterpart, Baptism will now save us also,'[30] showing that just as those who were not with Noe in the ark not only were not cleansed and sanctified by the water, but immediately perished in that flood, so now also whoever are not in the Church with Christ will perish without unless they are converted to the only and life-giving font of the Church through penance.

(16) But what is his error and how great is his blindness, who says that the remission of sins can be given in the synagogues of the heretics, and who does not remain on the foundation of the one Church, which was once founded by Christ upon the rock, can be learned from this which Christ said to Peter alone: 'Whatever thou shalt bind on earth shall be bound also in heaven, and whatever thou shalt loose on earth shall be loosed also in heaven,'[31] and again in the Gospel when Christ breathed upon the apostles alone, saying: 'Receive the Holy Spirit; whose sins you shall forgive, they are forgiven him; and whose you shall retain, they are retained.'[32] Therefore, the power of forgiving sins was given to the apostles and to the churches which these men, sent by Christ, established and to the bishops who succeeded them by ordination as vicars.

But the enemies of the one Catholic Church, in which we are, and the adversaries of us who have succeeded the apostles, claiming against us unlawful priesthoods for themselves and erecting profane altars, what else are they save Core and Dathan and Abiron, sacrilegious with an equal crime and about to pay the same penalty as those who agree with them? According to this, even then those who participated with them and were accomplices perished with them in a like death.

(17) And I am justly indignant in this respect at this so open and manifest stupidity of Stephen that he who so glories in the place of his episcopate and contends that he has the succession from Peter, on whom the foundations of the Church

---

30 Cf. 1 Peter 3.21.
31 Cf. Matt. 16.19.
32 John 20.22, 23.

were established, should introduce many other rocks and constitute new buildings of many churches while he maintains by his authority that baptism is there. For they who are baptized fill up without doubt the number of the Church; but he who approves their baptism confirms that the Church is also there from the baptized. He who thus betrays and deserts unity does not know that the truth of the Christian Rock is being obscured by him and, to some extent, destroyed. The Apostle confesses that the Jews, although blinded by ignorance and bound by the gravest crime, still have zeal for God. Stephen, who claims that through succession he has the See of Peter, is stirred up with no zeal against the heretics, when he grants them no ordinary, but rather the greatest, power of grace, in that he says and asserts that they wash away through the sacrament of baptism the stains of the old man, that they forgive former mortal sins, that by the heavenly regeneration they make sons of God, prepare again for eternal life by the sanctification of the divine washing.

If he concedes and grants these so great and heavenly gifts of the Church to the heretics, what else does he do but be in communion with those for whom he maintains and claims so much grace? And he hesitates now in vain to agree with them and to be a partaker with them in other matters and to assemble with them and, likewise, to join in prayers with them and to appoint a common altar and sacrifice.

(18) 'But,' he says, 'the Name of Christ accomplishes very much for the faith and sanctification of baptism, that whoever anywhere has been baptized in the Name of Christ immediately gains the grace of Christ,' although he can be met briefly in this position and be told that, if baptism given without in the Name of Christ is valid for the purgation of man, the imposition of hands in the Name of the same Christ ought to be valid there for receiving the Holy Spirit. And other things also which are done among the heretics will begin to seem just and lawful when they are done in the Name of Christ, according to what you said in your letter, unless in the Church

alone the Name of Christ is powerful to which Christ granted the power of heavenly grace.

(19) But as to what pertains to refuting the custom which they seem to oppose to truth, who is so vain as to prefer custom to truth, or, when he has perceived the light, not to leave the darkness? Unless after the coming of Christ, that is, Truth, the most ancient custom helps the Jews at all, that, having cast aside the new way of truth, they should remain in the old! This, indeed, you Africans can say against Stephen that, when the truth had been learned, you left the error of custom. But we join custom to truth and we oppose to the custom of the Romans the custom of truth, holding this from the beginning which was handed down by Christ and by the apostles. Nor do we remember that this began to be observed among us at any time, since it has always been so observed here that we recognized no other but the one Church of God and we counted no baptism holy except that of the Holy Church.

Clearly, since some of these doubted about the baptism of those who, even though they receive the new prophets, yet seem to know the same Father and Son with us, very many of us coming together in Iconium have diligently investigated and confirmed that every baptism which is administered outside the Church must be completely repudiated.

(20) But to what they assert and affirm for the heretics: that the Apostle said: 'Whether in pretense or in truth, Christ is being proclaimed,'[33] it is absurd for us to answer since it is evident that the Apostle in his Epistle in which he said this made mention neither of the heretics nor of their baptism, but spoke only of the brethren speaking with him either in perfidy or persevering in sincere faith; nor is it necessary to investigate this in a long tract, but it is sufficient to read the Epistle itself and to learn what the Apostle said from the Apostle himself.

(21) What, then, they say, will become of those who, coming from the heretics, have been admitted without the baptism of the Church? If they have died, they are considered in the

---
33 Phil. 1.18.

number of those who have, indeed, been catechumens among us but died before they were baptized—no small advantage of truth and faith to which they had attained after having abandoned their error—although, having been prevented by death, they did not obtain the perfection of grace.

But let those who are still remaining in the world be baptized with the baptism of the Church that they may obtain the remission of their sins, lest, remaining in their former error, through any presumption of another, they should die without the perfecting of grace. Otherwise, how great is the sin either of those who are admitted or of those who admit them that, although their stains are not washed away through the font of the Church and their sins are not confessed, with Communion rashly usurped, they defile the Body and Blood of the Lord although it is written: 'Whoever eats the bread or drinks the cup of the Lord unworthily, will be guilty of the body and the blood of the Lord.'[34]

(22) We have judged that they also must not be considered as baptized whom these who previously had been bishops in the Catholic Church afterward had baptized, still assuming for themselves the power of clerical ordination. And this is observed among us, that whoever, baptized by them, come to us as strangers having gained nothing, moreover, are baptized among us with the one and true baptism of the Catholic Church that they may obtain the regeneration of the life-giving fountain.

And yet, there is a great difference between him who, unwilling and compelled by the pressure of persecution, succumbed, and him who, bold by voluntary sacrilege, rebels against the Church or blasphemes with impious voice against the Father and God of Christ and the Creator of the whole world. And Stephen is not ashamed to assert this, to say that the remission of sins can be given through those who themselves have been disposed to all sins as if the font of salvation could be in the home of death.

---

34 Cf. 1 Cor. 11.27.

(23) What, then, will be made of what has been written: 'Abstain from strange water and do not drink from a strange fountain,'[35] if, having abandoned the sealed fountain of the Church, you receive for your own strange water and you pollute the Church with profane fountains? For when you are in communion with the baptism of the heretics, what else do you do but drink from their whirlpool and filth and you yourself, having been purged by the sanctification of the Church, become tainted with the contacts of the sins of others?

Do you not fear the judgment of God when you give testimony to heretics against the Church since it is written: 'The false witness will not be unpunished'?[36] Nay, rather, you are worse than all the heretics. For when, after having recognized their error, many come to you to receive the true light of the Church, you help the errors of those who come and, having obscured the light of ecclesiastical truth, you pile up the darkness of heretical night and, although they confess that they are in sins and have no grace and are, therefore, coming to the Church, you take away from them the remission of sins which is given in baptism as long as you say that they are already baptized and have gained the grace of the Church outside the Church. You who have denied to the thirsting the drink of the Church and have been a cause of death to those desiring to live do not perceive that their souls will be required at your hands when the day of judgment comes and, in addition, you are angry!

(24) See with what ignorance you dare to reprehend those who are struggling for the truth against a falsehood. For who ought to be more justly angry against the other one? Is it the one who supports the enemies of God or he who stands firmly against the enemies of God for the truth of the Church? Unless it is clear that the ignorant are also hostile and wrathful while they are easily turned to wrath through the want of wisdom and advice so that of no other more than yourself

---

35 Cf. Prov. 9.18, 19 LXX.
36 Cf. Prov. 19.5.

does the Divine Scripture say: 'An ill-tempered man stirs up disputes, and a hotheaded man heaps up sins.'[37] For what quarrels and dissensions you have provoked through the churches of the whole world! How great a sin, certainly, you have heaped up for yourself when you cut yourself off from so many flocks! You have cut yourself off also. Do not be deceived since, indeed, he who has made himself an apostate from the communion of ecclesiastical unity is truly a schismatic. For while you think that all may be excommunicated by you, you have excommunicated yourself alone from all.

Nor could the precepts of the Apostle fashion you to the rule of truth and of peace when he warned and said: 'I therefore, the prisoner in the Lord, exhort you to walk in a manner worthy of the calling with which you were called, with all humility of disposition and meekness, with patience, bearing with one another in love, taking sufficient care to preserve the unity of the Spirit in the bond of peace: one body and one Spirit, even as you were called in one hope of your calling; one Lord, one faith, one Baptism; one God and Father of all, who is above all, and throughout all, and in us all.'[38]

(25) How diligently Stephen has fulfilled these salutary commands and admonitions of the Apostle, observing in the first place, humility of mind and meekness! For what is more humble or more meek than to have disagreed with so many bishops throughout the whole world, breaking the peace with each one in various kinds of discords, now with the Orientals—which we trust did not escape you—now with you who are in the South, from whom he received bishops as legates sufficiently patiently and meekly not even to admit them to the speech of a common conference, as yet, even more mindful of charity and love, to instruct the whole brotherhood that no one should receive them into his house so that not only peace and communion, but even a roof and hospitality, were denied to them who came!

---

37 Cf. Prov. 29.22.
38 Cf. Eph. 4.1-6.

This is 'to have preserved the unity of the Spirit in the bond of peace,'[39] to cut off from the unity of charity and to act as a stranger to the brethren in all matters and to rebel against the sacrament and bond of peace with the madness of discord! Can there be one body and one spirit with such a man in whom, perchance, there is not one mind, so slippery and fickle and uncertain it is?

But as far as he is concerned, let us leave him. Let us examine rather that concerning which there is the greatest question. They who contend that those baptized by heretics ought to be so received as if they had gained the grace of legitimate baptism say that there is one and the same baptism with them and us and that there is no difference at all. But what does the Apostle Paul say: 'One Lord, one faith, one Baptism; one God.'[40] If the baptism of the heretics is one and the same as ours, without doubt, faith is also one. But if there is one faith, there is certainly one Lord. If there is one Lord, it follows that we say that He is one. But if this unity, which cannot be separated or divided at all, is also itself with the heretics, why do we contend any more? Why do we call them heretics and not Christians? Moreover, since we and the heretics do not have one God, nor one Lord, nor one Church, nor one faith, nor even one Spirit, nor one body, it is clear that baptism cannot be common to us with the heretics with whom there is nothing at all in common.

And yet Stephen is not ashamed to show patronage to such men against the Church and to destroy the brotherhood for the sake of supporting the heretics and to say, in addition, that Cyprian is a false Christ and a false apostle and a treacherous laborer. Knowing that he is all these things himself, he has taken the initiative to charge to another through lying those faults which he himself deservedly ought to hear. We all trust that you are well with all of us, with all who are in Africa, the bishops and all the clerics and the whole brotherhood,

---
39 Cf. Eph. 4.3.
40 Eph. 4.5.

that we may have those who are unanimous and agreeing perpetually united with us even from afar.

76. *Cyprian*[1] *to Nemesianus,*[2] *Felix,*[3] *Lucius,*[4] *another Felix,*[5] *Litteus,*[6] *Polianus,*[7] *Victor,*[8] *Jader,*[9] *Dativus,*[10] *his fellow bishops, and also to his fellow priests and deacons, and other brethren, stationed in the mines, martyrs of God, the Father Almighty, and Jesus Christ, our Lord and God, our Savior, everlasting greeting.*

(1) Your glory, indeed, would demand, most blessed and dearly beloved Brethren, that I myself should come to see and to embrace you if prescribed limits of place did not keep me also banished because of confession of the Name. But as far as I can, I manifest myself to you and, although it is not granted me to come to you in body and in movement, yet I come to you in love and in spirit, expressing in a letter my mind in which I exult joyfully in those virtues and praises of yours, considering myself a sharer with you in the union of love if not in suffering of body.

Could I be silent and repress my voice in silence when I know concerning my dearly beloved friends so many and such glorious things with which the divine condescension has honored you, so that part of you, indeed, have already gone before by the consummation of their martyrdom to receive the

---
1 257 A.D.
2 Cf. Letter 62, n. 7.
3 Felix of Bagai in Numidia, one of the nine martyr bishops of the mines of Sigua.
4 Lucius, bishop of Thebeste in Numidia, another of the nine martyr bishops present at the synod.
5 Another Felix, bishop of Marazana in Numidia, also a martyr in the mines.
6 Litteus, bishop of Gemellae, another of the nine martyrs.
7 Polianus, bishop of Milev in Numidia.
8 Victor, a confessor in the mines, perhaps also the bishop of Octavum referred to in Letter 62, n. 5.
9 Jader, bishop of Midila in Numidia. His name is Punic.
10 Dativus, bishop of Badal in Numidia, martyr in the mines.

crown of their merits from the Lord? A part still lingers in the fortresses of the prison or in the mines and in chains, exhibiting through the very delays of their tortures greater examples for strengthening and arming the brethren, advancing by the tediousness of their punishments to greater titles of merit, about to receive as many rewards in heavenly recompenses as the days now are numbered in their punishments!

I do not wonder, indeed, that these things have happened to you, most brave and blessed Brethren, according to the merit of your religion and faith, that the Lord should thus have drawn you to the sublime height of glories by the honor of His glorification, you who always flourished in His Church with the even tenor of a faith practiced, firmly observing the commandments of the Lord: innocence in simplicity, concord in love, modesty in humility, diligence in administration, vigilance in aiding the exhausted, mercy in cherishing the poor, constancy in defending truth, judgment in severity of discipline. And lest anything should be lacking to the example of good deeds in you, even in the confession now of voice and in suffering of body, you are stirring up the minds of the brethren to divine martyrdoms by showing yourselves leaders in courage that, while the flock follows its shepherds and imitates what it sees is being done by its leaders, it may be crowned with equal rewards of obedience by the Lord.

(2) But that, first beaten severely with rods and afflicted through punishments of this nature, you initiated the religious first beginnings of your confession is not a matter to be deplored by us. For the Christian body, whose whole hope is in the wood of the cross, is not terrified at clubs. The servant of Christ recognizes the mystery of his salvation; having been redeemed by the wood to life eternal, he is drawn by the wood to the crown.

What, in truth, is astonishing if you, gold and silver vessels, have been given to the mine, that is, the home of gold and silver, unless that now the nature of mines has been changed and places which before had been accustomed to give gold and silver have begun to receive them? They have also put shackles on your feet and bound your blessed members, also temples of God, with degrading chains as if the spirit would be also bound with the body or your gold would be stained by the touch of iron. To men dedicated to God and giving testimony to their faith by their religious virtue, these are ornaments, not chains. They do not join the feet of Christians to infamy, but glorify them for a crown.

Oh, feet, happily bound, which are released not by a workman, but by the Lord! Oh, feet, happily bound, which are directed to Paradise by this salutary journey! Oh, feet, bound for the present in this world, that they may be always free before God! Oh, feet, lingering with fetters and crossbeams for a time, but about to run quickly to Christ on a glorious journey! Let either hateful or malignant cruelty hold you here in its bonds and chains as much as it wishes; speedily from the earth and these punishments, you will come to the kingdom of heaven.

The body is not cherished in the mines with a bed and with cushions, but it is cherished by the refreshment and solace of Christ. Your tired members, worn by labors, lie on the ground, but it is no punishment to lie with Christ. Your members are filthy without baths, unsightly with dust and dirt, but, what without is defiled with bodily stain, within is spiritually cleansed. There bread is scarce but 'not by bread alone does man live, but by the word of God.'[11] Clothing is wanting for those who are cold, but he who puts on Christ is clothed and adorned abundantly. The hair of the half-shaved head stands erect, but, since Christ is the Head of the man, whatever is necessary well befits that head which is outstanding for the Name of the Lord.

With how great splendor will all this deformity, detestable and repulsive to the Gentiles, be recompensed! For how glorious and eternal a reward of honor will this worldly and short punishment be changed when, according to the voice of

---
11 Cf. Luke 4.4.

the blessed Apostle: 'The Lord will refashion the body of our lowliness conformed to the body of his glory'!¹²

(3) But, dearly beloved Brethren, there can be felt no loss of religion or of faith in the fact that opportunity is not now given there to the priests of God of offering and of celebrating the divine Sacrifices. You celebrate, indeed, and offer a sacrifice to God equally precious and glorious and most profitable for you who are about to receive the recompense of heavenly rewards since the Divine Scripture speaks and says: 'My sacrifice to God is a contrite spirit: a heart contrite and humbled, God does not despise.'¹³

You offer this sacrifice to God; you celebrate this sacrifice without intermission day and night, having been made victims to God and exhibiting yourselves as holy and immaculate victims, as the Apostle exhorts and says: 'I exhort you therefore, brethren, by the mercy of God, to present your bodies as a sacrifice, living, holy, pleasing to God. . . . And be not conformed to this world, but transformed in the newness of your mind, that you may discern what is the good and acceptable and perfect will of God.'¹⁴

(4) For it is this which especially pleases God; it is this in which our works prosper with greater merits for obtaining the favor of God; it is this which alone the reverent tributes of our faith and our devotion repay to the Lord for His great and salutary benefits since the Holy Spirit declares openly and bears witness in the Psalms: 'What shall I render to the Lord,' He says, 'for all the things that he hath rendered to me? I will take the chalice of salvation; and I will call upon the name of the Lord. . . . Precious in the eyes of the Lord is the death of his faithful ones.'¹⁵

Who would not willingly and promptly receive the chalice of salvation? Who, joyful and rejoicing, would not strive for that in which he himself may render something to His Lord?

---

12 Cf. Phil. 3.21.
13 Cf. Ps. 50.19.
14 Cf. Rom. 12.1, 2.
15 Cf. Ps. 115.3, 4, 6.

Who would not bravely and constantly receive a death precious in the sight of God to please His eyes who, looking down upon us from above, approves of us wishing to act in the conflict for His Name? He aids the struggling; He crowns the victors, repaying with a return of His fatherly bounty and goodness whatsoever He Himself has provided and honoring what He Himself has accomplished.

(5) For, that it is through Him that we conquer and that we come to the palm of the greatest struggle by overcoming the adversary, the Lord declares and teaches in His Gospel, saying: 'But when they deliver you up, do not be anxious how or what you are to speak; for what you are to speak will be given you in that hour. For it is not you who are speaking, but the Spirit of your Father who speaks through you.'[16] And again: 'Resolve therefore in your hearts not to meditate beforehand how you are to make your defense. For I will give you utterance and wisdom, which all your adversaries will not be able to resist.'[17] In this, indeed, there is the great hope of the believers and the greatest fault of the unbelievers not to believe Him who promises that He will give His help to those who confess Him and, on the other hand, not to fear Him who threatens eternal punishment to those who deny Him.

(6) All of these things, most brave and faithful Soldiers of Christ, you have conveyed to our brethren, fulfilling in deeds what you before taught in words, about to be the greatest in the kingdom of heaven since the Lord promises and says: 'Whoever carries them out and teaches them shall be called the greatest in the kingdom of heaven.'[18] Finally, having followed your example, a manifold portion of the people have confessed likewise with you and likewise have been crowned, joined to you with the bond of the strongest love and separated from their prelates neither by prison nor by the mines. Virgins are not lacking to this number in whom the hundred-

---

16 Cf. Matt. 10.19, 20.
17 Cf. Luke 21.14, 15.
18 Cf. Matt. 5.19.

fold has been added to the sixtyfold fruit and whom the double glory has carried forward to the heavenly crown.[19] In boys also, a courage greater than their age transcends their years with the praise of their confession, so that both sexes and all ages adorn the blessed flock of your martyrdom.

(7) What vigor of victorious conscience is now yours, dearly beloved Brethren, what sublimity of mind, what exultation in feeling, what triumph in heart that each one of you stands near to the promised reward of God, is safe concerning the day of judgment, walks into the mine with a captive body, indeed, but with a heart reigning, knows that Christ is present with him, rejoicing at the endurance of His servants, who are advancing by His footsteps and His ways to the eternal kingdoms!

Joyful you await daily the salutary day of your departure and, every moment about to leave the world, you hasten to the rewards of martyrdom and to the heavenly dwellings, after this darkness of the world about to see the most shining light and to receive a glory greater than all sufferings and struggles since the Apostle bears witness and says: 'The sufferings of the present time are not worthy to be compared with the glory to come that will be revealed in us.'[20]

Because now your speech is clearly more efficacious in prayers, and supplication is quicker to obtain what is sought in persecutions, seek more eagerly and ask that the divine condescension may perfect the confession of us all that, from this darkness and from the deceits of the world, God may free us safe and glorious also with you, that we who here bound by the bond of love and of peace have stood firm against the injuries of the heretics and the persecutions of the Gentiles may, likewise, rejoice together in the heavenly kingdom. I trust that you, most blessed and courageous Brethren in the Lord, are well and always and everywhere mindful of us. Farewell.

---

19 Cf. Matt. 13.8.
20 Cf. Rom. 8.18.

LETTERS   319

77.¹ *Nemesianus,² Dativus,³ Felix,⁴ and Victor,⁵ to Cyprian, their brother, everlasting greeting in the Lord.*

(1) You have always spoken in your letters with great understanding, according to the condition of the time, dearly beloved Cyprian. After they have read these diligently, depraved men are corrected and men of good faith are strengthened. For while you do not cease in your treatises to lay bare hidden mysteries, thus you make us grow in faith and men of the world come near to belief. For whatever good you have brought in your many books, you have unconsciously revealed yourself to us. For you are greater than all men in discourse, more eloquent in speech, wiser in counsel, simpler in wisdom, more abundant in works, holier in abstinence, humbler in obedience, and more innocent in your good deeds. You know yourself also, dearly Beloved, that it is our prayerful wish that we may see that you, our teacher and friend, have arrived at the crown of a great confession.

(2) For as a good and true teacher, you announced first, in your proceedings before the proconsul, what we disciples ought to say, having followed you to the judge, and, as a singing trumpet, you have stirred up soldiers of God supplied with heavenly arms for the battle of the combat and, in the front line of battle, with a spiritual sword, you have killed the devil. You have also arrayed lines of the brethren here and there with your words that plots might be extended against the enemy on every side and the corpses of the public enemy itself and the cut sinews might be trodden under foot.

Believe us, dearly Beloved, that your innocent soul, which has feared neither the first attacks of the world, nor refused to go into exile, nor hesitated to leave the city, nor shrunk from abiding in a desert place, is not far from the hundred-

---

1 257 A.D.
2 Cf. Letter 62, n. 7.
3 Cf. Letter 76, n. 10.
4 Cf. Letter 76, n. 3.
5 Cf. Letter 76, n. 8.

fold reward. And since it gave to many an example of confession, itself first incited martyrdom. For how many has it stirred up to gain martyrdom by its example! It not only began to be a companion of the martyrs already departing from the world, but it also joined a heavenly friendship with future ones.

(3) Therefore, those condemned with us give the greatest thanks to you before God, dearly beloved Cyprian, because you have refreshed struggling hearts by your letters; you have cured members wounded by cudgels; you have released feet bound with chains; you have smoothed the hair of half-shaved heads; you have illuminated the darkness of the prison; you have brought the mountains of the mine down to the plains; you have even brought fragrant flowers to noses and have dissipated the foul odor of smoke.

But now your ministry and that of our dearly beloved Quirinus[6] have brought about and followed up what you sent to be distributed by Herennianus,[7] the subdeacon, and Lucan,[8] and Maximus,[9] and Amantius,[10] the acolytes, to deliver whatever had been wanting for the necessities of the body. Let us then be, by our prayers, helpers of one another and let us ask, as you have requested, that we may have God and Christ and the angels as protectors in all our actions. We trust that you, Lord and Brother, are always well and mindful of us. Greet all who are with you. All of our people who are with us love you and greet you and wish to see you.

---

6 Quirinus, a Christian of Carthage who joined Cyprian in aiding bishops and martyrs in the mines.
7 Herennianus, Carthaginian subdeacon.
8 Lucan, Carthaginian acolyte who, with Amantius and Maximus, distributed alms of Cyprian.
9 Maximus, Carthaginian acolyte with Amantius and Lucan.
10 Amantius, Carthaginian acolyte.

*78.*¹ *Lucius² and all the brethren in the Lord who are with him, to Cyprian, their brother and colleague, greeting.*

(1) Your letter, which you sent to us through Herennianus,³ the subdeacon, and Lucan⁴ and Maximus⁵ and Amantius,⁶ the acolytes, came to us, dearly beloved Brother, when we were exulting and rejoicing in God because He had armed us for the combat and made us victors in the battle by His condescension. Having read it, we received a loosening of our bonds, a solace in affliction, and a protection in our necessity and we were stirred up and animated more strongly for whatever more punishment there might be. For, before our suffering, we were stirred up to glory by you who first offered us guidance for the confession of the Name of Christ. We, in truth, having followed the footsteps of your confession, hope for an equal grace with you. For he who is first in the race is also first for the reward; and you who first engaged have thence communicated this to us from which you have begun, showing actually the undivided love with which you have always loved us, that those who had one spirit in the union of peace might have the grace of your prayers and one crown of confession.

(2) But for you, dearly beloved Brother, the recompense for your works has been added to the crown of confession, an abundant measure which you will receive from the Lord in the day of reward. And you who have shown yourself to us in your letter manifested that shining and blessed heart of yours, which we have always known, and, according to its greatness, you spoke praises to God with us, not so much as we deserve to hear, but as much as you can say. For, by your words, you both have embellished what was least prepared in us and you have strengthened us to sustain the same sufferings which we

---
1 257 A.D.
2 Cf. Letter 76, n. 4.
3 Cf. Letter 77, n. 7.
4 Cf. Letter 77, n. 8.
5 Cf. Letter 77, n. 9.
6 Cf. Letter 77, n. 10.

endure, secure concerning a heavenly reward and the crown of martyrdom and the kingdom of God, in the prophecy which you, filled with the Holy Spirit, have promised in your letter. This will all be accomplished, dearly Beloved, if you keep us in mind in your prayers; this I trust you do, just as we certainly do.

(3) And thus, we have received, ardently desired Brother, that which you sent from Quirinus[7] and from yourself, a sacrifice from every pure deed. Just as Noe offered to God and as God was delighted in the odor of the sweetness and looked upon his sacrifice,[8] so He looks upon yours and is delighted to render to you the reward of this so excellent work. But I ask that you may command the letter which we wrote to Quirinus to be sent over. I trust that you, dearly beloved and ardently desired Brother, are always well and mindful of us. Greet all who are with you. Farewell.

79.[1] *Felix,*[2] *Jader,*[3] *Polianus,*[4] *together with the priests and all staying with us in the mine, to dearly beloved and most dear Cyprian, everlasting greeting in the Lord.*

Strong and safe with the help of your prayers, we greet you in return, dearly beloved Brother, through Herennianus,[5] the subdeacon, and Lucan[6] and Maximus,[7] our brethren. From them we received a donation in the name of an offering together with your letter which you sent, in which you condescended to comfort us as your children with heavenly words.

And we have given and we do give thanks to God, the Father

---

7 Cf. Letter 77, n. 6.
8 Cf. Gen. 8.20-22.

---

1 257 A.D.
2 Cf. Letter 76, n. 5.
3 Cf. Letter 76, n. 9.
4 Cf. Letter 76, n. 7.
5 Cf. Letter 77, n. 7.
6 Cf. Letter 77, n. 8.
7 Cf. Letter 77, n. 9.

Almighty, through His Christ because we have been thus comforted and strengthened by your encouragement, seeking from the brightness of your spirit that you may deign to keep us in mind with your constant prayers that the Lord may make good your confession and ours which He has deigned to confer upon us. Greet all who are staying with you. We trust that you, dearly beloved Brother, are always well in the Lord. I, Felix, wrote this. I, Jader, subscribed. I, Polianus, read it. I greet my lord Eutychianus.[8]

80. Cyprian[1] to Successus,[2] his brother, greeting.

(1) This fact was responsible for my not writing to you immediately, dearly beloved Brother, that all the clergy situated in the thrust of the struggle were wholly unable to depart hence, all prepared according to the devotion of their minds for the divine and heavenly glory. But know that they had come whom I had sent to Rome for this, to bring back to us the truth they had found out in whatever manner it had been decreed concerning us. For many and varied and uncertain things are bruited about by rumors.

But the things which are true in them are these: that Valerian[3] had sent a rescript to the Senate that bishops and priests and deacons should be punished immediately, but senators and outstanding men and Roman knights should lose their rank and should also be deprived of their goods and, if, after their means had been taken away, they still persevered as Christians, they should also be deprived of their heads; that matrons should have their goods taken away and be sent into exile; but the people of Caesar's household, whoever either

---
8 Eutychianus, greeted by the martyr bishops in the mines.

1 258 A.D.
2 Cf. Letter 57, n. 9.
3 Valerian, Roman Emperor during one of the worst persecutions under whose edict Cyprian was the first to suffer in Africa. The emperor's policy was to punish the leaders.

had confessed before or now confessed, should have their goods confiscated and be sent as prisoners, assigned to Caesar's estates.

The Emperor Valerian also added to his speech a copy of the letters which he sent concerning us to the governors of the provinces. Standing according to the firmness of faith for the endurance of suffering and expecting the crown of eternal life from the help and mercy of the Lord, we hope daily that these letters will come.

But know that Sixtus[4] was executed in the cemetery on August 6, and with him four deacons. But the prefects in the city are daily following up the persecution that, if any are brought to them, they are executed and their goods claimed for the imperial treasury.

(2) I request that these things may become known to our other colleagues through you that everywhere, by their exhortation, the brotherhood may be strengthened and prepared for the spiritual combat, that each one of us may think less of death than of immortality and, dedicated to the Lord with full faith and complete courage, may rejoice rather than fear in this confession, in which they know that the soldiers of God and of Christ are not slain, but crowned. I trust that you, dearly beloved Brother, are always well in the Lord.

81. *Cyprian*[1] *to the priests and deacons and all the people, greeting.*

When it had been reported to us, dearly beloved Brethren, that officials had been sent to bring me to Utica and I had been persuaded by the counsel of those dearest to retire for a time from our gardens since a just cause was present, I consented because it is fitting for a bishop to confess the Lord

---

4 Sixtus, Pope for one year after Stephen, first to suffer under Valerian, martyred August 6, 258 A.D. Under Sixtus, relations between Rome and Carthage were more congenial, although Sixtus upheld the Roman practice regarding baptism.

1 258 A.D.

there in that city in which he presides over the Church of the Lord and to glorify the whole people by the confession of their leader in their presence. For whatever a confessor bishop speaks in the very moment of confession with God inspiring, he speaks with the mouth of all. Otherwise, the honor of our so glorious Church will be mutilated if I, the bishop, in charge of another Church, after having received the sentence from my confession in Utica, thence should set out as a martyr to the Lord because, both for myself and for you, I pray with continual supplications and I wish it eagerly with all my prayers that I may confess among you and suffer there and thence set out to the Lord as I ought.

We, therefore, await here in hidden retreat the coming of the proconsul, returning to Carthage, about to hear from him what the emperors have commanded about the account of the Christian laymen and bishops and to say what the Lord wishes to be said at that hour. But you, dearly beloved Brethren, in accordance with the discipline which you have always received from me concerning the commands of the Lord and according to what you have learned very often from my discourse, keep quiet and tranquillity, lest anyone of you should stir up any tumult for the brethren or offer himself voluntarily to the Gentiles. For the one seized and captured ought to speak since, abiding within us, God, who wishes us to confess rather than to profess, speaks at that hour. But, for the rest, it is fitting for us to observe before the proconsul renders the sentence against me for the confession of the Name of God, with the Lord instructing, what we shall decide at close quarters. May our Lord Jesus make you remain safe in His Church, dearly beloved Brethren, and may He deign to protect you!

INDICES

GENERAL INDEX

Aaron, 7, 234, 249, 250, 273.
Abel, 17, 166, 173.
Abiron, 7, 233, 249, 251, 273, 306.
Abraham, 6, 166, 170, 175, 204, 205.
Acts of the Apostles, 7, 30, 176, 218, 234, 235, 266, 279, 284.
Adam, 219, 290.
Adelphius, 231.
adulterer, 13, 151, 152, 214, 238, 291, 205; peace not given to, 146.
adultery, 105, 146, 152, 183, 186, 188, 214, 215.
Aelius, 231, 232n.
Africa, xvi, xxi, 63n., 93n., 128, 187, 199n., 240, 265, 268, 271n., 308, 312, 323n.
Agrippinus, xxi, 265, 270.
Ahymnus, 154.
Alexander, 302.
Alexandria, xxi.
Alexius, 62.

altar, 109, 115, 197, 205, 220, 221, 222, 227, 232, 235, 250, 260, 266, 267, 269, 273; priests to be free for, 3, 4; profane, 9, 73, 109, 142, 183, 190, 220, 221, 222, 240, 245, 266, 269, 306.
Amantius, 320, 321.
Ampius, 157.
Ananias, 18, 166.
Antichrist, xx, 60, 163, 168, 174, 185, 190, 191, 195, 198, 237, 244, 251, 252, 257, 261, 262, 264, 266, 277, 287, 288, 291.
Anthropians, 271.
Antonian, xvi, 134, 259.
Apocalypse, 168, 210, 220.
apostasy, ix, xvii, 46.
apostates, x, 138, 141, 153, 159, 311.
apostles (disciples), xxii, 27, 39, 41, 97, 117, 150, 164, 167, 170, 173, 178, 179, 205, 208,

329

215, 225, 226, 228, 234, 235, 237, 249, 252, 266, 271, 272, 273, 276, 277, 278, 279, 286, 287, 298, 299, 306, 308; chosen by Lord, 8; commission of, 70; killing of, 17, 27; obedience to Christ, 21; prayer of, 32; washing of feet by Christ, 42.
Appelles, 271n., 290, 298.
Appelletians, 271.
Aristo, 61.
Augendus, xv, 105, 106, 112, 125.
Augustine, xix.
Aurelius, bishop, 157, 230, 231.
Aurelius, reader, xv, 66, 69, 97, 101.
Azarias, 18, 166.

baptism, x, xix, xx, xxi, xxii, xxiv, 147, 156n., 200, 215, 244-257, 259-266, 268-294, 297, 298-312, 324n.; of blood, 160, 282, 283; clinical, xx, 244n.; controversy over, xx, xxiii; Council of Carthage on, 265-268; of evil woman, 303; of heretics, x, xiv, xx, xxi, 157n., 244-257, 259-265, 268-294, 298-312; infant, xix, 216-219; in name of Trinity, 68, 70, 171, 303, 304; sanctification of, 185, 227; signified by water, 206, 207, 208; sprinkling, xx, 253, 254, 257; tradition of Rome and Alexandria, xxi.
Basilides, founder of Gnostic sect, 298.
Basilides, lapsed bishop, xx, 230n., 231n., 232, 235, 236, 237, 238.
Bassianus, 23, 62.
Bassus, 61.
Bayard, Canon, xxv, 167n., 230n.
Bel, 167.
Benjamin, 248, 249.
Benson, E. W., xvii, 57n., 93n., 230n.
bishops, xi, xiii, xiv, 48, 50, 67, 75, 78, 82, 85, 87, 93, 98, 99, 103, 104, 105, 107, 108, 109, 113, 114, 117, 120, 121, 122, 123, 125, 129, 130, 131, 136, 137, 138, 139, 140, 141, 149, 156, 157, 160, 165, 172, 190, 193, 194, 195, 196, 197, 198, 199, 215, 219, 221, 222, 223, 224, 225, 227, 229, 232, 240, 241, 242, 243, 246, 247, 248, 251, 259, 261, 262, 264, 265, 266, 267, 268, 270, 273, 274, 283, 285, 291, 295, 301, 306, 309, 311, 312, 313, 320, 324, 325; to be appointed, 58, 78; assembled for decisions, 51, 55, 65, 75, 78, 83, 115, 146; chosen by God, 226; contributions of, 202; decrees to be observed, 4, 110, 116; direct responsibility to God, xi, xxi, 147, 257, 268, 285; good example of, 23; independence of

INDEX 331

judgment for, xi, xxi, 147, 285; joy of in good, 36; lapsed, 231n., 234, 235-237; not to be distracted from altar, 4; obedience to, 13, 93; obligations of, 292, 293; ordinary minister of penance, x, 44, 45, 47, 48, 61, 92; ordination of, 86, 173-178; power of, 6, 7, 47, 92, 216; rescript against, 323; selection and preparation of, 232-239; temptations of, xviii, 191, 192; union with, 112; unlawful, 115, 118, 140, 149, 150, 180-187, 266; of Africa, x, xvii, xx, xxi, xxii, 4, 53, 55, 60n., 62, 93, 103, 106, 128, 136, 137, 146, 172, 187, 202; of Mauretania, x, xxi, 34; of Numidia, x, xviii, xxi; of Rome (Pope), xviii, xxii, 75, 78, 114, 116, 123, 124, 134, 136, 137, 138, 139.
blasphemer, 281, 287, 290, 291, 298, 299, 309.
blasphemy, 47.
Blood of Christ, xix, 32, 44, 48, 56, 145, 147, 159, 163, 200, 203, 204, 206, 208, 209, 210, 211, 213, 242, 248, 267, 309; of martyrs, 25, 26, 28, 81, 82, 92, 95, 160, 163, 191, 194, 213.
Body of Christ, 32, 48, 159, 170, 204, 211, 248, 271, 309, 316; mystical, 104, 114, 150, 151, 211, 311; profanation of, 44.
Bona, 63.
bread, 204, 205, 208, 209, 211, 248, 255, 309, 315; pretended consecration by evil woman, 303.

Caldonius, xiii, xiv, xv, 63, 64, 65, 67, 103, 106, 113, 114, 117, 120, 121, 156, 258.
Calpurnius, 59, 62.
Candida, 57, 58, 61.
Canticle of Canticles, 245, 294, 305.
Capitol, 58n., 184, 190.
Cappadocia, 295n., 302.
Carthage, ix, x, xvi, xxiiin., 19n., 60, 61, 63, 68n., 93, 104, 105n., 112, 113, 129, 156, 180n., 181, 182, 231n., 265n., 320n., 324n., 325; allegiance to Pope, xviii, 199; news of martyrdom of Fabian, 20n.; uniform policy with Rome, xiii, xiv, 66, 69.
Cassius, 258.
catacombs, ix.
Cataphrygians, 299.
catechumens, 22, 52, 71, 282, 309.
Cecil, xviii, 10, 156, 202, 230, 258.
Celerina, 100.
Celerinus, xiii, xv, 56, 57n., 59, 67, 68, 94, 99, 100, 122n.
Cerdo, 270n., 287, 298.
certificate, 46n., 54, 73, 135, 140, 141, 142, 144, 151, 181, 232n., 236.

Chalice (cup), xix, 44, 47, 48, 159, 163, 168, 205, 208, 209, 210, 280, 309; of martyrdom, 95, 159; of Salvation, 69, 159, 163, 203, 205, 206, 207, 208, 209, 210, 211, 213, 214, 215, 248, 316; water alone, not Blood of Christ, 203.

charity, xviii, 36, 92, 94, 104, 114, 121, 126, 132, 192, 195, 196, 198, 202, 245, 247, 248, 276, 285, 296, 311, 312.

chastity, 109, 146.

chrism, 260.

Christ, 12, 33, 35, 39, 41, 42, 43, 55, 60, 64, 68, 81, 102, 104, 109, 112, 114, 122, 123, 124, 125, 127, 128, 132, 133, 138, 143, 149, 158, 159, 163, 164, 165, 166, 168, 170, 171, 172, 173, 179, 184, 185, 186, 189, 192, 194, 195, 198, 199, 200, 201, 226, 227, 237, 241, 242, 244, 245, 249, 250, 254, 262, 263, 264, 266, 267, 270, 274, 275, 276, 277, 288, 289, 290, 291, 294, 300, 301, 303, 305, 308, 309, 320, 321, 323, 324, 325; baptized by John, 252; battle of, 25; brightness of, 95; coming of, xix, 167, 218, 271; confession of, 59, 63, 74, 80, 84, 99, 100, 126, 197, 281, 282, 313-318; consecration to, 11, 70, 304; doctrine of, 111, 174, 203, 208, 209, 210, 212, 214, 278, 280, 281, 292; establishment of Church by, 261, 306; fidelity to, xvii, 14, 24, 56, 71, 203, 215; grace of, 260, 307; Intercessor, 32, 145; joy in confessors, 26; Judge, 169, 230; Melchisedec as type of, 204, 205; members of, 114, 151; mercy of, 57, 58, 255; offering of, 212, 213, 246; prediction of persecution, xviii; punishment of evildoers, 12; rebellion against, 9, 13, 108, 118, 224, 279; reign of, 17; respect for priests, 8, 178; union with, xv, 18, 96, 293; suffering for, 98; suffering of, 206, 207, 211, 225.

Christians, ix, x, 37, 110, 143, 149, 172, 184, 251, 252, 254, 255, 280, 286, 288, 290, 291, 302, 312, 314, 315, 320, 323, 325; actor, xi, 5-6; difficulty to remain, xi, xii, 142; failures of, 38; lapsed, 56n.; in prison, 16n., 199n.; rescripts against, xxiii, 323; soldiers of Christ, xvii.

Church, ix, xvii, xx, xxi, xxiv, 14, 23, 27, 36, 45, 46, 48, 49, 50, 74, 76, 77, 89, 92, 93, 101, 102, 103, 105, 107, 109, 110, 114, 115, 118, 119, 120, 122, 123, 124, 125, 126, 127, 130, 131, 132, 133, 134, 136, 137, 138, 139, 149, 150, 153, 154, 159, 160, 170, 172, 176, 177, 178, 179, 180, 181, 183, 184, 186, 187, 188, 189, 190,

INDEX 333

192, 193, 195, 196, 197, 198, 202, 203, 208, 210, 211, 222, 223, 224, 225, 226, 237, 239, 241, 242, 244, 271, 272, 273, 274, 275, 276, 277, 281, 282, 283, 284, 285, 286, 287, 288, 289, 290, 291, 292, 293, 294, 298, 299, 305, 308, 309, 310, 311, 312, 314, 325; admission to, 13, 56n., 111, 114; confessors, glory of, 24, 28, 43, 99, 146; Cyprian's conception of, xxiv, 128; discipline of, xiii, 3, 4, 270; establishment of, 86, 306; faith of, 22; government of, 40, 85, 86, 90, 229, 240; harming of, 114, 129, 238; haste of lapsed to return to, 53; Holy Spirit with, xxii, 261, 300, 304; ministry of, 8, 98, 101, 103; mystical body, 229; ordination against, 112; peace of, 61, 75; prefigured by ark of Noe, 305; purity of, 109; rebellion against, 141, 268-269; respect for, 5; restoration of, 34; return of confessors to, xvi, 111, 117, 140, 158; safety of, 73; separation from, 9, 144; support for needy, 6; teaching on baptism, xxi, xxii, 246-257, 259-265, 301, 307; unity of, 132, 133, 228, 245, 246, 264; in Africa, ix, x, xxi, xxiii, 26, 93, 112n., 202; in Rome, funds of, 68n.

Cilicia, 300.
circumcision, xix, 13, 216, 218, 264.
Cittinus, 259.
Clementian, 154.
clergy, x, xv, 3, 4, 47, 48, 50, 51, 52, 54, 55, 62, 63, 86, 87, 99, 126, 131, 138, 240, 312, 323; distribution of funds to indigent, 15, 202; lapsed not to resume clerical state, xx, 236, 266, 267; penitent, xxi, 266, 267; preparation for, 72; of Carthage, x, xi, xii, xiii, xiv, 14, 19, 20n., 28, 40, 44, 45, 46, 51, 53, 55, 63, 64, 65, 68, 71, 85, 87, 89, 90, 97, 99, 102, 103, 105, 108, 109, 116, 117, 190, 202, 324; to care for people in Cyprian's absence, 15, 20, 34-36; of Rome, x, xi, xii, xiii, xiv, 20, 23, 53, 54, 55, 66, 67, 70, 72, 73, 85, 89, 90, 93n., 120, 121, 122, 123, 124, 129, 136, 137, 191.
Collecta, 62.
Colonica, 62.
Commandments (precepts) of the Lord, 11, 13, 14, 16, 30, 38, 43, 45, 50, 52, 54, 67, 68, 69, 70, 78, 85, 96, 97, 101, 107, 110, 164, 168, 171, 189, 192, 212, 215, 221, 232, 233, 234, 238, 248, 261, 266, 281, 287, 288, 291, 292, 293, 314, 325; failure to observe, 29, 30, 31, 44; respect for, 32.
Commemoration of Christ,

203, 209, 212, 214; of martyrs, xii, 35, 36, 100.
Communion (Holy), 13, 47, 48, 50, 84, 134, 136, 137, 140, 151, 152, 155, 158, 159, 160, 161, 266; given to penitent, 22; sacrilegious, 140, 309; withheld from Gaius and his deacon, xiv, 87; from lapsed, 137.
communion with the Church, x, xiii, 46, 52, 55, 88, 89, 91, 92, 105, 112, 113, 121, 127, 130, 132, 134, 135, 137, 144, 145, 149, 155, 180, 186, 216, 223, 225, 226, 227, 228, 229, 232, 236, 240, 243, 267, 287, 311; for actor, 5; rashly given, 74, 93, 136, 216; with the lapsed or with heretics, 48, 50, 55, 87, 89, 104, 105, 123, 134, 183, 229, 233, 238, 239, 250, 251, 277, 281, 286, 287, 288, 291, 299, 307, 310.
confession, x, 24, 29, 39, 44, 48, 51, 55, 58, 107, 118, 122, 123, 135, 140, 144, 153, 165, 193, 195, 196, 197, 198, 235, 281, 282, 313, 314, 317, 318, 319, 320, 321, 323, 324, 325; of Cornelius, xviii, 193-196; glory of, 18, 24, 36, 91, 199; of lapsed, 22, 38, 39; of the Lord, 15, 16, 56, 64, 69, 70, 74, 80, 84, 94, 98, 99, 100, 103, 156, 159, 160, 163, 313-318; of the martyrs, 27, 59; for minor offenses, 50; not made, 44, 48, 186; of Pupian, xix, 223; of sins before return to Church, 13, 32, 47, 53, 55, 61, 126; for those in danger of death, 51; virtue of, 19, 38, 96.
confessors, 29, 34, 36, 41, 42, 43, 46, 48, 49, 51, 53, 55, 58, 59, 61, 62, 64, 65, 66, 67, 69, 71, 75, 82, 83, 94, 99, 101, 102, 106, 108, 118, 119, 121, 122, 126, 127, 129, 132, 136, 139, 144, 154, 184, 193, 196, 197, 199, 223, 228, 325; corruption of, 54, 107; faith of, 75; later leading evil lives, 29, 38, 39, 42; in mines, xxiii, 313-318; obligations of, 37; in prison, xi, xii, xiv, xv, xvi, xvii, 15, 16, 18, 23, 24, 34, 40n., 41, 43, 68n., 74, 79, 85, 94; strengthening of, 82; yielding under torture, xvii, 155-156.
Confirmation (giving of the Holy Spirit), x, xxii, 255, 265, 272, 273, 274.
confiscation, 63.
conscience, 72, 107, 142, 162, 179, 187, 188, 216, 224, 230, 235, 236, 253, 318; glorious (brave), 28, 63, 80, 140; guilty, 11, 54, 77, 135.
Constantine, xxiiin.
Core, 7, 233, 249, 250, 251, 273, 306.
Cornelia, 59, 62n.
Cornelius, centurion, 266.
Cornelius, Pope, x, xvii, xviii, xx, 43n., 68n., 112, 114, 117,

INDEX 335

118n., 119, 121, 122, 123, 124, 125, 126, 127, 131, 134, 136, 137, 138, 139, 140, 141, 157, 171, 181n., 193, 196n., 198, 237, 240, 243, 246; election and consecration of, xv, xvi, 113, 115, 116, 120; milder policy of, 112n.
councils, 71, 85, 97, 131, 137, 230n., 231n., 265, 297; decisions, guide to unity, xi, xiv, 72, 297; need to settle problems of lapsed, 53, 55, 65, 72, 83, 136.
Council or Synod of Arles, xxiiin.; of Nicaea, 170n.; of Carthage, ix, xvii, xix, xx, xxiii, 10, 89n., 93n., 103n., 113n., 120n., 136, 137, 154, 155, 156, 157n., 182, 184, 216, 217, 219, 230n., 231n., 240, 258n., 259, 262, 270, 313n.; on baptism, xxi, 265-268; clerics to be free for priestly duties, 3, 4; of Rome, 112n., 137.
Credula, 61.
Crementius (Clementius?), 20, 23, 24, 55.
crucifixion of Christ, 176, 200, 225; of martyrs, 25.
Curubis, xxiiin.
Cyprian, Bishop of Carthage, ix-xxv, 20, 36, 47, 48, 62, 63, 71, 72, 79, 80, 82, 87n., 93, 98, 102, 103, 104, 105, 109, 112n., 120, 121, 122n., 123, 124, 125, 129, 141, 156, 157, 181, 189, 216, 226, 227, 230,

231n., 232, 236, 265, 312, 319, 320, 321; death of, ix, xxiii, 323; desire to consult clergy and people, 43, 44, 75, 89; example and encouragement of, 319-323; exile, ix, xi, xii, xv, xxiii, 10, 14n., 16, 19n., 20, 40, 41, 49, 54, 108, 319; letters, ix-xxv, 24, 46, 51, 54, 55, 62, 64, 65, 66, 67, 69, 71, 74, 75, 79, 83, 85, 87, 88, 90, 93, 99, 106, 107, 113, 114, 115, 117, 118, 119, 121, 127, 131, 134, 135, 136, 137, 154, 156, 171, 184, 191, 193, 196, 199, 202, 203, 214, 216, 219, 223, 230, 239, 244, 258, 259, 262, 265, 268, 285, 295, 298, 313, 319, 320, 321, 322, 323, 324; proscription of, 177, 178, 226; rescript against, 323n.

Daniel, 167, 197, 238, 296.
Dathan, 7, 233, 249, 251, 273, 306.
Dativa, 62.
Dativus, 313, 319.
David, 248.
deacons, xii, 12, 42, 46, 48, 68, 85, 89, 106, 120, 129, 135, 136, 187, 235, 266, 273, 295, 303, 304, 313; chosen by apostles, 8; duty of, xi, 8, 15, 20, 44, 50, 75, 83; executed with Sixtus, 324; of Gaius, xiv, 87; insolence of, xi, 6, 7, 8, 9; involved with women, 10, 12; rescript

against, 323; restoration of lapsed by, x, 51; unable to restrain evildoers, 42.
death, 41, 52, 66, 75, 81, 88, 96, 102, 103, 104, 105, 109, 141, 144, 147, 149, 158, 165, 166, 178, 191, 197, 200, 209, 219, 222, 239, 264, 267, 271, 280, 281, 291, 306, 309, 310, 316, 317, 324, 325; conquered by Christ, 26, 206; of Fabian, 23; of faithful, 17, 19, 26, 29, 35, 40, 80; fear of, 77; perseverance unto, 41; reconciliation for those in danger of, xii, xvii, 51, 159; spiritual, 57.
Decimus, 63.
Decius, x, xi, xiii, 26n., 56n., 60n., 75n., 232n.
Deferrari, Roy J., ixn., xxv.
Demetrius, 157, 258.
Denis (Dionysius), 125.
Deuteronomy, 7, 13, 175, 225.
devil, 32, 64, 77, 140, 142, 171, 172, 182, 183, 184, 191, 195, 198, 200, 221, 222, 226, 240, 255, 282, 291, 297, 319; corruption of, 5, 73, 108, 111, 137, 145; cup of devils, 47; enemy of faith, 77; excluded in baptism, 256; failure to overcome good, 36, 100; giving opportunity to, 11, 33, 152; hold over lapsed, xix, 220; struggle with, 59, 169, 170; woman possessed by, 302-304.
Dictionary of Christian Biography, xvii.
discipline, ix, x, xii, xiii, xxiii, 34, 40, 46, 47, 51, 52, 54, 56, 65, 66, 72, 74, 83, 97, 102, 108, 135, 148, 180, 213, 214, 238, 276, 283, 288, 291, 314, 325; ecclesiastical discipline to be preserved, 10, 12, 15, 43, 45, 55, 73, 87, 98, 174; failure of confessors in, 29, 55, 56n., 107, 129; of the good, 37; in keeping of divine precepts, 11, 37, 41, 50, 68n., 69, 91, 303; Lord, Master of, 32, 71; respect for ecclesiastical, 4, 5, 53, 60, 70, 72, 171.
doctrine, ix, 109, 111.
Donata, 62.
Donatulus, 154.
Donatus, African bishop, 157, 258.
Donatus, earlier Bishop of Carthage, 93n., 181.
Donatus, martyr, 61.
Donatus, priest of Carthage, 43.

Easter (Paschal season), xv, 57, 71, 107, 298; time for council, xvii, 112, 156.
Egnatius (Ignatius), 100.
Eleazar, 234.
Elias, 284.
Eliseus, 217.
Emerita (Merida), 59, 62, 231, 232n.
Epictetus, xix, 219.
Emmanuel, 26.

INDEX   337

Ephesians, 246.
Esau, 285.
Esdras, 292.
Etecusa, 57n., 58.
Eucratius, xi, 5.
Eutychianus, 259, 323.
Eutyches, 157.
Evaristus, 125, 127.
excommunication, 104n., 105, 113, 178, 182, 228, 291, 311; of deacon, 12; of Felicissimus, xv, 106, 172, 180, 188; of Gaius, 87n.; of Marcian and Novatian, xx, 112n., 240, 241; power of bishop to use, 9; Stephen's threat of, xxi, xxiii.
exile (banishment), xii, 54, 63, 64, 97, 98, 106, 108, 127, 141, 197, 228, 313, 323; of confessors, 24, 53.
Exodus, 213, 221, 232, 255, 267.
exorcism, 303.
Ezechiel, 161, 253, 259, 296.

Fabian, Pope, xii, xiv, 23, 69, 112n., 138, 181, 246; martyrdom of, 20n., 22n., 68n., 69n., 75.
faith, xv, 34, 41, 43, 46, 52, 54, 60, 64, 66, 69, 73, 77, 82, 88, 94, 100, 101, 103, 107, 116, 122, 127, 128, 131, 132, 134, 139, 146, 149, 152, 155, 156, 162, 163, 164, 169, 170, 173, 177, 179, 184, 185, 186, 188, 189, 192, 193, 194, 195, 196, 197, 198, 199, 200, 201, 202, 210, 211, 217, 220, 222, 224, 227, 228, 232, 236, 237, 238, 239, 244, 246, 251, 253, 254, 256, 257, 262, 264, 265, 266, 267, 268, 270, 271, 272, 273, 274, 275, 277, 281, 282, 283, 285, 288, 291, 292, 293, 296, 298, 300, 301, 303, 305, 307, 308, 309, 311, 312, 314, 315, 316, 319, 324; Christ, Protector of, 26; of the Church, 93; of clergy, 15, 40, 53, 113; of confessors, 16, 19, 24, 25, 26, 35, 74, 75, 81, 97; danger to, 31; good faith of virgins, 11; hardships of, 84; justification by, 205; neglect of, 29; of Paul, 27; perseverance in, 22, 23, 24, 32, 33, 35, 41; of the poor, 36; power of, 37, 70, 96, 136, 144, 166, 167, 204; regained, 63; of Romans, 23; subverted, 67, 80, 108, 126; of women, 18.
faithful (those who stand), xii, xiv, xv, xvii, 17, 22, 32, 86, 93, 97, 111, 136, 170, 190, 195, 198, 203, 226, 302, 303; poor to be cared for, 41; to be present at decisions of clergy, 53, 75, 76, 83.
Faustinus, African bishop, 156.
Faustinus, Bishop of Lyons, 239.
Faustus, 231.
Favorinus, xiv, 89.

fear, 60, 68, 77, 139, 165, 168, 194, 195; of death, 77; of the Lord, 21, 43, 53, 54, 67, 83, 134, 146, 185, 188, 192, 195, 215, 232, 234, 237, 239, 291, 292; necessity of, 48; not considered by some, 44.
Felician, 181.
Felicissimus, confessor, 19.
Felicissimus, trouble maker, xv, 43n., 93n., 104, 105, 106, 107, 108, 112, 117, 129, 172, 180, 181, 188.
Felix, African bishop, 154, 156, 231, 258.
Felix, Bishop of Bagai in Numidia, 313, 319, 322, 323.
Felix, Bishop of Caesaraugusta, 236.
Felix, Bishop of Marazana in Numidia, 313.
Felix, lapsed African Christian, 63.
Felix, ordained bishop to replace Basilides, 231.
Felix, priest of Spain, 231, 232n., 236.
Felix, unlawful bishop, 181.
Fidus, xix, 216.
Firmilian, xxii, 295.
Firmus, 61.
Florus, 154.
forgiveness of sin (absolution), 272, 273, 279, 306, 307.
Fortunata, 61.
Fortunatian, xix, 219, 222.
Fortunatus, Bishop of Capsa, 154, 156.

Fortunatus, Bishop of Thuccabor, 113, 114, 117, 120, 121, 157, 230, 258.
Fortunatus, subdeacon, 89, 90.
Fortunatus, unlawful bishop, xiv, 43, 180, 181, 182, 187, 188.
Fortunio, 61.
Fructus, 61.
funds for converted actor, xi, 5, 6; for imprisoned, xxiii, 15, 20, 34, 40n., 41, 82, 199n., 201, 320, 322; for needy, 15, 20, 22, 104, 202, 320; for persecuted, xviii, 34.
Futurus, 93.

Gaius, xiv, 87.
Galatia, 300.
Galerius Maximus, xxiiin.
Gargilius, 258, 259.
Geminius Faustinus, 3, 4, 231.
Geminius Victor, 3, 4.
Genesis, 203, 205, 210, 285.
Gentiles (heathen, pagans), x, 40, 98, 172, 206, 210, 211, 223, 225, 236, 245, 249, 263, 266, 279, 286, 296, 315, 318, 325; conduct of Christians among, 38, 45; God blasphemed among, 37; hatred of, 20; justified by faith, 205.
Getulicus, 62.
Gnostic sect, 270, 271n., 287n., 290n., 298n.
Gordius, 43.
Gospel, 32, 44, 45, 46, 65, 66,

INDEX 339

67, 69, 70, 81, 86, 90, 92, 98, 108, 110, 114, 126, 130, 143, 145, 147, 148, 160, 166, 169, 170, 173, 174, 175, 177, 178, 183, 186, 189, 201, 205, 207, 209, 212, 213, 215, 217, 221, 224, 225, 228, 233, 242, 243, 244, 245, 249, 252, 254, 255, 261, 266, 274, 278, 281, 282, 283, 286, 288, 292, 306, 317; discipline of, 91, 97; disobeyed, 54, 74, 118; martyrs for, 75; priests unmindful of, 50, 83; reading of, 101; unity of, 132.

grace, x, 37, 43, 52, 79, 82, 95, 147, 185, 209, 210, 218, 219, 227, 247, 248, 252, 253, 254, 255, 256, 257, 262, 263, 264, 270, 271, 272, 273, 274, 275, 277, 278, 283, 284, 296, 300, 301, 303, 307, 308, 309, 310, 312, 321; through baptism, xx, 68, 260; not to be denied to anyone, xix, 217; safety through, 20, 43.

hands, cast out by, 78, 141, 170; of God, 110, 206, 217, 218; healing, 77; impious, 18, 54, 63, 70, 74, 84, 122, 168, 183, 197, 221, 267, 310; imposition of, xx, 44, 47, 48, 50, 51, 53, 55, 235, 252, 263, 265, 272, 273, 274, 286, 287, 289, 290, 294, 300, 301, 304, 307; offering by, 166; pure hands, 16; receiving Holy Eucharist, 170.

Hartel, Von, W., xxv, 167n., 182n., 230n.

hatred, 53, 68, 168, 173, 229, 276, 291; attack of, 69; danger of stirring up, 15, 20.

heaven, 14, 33, 42, 69, 82, 91, 96, 126, 158, 164, 167, 171, 174, 209, 212, 215, 228, 232, 250, 255, 271, 278, 283, 295, 301, 306, 315, 317; power in, 70; reward of confessors, 16, 78, 80, 81, 86.

Helias, 237.

Hell, 11, 25, 78, 86, 153, 168, 170, 174, 175, 191; destruction of soul in, 17; powerless against Church, 86; powerless against confessors, 18, 25.

Herculanus, 103, 106, 157, 258.

Hereda, 61.

Herennianus, 320, 321, 322.

Herennius, 61.

heresy, xxi, 68n., 93n., 118, 122, 176, 177, 181, 191, 226, 236n., 240, 241, 244, 263, 268, 270, 271, 282, 283, 286, 287, 290, 291, 294, 298, 301, 305.

heretics, x, xiv, xvii, xviii, xx, xxi, xxii, 68n., 112, 113, 117, 122, 123, 124, 125, 126, 127, 128, 130, 132, 134, 142, 144, 149, 151, 159, 172, 180, 181, 182, 183, 186, 187, 189, 190, 192, 198, 237, 266, 318; baptism of, 157n., 236n., 244-257, 259-265, 268-294,

298-312; beginnings of, 8; evil influence on confessors, xvi.
Hippocrates, 254.
Holy Eucharist, x, 159, 160, 170, 204, 209, 210, 211, 212, 213, 260; given before penance is performed, 44, 48, 50; pretense of celebrating by evil woman, 303; source of strength in persecution, xvii; treatise on in letter to Cecil, xviii, 203-215; worthy reception of, xii.
Holy Innocents, 167.
Holy Orders, x, 14.
Holy See (Roman), xxii, 139, 186, 307; Chair of Peter, xi, 109, 124, 139, 186; deference to, xv; primacy of, xiv, xxiv, 109, 121, 129; vacancy of, xi, xiv, 20n., 69n., 75, 78, 85n., 136, 139.
Holy Spirit, 49, 68, 70, 124, 161, 170, 177, 190, 192, 200, 204, 205, 206, 207, 210, 215, 217, 222, 224, 238, 243, 245, 247, 256, 260, 261, 266, 271, 275, 276, 279, 281, 282, 283, 288, 289, 290, 299, 306, 307, 311, 312, 316, 317, 322; blasphemy against, 47; evils not from, 152; giving of, x, xxii, 225, 265, 272, 273, 274; instruction by, 10, 26, 253; not with heretics, 249, 251, 252, 300, 301, 302, 303, 304; rejection of evildoers by, 13; sins forgiven through, 252; in Solomon, 7; strength of confessors, 16, 17, 166, 167, 227.
Honoratus, African bishop, 157, 230, 258.
Honoratus, Numidian bishop, 199, 259.
Hortensian, 157, 258.
Hyginus, Pope, 287.

Iambus, 157, 231.
Iconium in Phrygia, 300, 308.
infants, baptism of, xix, 216, 217, 218, 219; martyrdom of, 167.
Irene of the Rutili, 106.
Isaac, 6, 170.
Isaia, 26, 174, 177, 206, 207, 212, 233, 287.
Israel, 210, 213, 248, 250, 253.

Jacob, 6, 170, 173.
Jader, 313, 322, 323.
Januaria, 62.
Januarius, African bishop (2), 230, 258.
Januarius, Numidian bishop, 199, 230.
Jeremia, 214, 215, 272.
Jeroboam, son of Nabat, 248.
Jerusalem, 249, 299.
Jews, 172, 173, 175, 207, 210, 233, 237, 249, 278, 279, 304, 307, 308; alienation from God, 37; circumcision of, xix, 218; despising of Samuel, 7.
Jezebel, 147.
Job, 296.

INDEX   341

Joel, 147, 148.
John, Apostle, 70, 145, 163, 179, 244, 261, 273.
John, Baptist, 198, 252, 284, 300, 301.
Joseph, 173, 230.
Josue, son of Nun, 286.
Jovinus, 181.
Jubaian, xxi, 268.
Juda, 205, 206, 248, 249.
Judas, 173, 234, 296.
Judea, 303.
Julia, 61.
Junius, 156, 258.

Kings, Book of, 7, 248.

lapse (of followers), xvi, 23, 55, 110, 134n., 140, 155; caused by weakness, xii, 22; of Fortunatian, 219; sorrow for lapse, xix, 49, 65, 86, 93.
lapsed, 52, 60n., 66, 78, 85n., 92, 93, 104, 109, 133, 136, 137, 147, 154n., 155, 158, 161, 169, 183, 184, 186, 190, 195, 216n., 224, 227, 239n., 240, 242, 243, 297; attempt at force by, xiv, 53, 55, 56, 86, 90, 160; bishops, 103, 231; caution in restoration of, xii, xiv, 92, 107, 108, 196n.; communion with, 48, 50, 55, 86, 87, 88, 89; deception of, xv, 47n.; destructon of, 34, 107; distinction of type of, xvii, 159; incited to confession, xviii, 22, 34, 107, 121, 135; need for penance of, xiii, 64; pardon for, xvii, 22, 44, 46, 146, 161; peace for, 43n., 44, 46n., 158-162; penance for, 34; power of devil over, xix, 220-224; priests in communion with, 50; problem of, xvi, 43n., 75, 76, 110; repentant lapsed, xiii, 22, 78, 111, 121, 154n., 222; restoration of by deacon, x, 51.
Laurentine, 100.
Lazarus, 175.
Levite, 3, 4, 253; of the Gospel, 145.
Leviticus, 221, 232, 267.
libellus, 46n.
Liberalis, 120, 156, 258.
Libosus, 231.
Litteus, 313.
Longinus, 112, 124.
Lot, wife of, 33.
Lucan, 320, 321, 322.
Lucian, African bishop, 157, 258.
Lucian, African priest, 262.
Lucian, imprudent confessor, xiii, 56, 58, 59, 60, 61n., 62n., 63, 66, 67, 68.
Lucilian or Lucian, 230.
Lucius, African bishop, 231, 258.
Lucius, Numidian bishop, 313, 321.
Lucius, companion to Felix, 63.
Lucius, Pope, x, xviii, xx, 196, 197, 243.

Macarius, 59, 62n., 68n., 126, 131.
Machabees, 167.
Machaeus, 112, 124.
Magnus, xx, 244.
manna, 255.
Manthaneus, 157.
Mappalicus, 26, 27, 61, 66.
Marcellus, 231.
Marcian of Arles, xx, 239, 240, 241, 243.
Marcion of Pontus, 270, 271, 287, 290, 291, 298.
Marcionites, 271.
Maris, 62.
Mark, African bishop, 258.
marriage (nuptials), x, 11, 151, 172, 201, 210.
Marrutius, 156, 258.
Martial (Felix), xx, 231n., 232, 236, 237, 238.
Martial, martyr, 61.
martyrs, xiv, 18, 24, 26, 27, 28, 35, 45, 49, 51, 52, 53, 55, 56, 57, 60, 61, 63, 64, 66, 68, 69, 70, 82, 87, 91, 92, 97, 98, 99, 103, 139, 144, 159, 164, 167, 170, 198, 199n., 227, 243, 282, 313, 320, 323, 324, 325; anniversaries of, 35, 36, 100; bodies to be buried, 22, 35; courage of, xi, 27; death of, 80; exposed to hatred, 48; guided by deacons, 44; importuned by lapsed, 54; letters to, x, 24, 43; petitions given by, 46, 67; requests for lapsed, 50, 51; sanctified by torments, 17.
martyrdom, ix, xiv, xxiii, xxiv, xxv, 69, 75, 95, 97, 98, 100, 135, 146, 159, 160, 166, 197, 198, 199, 223, 226, 237, 243, 246, 313, 314, 318, 320, 322; consummated in prison, 35; exhortation to, 162-171; of Fabian, 20n.; triumph of, 167.
Mary, 59, 62.
Mattathias, 237.
Matthew, 123.
Mauretania, 120, 231n., 266, 268.
Maximus, Carthaginian acolyte, 320, 321, 322.
Maximus, Numidian bishop, 199, 258.
Maximus, priest and confessor, xv, xvi, 59n., 68, 69, 79, 85, 94, 105n., 112, 118, 122, 123, 124, 126, 131, 136, 180, 181.
Melchisedec, 204, 205.
mercy, 48, 51; divine, 28, 39, 40, 49, 86, 89, 93, 96, 98, 103, 108, 110, 112, 130, 136, 143, 148, 153, 155, 162, 196, 210, 214, 217, 219, 222, 240, 241, 243, 254, 255, 256, 257, 272, 276, 283, 314, 316, 324; false, 74; to be gained by peace, 31; for the lapsed, xiii, xiv, xvii, 30, 31, 52, 142, 143, 195; prayers for, xviii, 30, 52, 54.
Mettius, 117, 118n., 119.
mines, bishops and brethren

INDEX 343

in, xxiii, 61, 199n., 313, 314, 315, 317, 318, 320, 322, 323n.
minister, x, 89, 107, 254, 267; of devil, 222; diligence of, xii, 20; faith of, 254; of Old Law, 7; service of altar, 3, 221; worthiness of, xxi, 250-257.
ministry, 3, 34, 89, 99, 138, 203, 235, 249, 250, 320; of deacon, 6; of Levites, 4; of priests and deacons, 41, 71.
Misael, 18, 166.
Modianus, 199, 258.
Monnulus, 157.
Montanus, Christian, 56.
Montanus, founder of heresy, 299n., 300.
Moses, confessor and martyr, xv, 68, 69, 79, 85, 94, 122n., 136.
Moses, Hebrew, 143, 232, 234, 249, 251, 253, 256, 273, 279.

Nabuchodonosor, 18, 166.
Nampulus, 199, 259.
Naricus, 20.
Nemisianus, 199, 259, 313, 319.
Nicephorus (Niceforus), 117 n., 118, 124, 127.
Nicomedes, 156, 230, 258.
Nicostratus, xvi, 68, 79, 85, 118, 125, 128.
Ninus, 154.
Noe, 203, 204, 210, 245, 294, 296, 305, 306, 322.
Novatian, xx, 59n., 68n., 105n., 112, 113, 119, 122, 124, 125n., 127, 135, 136, 149, 180, 190, 195, 236, 239, 240, 241, 243, 244, 246, 248, 249, 250; evil influence of, xvi, 134; rebaptizing by, xxii, 269; schism of, xv, 112n.
Novatus, 43, 112n., 113, 119, 125, 127, 128, 129, 130.
Numbers, 233, 234, 253, 260.
Numeria, 57, 58, 60.
Numidia, xviii, xxi, 93n., 120, 182, 265, 266, 268, 313.
Numidicus, xv, 102, 103, 106.
Nun, 86.

Oblation, 208, 213, 222; of lapsed, 87; of martyrs, 36.
Ophites, 271.
Optatus, bishop, 154.
Optatus, confessor, 71, 90.
ordination, xv, 246, 247, 250, 265, 266, 267, 273, 291, 300, 306, 309; of bishops, 86, 177, 224, 233, 235, 237; of Cornelius, 121, 138; of Levites, 3; of priests, 4, 97, 98, 234; unlawful, 112, 139.
Osee, 233, 235, 251.

Paconius, 10.
Pamelius, 93n.
Paradise, 95, 274, 283, 294, 305, 315; revealed to Paul, 42.
pardon, xvii, xx, 56, 57, 74, 83, 111, 137, 146, 147, 148, 152, 155, 195, 214, 253, 267,

276, 281; recommended for repentant in danger of death, xvii, 158-162; result of discipline, 34; result of penance, 22, 76.

Passion of Christ, 8, 42, 80, 175, 242, 283, 296; of the martyrs, 100; sacrifice of the Lord, 203-215.

Passover, 246.

patience, 52, 65, 76, 77, 84, 292, 311; of bishops, 9; Cyprian's treatise on, 285; example of Christ, 8; plea for, xii.

patients *(clinici)*, 254, 257.

Paul, African bishop, 231.

Paul, Apostle, 9, 11, 14, 17, 27, 32, 38, 47, 49, 68, 73, 110, 116, 128, 132, 143, 144, 145, 150, 151, 152, 154, 163, 169, 171, 178, 179, 185, 186, 192, 193, 200, 204, 208, 209, 213, 228, 236, 238, 239, 246, 247, 256, 257, 264, 276, 277, 282, 284, 285, 288, 289, 290, 292, 293, 299, 300, 301, 304, 307, 308, 311, 312, 316, 318; perseverance of, 42, 81; respect for high priests, 7, 8, 176, 225.

Paul, martyr, xiii, 60, 61, 66, 68, 90.

Paul, martyr with Aristo, 61.

Paula, 106.

peace, civil, xi, 15, 28, 33, 34, 40, 47, 48, 53, 54, 55, 65, 72, 98, 101, 109, 110, 111, 120, 122, 128, 129, 131, 136, 229, 302; to be asked for, 76; need to provide for, 20, 75, 159; of the Lord, 31, 39, 55, 61, 111, 118, 122, 129, 132, 133, 161, 162, 165, 167, 177, 193, 215, 230, 244, 247, 250, 264, 267, 268, 285, 295, 299, 311, 312, 318, 321; rebellion against, 9; reconciliation with the Church, xiii, xvii, 43n., 44, 45, 48, 51, 53, 55, 60, 61, 62, 65, 66, 68, 77, 87, 90, 92, 93, 105, 108, 131, 133, 137, 144, 146, 149, 152, 153, 154, 155, 157n., 158-162, 165, 184, 186, 190, 194, 215, 218, 226, 227, 229, 240, 241, 243, 266, 267; for the dying, 55, 136, 141; false, 109; given by bishop not to be taken away, xix, 216; names to be designated, 45; not given rashly, 63, 64, 135; usurped, 50, 55, 67, 83, 91, 108.

penance, x, xiii, xvii, 46, 65, 77, 87, 88, 112, 135, 146, 147, 149, 151, 152, 153, 154n., 155, 179, 183, 185, 188, 189, 190, 195, 216, 219n., 223, 229, 236, 239, 241, 243, 281, 283, 286, 287, 294, 297, 306; to be done by insolent deacon, 8; by virgins, 12, 13; indication of sorrow of the lapsed, xvii, 34, 46, 47, 51, 52, 53, 55, 63, 64, 78, 93, 140, 184, 237, 263; in minor offenses, 50; nec-

INDEX 345

essary for lapsed, 22, 158; not done, 44, 48; refusal to do, xii, 90, 108.
people, of Arles, 239, 241; of Assurae, xix, 219; of Asturica, 231; of Carthage, x, xv, 42, 43, 45, 46, 49, 50, 51, 53, 64, 89, 97, 98, 99, 102, 106, 110, 112, 113, 116, 117, 126, 127, 165, 188, 202, 216, 228, 308, 324, 325; of Emerita (Merida), 231; of Furni, xi, 3; of Gaul, xx; of Legio, 231; of Rome, x, 126, 127, 129, 138, 186, 240; of Thibaris, xvii, 162.
persecution, ix-xxiii, 11, 19n., 20, 26n., 34, 47, 48, 49, 56, 57n., 58n., 59n., 62n., 63, 68n., 72, 76, 78, 81, 89n., 90, 99, 101, 102n., 108, 109, 111, 112, 122n., 129, 130, 134n., 135, 136, 143, 144, 149, 154, 155, 158, 163, 164, 165, 167, 168, 171, 177, 182, 183, 184, 190, 194, 198, 213, 223n., 226, 229, 230, 232n., 238, 302, 309, 318, 323n., 324; cause of lapse, 49; Cyprian's retirement in, 10, 20; end of, 44; extinguished by blood of martyrs, 25, 95; relief for sufferers in, 20n.; source of future glory, 18, 32, 36, 166.
Perseus, 181.
perseverance, 42, 76, 111; final, 37; of martyrs, xv, 15, 16, 18, 25, 35, 81.

Peter, African bishop, 230.
Peter, Apostle, xxii, 21, 38, 86, 109, 139, 164, 178, 218, 228, 234, 245, 261, 264, 266, 272, 273, 279, 294, 299, 306, 307; Chair of, 186; Lord's warning to, 32.
petitions from martyrs, xii, xiii, 44, 46, 51, 53, 54, 55, 56n., 58, 66, 74, 77, 82, 87, 112n., 216; careless distribution of, 54; to be honored for those in danger of death, 52, 55; names to be designated, 46; reserved for bishop, 45.
Pharao, 255, 257.
Philip, 273.
Philumenus, xiv, 89.
Phinees, 274.
Polianus, 313, 322, 323.
Polycarp, 120, 157, 230, 258.
Pompey, xxii, 113, 115, 121, 285.
Pomponius, 10, 157, 230, 258.
Pontus, 302.
poor, xi, 19n., 20, 35, 36, 41.
prayer, xii, xviii, xix, xxv, 29, 33, 36, 40, 45, 47, 58, 76, 77, 79, 93, 94, 96, 98, 107, 110, 111, 126, 131, 135, 140, 148, 183, 189, 191, 193, 196, 199, 202, 220, 221, 222, 233, 274, 307, 318, 320, 321, 322, 323, 325; of the lapsed, 77; neglected, 107; for perseverance, 19, 30, 31; perseverance in, 32, 34; priests to have time for, 3, 4.

priests, 23, 44, 46, 48, 63, 71, 75, 85, 89, 102, 103, 106, 107, 108, 111, 113, 114, 120, 122, 135, 136, 137, 145, 176, 185, 186, 187, 198, 199, 204, 205, 212, 225, 226, 229, 230, 231, 232, 233, 234, 235, 237, 250, 262, 266, 267, 273, 291, 303, 313, 316, 322, 324; assistance to poor, 19n., 20; to prisoners, xi, xii, 15; Christ, High Priest, 212; duties, 50, 83, 160; honor of, 7, 8; interference with duties of, xi, 3, 4, 7; not respecting bishop, 50, 88; obedience to, 13, 14, 52; rescript against, 323; restoration of lapsed by, 51, 153; sinful, 108, 221, 260; unable to restrain evildoers, 42, 83; vigilance of, 54, 55.

priesthood, x, 102, 107, 109, 112, 117, 130, 139, 220, 221, 225, 232, 233, 250, 262, 285; dignity of, xi, 7, 8, 50, 115, 138; importance of, xv, 97-102; penalty of scorning, xi, 7, 13; sacerdotal vigor of, 54, 115; unlawful, 245, 306.

Primitivus, 113, 120.

Primus, Bishop of Misgirpa, 230, 258.

Primus, Novatianist, 125.

Prisca (Priscilla), 300.

Priscus, 157.

prison, confessors in, xi, xiii, xxiii, 15, 16, 19, 22, 24, 27, 34, 35, 40, 41, 42, 56, 61, 66, 68, 74, 75, 79, 82, 84, 85, 94, 95, 96, 99, 123, 132, 146, 155, 201, 227, 314, 315, 317, 320.

Privatian, 154, 157.

Privatus of Lambaesis, 43n., 93, 181, 182, 199n.

Proculus, 199, 258.

prophets, 167, 188, 206, 207, 212, 214, 233, 264, 272, 284, 297, 308; false, 109, 143, 278, 300, 301; false woman, 302, 303; foretelling of persecution, 27; killing of, 17, 81.

Psalms, 10, 26, 148, 204, 210, 213, 214, 238, 247, 260, 295, 316.

Puppian, Florentius, xix, 223, 226, 228.

Quietus, 231.
Quintianus, 62.
Quintus, xxi, 134, 156, 231, 258, 262, 266, 268.
Quirinus, 320, 322.

Rahab, 246.
reader, xv, 62, 63, 66, 71, 98, 99, 101, 102.
rebaptism, xx, xxi, xxii, xxiii, 236n., 262, 265, 268, 273, 284; by Novatian, 112n.
reconciliation of lapsed, xii, xiii, xiv, xvii, 43, 121; of sinners, ix, 131, 152.
Redemption, 212.
remission of sins, 219, 252, 260, 264, 270, 271, 273, 275, 277, 278, 279, 280, 281, 284,

290, 291, 297, 300, 301, 303, 306, 309, 310.
Repostus, 106, 182.
Resurrection, 70, 213, 218, 252, 271, 272, 279; at last day, 166.
Rogatian, Carthaginian deacon, 295, 304.
Rogatian, confessor, xii, 16, 19, 20, 36, 103, 106.
Rogatian, Numidian bishop, xi, 6, 157, 231, 258, 259.
Rogatus, 157.
Roman Church, xx, xxi, 68n., 74, 308.
Rome, ix, xxi, 56n., 58n., 59n., 62n., 85, 93n., 100n., 113n., 117n., 120, 128, 137, 138, 139, 181n., 182, 232, 287, 298, 323, 324n.; news of Cyprian's exile, 20n.; position concerning lapsed, xiv, 22, 23, 93, 94; precedence over Carthage, 129; recognition of baptism of heretics, xx, 288, 290, 300, 304, 307, 308, 309; union with, xi, xiii, 137.
Rufinus, 68, 79, 85.
Rusticus, 303.

Sabbath, 218.
Sabellian, heresy, 270.
Sabina, 62.
Sabinus, 231n., 232, 235, 236.
Sacrament, x, 177, 212, 213, 248, 253, 262, 266, 271, 275, 281, 282, 283, 288, 291, 293, 294, 305, 312; baptism, xix, xx, 301, 304, 307; efficacy of, xx, 250, 251, 261; Holy Eucharist, xviii, 203, 204, 209, 210, 211; penance, 77; worthiness of minister, xxi, 251, 252, 260.
sacrifice, 38, 160, 199, 202, 204, 205, 213, 221, 234, 267, 269, 307, 322; contrite spirit, 17, 316; Paul, a sacrifice to the Lord, 27; Holy Sacrifice of the Mass, x, xix, 44, 48, 49, 94, 100, 160, 170n., 203-215, 221, 229, 232, 233, 237, 247, 316; not to be offered for Victor, 4; offered for confessors, 15, 36; offered for lapsed, 50; pretended sacrifice by evil woman, 303; priests to be devoted to, 3, 4; pagan or sacrilegious, 57, 58, 63, 74, 84, 92, 129, 134, 135, 140, 141, 142, 144, 151, 158, 170, 177, 178, 181, 182, 183, 185, 186, 188, 220, 221, 233, 240, 245, 250, 251, 266, 269, 273.
sacrilege, 54, 190, 309.
saints, 58, 78, 295.
salutations of *Letters*, xxiv, xxv.
salvation, xxv, 34, 44, 47, 50, 91, 92, 108, 109, 111, 135, 140, 158, 159, 169, 170, 178, 179, 205, 222, 226, 240, 249, 253, 256, 278, 282, 314, 316; only in Church, 13; danger to, 31; through discipline, 10, 13, 29, 42, 88; glory of,

19, 82; instruction for, 50, 88; solicitude for, 14, 110, 137.
Samaria, 249, 273.
Samuel, 7, 175, 225.
Sattius, 157, 230, 258.
Saturninus (four bishops of this name), 156, 157, 231, 258, 259.
Saturninus, Carthaginian confessor, 59, 61, 66, 69.
Saturus, 62, 71, 72, 85, 90, 171.
Saul, 7, 37.
scandal, ix, xvii, 187; avoidance of, 11, 12, 14, 115, 120; of evil confessors, 39; spreading of, 116.
schism, ix, xi, xvi, 68n., 114, 120, 122, 125, 142, 172, 176, 188, 226, 244, 248, 250, 263, 290, 291, 300n.; abandoning of, 126.
schismatics, x, xvi, xviii, 124, 127, 130, 132, 144, 150, 180, 244, 249, 250, 251, 252, 265, 311; baptism of, 259, 261, 262, 265; beginnings of, 9; communion with, 123.
Scripture, xi, xix, xx, 13, 17, 41, 44, 48, 64, 83, 88, 137, 143, 152, 153, 174, 203, 204, 205, 206, 207, 210, 214, 217, 221, 244, 246, 248, 250, 259, 273, 285, 311, 316; Cyprian's use of, xviii, xxiv.
Secundinus, 157, 230.
Sedatus, 10, 230, 258.
sedition, 67.
Serenian, 302.

Sergius, 16.
Severianus, 58.
shepherd, 50, 104, 142, 187, 197, 229, 247, 263; appointed by Christ, 10; Christ, Good Shepherd, 21, 294; responsibility of bishops as, xvii, 21, 44, 111, 158, 161, 226, 241, 242, 263, 314.
Sicily, 75.
Sidonius, 68n., 122, 123, 126, 131.
Sixtus, Pope, xxiii, 324.
Soliassus, 106.
Solomon, 7, 37, 192, 205.
Sophia, 62.
Sophronius, 106.
Soranus, 254.
Spesina, 62.
Statius, 58.
Stephen, African bishop, 113, 115, 121.
Stephen, Pope, x, xx, xxi, 232n., 236, 239, 243n., 265, 285, 288, 290, 324n.; teaching on baptism, xxi, xxii, 296-312.
Stoics, 143.
Successus, xxiii, 156, 230, 258, 323.
suffering, xiv, xv, 28, 95, 97, 108, 164, 165, 167, 168, 171, 195, 227, 281, 282, 283, 314, 315, 318, 321, 324, 325; for Christ, xv, xxiii, 19, 24, 94; perseverance in, xii, 146; strengthened by the Holy Spirit, 17.
Superius, 154.

INDEX

Susanna, 109.

Tenax, 231.
Tertullus, 10, 35, 41, 157, 258.
theater, 5.
Therapius, xix, 216.
Thomas, 100.
Three Fates, 58.
Timothy, 9, 292.
torment (torture), xii, xiii, xv, xvii, 26, 35, 59, 61, 69, 92, 96, 98, 99, 100, 103, 139, 154n., 156, 168, 169, 171, 197, 201, 228, 251; of confessors, 16n., 17, 24, 25, 28, 29, 35, 54, 66, 75, 80, 81, 155, 167; of hell, 77, 78, 175, 185, 191, 220, 314, 315, 320, 321.
Trinity, 271, 275, 279, 301, 313.
Trofimus, xvi, 134, 140.
Twelve Prophets, 177.

unity among bishops, xxii, 34, 150, 241, 312; of chosen people, 248; of Church, 13, 30, 114, 115, 117, 119, 121, 123, 127, 128, 132, 133, 137, 149, 150, 154, 173, 177, 193, 194, 200, 228, 229, 245, 246, 247, 248, 250, 259, 261, 262, 264, 265, 269, 272, 273, 274, 275, 281, 286, 288, 291, 293, 294, 295, 296, 297, 299, 305, 306, 307, 311, 312, 313, 321; of God, 9; plea for return to, 118; return to unity, 126; Rome as chief See of, xi, xxiv, 109, 114, 124, 134, 186.
Uranius, 62.
Urban, xvi, 68n., 122, 123, 126, 131.
Utica, xxiii, 324, 325.

Valentine, 290, 298.
Valentinians, 271, 290.
Valerian, x, xxiii, 323, 324.
Venantius, 231.
Venustus, 61.
Verianus, 157.
Victor, African bishop, 10, 106, 156, 199, 230, 258, 313, 319.
Victor, companion of Cyprian's exile, 40n.
Victor, lapsed African priest, xix, 216.
Victor, martyr with Aristo, 61.
Victoria, 63.
Victoricus, 157, 231.
Victorinus, 61.
Vincent, 162n., 231.
Virgin, Blessed Mary, 26, 271.
virgins, 146, 172, 184, 201, 228, 304, 317; abuses among, xi, 10-14.
virginity, x, xi, 10, 11, 138, 146.
Virtius, 106.

water, 206, 210, 213, 245, 254, 255, 257, 259, 260, 263, 265, 269, 273, 274, 275, 282, 289, 290, 293, 294, 297, 304, 306, 310; matter for baptism, xix, 206, 207, 208, 210, 211, 246, 253, 254, 256, 266, 269,

272, 305; used alone for
Sacrifice, xviii, 203, 204,
209.
wine, 95, 203, 204, 205, 206,
208, 210, 211, 213, 214, 220,
248; of the wrath of God,
168.

Zachaeus, 205.
Zacharia, 189.
Zetus, 125.

INDEX
OF HOLY SCRIPTURE

(BOOKS OF THE OLD TESTAMENT)

Genesis, 33, 204, 206, 230, 274, 285, 322.
Exodus, 183, 213, 220, 221, 232, 246, 267, 281.
Leviticus, 221, 232, 261, 267, 273.
Numbers, 143, 234, 250, 251, 253, 254, 260, 273, 274.
Deuteronomy, 5, 7, 13, 110, 111, 152, 175, 225, 274.
Josue, 247, 286.
1 Kings, 7, 175, 225.
4 Kings, 217, 248.
2 Paralipomenon, 189.
3 Esdras, 292.
Tobias, 147.
Psalms, 11, 17, 26, 30, 58, 116, 148, 174, 204, 209, 213, 214, 238, 247, 260, 295, 297, 305, 316.
Proverbs, 14, 144, 192, 205, 227, 259, 310, 311.
Canticle of Canticles, 245, 294, 305.
Wisdom, 10, 17, 147.
Sirach (Ecclus.), 7, 41, 188, 192, 227, 263.
Isaia, 26, 37, 38, 65, 88, 174, 177, 183, 185, 206, 207, 212, 220, 233, 288, 295.
Jeremia, 10, 109, 215, 259, 272.
Ezechiel, 21, 142, 152, 161, 242, 253, 260.
Daniel, 19, 109, 166, 167, 197.
Osee, 177, 233, 235, 251.
Joel, 148.
Habacuc, 174, 243.
Malachia, 185, 291.
1 Machabees, 174.

(BOOKS OF THE NEW TESTAMENT)

Matthew, 8, 16, 17, 26, 30, 33, 35, 38, 42, 47, 70, 77, 78, 81, 83, 86, 110, 123, 130, 143, 146, 148, 158, 160, 167, 168, 175, 177, 183, 187, 192, 200, 205, 207, 208, 212, 215, 224, 242, 245, 249, 271, 278, 280, 281, 284, 286, 306, 317, 318.

Mark, 47, 110, 212, 213, 233, 278, 288, 301.

Luke, 22, 29, 30, 32, 33, 39, 42, 77, 87, 126, 143, 147, 164, 175, 205, 217, 226, 243, 244, 261, 280, 283, 292, 295, 305, 315, 317.

John, 8, 17, 21, 25, 30, 37, 39, 42, 151, 163, 168, 176, 178, 179, 203, 207, 212, 215, 221, 224, 225, 228, 233, 247, 252, 261, 266, 272, 274, 278, 280, 282, 292, 297, 306.

Acts of the Apostles, 8, 30, 176, 218, 226, 234, 235, 273, 279.

Romans, 18, 32, 37, 38, 73, 81, 145, 163, 171, 179, 228, 238, 239, 257, 316, 318.

1 Corinthians, 12, 22, 27, 44, 47, 48, 49, 143, 145, 151, 171, 175, 192, 200, 209, 214, 256, 264, 282, 285, 293, 297, 301, 309.

2 Corinthians, 49, 151, 200, 277, 304.

Galatians, 14, 39, 68, 145, 179, 200, 205, 209, 213, 236, 289, 304.

Ephesians, 11, 33, 111, 116, 128, 150, 151, 169, 223, 246, 290, 311, 312.

Philippians, 38, 276, 308, 316.

Colossians, 32, 143, 151.

2 Thessalonians, 42, 185, 192.

1 Timothy, 9, 111, 276, 288.

2 Timothy, 3, 21, 27, 109, 133, 150, 192, 277, 292.

Titus, 192, 218, 236, 247, 287, 289.

Hebrews, 31.

1 Peter, 38, 164, 245, 294, 306.

2 Peter, 29.

1 John, 70, 145, 163, 179, 244, 261, 277.

Apocalypse, 28, 35, 42, 52, 81, 88, 147, 169, 211, 220.

THE FATHERS OF THE CHURCH

(A series of approximately 100 volumes when completed)

Volume 1:   THE APOSTOLIC FATHERS   (1947)
    The Letter of St. Clement of Rome to the Corinthians
    The So-called Second Letter of St. Clement
    The Letter of St. Polycarp to the Philippians
    The Martyrdom of St. Polycarp
    The Didache or Teaching of the Twelve Apostles
        translated by F. Glimm
    The Letters of St. Ignatius of Antioch
    Letter to Diognetus
        translated by G. Walsh
    The Shepherd of Hermas
    The Fragments of Papias (first printing only)
        translated by J. Marique
                                                                 ˙OCLC 367814

Volume 2:   SAINT AUGUSTINE   (1947)
    Christian Instruction
        translated by J. Gavigan
    Admonition and Grace
        translated by John Courtney Murray
    The Christian Combat
        translated by R. Russell
    Faith, Hope and Charity *(Enchiridion)*
        translated by B. Peebles
                                                                  OCLC 728405

Volume 3: THE WRITINGS OF SALVIAN THE PRESBYTER (1947)
    The Governance of God
    Letters
    The Four Books of Timothy to the Church
        translated by J. O'Sullivan
                                                                  OCLC 806839

Volume 4:   SAINT AUGUSTINE   (1947)
    The Immortality of the Soul

   translated by L. Schopp
 The Magnitude of the Soul
   translated by J. McMahon
 On Music
   translated by R. Taliaferro
 The Advantage of Believing
   translated by L. Meagher
 On Faith in Things Unseen
   translated by R. Deferrari, M–F. McDonald
              OCLC 856032

Volume 5:   SAINT AUGUSTINE   (1948)
 The Happy Life
   translated by L. Schopp
 Answer to Skeptics *(Contra Academicos)*
   translated by D. Kavanagh
 Divine Providence and the Problem of Evil
   translated by R. Russell
 The Soliloquies
   translated by T. Gilligan
              OCLC 728405

Volume 6: WRITINGS OF SAINT JUSTIN MARTYR (1948)
 The First Apology
 The Second Apology
 The Dialogue with Trypho
 Exhortation to the Greeks
 Discourse to the Greeks
 The Monarchy or Rule of God
   translated by T. Falls
              OCLC 807077

Volume 7:   NICETA OF REMESIANA (1949)
 Writings of Niceta of Remesiana
   translated by G. Walsh
 Prosper of Aquitaine: Grace and Free Will
   translated by J. O'Donnell
 Writings of Sulpicius Severus
   translated by B. Peebles
 Vincent of Lerins: The Commonitories
   translated by R. Morris
              OCLC 807068

Volume 8:   SAINT AUGUSTINE   (1950)

          The City of God (books 1–7)
            translated by D. Zema, G. Walsh
                                      OCLC 807084

Volume 9:   SAINT BASIL ASCETICAL WORKS   (1950)
            translated by M. Wagner
                                      OCLC 856020

Volume 10:   TERTULLIAN APOLOGETICAL WORKS   (1950)
          Tertullian Apology
            translated by E–J. Daly
          On the Soul
            translated by E. Quain
          The Testimony of the Soul
          To Scapula
            translated by R. Arbesmann
          Minucius Felix: Octavius
            translated by R. Arbesmann
                                      OCLC 1037264

Volume 11:   SAINT AUGUSTINE   (1957)
          Commentary on the Lord's Sermon on the Mount
          Selected Sermons (17)
            translated by D. Kavanagh
                                      OCLC 2210742

Volume 12:   SAINT AUGUSTINE   (1951)
          Letters (1–82)
            translated by W. Parsons
                                   · OCLC 807061

Volume 13:   SAINT BASIL   (1951)
          Letters (1–185)
            translated by A–C. Way
                                    OCLC 2276183

Volume 14:   SAINT AUGUSTINE   (1952)
          The City of God (books 8–16)
            translated by G. Walsh, G. Monahan
                                  OCLC 807084

Volume 15:   EARLY CHRISTIAN BIOGRAPHIES   (1952)
          Life of St. Ambrose by Paulinus
            translated by J. Lacy
          Life of St. Augustine by Bishop Possidius

Life of St. Cyprian by Pontius
   translated by M. M. Mueller, R. Deferrari
Life of St. Epiphanius by Ennodius
   translated by G. Cook
Life of St. Paul the First Hermit
Life of St. Hilarion by St. Jerome
Life of Malchus by St. Jerome
   translated by L. Ewald
Life of St. Anthony by St. Athanasius
   translated by E. Keenan
A Sermon on the Life of St. Honoratus by St. Hilary
   translated by R. Deferrari
                                                OCLC 806775

Volume 16:   SAINT AUGUSTINE   (1952)
   The Christian Life
   Lying
   The Work of Monks
   The Usefulness of Fasting
      translated by S. Muldowney
   Against Lying
      translated by H. Jaffe
   Continence
      translated by M–F. McDonald
   Patience
      translated by L. Meagher
   The Excellence of Widowhood
      translated by C. Eagan
   The Eight Questions of Dulcitius
      translated by M. Deferrari
                                                OCLC 806731

Volume 17:   SAINT PETER CHRYSOLOGUS   (1953)
   Selected Sermons
   Letter to Eutyches
                   SAINT VALERIAN
   Homilies
   Letter to the Monks
      translated by G. Ganss
                                                OCLC 806783

Volume 18:   SAINT AUGUSTINE   (1953)

Letters (83–130)
    translated by W. Parsons
                        OCLC 807061

Volume 19:   EUSEBIUS PAMPHILI   (1953)
    Ecclesiastical History (books 1–5)
        translated by R. Deferrari
                        OCLC 708651

Volume 20:   SAINT AUGUSTINE   (1953)
    Letters (131–164)
        translated by W. Parsons
                        OCLC 807061

Volume 21:   SAINT AUGUSTINE   (1953)
    Confessions
        translated by V. Bourke
                        OCLC 2210845

Volume 22:   FUNERAL ORATIONS   (1953)
    Saint Gregory Nazianzen: Four Funeral Orations
        translated by L. McCauley
    Saint Ambrose: On the Death of His Brother Satyrus I & II
        translated by J. Sullivan, M. McGuire
    Saint Ambrose: Consolation on the Death of Emperor
    Valentinian
    Funeral Oration on the Death of Emperor Theodosius
        translated by R. Deferrari
                        OCLC 806797

Volume 23:   CLEMENT OF ALEXANDRIA   (1954)
    Christ the Educator
        translated by S. Wood
                        OCLC 2200024

Volume 24:   SAINT AUGUSTINE   (1954)
    The City of God (books 17-22)
        translated by G. Walsh, D. Honan
                        OCLC 807084

Volume 25:   SAINT HILARY OF POITIERS   (1954)
    The Trinity
        translated by S. McKenna
                        OCLC 806781

Volume 26:   SAINT AMBROSE   (1954)

            Letters (1–91)
                translated by M. Beyenka
                                                OCLC 806836
Volume 27:   SAINT AUGUSTINE   (1955)
            The Divination of Demons
                translated by R. Brown
            Faith and Works
            The Creed
            In Answer to the Jews
                translated by L. Ewald
            Adulterous Marriages
                translated by C. Huegelmeyer
            The Care to be Taken for the Dead
                translated by J. Lacy
            Holy Virginity
                translated by J. McQuade
            Faith and the Creed
                translated by R. Russell
            The Good of Marriage
                translated by C. Wilcox
                                                OCLC 855069
Volume 28:   SAINT BASIL   (1955)
            Letters (186–368)
                translated by A–C. Way
                                                OCLC 2276183
Volume 29:   EUSEBIUS PAMPHILI   (1955)
            Ecclesiastical History
                translated by R. Deferrari
                                                OCLC 708651
Volume 30:   SAINT AUGUSTINE   (1955)
            Letters (165–203)
                translated by W. Parsons
                                                OCLC 807061
Volume 31:   SAINT CAESARIUS OF ARLES I   (1956)
            Sermons (1–8)
                translated by M–M. Mueller
                                                OCLC 806828
Volume 32:   SAINT AUGUSTINE   (1956)

　　　　Letters (204–270)
　　　　　　translated by W. Parsons
　　　　　　　　　　　　　　　　　　　　OCLC 807061

Volume 33:　　　　SAINT JOHN CHRYSOSTOM　　　(1957)
　　　　Commentary on St. John The Apostle and Evangelist
　　　　Homilies (1–47)
　　　　　　translated by T. Goggin
　　　　　　　　　　　　　　　　　　　　OCLC 2210926

Volume 34:　　　　　SAINT LEO THE GREAT　　　(1957)
　　　　Letters
　　　　　　translated by E. Hunt
　　　　　　　　　　　　　　　　　　　　OCLC 825765

Volume 35:　　　　　　SAINT AUGUSTINE　　　　(1957)
　　　　Against Julian
　　　　　　translated by M. Schumacher
　　　　　　　　　　　　　　　　　　　　OCLC 3255620

Volume 36:　　　　　　　SAINT CYPRIAN　　　　　(1958)
　　　　To Donatus
　　　　The Lapsed
　　　　The Unity of the Church
　　　　The Lord's Prayer
　　　　To Demetrian
　　　　Mortality
　　　　Works and Almsgiving
　　　　Jealousy and Envy
　　　　Exhortation to Martyrdom to Fortunatus
　　　　That Idols Are Not Gods
　　　　　　translated by R. Deferrari
　　　　The Dress of Virgins
　　　　　　translated by A. Keenan
　　　　The Good of Patience
　　　　　　translated by G. Conway
　　　　　　　　　　　　　　　　　　　　OCLC 3894637

Volume 37:　　　　SAINT JOHN OF DAMASCUS　　　(1958)
　　　　The Fount of Knowledge
　　　　On Heresies
　　　　The Orthodox Faith (4 books)
　　　　　　translated by F. Chase, Jr.
　　　　　　　　　　　　　　　　　　　　OCLC 810002

Volume 38:　　　　　SAINT AUGUSTINE　　　(1959)
　　　Sermons on the Liturgical Seasons
　　　　　translated by S. Muldowney
　　　　　　　　　　　　　　　　　OCLC 810000

Volume 39:　　　SAINT GREGORY THE GREAT　(1959)
　　　Dialogues
　　　　　translated by O. Zimmermann
　　　　　　　　　　　　　　　　　OCLC 3713482

Volume 40:　　　　　　TERTULLIAN　　　　(1959)
　　　To the Martyrs
　　　Spectacles
　　　　　translated by R. Arbesmann
　　　The Apparel of Women
　　　The Chaplet
　　　Flight in Time of Persecution
　　　　　translated by E. Quain
　　　Prayer
　　　Patience
　　　　　translated by E. Daly
　　　　　　　　　　　　　　　OCLC 810006;804160

Volume 41:　　　SAINT JOHN CHRYSOSTOM　　(1960)
　　　Commentary on St. John the Apostle and Evangelist
　　　Homilies 48–88
　　　　　translated by T. Goggin
　　　　　　　　　　　　　　　　　OCLC 2210926

Volume 42:　　　　　SAINT AMBROSE　　　　(1961)
　　　Hexameron
　　　Paradise
　　　Cain and Abel
　　　　　translated by J. Savage
　　　　　　　　　　　　　　　　　OCLC 806739

Volume 43:　　　THE POEMS OF PRUDENTIUS　　(1962)
　　　The Book of Hymns for Every Day
　　　The Book of the Martyrs' Crowns
　　　　　translated by C. Eagan
　　　　　　　　　　　　　　　　　OCLC 806750

Volume 44:　　　　　SAINT AMBROSE　　　　(1963)
　　　The Mysteries
　　　The Holy Spirit

   The Sacrament of the Incarnation of Our Lord
   The Sacraments
    translated by R. Deferrari
               OCLC 2316634

Volume 45:   SAINT AUGUSTINE   (1963)
   The Trinity
    translated by S. McKenna
               OCLC 784847

Volume 46:   SAINT BASIL   (1963)
   Exegetic Homilies
    translated by A–C. Way
               OCLC 806743

Volume 47: SAINT CAESARIUS OF ARLES II (1963)
   Sermons (81–186)
    translated by M. M. Mueller
               OCLC 2494636

Volume 48: THE HOMILIES OF SAINT JEROME (1964)
   Homilies 1–59
    translated by L. Ewald
               OCLC 412009

Volume 49:   LACTANTIUS   (1964)
   The Divine Institutes
    translated by M–F. McDonald
               OCLC 711211

Volume 50:   PAULUS OROSIUS   (1964)
   The Seven Books of History Against the Pagans
    translated by R. Deferrari
               OCLC 711212

Volume 51:   SAINT CYPRIAN   (1964)
   Letters (1–81)
    translated by R. Donna
               OCLC 806738

Volume 52: THE POEMS OF PRUDENTIUS (1965)
   The Divinity of Christ
   The Origin of Sin
   The Spiritual Combat
   Against Symmachus (two books)
   Scenes from Sacred History Or Twofold Nourishment
    translated by C. Eagan

		OCLC 806750
Volume 53:	**SAINT JEROME**	(1965)

    On the Perpetual Virginity of the Blessed Mary
Against Helvidius
The Apology Against the Books of Rufinus
The Dialogue Against the Pelagians
translated by J. Hritzu

		OCLC 806757
Volume 54:	**LACTANTIUS**	(1965)

    The Workmanship of God
The Wrath of God
The Deaths of the Persecutors
The Phoenix
Appendix
translated by M–F. McDonald

		OCLC 806760
Volume 55:	**EUGIPPIUS**	(1965)

    The Life of Saint Severin
translated by L. Bieler, L. Krestan

		OCLC 806735
Volume 56:	**SAINT AUGUSTINE**	(1966)

    The Catholic and Manichaean Ways of Life
The Way of Life of the Catholic Church
The Way of Life of the Manichaeans
translated by D. Gallagher, I. Gallagher

		OCLC 295838
Volume 57:	**THE HOMILIES OF SAINT JEROME**	(1966)

    Homilies 60–96
translated by L. Ewald

		OCLC 412009
Volume 58:	**SAINT GREGORY OF NYSSA**	(1967)

    On Virginity
On What It Means to Call Oneself a Christian
On Perfection
On the Christian Mode of Life
The Life of Saint Macrina
On the Soul and the Resurrection
translated by V. Callahan

    OCLC 806734

Volume 59:   SAINT AUGUSTINE   (1968)
    The Teacher
    The Free Choice of the Will
    Grace and Free Will
        translated by R. Russell
        OCLC 712674

Volume 60:   SAINT AUGUSTINE   (1968)
    The Retractations
        translated by I. Bogan
        OCLC 712676

Volume 61: THE WORKS OF SAINT CYRIL OF JERUSALEM I (1969)
    Procatechesis
        translated by A. Stephenson
    Lenten Lectures 1–12 (Catecheses)
        translated by L. McCauley
        OCLC 21885

Volume 62:   IBERIAN FATHERS I   (1969)
    Writings of Martin of Braga
        Sayings of the Egyptian Fathers
        Driving Away Vanity
        Exhortation to Humility
        Anger
        Reforming the Rustics
        Rules For An Honest Life
        Triple Immersion
        Easter
    Paschasius of Dumium
        Questions and Answers of the Greek Fathers
    Writings of Leander of Seville
        The Training of Nuns and the Contempt of the World
        Sermon on the Triumph of the Church for the Conversion of the Goths
        translated by C. Barlow
        OCLC 718095

Volume 63:   IBERIAN FATHERS II   (1969)
    Braulio of Saragossa
        Letters of Braulio
        Life of St. Emilian
        List of the Books of Isidore of Seville
    Writings of Fructuosus of Braga

Rule for the Monastery of Compludo
General Rule for Monasteries
Pact
Monastic Agreement
translated by C. Barlow
                                                            OCLC 718095

Volume 64:   THE WORKS OF SAINT CYRIL   (1970)
                        OF JERUSALEM II
            Lenten Lectures (Catcheses) 13–18
                translated by L. McCauley
            The Mystagogical Lectures
            Sermon on the Paralytic
            Letter to Constantius
                translated by A. Stephenson
                                                            OCLC 21885

Volume 65   SAINT AMBROSE   (1972)
            Seven Exegetical Works
                Isaac or the Soul
                Death as a Good
                Jacob and the Happy Life
                Joseph
                The Patriarchs
                Flight from the World
                The Prayer of Job and David
                translated by M. McHugh
                                                            OCLC 314148

Volume 66:   SAINT CAESARIUS OF ARLES III   (1973)
            Sermons 187–238
                translated by M. M. Mueller
                                            OCLC 1035149; 2494636

Volume 67:   NOVATIAN   (1974)
            The Trinity
            The Spectacles
            Jewish Foods
            In Praise of Purity
            Letters
                translated by R. DeSimone
                                                            OCLC 662181

Volume 68:   SAINT JOHN CHRYSOSTOM   (1978)
Discourses Against Judaizing Christians
translated by P. Harkins
OCLC 3003009

Volume 69:   MARIUS VICTORINUS   (1981)
Theological Treatises on the Trinity
Letter of Candidus the Arian to Marius Victorinus Rhetor On the Divine Begetting
Letter of Marius Victorinus Rhetor of the City of Rome to Candidus the Arian
Letter of Candidus the Arian to the Most Illustrious Marius Victorinus
Against Arius Book I A
Against Arius Book I B
Against Arius Book II
Against Arius Book III
Against Arius Book IV
On the Necessity of Accepting the Term *Homoousios*
Hymns on the Trinity
translated by M. T. Clark
OCLC 5029056

www.ingramcontent.com/pod-product-compliance
Lightning Source LLC
Chambersburg PA
CBHW030527010526
44110CB00048B/660